To - George and Je...

Christmas - 73

FROM: Mar- Ghi Feed
Mar- Ghi Ranch
+
Mario + Eva

THE ARABIAN • WAR HORSE • TO SHOW HORSE

THE ARABIAN

WAR HORSE

TO SHOW HORSE

By

GLADYS BROWN EDWARDS

2040

714- 676-5712
304-744-4290 teres

PUBLISHED BY
RICH PUBLISHING, INC. COVINA, CALIFORNIA 91723
Editorial Directors
RAY R. RICH
DAN COTTERMAN

2/3 -
1450
P.O. Box 555

PREFACE

The idea for this book was conceived in the minds of some members of the Arabian Horse Association of Southern California who felt that the Association could best commemorate its silver anniversary by under-writing the production of an interesting, lasting and authoritative contribution to Arabian horse literature.

Gladys Brown Edwards was the obvious choice for this important task as she has long been recognized by student and breeder alike as one of the foremost authorities on the Arabian horse.

The following book, then, is the culmination of many years of study, research, travel and personal observation on the part of the author. She has succeeded in presenting an exhaustive yet very readable accounting of the origins of the breed, its history up to and including importations to America of early sires and brood mares, and the individuals who were responsible for their importations. Included are lists of all importations to the present time, countries of origin, charts of leading sire lines and lists of leading brood mares. The later chapters provide comments on performance, including Arabian racing, a history of Arabian horse shows in America and highlights of many outstanding individuals.

This book will quickly take its rightful place as one of the major contributions to the field of Arabian horse literature.

EDITORIAL COMMITTEE

WILLIAM AINLEY
JACK M. TALLON
JAMES M. KLINE

INTRODUCTION

In an age of specialization and when extravagant statement and the use of superlatives seem to be the order of the day, Gladys Brown Edwards must be regarded as most unusual. It is doubtful if there is another in her field who combines so many and such a variety of talents relating to equines, with such a long and thorough experience with horses in general and Arabians in particular. Not only is she an accomplished writer, artist, illustrator and sculptress in the equine field—a combination which in itself is a rarity—but she also has become, through a lifetime of dedicated and intensive study, a fountain of knowledge and understanding regarding the practical side of horse conformation and anatomy as well as a storehouse of information dealing with the modern history and development of the Arabian horse in America and the background of the breed generally.

To properly understand and appraise her unusual talents and accomplishments one needs to be familiar with some of the highlights of her long and interesting career. After graduating from Chouinard Art Institute in Los Angeles, where her interests of choice centered on equines, she joined the administrative staff of the Kellogg Arabian Horse Ranch at Pomona, which had been built and stocked at great expense by the cereal magnate whose name it bore. Subsequently this ranch was to become world famous as an Arabian nursery and to serve as probably the most influential factor in introducing, advancing, and gaining respect for the Arabian breed among practical horsemen in America. She continued her service there for many years which included the owner-sponsorship of the University of California and the period during which the installation was operated as a Remount depot by the United States Army under command of the undersigned.

During that long period she took fullest advantage of the rare opportunity offered to study and become familiar with the Arabian breed—its background, bloodlines, characteristics, strengths and weaknesses—and to establish and maintain contact with the men and women who had been prominent and effective in introducing and developing the Arabian breed in America. She not only got acquainted with them but also with their horses. She made the most of the rare oppoprtunity to acquire a fine understanding of many other light as well as draft breeds of horses, together with a broad experience and much valuable training in practical horse breeding and husbandry. Concurrently she developed her artistic talents and became widely and favorably knoyn as a horse artist and sculptress—her skill in the latter field being extended to include not only models of most light horse breeds represented in America but also to breeds of cattle and dogs. Meanwhile, she acquired considerable skill and much experience as a rider and driver.

Gladys Brown Edwards was determined to leave no available horse field unexplored. She missed no chance to study the background of the equine species, and the various breeds thereof as well as their characteristics. As she studied them she recorded and catalogued her observations, both mentally and on paper. She passed up no opportunity to observe or participate in the judging of individual horses or groups and the reasons for the ratings. Later she began to write about horses and though many of her articles dealt with Arabians, their basic subject matter most often related to conformation and its effect on performance. Her exceptional artistic ability, combined with her practical understanding of equine anatomy and conformation, enabled her to illustrate her articles in most interesting and attractive fashion and to give physical form to her thoughts on conformation and type and thus add to their meaning and value. A fine example of her work in this field was furnished by her outstanding and beautifully illustrated study "Anatomy and Conformation of the Horse" which ran serially in *The THOROUGHBRED of California* from December, 1966 through January, 1968.

In recent years, she collaborated with the late H. H. Reese and others in the authorship of several books; and as a sort of change of pace and to indulge her side-hobby as a dog fancier, she authored and illustrated *"The Complete Airedale."* She judged Arabian horse classes and shows for a number of years, and has visited Arabian breeding establishments in England, Poland, West Germany, and Holland as well as various points in the United States.

Gladys Brown Edwards as a result of long study and observation, has developed several practical and realistic theories concerning the origin of the Arabian breed, a highly controversial subject on which much has been written over the centuries by writers, many of whom we suspect were inclined to dip their pens more in the inkwells of romanticism and fiction than in those of fact. Anyway, Gladys Brown Edwards is not one who subscribes to the sort of "immaculate conception" theory which many Arabian breed addicts tend to embrace. She has a more practical approach to the subject and this is reflected in her book in the chapters in which she touches on the early history and development of the breed. As valuable source material she is including in her book a list of Arabians imported into the United States—an Herculean task in itself, as well as charts of championship lines tracing back to the desertsbred sires, and the more prominent families.

As one who is thoroughly familiar with the background, capabilities of Gladys Brown Edwards I have every confidence that her latest book is one that every horse lover will want to add to their library, whatever their breed or type allegiance may be.

COLONEL F. W. KOESTER

FOREWORD

It will not take the reader long to appreciate the fact that while I may be an author, I am not a writer. Statistics and research are more in my line, along with an unquenchable curiosity as to how a compilation of figures may turn out. This last resulted in the Sire Line and similar statistics. The fun of these things, while doing them, is that you never know who will win until the results are totaled.

The history chapter is an acute abridgement of a ream of material on this subject. The program was embarked upon ten years ago in order to find new archeological verification of the opinion of Lady Wentworth and others that the Arabian horse was originally found wild in the arid interior of the Arabian peninsula. Unfortunately for this theory the operation backfired, and instead all new material seemed to provide incontrovertible proof that the ancestral Arabian may have evolved south of the Caucasus, but not that far south. Moreover, zoologists, historians and a few others who hold to the impossible theory that the hot-blooded horse found in the Near East was the immediate offspring of the Tarpan or Przewalski horse, are equally erroneous. But as to my original intention of finding absolute proof of the "Arabian wild horse" ancestry, it went poof. I had no recourse but to agree with geologists, archeologists, and historians regarding the impossibility of wild horses existing from prehistoric times in the central plateaus of Arabia. It was a case of "if you can't beat 'em, join 'em," even though the joining was not necessarily voluntary.

Along with the inadequacies of this book—some due to space limitations—others due to my own limitations, there is the problem of inconsistencies. But in this I am not alone. The following discourse between T. E. Lawrence (of Arabia) and his publisher is apropos and delightfully light hearted despite the hysteria it gave the proofreader. This was a publisher's note in *Revolt in the Desert* in which it was explained that the spelling of Arabic names "varied with the whim of the author" and what Lawrence's answers to the proofreader's notes were:

> "QUESTION: I attach a list of queries raised by F. who is reading the proofs. He finds these very clean, but full of inconsistencies in the spelling of proper names, a point which reviewers often take up.
> ANSWER: Annoted: not very helpfully perhaps. Arabic names won't go into English, exactly, for their consonants are not the same as ours, and their vowels, like ours, vary from district to district. There are some 'scientific systems' of transliteration, helpful to people who know enough Arabic not to need helping, but a wash-out for the world. I spell my names anyhow, to show what rot the systems are.

QUESTION: Slip 1. Jeddah and Jidda used imparitally through-out. Intentional?
ANSWER: Rather!

QUESTION: Slip 16. Bit Wahei*da*, was Bir Wahei*di*.
ANSWER: Why not? All one place.

QUESTION: Slip 20. Nuri, Emir of the Ruwalla, belongs to the 'chief family of the Rualla.' On Slip 33, 'Rualla horse,' and Slip 38, 'killed one Rueili.' In all later slips 'Rualla.'
ANSWER: Should have also used Ruwala and Ruala.

QUESTION: Slip 28. The Bisaita is also spelt Biseita.
ANSWER: Good.

QUESTION: Slip 47. Jedha, the she camel, was Jedhah on Slip 40.
ANSWER: She was a splendid beast.

QUESTION: Slip 78. Sherif Abd el Mayin of Slip 68 becomes el Main, el Mayein, el Muein, el Mayin and el Muyein.
ANSWER: Good egg. I call this really ingenious.

In the face of such replies to the publisher's well intentioned questions, further expostulation was clearly impossible."

I am sure I will cause as many problems, not only by my own inventions but through the infinite variety of spelling in source material.

G.B.E.

GLOSSARY

This is not a complete list, but merely those expressions which may be unfamiliar to the newcomer.

ARAB or ARABIAN	Either term is correct in regard to horses. Some countries use one in preference to the other. It is sometimes through that Arab is used only in regard to the people of that name. However Hitti, in *History of the Arabs*, distinguishes between the use of Arabian for the inhabitants of the peninsula and of Arabs for all the Arabic-speaking peoples.
ASTERISK	The star (*) in front of a horse's name, indicating that it was imported to the United States or Canada. The plus sign (+) following an Arabian's name, indicates Legion of Merit.
BREEDY	Bloodlike—showing good breeding. Blood in this sense refers to Oriental blood. A breedy horse would be very refined throughout, dry of head and neck, and showing great quality.

COLT

An ungelded male equine under four years of age. In racing this age is extended one year, a colt not becoming a horse until five. Otherwise a colt becomes a stallion at four. A young gelding is not a colt.

DISTAFF

The dam's half of the pedigree. This is not synonymous with tail female, or family line. Instead it includes all the ancestors in the lower half of the pedigree.

DRY

The clean-cut, well-chiselled appearance of the head, showing bone structure and veins. The skin is thin, the hair fine. A dry neck is light, with fine throatlatch. Dry quality of the legs shows every tendon and ligament distinctly, and the skin is thin, the hair fine. The opposite of meaty (as to head) and gummy (as to legs).

EASTERN

A horse of the Near East or North Africa, especially the Arabian, Turk (so-called), and Barb.

FAMILY

The tail female line. This is traced back through the dam, *her* dam, granddam, great-granddam, and so on, back down to the taproot mare. It is always the line of names along the bottom of the pedigree. The taproot mare is the bottom name on the most distant generation. Among Arabian horses the strain is inherited through the tail female line, never via the sire.

FILLY

A female equine under four years of age. Except on the track, she becomes a mare at four. In the former case, five is the age of maturity. The track terminology is based on maturity as shown by the teeth, a full mouth being attained at five.

FOAL

A colt or filly under one year of age. Further described as a colt foal or filly foal, depending on its sex. It can also be described as a suckling foal or a weanling foal, or the word foal can be left off, and only the terms suckling or weanling used, together (if desired) with its sex, such as weanling filly, suckling colt. On January first a foal automatically becomes a yearling, regardless of his actual age in months.

HALF BROTHER (or SISTER)

In the language of high bred horses (but not draft horses or other coldbloods) a half brother has the *same dam* as that of another horse, but a different sire. Those by the same sire but out of different mares are *not* included under this heading. They are designated as "by the same sire" or the sire is named, if he is better known than the horse in question.

There is a specific reason for this precise terminology, and that is to give proper emphasis to the dam. There can be several hundred foals by the same sire, but at most around twenty (and an average of much less) from a broodmare. Therefore foals from the dam of especially good horses are always eagerly sought.

There are closer relationships as well, such as three-quarter brothers (and sisters), or seven-eighths, and so on. In such instances however no distinction is made as to sire or dam, since the relationship is through both.

MEATY
The opposite of dry in regard to head. A meaty head has about as much chiselling and vein definition as does an egg; the muzzle is thick, and the ears are usually coarse.

ORIENTAL
The same as Eastern in regard to horses. It does not mean Chinese despite the connotation.

PLAIN
Lacking in breed type, but not actually coarse. An Arabian with a straight neck and an oblong but breedy head would be *plain*. But one with a meaty head; short, thick neck; too-heavy bone; and hairy fetlocks would be *coarse*.

QUALITY
Refinement, as shown by satiny coat, silky mane, breedy head, neat ears, fine (but not too light) bone, and fetlocks free of long or coarse hair.

SIRE LINE
The tail male line, as traced by the top line of names in the pedigree. The sire, *his* sire, grandsire, and so on, back to the taproot sire. This line is represented by the top name on the stack of names of each generation, with the foundation sire being the one named at the top of the most distant generation. The sire line is the same as the inheritance of a surname.

STRAIN
Among Arabian horses, this is generally synonymous with family and is traced in the same fashion. However a strain otherwise is defined as "a line of individuals of a certain species or race, differentiated from the main group by superior qualities, especially as the result of artificial breeding."

TAIL MALE
See Sire Line.

TAIL FEMALE
See Family.

TYPE
The unique characteristics which set a breed apart. In the Arabian it includes the triangular head; the light, arched neck; the level croup and high-carried tail; and extreme quality.

TYPY
Having characteristics of the breed to which the animal belongs. An Arabian can be breedy without being typy, but it cannot be typy without being breedy.

UNDERYEARLING
No such animal: See Foal.

TABLE OF CONTENTS

xiii

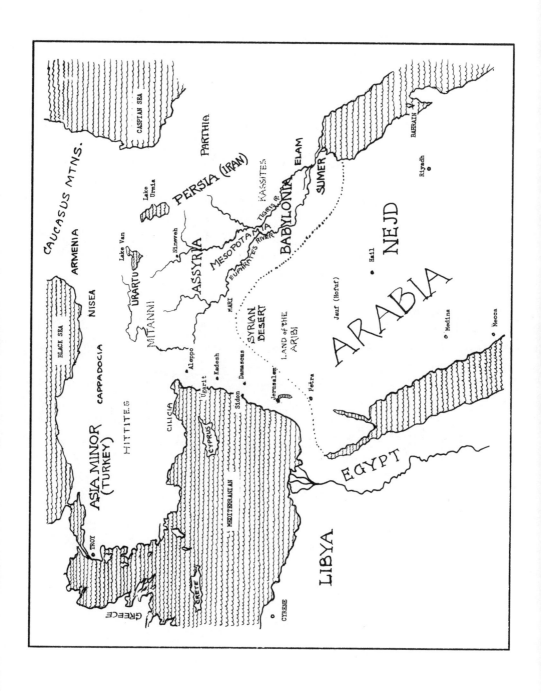

I
FROM MYSTERY TO HISTORY

Opinions on the origin of the Arabian horse range from the ridiculous to sublimely impossible, most historians shrugging it off with such platitudes as "shrouded in mystery" or "lost in the sands of time," not wishing to take any definite stand on the subject. And considering the radical extremes—from myths as fantastic as any from Greece—to the naturalists' pedantic viewpoint of Tarpan parentage, they can hardly be blamed for taking the less dangerous course.

From a study from all angles—ecology, geology, anthropology, archaeology and a few other "ologies" including hippology but not mythology, and most recent discoveries in archaeological digs in the Near East, it is only possible to assume that the ancestral Arabian—or "proto-Arabian" —was a wild horse indigenous to northern Syria and southern Turkey and possibly the piedmont regions to the east as well. The ecology was ideal for horses, the climate reasonably mild, rains sufficient to make the region a fertile grassland where ancestral forms of wheat, barley and other cereal grains flourished. This was along the northern edge of the Fertile Crescent, that area of well-watered land (either by rains or irrigation) looping up from Mesopotamia (modern Iraq) along the Euphrates then west to a broad strip along the coast, and down to Egypt. Inland was dry steppe or plain, but not as arid as it was to become through countless centuries of over-pasturing, and the devastation of war.

All prehistoric art showing the northern varieties of horse indicated these ranged from what is now known as the Przewalski horse, to a rather neat though chunky type with fairly good head and neck. Their colors were dun of all shades and dull black. Many of the duns (some of which were almost bay or chestnut, but very washy, with light underbody)

Two types of horses, engravings from Les Combarelles (L) and El Buxu (R)

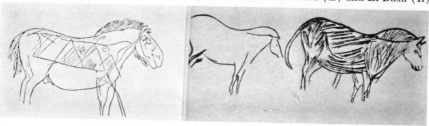

1

The so-called "Spotted" mares of Pech-Merle

had the characteristic shoulder stripe and dark neck. All these horses had upright manes with no foretop, and tails shorter than those of the modern horse. None had white markings. A few rare examples of seemingly spotted or piebald horses have so far been proven otherwise, the "spotted" horses also being surrounded by spots, the work apparently being that of a spot-happy artist; while the supposed pinto seems merely to have been originally dark, some of the paint having flaked off. So there's the picture. The northern horses appear to have been small solid-colored animals (aside from light shadings or dark points) with upright mane and no tail carriage. They had no withers, were stocky and generally carried their heads low, although there were exceptions. Some had large, hideous heads, others were quite pretty. Croups ranged from fairly level to steep. None had heavy fetlocks, although all had profuse and long winter coats in representations of that season.

Contrast these with the graceful and aristocratic horses shown in early Egyptian art. Except for plain heads (in the majority of cases), these elegant animals are Arabians of the most elite type. The first paintings, sculptures, and hieroglyphics of horses occúrred in Egyptian art and literature after the expulsion of the Hyksos, in the sixteenth century B.C.

Having compared the two, take the figures of most historians, who say that "the horse and chariot was introduced into the Near East by the Indo-Europeans in the twentieth century B.C." This is not true in either instance—the chariot having envolved from early and crude

2

Fiery horses and docile mules from tomb of Neb-Amon, 15th Century, Egypt

beginnings in Sumer (near present Kuwait), while horses were known there and in the rest of the region from *at least* the "Old Babylonian" period (c. 1800 B.C.-1700), as will be noted shortly. It will be seen that only three hundred and fifty years separate the alleged introduction of horses into a supposedly horseless land, and the appearance of the prancing horses of Egypt.

It is hard to understand how scientists, historians and others writing about the lineage of the Arabian horse, can so stoutly maintain that the Arabian's immediate ancestors were either all-Tarpan, or Tarpan-Przewalski, which is more of the same. For the ancestral Arabian, as shown in all Egyptian art, could hardly have been obtained from such parentage in any case, but especially and certainly not in the short period of three hundred and fifty years. It is quite easy to evolve a new type by deliberately breeding for that ideal, by having horses available with those characteristics, with which the Tarpans could be crossed. These others would have had to possess everything in the matter of type and much in conformation that was opposite to that of the so-called Tarpan in order to have made such a complete change in the new breed. It could not be done in any other fashion, except by mass-mutations which is in the field of science-fiction and unlikely to have happened; therefore,

3

if a new breed were crossed on the Tarpans, it is an admission that it already existed in the locale. So why go to the trouble to duplicate it?

There is another reason to believe that a native Near Eastern horse was present, and that is the matter of color, markings, the long mane and tail. In contrast to the cave paintings and rock drawings of Europe, wherein the horses were depicted as previously described; a pebble engraving was found in a cave on the coast of Southern Turkey, which shows a running or leaping horse with high-held head and long flowing mane and tail. This is dated roughly 8000 B.C., as also are horse bones (definitely not asinine, or hemione) found in connection with Natufian culture in Palestine. These bones were identified as those of wild horses, of course, not domesticated, but *horses* at least. More recently a new archaeological dig in Selenkahiye, Syria turned up horse bones as well as artifacts featuring horses. These horses were domesticated, as indicated by the halters on the models, and are dated about 2000 B.C. This is the earliest evidence of domesticated horses in the Near East—and occured before the Indo-European invasions.   Przewalski Horse

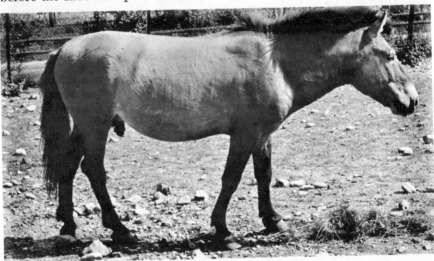

To return to color: while the majority of Egyptian paintings or colored bas-reliefs show solid-colored chestnuts or bays, and an occasional pinto, at least one of the tombs at Thebes has more diversity in markings and color. Some of the horses are blaze-faced and have short socks; some are flaxen-maned chestnuts, usually with white markings; and a few are so-called albinos. That these are albinos rather than aged greys is indicated by their pink muzzles and red-rimmed eyes. Many of the horses have the so-called "human eye," in which too much of the white shows, but this could be artistic license, as even today artists cannot seem to realize that few animals have the same sort of eye as that of man. Some of the eyes even seem to be blue ("glass" or "china"). The white horses invariably have henna-dyed manes and tails, almost scarlet in hue.

Zoologists emphasize that white markings and pied coats are indicative of domestication, only rarely occuring in the wild. When they do appear, the animals sporting these distinctive coats are eagerly sought as "big medicine," as an unusual trophy of the chase, or if suitable, for a really different fur coat. More often they were killed early. For instance stallions are inclined to immediately kill a white or light-colored foal, if the normal colors were dark. On the other hand, under domestication, breeders were apparently pleased by any unusual marking. Not only was it unique, but it made the animal easy to identify. Whatever the reason, all domestic animals, even dogs, cats and chickens have displayed a remarkable inclination to depart from their original colors, once they are domesticated. The mere fact that they were under the care of man could hardly account for it, but the selection of breeding stock would have a definite bearing. Man has always been intrigued by the unusual, and there is no reason to believe that our most distant ancestors were any different in this respect.

Pinto on Egyptian Vase   Pinto horses, ca. 1400 B.C. tomb of Menna, Egypt

With liberal white being a feature of some of the early Egyptian horses, it can be assumed that a similar situation existed throughout the Near East, for after all the Egyptians not only obtained their horses from Syria and environs in the first place, but continued to renew their stock from there. Therefore, in view of the fact that white markings were an indication of early domestication, it can be presumed that the ancestral Arabian (the native Near Eastern horse) had been bred by man much longer than had the northern horses. The latter, even in modern times, ranged in half-wild herds, the stallions chosen by natural selection, on the order of "to the victor belongs the spoils" with only fighting ability

5

as the deciding factor. This is quite different from the custom elsewhere under domestication, in which carefully selected stallions were used as herd sires; where color, speed, power, temperament or whatever was most important at the time influenced the choice. Thus the horses of the northern steppes were not domesticated in the same sense as were those of the south; moreover, they retained their dun hues and did not acquire different colors or white markings until they had been crossed with the Near Eastern horses.

Professor William Ridgeway steadfastly maintained in *The Origin and Influence of the Thoroughbred Horse* that the Arabian horse originated in North Africa, specifically Libya. Other writers have with equal tenacity despite heavy odds against them, held out for Arabia as the equine Garden of Eden. The Libyan theory can quickly be disposed of, for horses were introduced into Egypt from the east, not west, the Near East being overrun with horse-drawn chariots by the time Egypt acknowledged their existence. By evidence of the Pharoahs' records, horses were not among the spoils of war in the first Libyan conflict; in the second, in 1223 B.C., twelve horses "of the killed Libyan chieftan and children" were captured, while in the third war with these people of the west, Egypt acquired "183 horses of Meshwesh." By contrast in successful wars with eastern nations, the Egyptians constantly collected horses and chariots, the "Spoil of Megiddo" alone accounting for "2,041 mares, 191 foals, 6 stallions." (A strange ratio—no wonder there were so few foals. Possibly there was an error, and should have been 241 mares. But this exact number is always given.) The crudeness of the drawings of four-horse chariots in Saharan rock art give the impression that they were ancient work, but they are dated as recently as 1200 B.C., long after Egypt had horses; all other references to horses and chariots in North Africa are even more modern. So Ridgeway's theory of the Arabs acquiring horses from Libya seems to have been caught in reverse gear.

Wilfrid Blunt's summing up of the Arabian origin of the breed is pertinent and succinct: "I think we may be content with accepting the usual belief that Arabia was one of the countries where the horse was originally found in his wild state, and where he was caught and tamed. *By Arabia, however, I would not imply the peninsula,* which, to every account we have of it, is not at all a country suited to the horse in his natural condition. There is no water above ground in Nejd, nor any pasture fit for horses except during the winter months; the mares kept by the Bedouins are fed, during part of the year at least, on dates and camel's milk." This comment is from *Bedouin Tribes of the Euphrates.*

The proponents of the theory that the Arabian horse originated as a wild species in the interior of Arabia, in that inhospitable area that has never been able to sustain wild horses in historic times, argue that this region was once a lush and green pastureland. They point to geologists' admission that in Recent times the now dry rivers ran full, fed by the

6

constant rainstorms, and that the vegetation was tropical in nature. What they fail to realize is that word "Recent" technically refers to the geologic period extending from the end of the Ice Age to the present, roughly ten thousand years. As far back as history goes, the climate of the area has been the same, allowing however for the usual fluctuation, and archaeological evidence indicates that early residents of Palestine and other ancient centers of civilization, were plagued by lack of water. The presence of cisterns for catching rain water (as for instance in Jericho, 8000 B.C.), and the existence of canals for irrigation dating into most remote antiquity prove that the climate was anything but wet at the time towns were first built in the area. Long before that of course, during the Ice Ages, the pluvial periods doused both the Sahara and Arabia (which is an extension of that great wasteland) with plentiful rain, but that was long before anyone was interested in domesticating horses. From that point on increasing desiccation precluded the existence of any wild animals so dependent on adequate water as are horses, in the interior desert regions. In the regions well watered by rain storms— such as the "Syrian Saddle" and the piedmont regions as well as plateaus above the Fertile Crescent, the situation was different and was ideal for wild horses.

The horse is said to be the least patient of thirst of any of the animals of the region. In summer it has to be watered twice a day, although in extreme emergencies it has been known to go as long as forty-eight hours without water in moderate weather. In winter, when pasture is plentiful and succulent, horses can go without water for several days. But once this forage dries, and the rainpools also, there is no source of water for wild horses in central Arabia or even in the Syrian desert. There are wells, but these are very, very deep, entailing the use of an extremely long rope with which to pull up goatskins of water, which of course would be impossible for horses to use. Moreover they often fill up with sand and have to be re-dug. Wild asses, gazelles and similar desert creatures can exist with little or no water, but horses must drink or die. Nor can horses live on the sparse and often salty vegetation that appeals to the camel, nor keep alive on the amount of forage that can support wild asses and gazelles. Under domestication, horses obviously can exist in the desert, as they have human assistance in obtaining water and furnishing food. They also have the welcome and invaluable cooperation of the camels.

In view of this, the premise that the Arabian horse is a separate species which emerged full-grown and without evolution from a mare's nest in Nejd cannot be accepted. It is quite possible though, that the Arabs were acquainted with wild horses long before they even domesticated the camel, when they were still "Amorites" in Syria; and as such, some of them had ridden horses. The date on which the Bedouins first penetrated into the interior of Arabia depends upon the time camels were bred in sufficient numbers to make life in the desert possible. For camels were everything to the desert nomad—meat, drink, transportation, wealth, wool (of a sort), and sacrificial animal. The camel was a filtering machine for filthy, brackish, salty water, converting it into potable milk drunk by man and mare alike to either replace water when that was scarce or undrinkable for anything but camels, or food, when that too was unavailable for the mare. The milk also had other uses than in its liquid form such as dried pellets. Camels actually prefer the desert vegetation to that of more fertile country and saline water to fresh, drinking water so bad that horses won't touch it.

Most people seem to believe that the Arabs migrated out of Central Arabia, but instead, they migrated into it, from the north and outskirts. The Semitic invasions of Mesopotamia started on the south-western borders of Arabia, the first going up the east coast into Sumer, blending with the population there, eventually founding Akkad before going up-river and founding Babylon. The next wave, about a thousand years later (c. 2500 B.C.) went up the western edge, cutting north via Mecca on what became the Incense Route, and going into Syria and Palestine. These Semites had their capital in Amurru, near Damascus, and were known to the people of Mari as Amorites—westerners. The third wave was comprised of the Aramaeans. Some of these Semites became the Hebrews, others Phoenicians, Assyrians, Arabs, and so on. The Arabs went down into Arabia upon their adoption of camel culture.

As early as 1780 B.C. Zimri-Lim, the king of Mari (an important city-state on the Euphrates due east of Palmyra) was reprimanded by his ministers for wanting to ride a horse as did some of his subjects, the Hanaeans (who were Amorites) on the plains west and south of Mari. The king was told to either ride a mule or drive a chariot. This was probably in defense of kingly dignity since it is very easy to lose face (though this may not be the part of the anatomy affected) if bucked off the slippery back of a horse. Records of about the same period speak of "grooms and horses from Amurru," while other references also mention horses, indicating that Syria then was a natural horse country. One of these is amusing, though not funny to the king involved. A letter from the king of Qatna (near Kadesh in Syria) in 1530 B.C., said:

> "This thing is unthinkable! But yet I must speak so that I may relieve my heart. You desired from me, at your request, two horses, and I have sent them to you. Now you have had 20 minas of lead brought to me. The price of a horse here with us is 600 shekels of silver, but you had only 20 minas of lead brought to me."

This was to Ishme-Dagan, king of Assyria (when that country was in its infancy), and may indicate that horses were then more numerous to the west than in Mesopotamia. It is also of interest in giving the price of a horse at that early time, and it is no wonder that the common man could not own a horse. In Babylon, somewhat later, a donkey was 30 shekels

8

and a slave was 40, but slave value depended on fortunes of war, in direct ratio to the number of captives obtained.

The chariot was invented in Sumer, long before it was modified, or rather improved, by peoples in the regions to the north of the Fertile Crescent, either the Hittites in Turkey, or the Hurrians (Mittanians) to their east. One reason why the horse was not employed earlier in Sumer and Susa, was the method of control. This was by a ring through the nose or upper lip; and while it may have worked for cattle, mules, donkeys or onagers, it certainly would have been impractical on the hot-blooded horse. Moreover, horses were of little use in pulling the lumbering, solid-wheeled chariots of Sumer, the light horse being inclined to lunge and rear in moving a heavy load; while a more phlegmatic animal digs in and pulls. Whether the new, light chariot was created after the bit had been invented will never be known, but this, plus use of new metal tools, such as the saw and wood-working implements, definitely played a part in creating a formidable war machine; and the horse suddenly became a vital part of the economy, a war industry, so to speak. The first chariots, like their motive power, were very light. One could be carried on the shoulders of a man, but by late Assyrian times they had become both large and massive.

A census of the horse population can be ascertained to a degree from Assyrian records, these rapacious warrior-kings being meticulous in reporting their campaigns including all booty and tribute. Accordingly, the locales where the best and most horses were obtained is well outlined; the consistently most lucrative from the horse-acquisition point of view

Sumerian four-wheel "war-wagon" as shown in the "Standard of Ur"

was northern Syria, the regions northeast of Assyria and in southern Turkey, all logical horse-raising terrains. Significantly Arabia contributed camels in great numbers, but never, apparently, a horse. Even after Alexander's time Syria was good horse country, the royal stud of Seleucis Nicator consisting of 30,000 mares and 3000 stallions; and Syria even up into the twentieth century was the summer range of the Anazeh and other tribes, as was part of Mesopotamia, favored by the Shammar.

Assyria in its early days may have had to buy horses, but its later kings simply took them by force, or through tribute, which is indirect force. The first reference to Arabs was the thousand camels taken from "Gindibu the Arabian" by the army of Shalmaneser III (858-824 B.C.), the Arabs first being called "Aribi," a word that meant nomads, just as centuries later bedouin meant the same thing, or else raider which was also too fitting. From that time on, until the fall of the Assyrian Empire in 612 B.C., the Aribi were often mentioned, usually as to tribute of camels or in their being chased into the desert as this instance reported by Sennacherib in his last campaign against the nomads, around 685 B.C.: "Telknunu, the queen of Arabia, in the midst of the desert, from her I took away a thousand camels. The fear of my dominion cast her down, and Khazail also. They left their tents and fled to Adummatu whose location

The change in weight of chariots and horses in 200 years. Left, time of Shalmaneser III (858-824 B.C.). Right, Ashurbanipal (668-626 B.C.)

is in the desert, a thirsty place where there is neither provision nor places to drink." This has been defined as in the Wadi Sirhan, which is partially in Jordan and partially in the very north of Saudi Arabia, and which is truly a thirsty place, but not in the heart of Arabia, as one might think. Arabian tribute never included horses, although the occasional grouping of Arabian loot with that of horse locales or peoples has led some writers to this erroneous conclusion.

The Assyrian horses at first, judging by art, were fairly refined, with level croups and fairly good tail carriage. Their necks were arched and their heads no more Arabian than those in Egyptian art (with the usual rare exceptions) but still breedy. Through the years, with increased armor and heavier chariots, the horses too increased in heft, gradually losing their resemblance to the airy-fairy prancing horses of Egyptian repre-

10

sentations. However it should be remembered that the Egyptian artistic format for humans was tall and slender, their horses equally slight, while the opposite was true of the Assyrian concept—their artists had a heavier, muscular man as the ideal, and the horses, even the wild animals, also had more substance than their western antecedents. Aside from this, both schools were adept at distinguishing the difference between donkeys and horses in more than just ears—the backline and tail carriage was well differentiated, and the head carriage, especially in Egypt, was very high for the horses, very low for the donkeys. Even the difference in temperament was shown—the horses always under tight hold even when the driver was out of the chariot, the donkeys or mules placid, with the driver in several instances sitting on the back of the chariot, paying no attention to them. So we can assume that portrayals of horses in art were reasonably faithful, though stylized.

It is through art also that the diffusion of the horse of distant Arabian type can be traced throughout the western Mediterranian area. As early as 1600 B.C. beautiful little "Arabians" with high heads and equally high tails are shown on jewelry and other artifacts, one being a seal ring in Mycenae; an ivory game-box also shows a chariot team at the flying gallop, this being from Crete; and from Ugarit (an important city near present Latakia on the Syrian coast) came many beautiful gold and silver engraved bowls, showing the same type of slender, graceful and fiery horse. Immediately after the dark ages of Greece (c. 1200 to 800 B.C.) horses again were depicted, but crudely for a couple of centuries, then came the approach to the golden age and horses were everywhere in Greek art, including their beautiful coins. Here the race horses, and at first the war-horses (of chariots) were still of the original Near-Eastern type, but as time went by and wars called for more armor, the horses too became heavier. But not the racing stock—these were as ever, though lacking the very high tail carriage of the early Egyptian style (of close to a millenium before). The colors of the Greek horses are well known through literature, but in art about all that can be told is that some were white, some were parti-color (pinto) and others were dark. This is about the same as those of earliest Egyptian horses. The deservedly famous horses of the Parthenon are beautifully done, although they are not always beautiful horses, being usually rather plain of neck, which was not ordinarily the case with the much lighter race horses. The Parthenon horses are mostly cavalry animals, or "officers' chargers" so well described by Xenophon. It was about this time that heavy cavalry everywhere was becoming beefed-up in order to sustain the weight of their fully-armored riders as well as their own protective equipment. The light cavalry nevertheless remained less encumbered with armor and continued to be fast and manueverable, heckling the enemy like swarms of bees.

Persia can take the credit, or blame, for the sudden increase in bulk of the war horses, both for cavalry and then less fashionable chariotry.

11

GREEK AND ROMAN COINS

(1) Mare and foal, Thessaly 400-344 B.C.; (2) Calabria, 272-235 B.C.; (3) Calabria, jockey crowning race horse with wreath;. (4) Race horse of Philip II of Macedon. Winner in Olympic Games 356 B.C.; (5) Rome, Warrior slaying Gaul 61 B.C.; (6) Rome. Victory in triga; (7) Race chariot, Philip II, Olympic winner; (8) Coin of Calpurnius, Rome. Race horse, jockey carrying victory palm branch. 90-89 B.C.; (9) High-tailed horses, Mycenae (Greece) 1600 B.C.

COINS OF NORTH AFRICA, SPAIN AND PARTHIA

1—Cyrene, North Africa, Before 308 B.C.
2—Zeugitana, Carthage, North Africa. 340-242 B.C.
3—Spain, 204-154 B.C.
4—Parthia, c.100 A.D.

True cavalry had been used by the later Assyrians, before that horsemen were little more than mounted infantry, each archer being assisted by having another rider hold his horse, at least when shooting. Some historians believe that cavalry was employed after the Assyrians had contact with the northern nomads, mainly the Cimmerians, who had invaded and taken over Asia Minor in the eighth century, Urartu (around Lake Van) being overrun in the time of the Assyrian king Sargon II (721-705 B.C.) as reported to him by a communique. This country was of special interest, for Sargon said: "...their horses, in advancing, wheeling, retreating or battle disposition...are never seen to break out of control," and in commenting on the skill of Uratrians in training horses—"Their like does not exist for skill with cavalry horses." This locality is just below Nisea and the once-larger domains of Armenia, both famed as horse countries. As descendants of the Mittanians (Hurrians), there is no wonder at the Uratrians' skill with horses. Whether or not the first use of real cavalry coincided exactly with the arrival of the Cimmerians, the dates were very, very close. Moreover, an important fact in regard to the changing type of the war-horse was that the notorious Nisean horses were developed in Nisea (and similar types in Armenia) shortly thereafter. These were described by Strabo—several centuries later—as somewhat less than beautiful though so described by writers copying from him: "The Nisean horses, best and largest of the (Persian) king's province, were bred here (Media) according to some writers, but others say they came from Armenia. Their shape is peculiar, as is that of the Parthian horses compared with those of Greece and others in our country." "Peculiar" does not indicate beauty, for the "peculiar" Parthian horses were overgrown blobs, with rumps that would make a goose green with envy; furthermore, these Parthian animals tucked their tails, rather than carried them. But they were *heavy* horses, and that is what the Persians wanted . . . for by the time of Persian wars the heavy cavalry was totally armored—horse and rider—with combined scale and plate armor. Under this impost the lighter or weaker animals would go down and be trampled by their own fellows, just marching to the battlefields, not to mention under duress.

It was this new ideal for the war-horse that spelled finis for the light, tough and much more handsome original Near Eastern horse, as the all-purpose beast-of-combat. Light cavalry was still maintained, but was outweighed, more than literally, by the new breed.

Another factor that must be considered in this changing type was an additional inflow of northern cold bloods, courtesy of the Scythians. These relatives of the Cimmerians, enticed by tales of plunder and high-living, followed shortly after their kinfolk, but slightly farther to the east, going into Media (part of Persia, or rather, Iran) then down to the foothills and the domains of Assyria. The Scythians were horse-nomads in every sense . . . they rarely walked when they could ride; they ate horse-meat and drank mares' milk, so no other livestock was necessary; they made a popskull beverage from fermented mares' milk on which they could get as high as any Roman carouser; and they shared with the Sarmatians the credit for being the first to geld horses. As Strabo wrote, "although their horses are small, they are exceeding quick and hard to manage," and castration at least made them more manageable. The Scythians were also the first the scalp victims, but that is beside the point. Their horses by this time were crossbred (this being 1300 years after horses were domesticated in the Near East) for they had trading contact with the Greeks and other civilized countries for many years. Their domain reached from Europe to the Volga (their relatives, the Sarmatians, taking over the more eastern steppes), mainly around the Black Sea and above. Ranging deep into Europe, they had every opportunity of acquiring European horses, from the south, Grecian stock, and from the east, the most Mongolian of Mongol ponies—even some similar in every way to Przewalski horses.

Why this by-road into the Steppes? Because the Scythians did not make a hit-and-run raid into Assyria—they stayed for a quarter century, and not only in Assyria but throughout the Near East, reaching the border of Egypt in 630 B.C., as reported by Breasted in *The History of Egypt*, where they were bought off by the pharoah. These Scythian excursions were during the declining period of the Assyrian Empire and no other nation had the power to defy them. As the historian Ragozin puts it: "We do not know in what way Palestine and Syria were rid of their terrible visitors. They are said to have held western Asia under their sway for a number of years, during which time their insolence and oppression spread ruin on every side. For, besides the regular tribute, they exacted from several nations additional imposts which they fixed at pleasure; and further they scoured the country and plundered everyone of whatever they could." Moreover they pastured their horse herds where they pleased, whether it was on growing grainfields, gardens, or orchards. The possibility of admixture of the horse populations can hardly be under-rated. While it is probable they brought only a portion of their herds south including geldings, in view of the Scythian eating habits, breeding stock was also brought along for milk and its by-products and meat.

The actual effect on the horses of the Near East, as reflected in art, was shown in the handsome bas-reliefs of the Persian edifaces at Persepolis, which were started in the time of Darius (558-486 B.C.) and continued by his successors, but although the whole city was destroyed by Alexander, the sculptures fortunately remained reasonably intact. Here are depicted the bringers of tribute to the Persian kings, often the gifts being horses, in these processions carved from rock. Every horse is a stolid, phlegmatic animal, coarse of head, but not long-headed; thick-necked, mutton-withered; long-backed, and goose-rumped. They have the tail carriage of a mule backed up to a raging blizzard . . . in other words no tail carriage at all. Their substance would be admired by admirers of horse meat, if not horse flesh, for substance they have in overabundance. But not one of the horses is tall, indeed a few are not much taller than rams in the same procession, and since some of these are believed to be the well-publicized (though peculiar) Nisean horses, it would seem that they were big only sidewise—through the beam, and in general heft. Moreover as Nisean foals were the main course in the feast of Mithras (20,000 anually sent for this event) it stands to reason a stocky, thick-set foal would be a better meat animal than a slim leggy one.

The equally peculiar (compared to Grecian horses of Parthia, at least the mounts of kings, as so often shown hunting or in battle, were overgrown bulbous blobs, built like a series of conjoined balloons, their tail-set near the hocks, and tails clamped to the body. Like their Persepolis predecessors, their heads were very short, sometimes Roman-nosed, the muzzle coarse, the ears set far back, creating a receding forehead which heightens the impression of a Roman nose. These horses were the result of another dose of Scythian horse stock, through the invasion of eastern Persia by the Saka tribe, more relatives of the Scythians. The Parthians were said to be a nation of horse-archers, being able to shoot not only from front and side, but also in retreat (real or simulated), turning and shooting to the rear without losing their balance. This is the famous "Parthian shot," perfected earlier however by the Scythians, and shown in metalwork of these people.

The Sassinids, which replaced the Parthian domination of Persia, had the same sort of curvaceous steeds, even more rotund, if possible. The conquest of Persia by the Arabs wrought another drastic change in horse type, as reflected in the delightful miniatures of Persia, wherein the horses are without a doubt Arabian, but retaining somewhat too much substance, being very deep of body. Their quality, arched necks and level croups with good, if not high, tail carriage shows the influence of Arabian crossing.

Returning to the Arabs, as of the last Assyrian records they had never had a horse up to that date—around 612 B.C. It may have been in the turbulent period therafter, when the Assyrians could no longer guard their empire, and when Scythians were still scouring the countryside, that the Arabs were able to steal horses occasionally. Babylonia revived after Nineveh fell and exercised some influence, but may not have kept the Arab raiders down as well as did the Assyrians, the wily Arabs either escorting caravans or giving paid-for "protection" when crossing their zones of control. Aside from this they robbed whatever was unguarded, whether caravan or town.

If the majority of the foundation stock was obtained this early (which seems improbable, in view of subsequent history), the Steppe blood

15

(which included both European and Asian as well as intermediate) would have been at a minimum. However subsequent invasions brought in more horses, including Alexander's cavalry and the two hundred horses he was given in Libya on his side-trip through Egypt to North Africa. The royal stud of his successor, Seleucis Nicator, with 30,000 mares, and 3000 stallions, shows the size of just one of the stud farms, of which there were many, in the Near East and environs. The Greek horses had been founded on Near Eastern blood, though later acquiring northern blood—except (judging by appearance) in their racing stock, the same being true of the early North African horses.

A blow to the theory of early acquisition of horses by the Arabs is the fact that Greek and Roman writers were emphatic that horses did not exist in Arabia, nor did Arab warriors use them, all being camel riders. The later Romans may have mentioned Arabian horses, but not the well-known writers of pre-Christian and early Christian times. Such a late date would have allowed much more time for homogenization of blood of horses from north, south, east and west. But only the Near Eastern could survive, no matter how much foreign blood was there, it was boiled out in the desert pasteurization process, the type reverting to that which was natural for the locality, even though the blood was mixed originally.

There was no such place by name as Arabia until 530 B.C. when a Persian document designated it "Arabaya," though references to "Arabia" as the land occupied by certain tribes had been previously made by Assyrians. These last were not in Arabia itself however. The Aribi of Assyrian times did most of their nomading in Syria, Jordan and Mesopotamia, penetrating gradually south as the Assyrians drove them farther into the deserts. So, the Arabs until then, were a rootless people, who lived off their camels or sheep and goats, just the nomads their name implied. They may have learned a thing or two from the Scythians, those fierce people whom they could not have avoided in the duration of a quarter-century; and one of these lessons would have been the great advantage of horses over camels as war mounts. Camels are unsatisfactory fighting platforms; whatever advantage their height may give is lost by their lack of agility and the inability of the rider to get close to his adversary (unless he too is on a camel). The custom was to dismount and fight hand to hand. With horses this was changed; moreover, if you lost the fight you could get away from there, fast. Horses also were faster than camels at short distances, making them good for raiding.

Scythian tactics were so much like the Arabian hit-and-run methods that the similarity suggests that the Arabs learned their original horsemanship, possibly the hard way, or else by observation, from these masters of the horse. Scythian cavalry was appreciated by the Persians, for "a thousand picked Scythian horsemen" were selected along with two thousand Cadusii cavalry, for attack against the Macedonian forces.

Hittite Horses, c. 850 B.C.

A horse of Elam (Southeast of Babylon) (L), A Persian mount (590-330 B.C.) (R).

Type of horse shown on the
apadana at Persepolis, Persia,
c. 470 B.C.

17

These particular Scythians were from a settlement in Persia, most of others having returned to the steppes, taking southern horses with them—the possible ancestors of the "heavenly horses" of Ferghana, which were light and fine-haired, quite unlike the northern ponies.

There are some writers, rather out of touch with reality (or with research), who are positive that the Arabs did not have horses until after the time of Mohammed, this profound opinion based on the fact that Mohammed had only two horses in his army during his first battles. What is inexplicably overlooked is the number of horsemen (200) among the opposing forces, and before that, a "troop of horse" set out on Mohammed's trail when he fled to Medina from Mecca. Mohammed rode a camel on this journey—the Hejira—and was accompanied by Abu Bekr, also aboard a ship of the desert. Yet some American breeders of Arabian horses have claimed descent for their stock from "the horse Mohammed rode from Mecca to Medina." If that steed were a horse, that might explain the presence of ewe necks, straight shoulders, calf-knees, roach backs, very short steep croups, and sickle- and cow-hocks in the breed, but unfortunately the cause is elsewhere. But this shows how gullible people can be, also that they never read history. In addition to horses of the troops opposed to the Moslems, the presence of horses in Arabia before Islam is proven in the poems in the "suspended books" (pre-Islamic) in the Kaaba at Mecca, in which horses are often mentioned and the life as described was exactly that of later times. Even horse races were excitingly detailed. In addition, to clinch the argument; during the Moslem wars, the booty allowed a horseman was three times that of a footman, and the owner of a horse of "the right Arabian breed" was allowed twice as much as other horsemen. This would indicate that horses had been bred in Arabia and environs by the Bedouins for many generations at this date, the seventh century A.D. It also proves that they had foreign horses too, as thousands were captured which were not "the right Arabian breed."

Whenever the Arabs first got horses, the foundation stock certainly was close enough to the old proto-Arabian in appearance to have continued to breed with appreciable dominance. A primitive standard of perfection must have been in their mind's eye, for admiration of high tail carriage was strong enough that they went to considerable trouble to insure it. This was done in Nejd, as reported by the Blunts, although they could not seem to believe such a practice was indulged in by artless Arabs. Yet they remarked on the uniform and unusual tail carriage of the horses of Nejd. This aid to nature was employed by some other tribes also, as recounted by several other writers. One of these was J. L. Burckhardt, who wrote, in Notes on the Bedouin and Wahabys (1830):

> Immediately after the birth of a foal, the Arabs tie the ears
> together over its head with a thread, that they may assume a fine

pointed direction; at the same time press the tail of the foal up-
wards, and take other measures whereby it may be carried high.

In Volume I of Prince Mohamed Ali's book *Breeding of Pure Bred Arab Horses* he states:

> As soon as the foal is born, after having the umbilical cord
> cut, it is the usual custom to massage it gently with the hands,
> which have previously been smeared with fat or butter. The tail
> should be gradually bent upwards and forward . . . The foal's
> spine must be massaged for nine days and the raising of the tail
> continued.

This is augmented in the second volume by:

> The Arabs, as I said previously, lift the foal's tail when it is
> newly born and turn it back for nine or ten days. This is done to get
> the nerves of the tail, before becoming strong, to take the desired
> position. Some Arabs also later on, when the horse is grown up,
> or let us say, at least a yearling, burn under the tail with a red-hot
> iron. A horse lover never likes a tail that has been burnt or nicked.
> You can immediately spot it, as the tail looks like a piece of wood
> that has been tacked on the body—it has no life or flexibility . . .
>
> The reason Orientals like their horses to have fine upstanding
> tails is that no horse having this would have drooping quarters,
> which is looked upon as a defect. Most of the horses which carry
> their tails well are slightly hollow-backed . . ."

The Prince's comments on this subject were related a hundred years after
Burckhardt's notes and slightly over fifty years after the Blunt references
to the same subject, so apparently it was a widespread and long-standing
custom. This practice could effect the still soft bones of the sacrum and
tail-head, but it is hard to see how it would affect inheritance. Apparently
the Bedouins also *bred* for high tail carriage, not depending entirely on
artificial aid, otherwise the breed today would not have the characteristic
high tail carriage.

That the Arabs picked up additional horses as part of their loot,
mostly in Syria, there is no doubt; and there is equal reason to believe
that many of these were taken back into Arabia, for horses were too
precious to discard. They were vital to the protection of camel herds and
the pleasurable raids for the gain of more camels and horses. In this way
the breed gained new blood, but after all, it was the same basically as the
original collection, so no drastic changes in type occurred. The old
Arabian, the Kehilan-Ajuz, was even then more esteemed than the new
acquisitions—not because it was better-looking or more useful—but just
because the individuals thereof were known, or known of, for several
generations.

As to actual strains or families, however, there has been no reference
in any writings at all to strains other than the Kehilan (and even that
not by name) in the time of Mohammed, nor any even as late as 1330

MARES OF THE RUALLA, 1911

A.D. when the Sultan el Naseri had pedigrees traced, though they turned out to be more fiction than fact, and were based entirely on a horse and a mare saved from the flood occasioned by the bursting of the Marib dam in Yemen in 542 A.D. This flood in Arab legend became confused with the Biblical flood, and as one of the mares involved was allegedly owned by a greatgreatgrandson of Noah, the generation gap here is several thousand years in width. In the fourteenth century by el Naseri records, there were no strains at all. He did however mention the "old breed" (Kehilan-Ajuz) and a "new breed" (Kehilan-Jadeed). By 1700 however, there was definitely were strains, as the world-famous Darley Arabian, foaled in that year, was of the Maneghi strain.

Lady Wentworth spoke of a reference to the Jilfan strain in the 1600's. Early travellers to Arabia and environs would usually write of two or three "breeds," as they termed the strains, one being the Kehilan, also called the Koheyl, Kohloni and a host of other varied spellings. The other would usuually be the "Nejdee," or horse of Nejd, this latter supposed to be the most pure because of the isolation of Nejd in central Arabia, so that no foreign horse could approach the allegedly matchless mares of Nejd. This ascribing of 'breeds" to the horses of Arabia naturally led to attempts to define the differences among the various "breeds" just as would have been the case in discussing breeds of any other area. It would also lead to a natural surprise to find that these so-called breeds were constantly crossed with one another, and such surprise was often expressed by

20

writers. However when it is realized that these are merely different families of the same breed, then the situation is clarified. Unfortunately this did not occur until the idea of "breed type" for each strain had become widely broadcast.

There are many strains or families, but the most common are Kehilan and the Seglawi in their various substrains. The Maneghi was popular to the point of fanaticism in the 1800's, especially after it was discovered that the Darley Arabian was of that strain. It is generally conceded that the Kehilan-Ajuz is the original strain, since the name means "the old Kehilan," or as generally defined, "the old Arabian breed," since strictly speaking "Kehilan" means purebred, in this case purebred Arabian since the Bedouins recognised no other breed. The Seglawi, the Abeyan, the Maneghi and all the other main strains are conceded to be descended from the Kehilan-Ajuz but there is no absolute proof that this is so. The Bedouins merely shrug and say "they are all Kehilan"—meaning they are all of the same breed—the "pure breed."

The Abbas Pasha stud books give unexpected sidelights on many features of Bedouin horse culture and customs. One of these was the habit of tribesmen to let it be known that a mare of a much esteemed and rare strain was "only a Kehilan," in order to prevent its being seized by some covetous ruler. Often war would be started on some pretense just to enable the aggressor to capture such a mare if her true strain were known. Other times the mare might have been captured from a noted breeder, and who would at once claim her if he knew where she was, so the newly acquired mare would be termed a Kehilan (strictly speaking, it would be the feminine form—Kehilet). From these several instances, it might be assumed that the "Old Kehilan" was more than just the original breed; it was also general classification for horses of all strains under certain circumstances. Under such conditions the animals would be considered Asil or purebred, but with no further history. It can be assumed therefore that many a Kehilan-Ajuz could actually be originally of some other strain, due to the owner hiding its real strain, or, under other circumstances, where nothing more is known other than that it is purebred—of "the old breed"—Kehilan-Ajuz.

The inviolability of Nejd is another misconception, for it was rudely violated in the early 1800s. This was due to the over-activity of the Wahibi sect which kept Arabia in a turmoil of wars, the Wahabis being inspired to bring back the ol' time religion of Mohammed. The Turks, who ruled all the roosts of the Near East and Asia Minor, except central Arabia, thought the Wahabis needed to be tranquilized, and set about it via Egypt and the Pashas, who were also subjects of the Turks' Ottoman Empire. Several expeditions were sent to Arabia, the first getting no farther than the coast; the second in 1813, under the command of the redoubtable Muhammed Ali Pasha, didn't get into Wahabi country—Nejd—either. Both attempts brought horses to Arabia, the first with

21

eight hundred horsemen, the second with two thousand. But in 1815 Tusan Pasha, a son of Muhammed Ali, marched into Qaseem (between Medina and Hail, in Nejd), with six hundred cavalry plus infantry, plus left-over cavalry from the former expeditions. The Wahabi leader relinquished all claim to Medina and Mecca and recognized the Sultan of Turkey as overlord. The next foreign invasion went even deeper into Nejd, and across it to Hasa. This was in 1816, led by another son of Muhammed Ali, Ibrahim Pasha. With him were fifteen hundred Libyan horsemen in addition to his two thousand infantry. He (as was Tusan) was joined by Harb and Muteyr tribesmen who had become disenchanted with the fanatic Wahabi movement, and also some Attaiba and Shammar. This army stayed in Qaseem from June, 1817 until the following March, and by April had taken the Wahabi capital, Deraiya. Abdullah Ibn Saoud was not captured until September however, and the army then went on to Hasa, not being recalled until the next August.

It has been the custom of North Africans to ride stallions, just as the Bedouins of Arabia and the Syrian deserts almost exclusively ride mares. With the foregoing number of North African (Libyan) horses, plus the remaining Egyptian cavalry (many horses having starved to death on the earlier campaigns or died from other causes) staying in Nejd for such a long period, there was bound to be accidental fraternizing between the horses and mares of the allies, as well as with the Wahabi mares after battles, when riders had been unhorsed, wounded or killed. Not to mention other types of such accidents. This situation may have been an underlying cause of Bedouin pedigree-tracers being insistent on owners swearing that mares had never been "interfered with" by an unapproved stallion. Lack of approval however could depend on many things—a disliked strain, or disliked owner of the horse, or lack of complete history of the horse, and unknown substrain, or it could be just a very bad horse. The Arabs were firm believers in telegony, the supposed transmission of hereditary characteristics of one sire to foals subsequently borne by the same mare. As a consequence of this erroneous theory, they were extraordinarily concerned about previous marital adventures of a mare which they may have acquired or of which they own descendants. The histories of the mares obtained by Abbas Pasha, as published by Prince Mohamed Ali, reflect this undue interest. Moreover the frequency of references to accidental matings may refer to the time of the invasion of Nejd, or they could have merely proven that not only were there more stallions kept in those days, but they were less carefully guarded. At any rate accidents did happen, with the resultant declassing of the delinquent mare and all her subsequent produce. Often however, descendants of such a tarnished strain would become clean again through virtue of superior qualities, such as being very fast "and therefore good for raiding" as one tribesman put it. The same reason brought previously unknown strains into the fold, after several generations of being known.

The strain in this instance meaning a family of horses bred by a certain breeder, clan, or tribe—in other words a substrain, usually named after the breeder or current owner. In fact this is the way most substrains —such as the Maneghi-Hedruj horses of Ibn Sbeyel of the Gomussa tribe, which eventually became Maneghi-Sbeyel, acquired their names; ditto Seglawi-Jedran—the Seglawis of Jedran.

At any rate, the fact that foreign horses were in Nejd is incontrovertable; moreover, the main group was there for over two years, the previous expeditions for somewhat shorter periods. It was a two-way affair however; for around two hundred fine Arabians were taken to Egypt. Although these were eventually lost to the breed, the impression they made on Abbas (later to become Abbas Pasha I) was great. Through Abbas assistance to the Wahabi prince, he earned the latter's gratitude to the extent he was able to buy up some of the best horses of the tribes, including all but two (or so it is said) of the celebrated Seglawi-Jedran family. Abbas also bought up what must have been most of the parti-color Arabians in the breed, at least eleven; for after that time this coloration was rare in the desert (or anywhere else). Its influence is seen however through the Abbas Pasha lines of MESAOUD and MAHRUSS(the latter's granddam being one of those pintos), in the occasional under-body (or low on the side) white patches.

In Daumas' *Horses of the Sahara* a letter (dated 1861) is quoted which states that "For the past forty or fifty years only" did the Arabs of Nejd esteem and use pure blood. This is a rather surprising statement but one which coincides with the Egyptian invasions, and doubtless the idea was to eliminate the foreign crosses, if known; if this report is true. At any rate this would date pure breeding in Nejd from 1810 or 1820. The joke of this is that the rulers of Nejd obtained their horses from the tribes to the north—the Anazeh and Shammar, who had left Nejd around a couple of hundred years before for better, if not greener, pastures in the plains and deserts of Syria and Mesopotamia. All the shieks questioned by the Blunts about the "Nejd breed" scornfully said there was no such thing—that the Wahabis had obtained their horses from the Bedouins, and their bloodlines were the same, but the foals bred in Nejd were stunted, maturing smaller than the others, due to the lack of good feed (and the poor care) in the towns, even in the kings' studs, which in fact were about all there were in Nejd at that date.

Lady Anne and Wilfrid Blunt spoke of the devastation to the horse population due to the Wahabi wars, which had been followed immediately by the purchases of Abbas Pasha of Egypt, saying that inbreeding was ruining the Arabian horse in the desert. One reason was the lack of stallions (one per 200 mares), and the other was an over-emphasis on certain esteemed strains. This esteem was not based on conformation or much of anything else except pedigree in most cases. They still admired speed, and there are many references (in the Abbas books) to the eventual esteem given a substrain because the horses were "fast, therefore good for raiding."

Horses bred in the comparatively lush pastures of Mesopotamia were scorned by the Bedouins, not necessarily because they thought them impure, but because they were not as tough as their own mares. This was brought out by Doughty in *Arabia Deserta* in which he said, "... although of good stature and swifter, they are not esteemed by the inner Arabians. Their flesh being only of 'greenness and water' they could not endure in the sun-stricken languishing country. Their own daughters-of-the desert, albe they are less fairly shaped, are, in the same strains, worth five of the other." So type, as we consider it, had nothing to do with esteem, nor did beauty if a horse could not tolerate desert hardships.

The Arabian is the first man-made breed as well as the oldest. It is man-made due to the abnormal environment which produced it, with its very life dependent on man. Except in the rainy season when rain-pools provided water and the forage was succulent enough that at times the mares could go days without water, they were dependent on members of the household (tenthold?) to provide both feed and water. When the dry grass was scant or non-existent the mares still were turned out to graze or at least wander, though they were either hop-shackled or, for more restriction, tied head to hock with a rope just long enough to allow the mare to graze but not to go faster than a gimpy walk. When there was no forage at all, they were fed dates and camel milk, the milk also taking the place of water when that was unavailable or too brackish for horses to tolerate. Such water is relished by camels, even if very salty, and so is thorn-bush and salty bushes, which are unappreciated by horses, but by which they benefit indirectly through the camel dairy products. Stallions were noisy nuisances that could cause all sorts of problems should one happen to get loose, not the least of which was "interfering" with mares. According to several writers, some of whom lived with the Bedouins for a period, the stallion would be kept as far as possible from the mares, preferably in a wadi (ravine) if one were available, so as to be out of sight. He was in the care of a slave, and the fact that a nosebag was kept on his head at all times, not just for feeding, served to both muffle his neighs and blunt his bite. He was ordinarily shackled by a hind pastern, chained to a stake, but a real tough customer would be shackled fore and aft, barely able to stamp flies. By the turn of the century some tribes did not maintain stallions, selling colts as soon as they were old enough to make the trip to sales centers, or killing them at birth, if water and feed were scarce. A Spanish expedition to Arabia for the purpose of buying horses made this report:

> It is to be noticed that they (the Sabaa) did not have horses, because in these tribes of Bedouins they do not keep them. Generally the colts are sold as weanlings or at the most at two years. The nervousness, the spirit of stallions cause them to be isolated

24

HORSES IN NEJD, 1962

All except the bay stallion (top right) are in the king's stables at Al Kharj. The bay is the top sire at Hofuf. The grey stallion was the old king's special mount and is a herd sire. He is shackled around the right fore pastern.

25

from his fellows and bands of mares and have made the horse a dangerous animal, of irascible character, so fearsome and so fierce when they come near others of the same sex. For this reason the Bedouins do not keep males, having to breed their mares from famous stallions in the litoral (sea coast) or the interior.

This was written in 1905, just a year before Homer Davenport made his quick trip to the Near East, and certainly he had no trouble locating stallions, nor were they ill-tempered. In fact *HALEB was from this very same tribe, although he was not obtained directly from the Sabaa. *GOMUSSA was from the same source, but also indirectly. However most of the Davenport stallions were from other tribes, or from towns.

The care given horses in the desert was nil, and this casual treatment combined with the hardships encountered there resulted in a survival of the fittest situation created by man, so this too could be called man-made. It assuredly was not the ecological environment which horses would have chosen for themselves. However it was this combination of circumstances, plus the work required of the war mares under the most severe conditions, that created the toughness of the breed and gave it the reputation it has maintained for centuries.

As the oldest breed of horse in existence, the Arabian need have no apologies for the long-ago minor crosses on its original Near-Eastern blood, plus rare subsequent additions along the way. For all we know, these foreign crosses may have added stamina, though certainly not beauty, to the Bedouin's foundation stock. But whether it did or not, the mixture was there. Every other breed, whether founded originally on appearance or performance, also consisted of a combination of bloodlines or types to begin with. Or the breeds may have been ecotypes of a sort —a creation of their environment—but nevertheless they usually would have been of mixed blood to start with. When a breed was deliberately produced according to a fixed design, the breeders could add any other blood they wanted which they thought would add the desired improvement; and the same was true of a breed in which performance was the main attribute. As soon as the type had become fixed and a breed created, further outcrosses were usually not needed. This was true of the Thoroughbred. At first all types of Oriental horses were imported, but after several generations it was found that fresh infusions of this blood only slowed down horses of subsequent generations, so the "book was closed," so to speak, even before there was such a thing as a stud book.

It should be remembered that our present system of recording purebred stock is based on Weatherby's Stud Book of England (the General Stud Book), the first volume of which was published in 1803, after the Thoroughbred had been a true breed for over a century. The research involved in tracing the histories of the horses listed in the first volume was not too different from the problems encountered in obtaining the records of the antecedants of the horses Abbas Pasha obtained in the desert—except that there were more of them and over a much longer period in the case of the Thoroughbred.

If it took the practical English a hundred years to get around to the idea of inventing a system of recording the ancestry of Thoroughbred horses, it is no wonder it took some time longer for similar systems of registration to evolve elsewhere. Up to that point, there was no central organization for the purpose of promoting and registering animals, and no stigma occasioned by outcrosses of foreign blood. There were certain breeding establishments which bred Oriental horses in Europe, nearly always owned by aristocracy, and these as much as possible consisted of Arabian, or what was considered Arabian stock. In Poland for instance, written records were kept by each stud farm, originating as far back as 1810 at least, but there was no central and official registry for Arabian horses in that country until 1926. Germany has bred Arabians for a similar period and still it has no official registry for Arabians alone. Strange though it may seem, that johnny-come-lately among Arabian horse breeding countries, the United States of America, was the first to have an all Arabian registry. Prior to that, as was the case in England, Arabians were merely "Thoroughbreds" registered in either the Jockey Club or the General Stud Book, as the case might be, but in the Oriental section.

The Arabian breed itself may be only two thousand years old, but its high prancing ancestors, the epitome of Arab type, were around much longer. While it is true that it cannot be called a sub-species, as some wishful thinkers contend, it is never-the-less the oldest recognized breed in existence, and the foreign matter that was part of the Bedouin's original foundation material must certainly have been burned out long ago in the crucible of the desert.

Those who claim the Arabian horse is a distinct sub-species claim that "all Arabian horses have one less lumbar vertebra." This is another of the many false statements made about the breed. A study made by Dr. Robert M. Stecher of the skeletons of fourteen purebred Arabians (most of them English or American breds, or imports) showed three of these have the much-heralded five lumbar vertebrae, while eleven had six, the number usually attributed to the domestic horse in general. However some of the latter had five, rather than six, to further confound the issue. By adding the vertebrae count from other registered Arabians, the total number counted rises to twenty-two. Of these the ones with six lumbar vertebrae are: *ASTRALED, *ABU ZEYD, *HALIM, GHARIFET, MANNAKY JR., RISALA, DWARKA DB, KIBLA, RISSAM, JADAAN, RAHIKA, and *DEYR DB. Those with the "short count" of five are: *NIMR, AJJAM, MARHABA, RIYALA, RIM, RISHAFA, BINT NURA, SKOWRONEK, SOMRA, and RISSILLA. As a note of interest, the Przewalski horse was at first thought to have only five lumbar vertebrae also, but this was based on examination of *one skeleton only*. Dr. Stecher counted the vertebrae of thirty-two of these animals and the result was sixteen with six, and sixteen with five. Asses were generally placed in the "five" group, but now an occasional one with six has been found. In any case, bragging about having the same vertebrae count as the Przewalski horse and the donkey doesn't help the cause of the Arabian too much, regarding shortness of back. By the way, one skeleton named Pride of the Desert may be that of *HALEB. If so it is of interest, in that it has six lumbar vertebrae, yet he was eulogized for his remarkably short back. This one is not included in the foregoing list.

Another misconception regarding Arabian horses is that they are always the standard colors of bay, chestnut, grey, or rarely black. The Abbas Pasha records prove that parti-colors were once reasonably numerous. Other old records attest to the presence of roan, or at least, very heavy roaning of the body. The parti-colors obtained by Abbas were of the most esteemed bloodlines, so the Registry's comment (in a summary of the breed) that "Parti-colors are crossbreds" is obviously wrong. A parti-color can be part-bred of course. So can a horse of any other color.

There is no other breed so afflicted with wild statements and fantasies, all solemnly accepted as fact. It should be realized that the Arabian may be the oldest breed of horse, but it is still mortal, not divine, and it had its beginnings in the same manner as other types of horses. But that it is the most beautiful of breeds, with a truly romantic history (in fact, not fantasy), surely no one can deny.

EGYPTIAN BROODMARES

BINT GAMILA (Ibn Nadra-Famila)   NEGMA (Dahman el Azrak- Bint Yamama)
(Dam of Ibn Rabdan)   (See photo on page 59)

28

II

THE EARLY AMERICANS

The first importations of Arabian or other Oriental horses were registered by the Jockey Club, no registry for Arabians alone being available until 1908, when the Arabian Horse Club of America was founded (no Registry in its name then). As a matter of fact, the latter was the first all Arabian registry in the world.

The majority of the early imports were of doubtful authenticity, but there were some nevertheless which may have been purebred. The first group importation of undeniable Arabians was that of A. Keene Richards of Kentucky, who made two trips to the Near East and personally selected the horses. They were seemingly as excellent a group as would be expected from a world traveller who was a connoisseur of horses, especially the Thoroughbred. The horses were brought over in 1853 and 1856, including several colts and stallions but only two mares. It is interesting to note in the translation of one pedigree, that of HAMDAN, that Kehilan-Ajuz is properly translated as "the old Kehilan," so this must have been before the silly story of the "old woman" as the meaning of Ajuz had become part of Arabian folklore. A few of the descendants of these Arabians did well on the turf, but unfortunately this was on the eve of the Civil War. During the course of the war the papers of many Thoroughbreds were lost, which meant (as in the case of Arabians in the Spanish civil war) that the identification of a good percentage of purebreds could not be positively made, resulting in great losses to the breed. This also caused the American Thoroughbred to be discriminated against by the English, because of a few consequent "holes" in the pedigrees. The Richards' imports would have been of inestimable value in starting a breed registry here, if they could have bred on, but their offspring were integrated into the Thoroughbred (that being the purpose of the whole project). The one Arabian line (from the two mares, by Arabian sires) also was lost because of the war. Accompanying Richards on the second trip, the great portrait painter of horses, Edward Troye made some on-the-spot paintings during the trip, including one of the Arabian MASSOUD who was among the horses imported.

The next first was the grey stallion *LEOPARD. His claim to that distinction was due to his being the first of the early imports to breed into the bloodlines of modern Arabians. Adding to *LEOPARD's lustre is the fact that he was personally selected by General (and then ex-

29

President) Grant when he was on a world tour, stopping in Constantinople (Istanbul) for a visit with Abdul Hamid II, the Sultan of Turkey. General George Bryant, a friend of Grant's quoted him as saying, "I visited the Sultan of Turkey at Constantinople and with him at his stables, where there were at least a hundred horses, in March, 1878. It was given to understand through the interpreter that the Sultan desired to present me with a stallion and I was asked to select one. I was told that there was no horse in the stable whose pedigree could not be traced for six hundred years. I selected the dapple-grey five year old Arab 'Leopard'. After I had signified my choice the Sultan said, 'I will pick one' and selected the blue-grey four year old 'Linden Tree'...." The horses were cared for in America by General E. F. Beale in Washington, D.C. Both were widely used at stud in the area, mostly to trotting-bred and Thoroughbred mares, with their get bringing high prices. The sum of $10,000 was refused for a son of *LEOPARD, out of a Clay Standardbred mare. This horse was named after the Sultan, ABDUL HAMID II, and won the gold medal at the Buffalo International Horse Show. KASIM was another for which a like amount was refused, he being a grandson of *LEOPARD and winner of first for Pony Stallions at the New York National Horse Show in 1898. Every time *LEOPARD and *LINDEN TREE (a Barb) were shown, *LEOPARD was the winner, being described as the "finer and more graceful of the two in build and action and had a better disposition." The get of *LINDEN TREE had more size and substance than those by *LEOPARD, according to Thornton Chard.

*LEOPARD would have been lost to the Arabian breed if it had not been for Randolph Huntington, breeder of the Clay family of Standardbreds (though the breed was not so named, at the time) which had close-up Arabian, Barb and other Oriental blood. Huntington was a student of the horse and was firmly convinced that bringing in fresh Arabian blood would help stamina. From this beginning he became interested in the Arabian for itself. Huntington was a great admirer of *LEOPARD, and imported the mare *NAOMI to breed him, the resulting foal being ANAZEH No. 235, foaled in 1890, a handsome chestnut with true Arabian fire and style. Although there is no direct sire line to this horse today, many Arabians trace to him through the middle of the pedigree.

Huntington described *LEOPARD thusly, "He was a beautiful dappled grey (in 1880), fourteen and three-quarter hands high; his symmetry and perfectness making him appear much taller.... He needed no quarter-boots, shin-boots ... or protection of any kind; and yet the same movements this Arabian went through (at play) would have blemished every leg and joint upon an American trotting horse ... the knee action was beautiful: not too much, as in the toe-weighted horses, nor stiff and staky, as in the English race horse, but graceful and elastic, beautifully balanced by movement in the hock and stifle." He was a

Seglawi-Jedran, foaled in the desert in 1873. Huntington's interest in action was due to his involvement with Standardbreds, with which he crossed *LEOPARD as well as *LINDEN TREE.

As already indicated, Huntington was so enthusiastic about the Arabian cross on his Standardbreds that he decided to also breed purebred Arabians, with the intent of having some purebred *LEOPARD foals. *NAOMI, the chestnut mare he chose, had been used as a hunter in England. Her "fencing" had won the admiration of even the anti-Arabian people (which included most horsemen at the time) even though at the time she was then unprepossessing and in a lean and gaunt condition. She had been bred by A. Sandeman and was owned by the Rev. F. F. Vidal. Her sire was YATAGHAN, her dam HAIDEE.

KHALED (*Nimr-*Naomi)   *NAOMI (Yataghan-Haidee)

YATAGHAN and HAIDEE were part of an importation from the desert to England by Major Roger D. Upton (author of *Newmarket and Arabia* and *Gleanings from the Desert of Arabia,* who was commissioned by Albert Sandeman, M.P., and Henry Chaplin, M.P. The cost of the importation was $62,000 in gold, an enormous amount for those days, in 1875. It has been customary to give YATAGHAN's strain as Maneghi, thus making *NAOMI "pure-in-strain" since sire and dam were supposedly of the same strain and substrain. However it now turns out that YATAGHAN, a chestnut, was a Kehilan. A letter from Upton lists the horses of the importation:

> I have tried to get a Maneghi-Hedrudj of the family of Ibn Sbeyel of the Gomussa tribe of the Sebaa Anezeh which I hold to be the best breed in the Desert. I have succeeded and one of them is now in my stable. I had enquired at the same time about mares; and two have come of the same family. The four are as follows: No. 1. Chestnut stallion, 4 yrs. old, 14.2. His dam a Kehilet Jeabah taken from the Heissa Anezeh, and his sire the famous Keheilan Hellawi of the Shammar tribe. No. 2. Pearl Grey stallion with black mane and black tail, tipped with white, 4 years old, 14.2. His dam 'Managhi Hedrudj' of the Ibn Sbeyel family of the Gomussa Anazeh, and his sire of the same breed, now in the stud of the

31

King of Italy. No. 3. Bay mare, 5 years old, 14.1½. Same breed as No. 2 but sire and dam not the same. No. 4. Chestnut mare, 4 years old, 14.3. Same breed as No. 2 and 3, but dam and sire not the same. Noted for speed and bottom.

In this country (Arabia) mares are never so handsome as stallions and these are the best looking I could get. The chestnut mare, however, was not selected for her shape—but for her speed and bottom.

The name (Maneghi) means "long-necked" while Jeeban meant "proved" and Hellawi "the sweet."

For some inexplicable reason, the parents of *NAOMI are usually written as being "full brother and sister," possibly a misinterpretation of "same family," but actually they were not even of the same strain.

The only picture of YATAGHAN, often published, shows him to be a chestnut. His description in the General Stud Book is: "A chestnut horse, now 7 years old, a Greban, his dam of Greban family, his sire of the Hellawee family," with *NAOMI his only registered get. The horse pictured is no beauty and has accordingly been used by strain-faddists as "proof" of the plainess of the maligned Maneghi strain. It is quite a blow to them to find that he was not of that strain by either sire or dam. Upton wrote glowingly of the sire of "the chestnut colt," calling the stallion "this Kehilan Greeban," so there is no possibility of there being a mix-up in color and strain. A note by Vidal says that "No. 2 refers to YATA-GHAN, No. 4 in the same letter refers to HAIDEE," so the question is, what happened to the original, grey horse named YATAGHAN? There is also some confusion on the part of the Rev. Vidal regarding a facsimile of the pedigree of his mare ZULEIKA of the same group who was one of the Maneghi mares. The pedigree quite plainly states it was for a bay mare, Kehileh-Nauwak, sire a Daba Nauwak, bred by the Shiek Suleyman Ibn Merschid of the Gomussa tribe. How he could have made such a mistake is strange, for this was the pedigree of KESIA, dam of KESIA II, whose son IMAMZADA and daughter *SHABAKA were imported to America by Spencer Borden. RUTH KESIA, a daughter of BORAK who was a daughter of KESIA II, was the dam of the remarkable performance horse SHAHZADA (who founded a line in Australia) and *NURI PASHA, the favorite stallion of A. W. Harris.

The breeder of ZULEIKA was the same shiek who was eventually persuaded to sell the handsome bay filly QUEEN OF SHEBA to Lady Anne and Wilfrid Blunt after they saw her in the desert in 1879.

The oft-repeated but erroneous statement that the parents of *NAOMI were "full brother and sister" has been used by proponents of in-and-in breeding (very "in" incest) as alleged proof of very close, even incest breeding being practiced in the desert. But this, the main exhibit of that premise, has now gone poufff.

32

Returning to *NAOMI, in 1893, Huntington brought over *NAOMI's daughter *NAZLI (by Maidan), *NIMR(*Kismet-*Nazli), and *GARA-VEEN (*Kismet-Kushdil). KUSHDIL was another daughter of *NAOMI, her sire being the desertbred KARS. *KISMET may not qualify for the asterisk (*) which denotes an Arabian as being imported to the United States, since he died within two hours after landing, having contracted pneumonia during the last days of the voyage; but he lives on through his foals sired in England and deserves due recognition, as he was a remarkable horse. But first let us consider MAIDAN.

MAIDAN was described in the General Stud Book as a "Chestnut horse foaled 1867 and bought by Abd er Rahman of Bombay by Colonel Brownlow in 1871, who received a certificate that he was a thoroughbred. He was then sold to Major Brough who sold him to Captain Fisher. He won the Kadis Cup and was then purchased by Lord Airlie. He was three years in Afghanistan, and was imported to England by Hon. Eustace Vezey, at whose death he was purchased of Mrs. Vezey by Miss Dillon." The term thoroughbred of course here means pure Arabian not Thorough-bred. The strain of MAIDAN was not known but according to Spencer Borden he was "said by some to have been a Manaki Hedruj, though this is doubted by others because of his great beauty, the Manaki being a family of rather plain appearance, though great race horses." The amusing thing here, and seen again and again under similar circum-stances, is that because of an early description of the strain as plain, writers (even owners) continued to believe this even when minutely describing horses of this strain as the best in the country, the most admired and so on; when the horse is of unknown strain, but believed to be Maneghi because of superior performance, yet is handsome too—then "he can't be, because he's too good-looking."

MAIDAN started his racing career at two, in 1871, according to Spencer Borden, but this does not tally with his given birth date. For three years MAIDAN continued to win until other owners refused to race their horses against him, so at this point Colonel Brownlow used him as a charger. With full equipment plus the colonel, MAIDAN had to carry 266 pounds. Since he was used as an officer's charger for twelve years in campaigns in Afghanistan and India, it can be seen he was a tough horse with won-derfully sound legs. During this time as a charger, he was run in gentle-men's races, winning a Hunt Cup and a four-mile steeplechase across rough terrain. When MAIDAN was acquired by Lord Airlie he was seventeen, according to Borden, and was again put in race training and won both on the flat and in steeplechase before being sold to Mr. Vezey and taken to England. There is a discrepancy between the "3 years in Afghanistan" of the G.S.B. statement, and the "11 years in Afghanistan and India" of Borden's, but the forgotten India years may make up the difference. MAIDAN was a horse of heroic stature in performance.

*KISMET, with a two branch sire line nevertheless represented mostly in the pedigree of *NAOMI descendants, deserves mention too, for he was another outstanding racer, but did not have the extracurricular experiences that MAIDAN did. *KISMET was " a dark chestnut horse, three white legs and blaze, foaled in 1877, sent from Arabia to Abdool Rahman of Bombay, in October 1882, then purchased by Mr. Broadwood, 12th Lancers. Won the Mysore Cup, Mysore Purse, Deccan Handicap, Bombay Derby and four of the Agha-Khan's Plates in 1883-1884. Imported April 1884 by Mr. Broadwood, and sold to Sir R. Dick Cunyngham, for whom he won matches in England at Newmarket and Sandown Park in July 1886, beating the Arabian horse Asil . . ." He had been sold to a Mr. Corbet, who sold him to the Rev. F. F. Vidal, who stood the horse at stud until 1891, when he was persuaded to lease him to Huntington. No strain at all is given for *KISMET in the G.S.B., any more than there is for MAIDAN, the certificate that they were "thoroughbred" being considered sufficient. In such cases thoroughbred meant "Arabian," this being the original "thorough-bred from Oriental blood," and was so used in Arabia, confusing though it may be. Often the horse dealers for Indian markets would not bother to even ask the strains of colts purchased from the Bedouins, their main interest being only in assurance of purity plus the potential for racing. So it is doubtful if the strains of these horses ever could be proven, though both have been called Maneghi, and for the same reason—outstanding performance. *KISMET moreover was recorded as being of this strain in the A.H.C.R. studbook, but one thing was evident. Huntington *wanted* the horse to be Maneghi, since he was (or thought he was) inbreeding to this strain, and therefore may have indulged in some wishful thinking. Referring back to *NAOMI, it was probably a shock to Huntington when he discovered that his pure-in-strain mare was sired by a Kehilan, not a Maneghi.

The *NAOMI family is represented by many champions tracing to her in tail female (the bottom line of the pedigree), the most important being through the *NAZLI branch, inbred to the Huntington horses. This is the line of OURIDA, whose grandsons IMARAFF and RAFFI are two of America's leading sires. OURIDA's granddam NIMNAARAH is by NAAMAN (who has *NAOMI as both granddams) out of NIM-RETTE, whose pedigree shows *NAOMI as three of her granddams, and is further inbred, this time to MAIDAN, so NIMNAARAH is double ANAZEH, triple MAIDAN and quintuple *NAOMI. OURIDA herself is the result of a complete outcross, being by RIBAL (*Berk-*Rijma), but the brothers RAFFI and IMARAFF are linebred, being by *RAFFLES out of IMAGIDA, whose sire is out of *RAFFLE's dam *RIFALA. RAFISSA, dam of RIFRAFF, another leading sire, is also of the NIM-NAARAH branch.

An importation that was not intended as such—in that the horses were expected to have been returned to the Near East—was the group brought over in 1893 for the Chicago World's Fair by the Hamidie Society of

*OBEYRAN D.B.   ABEYAN (*Abbeian ?)

Syria. There were forty-five horses originally in this lot, some of them
not purebred Arabians but suitable for the performance and exhibition
planned. Of these only a few survived the fire that followed the financial
problems of the Hamidie Society, all the remaining horses being sold
at auction. Luckily the best ones were obtained by breeders interested
in promoting a nucleus of Arabian horses rather than crossbreeding.

By right of priority, *LEOPARD should have been No. 1 in the
Stud Book when it was finally established, but instead the honor went
to what was considered the best mare in the Hamidie importation—
*NEJDME, with another Hamidie import as No. 2, while others of
this group were registered later and have higher numbers. There are
several discrepancies in the records of some of these horses, many of
them in regard to No. 1 herself. The auction catalog agrees with the
strain of *NEJDME's dam, but does not give the strain of her sire, which
is listed as Seglawi-Jedran in the Stud Book; she is said to have been
foaled in 1887, according to the catalog; in 1881, in the Stud Book. Her
breeder is given specifically as Hedje Mehmed, Damascus, Syria in the
Stud Book, but according to the Bedouin in charge of the horses, she was
bred by the Anazeh; and moreover, was sired by a Kehilan, not a Seglawi.
The later date is generally believed the correct one for *NEJDME's age.
She is credited with having thirteen foals; and even discounting the
two that were apparently those of her granddaughter NEJDME III (No.
54, sired by *OBEYRAN out of NANSHAN, she by *GARAVEEN ex
*NEJDME) and listed in Vol. IV under the names of both NEJDMEs,
such a number would still be a lot of foals from a mare who was
13 at time of importation and 16 before she could even be got in
foal. Hence the theory that the more recent date is the correct one.
As indicated, two of the foals accorded *NEJDME No. 1 are also
credited to the "third" NEJDME; and in addition, a third foal supposedly
of *NEJDME is that of her granddaughter although it is not listed under
the latter's name. So her amazingly long productive life, which would

have had her produce her last foal when she was 32 by dating her 1881, was not long after all. By giving her the more probable birth date, of 1887, her last foal (1913) was produced when she was 26. But since it was not hers but rather NEJDME III's, her last foal arrived when she was 19 by "1887 dating" or 25 by the older date. Numerous champions trace to *NEJDME in direct tail female, but the majority of mares of this line have produced only one champion each, rather than multiples. The leading sire KAHAR is of this family.

Other descrepancies occur in the registration of Hamidie horses. *OBEYRAN is another with date problems. He is registered as being foaled in 1879, and his strain as Abeyan-Sherrak. In the catalog his strain is shown as the more probable (in view of his name) Seglawi-Obeyran and the date as 1889. Throughout the rest of his life—especially in his later years—there were expressions of amazement of his astounding preservation, which is not surprising when it is realized that when he was thought to be 25 he was only 15, or 20 when his owners thought he was 30.

The case of *MANNAKY is much more complicated. The horse of that name but slightly different spelling in the catalog was *MANAKEY, "a sorrel stallion, both hind feet white, 14¾ hands, foaled 1888; breed Managhi-Slaji," who brought the highest price of all the stallions of the importation—$550, the highest-priced mare being *NEJDME at $1200. Homer Davenport gave this same horse as the sire of his mare ZITRA (as " 'Mannakey', a chestnut horse, a Maneghi Slaji, imported and shown under the same conditions as stated with Galfia") in his farm catalog. The "sorrel" MANAKEY was purchased along with *OBEYRAN and *GALFIA by H. A. Souther who was acting as bidder for Peter Bradley. So what's the problem? The usual, mismatched facts. The import of the same name (but slightly different spelling) *MANNAKY No. 294 is registered as a "chestnut Hamdani-Simri stallion, foaled 1893, Desertbred and imported by the Hamidie Society for the Chicago World's Fair." If this account were correct, he would have been a foal when imported, or else imported en utero, but there were no notes referring to foals in the group. Besides the foregoing is another MANAKEY (same as the Hamidie spelling) No. 62, sired by MANNAKY JR. No. 292, out of ZITRA, the mare owned by Davenport and said by him to be by the Hamidie stallion, as already stated. Although the sire of MANNAKY JR. is given by the Stud Book as simply MANNAKY d.b. (no number) "Junior" is presumably a full brother of ZITRA, who, to further confuse the issue, is registered as being by *MANNAKY No. 294, this stallion also credited as her sire and of MANAKEY No. 62 under his own heading. To sum up, these horses are:

In Hamidie catalog: *MANAKEY, a chestnut (sorrel) Maneghi-Slaji, foaled 1888, imported 1893. D.B.

In Stud Book: *MANNAKY No. 294 ch. st. foaled 1893, desertbred. Hamdani-Simri.

36

In Stud Book: MANAKEY No. 62 ch. st foaled 1907. Bred by Homer Davenport. Hamdani-Simri.

In Stud Book: MANNAKY JR. No. 292 ch. st. foaled 1895. Bred by Homer Davenport. Hamdani-Simri.

"Junior," No. 292, is out of *GALFIA, a Hamdani-Simri (using the usual spelling of strains, not the feminine form which would further confuse the issue); and MANAKEY No. 62, whose name is spelled the same way as that of the Hamidie import, was out of ZITRA, the daughter of *GALFIA, and therefore also a Hamdani-Simri.

What seems to have happened is that the old stallion, the Maneghi, was confused with his grandson of the same name but different strain. Why is this apparently the case, rather than the "imported" No. 294 who is recorded as the sire of ZITRA and "Junior"? Because this horse, No. 294, would have had to sire MANNAKY JR. when he was only a yearling —not impossible, but improbable. For No. 294 was "foaled in 1893" while MANNAKY JR. was foaled in 1895. So it would seem that there was confusion all around, and the alleged "import," the Hamdani-Simri *MANNAKY, actually never existed, while the *MANAKEY Maneghi-Slaji was never registered, though his get were.

A mare of this same Maneghi-Slaji strain was *PRIDE, in the Hamidie importation. She is registered as No. 321, a chestnut "bred in the desert; imported for the World's Fair, . . ." etc., 1893. The problem with this mare is that there is no record of her anywhere, there being no mare of her color and strain (in right combination) in the Hamidie auction list. By stretching credulity somewhat it is possible to imagine she may have been sold before the auction, but since the horses were in the hot little hands of rapacious creditors for some time before the sale, this seems rather unlikely. A. G. Asdikian, a member of the Turkish Embassy in Chicago, who was very interested in the horses and wrote a detailed report on them, spoke of No. 24, "a little dark bay mare, my second choice among the females (the first being *NEJDME). She belonged to the Managhi-Hedrij breed and was as handsome an Arab brood mare as I ever saw. Like the rest of the pedigreed horses she was purchased from the Anazeh by Hadji Hassan. The third best mare was No. 26 which went to Boston . . ." This last was *GALFIA (Spelled GALLFEA in the auction catalog). There might be some chance of No. 24 having been confused with the mare eventually known as *PRIDE, but color and substrain ruin that premise. The dark bay mare unfortunately was never registered, having been sold to a C. S. Jones of Chicago who bought a couple more horses which also were never heard of again—in Arabian records.

A horse registered in the Stud Book as being imported by Homer Davenport is *ABBEIAN No. 111 as "gr. Abeyan-Dahwak st; Sire, desert bred; Dam, desert bred; Bred in the desert, foaled in 1889. Imported 1906 by Homer Davenport .. ." The reason for doubting the 1906 importation date is, first, that there is a grey stallion of this exact spelling in the Hamidie catalog, though foaled in 1888, and whose strain was Abeyan-Dahra. He was not one of those known by Asdikian to have a pedigree, thus was not one of the desert purchases of the Bedouin who bought those "with pedigrees" (mostly from the Anazeh) and accompanied the horses to Chicago. There were only eleven of these, three having been lost in the fire which destroyed many of the horses, purebred and grade alike.

By the Hamidie dating, *ABBEIAN would have been five years of age when imported. If Davenport had imported the horse of identical name and near-identical substrain, he would have been seventeen at the time. (Spelling being so varied, this is not serious—i.e. whether Abeyan-Dahra or a different spelling, Abeyan-Dahwak), and the dates regarding the Hamidie horses have been more at odds than the one-year difference here.) No reference of such an aged stallion was made by Davenport, and indeed rarely was a horse this old brought such a distance or even from England, unless he was a proven sire of superior stock or of great fame as the case of *KISMET.

Davenport was meticulously careful to get the strain of the sire and dam of each import, also the breeder by name if possible, otherwise the tribe. But the case of *ABBEIAN is quite different—both his sire and dam are merely "desert bred," no breeder, not even a tribe, is given. Nor was this horse registered at the same time as the Davenport desert-breds, but rather in 1911, when three of his foals were registered by the Hingham Stock Farm. The Hamidie horses, in contrast to Davenport's, were invariably just "bred in the desert" with exception of one account of *NEJDME.

As it happens, before his trip to the desert, Davenport owned a grey stallion named ABEYAN, always (naturally) described as being of the Abeyan strain. He also owned *OBEYRAN, the two names being confused at times, and ABEYAN is specifically mentioned as having sired a half-Arabian colt which won at a large horse show. Both these grey stallions were often pictured in Davenport's ads, before he brought in his own desertbreds. In view of the foregoing coincidences and discrepancies, it would seem that the Hamidie horse of identical name and near-identical statistics, is *ABBEIAN No. 111 also ABEYAN. He is noted as the sire of JADAAN, the mount of Rudolph Valentino in "The Son of the Shiek," and of SHERIA, founder of the most prolific champion-producing line of the Davenport mare *URFAH's descendants. The 1937 Travelers Rest catalog gives the Hamidie horse as *ABBIEAN, the sire of JADAAN. No other premise is noted.

Spencer Borden, who wrote several books on the Arabian horse and its use, imported several Arabians around the turn of the century, bringing over *SHABAKA in 1898, who became the dam of SEGARIO (by *Nimr), among others. She was by the desertbred MAMELUKE (in the

38

G.S.B.: "A high-caste Arab, imported from India by Lord Hebrand Russell") out of KESIA II. From 1905 to 1911 Borden brought over from England several more, the most important being *ANTIKA, *RISALDA, *HAURAN, *BUTHEYNA, *ROSE OF SHARON, and *RUMELYIA from the Crabbet Park Stud, and *IMAMZADA, *HAIL, and *RAKSH from the Hon. Miss Dillon. *HAURAN was a son of the tough if not beautiful mare HAGAR ridden by Lady Anne Blunt in the desert and often mentioned in her book *Bedouin Tribes of the Euphrates.* *BUTHEYNA founded a very strong family of champion-producers. *ROSE OF SHARON is in the pedigree, usually several times over, of nearly every horse bred at Crabbet, and she was imported when she was twenty years old, her worth having been brillaintly displayed by the quality of her sons and daughters in England. Even at this advanced age she was worth importing, producing the en utero import by HARB, *RODAN, and then ROSA RUGOSA by *IMAMZADA (Imam-Kesia II). *RODAN was an important sire to whom many of today's best horses trace ancestry, and ROSA's claim to fame is through her son SIDI (by Khaled, a son of *Nimr and *Naomi) who sired REHAL (out of *Ramim, a daughter of *Berk) whose get usually had excellent trotting action. This would be expected from the *BERK cross, but *NAOMI was extolled for her "fine, square trotting action" with Huntington saying that if he could have trained her when she was young he could have made a mark with her, speaking of the Standardbred standard record or mark. So the *NAOMI blood would nick well for action.

Borden also imported the first Egyptian-bred Arabian mare to come to America. This was *GHAZALA, bred by Ali Pasha Sherif but imported by the Blunts to Crabbet Park in England, and purchased from them. This was also the case of *SHAHWAN, whose beautiful portrait was used for years as an example of Arabian type, and who had been imported by J.A.P. Ramsdell in 1895. Although *SHAHWAN died before he had sired more than three foals in America, he lives on through descendants in Crabbet pedigrees.

Returning to *GHAZALA, this mare though bred by Ali Pasha Sherif is listed as being foaled at the Blunt's Sheyk Obeyd Stud in Cairo, in 1896. She was sold to Borden in 1909. *GHAZALA's dam, BINT HELWA, was also taken to England by the Blunt's and, having broken a foreleg in jumping a fence on arrival, she was thereafter known as "the Broken-legged mare." Having survived this usually-fatal affair, on healing her forehand was permanently misshapen. Old BINT was no beauty, judging by her several pictures. Her head was long and plain (despite Borden's opinion); but her conformation—aside from the aforementioned disfiguration—was apparently good. *GHAZALA was of excellent conformation, but she too had a rather plain head. Her daughters GUEMURA (by Segario) and GULNARE (by *Rodan) were typy and founded influential families. They were also noted for their sons—GUEMURA for GHAZI (by *Rodan), GHAYR (by *Astraled, therefore a ¾ brother of Gulastra), GHARIS (by *Abu Zeyd) and CHEPE NOYON (by Kolastra). GULNARE is dam of the great sire GULASTRA (by *Astraled) and the brothers GHADAF and GHAWI by RIBAL (*Berk-*Rijma). The leading sires GA'ZI and HANDEYRAFF trace to *GHAZALA in tail female.

The horses of the World's Fair exhibition may not have in themselves been so very influential, but their effect on prospective Arabian breeders certainly was. One of these was Homer Davenport, a well-known political cartoonist who was also a decidedly good hand at drawing a horse. He had been entranced by the Hamidie imports and had often viewed the performance staged by the troupe. He acquired a few Arabians thereafter, and it was not long before he was inspired to go to the source and import a number of Arabians on his own. With the approval of President Theodore Roosevelt and the financial backing of Peter Bradley of the Hingham Stock Farm, Davenport left for Turkey, from whose Sultan it was necessary to get permission to buy horses in the desert since Turkey's domain extended over the Middle East. After considerable red tape entanglement, he was able to get a permit to export six or eight horses. This in itself was something of an accomplishment since no horses had been allowed to be exported from the Ottoman Empire for thirty-five years (or so it was said, but France obtained some, so did Argentina). Traveling from Turkey to Syria, Davenport through a lucky blunder in protocol contacted Achmet Haffez, the

DAVENPORT STALLIONS

*HAMRAH

*HALEB

*MUSON

*EL BULAD

diplomatic ruler of the desert, before he called on the Governor of Aleppo. This so pleased Achmet Haffez that took personal charge of the expedition, making certain that Davenport met the shieks of the Anazeh tribe, which was at that time on its annual trek to its summer grazing grounds near Aleppo—only a twelve-hour horseback trip away, in fact. The chestnut mare *WADUDDA was a gift from Achmet Haffez, but the governor, not to be outdone and apparently not upset because of the diplomatic error, gave Davenport the Maneghi stallion *HALEB, known as "The Pride of the Desert". His name is Arabic for Aleppo, giving the impression it possibly should be pronounced "ha'LEB",' not "HAH-leb" or "HAY-leb" so often heard in reference to this horse.

*WADUDDA, except for long cannons, was a well-conformed mare though not especially typy, other than having a level croup and a high-carried tail. Both her neck and profile of head were straight, and her muzzle was boxy, her head rectangular, rather than triangular. There is no denying that she was plain-headed, and this effect was augmented by her eyes which showed too much white—the "human eye." Such an eye is not a fault, but it is an eyesore (if you will pardon the pun) to many Arabian horse owners, no matter how much it is said to have been admired by the Bedouins. It should be emphasized too, that the eye which shows the sclera, as does this sort, is *not* a "wall eye." The latter is a blue eye, generally called "glass," "china," or even a "white" eye, though it is hardly white in the true sense. Moreover a blue eye is perfectly sound. The latter is objected to because of its blank, staring look; the "human-eye" because it gives the horse a wary, even wild expression, and it also makes the eye appear smaller than its totally dark counterpart. Some of *WADUDDA's descendants inherited her type of eye; one of these was SANKIRAH, whose head was Roman nosed as well; it was very coarse throughout, and this sort of eye did nothing to enhance her appearance. It is surprising that anything good descended from SANKIRAH for her head was not her only misfortune. Her neck was heavy and upside down, her back long, and her hind legs so sickle-hocked she seemed to always be about ready to sit down. She was incest bred, her dam MOLIAH having been bred to her own sire, *HAMRAH; and SANKIRAH inherited every fault of that stallion in double dose. On the other hand MOLIAH was a very good mare in practically every point. Apparently SANKIRAH was not dominant in most of her bad points (except sometimes for crooked hocks) and her most distant descendants do not resemble her in the least. This is not surprising since they have the benefit of top crosses to the most noted sires in the breed, mainly of the *RAFFLES and *RASEYN lines, but also through ABU FARWA, FADEHEILAN, *FERDIN and so on. The same was true of other lines descending from *WADUDDA through her several daughters, though none had the handicap to overcome that the SANKIRAH branch had in the beginning, since many were good mares. These were AMRAN (by

41

*Deyr), DOMOW (by *Abu Zeyd), AARED (by *Obeyran) and one other branch of the MOLIAH dynasty. The AARED branch descends down through her daughter SEDJUR to BINT SEDJUR, where the line divides into three. Of these the most famous by far is founded by the great broodmatron BINT SAHARA (by Farawi, a son of Farana), the leading producer of champions in the breed with nine to her credit, while a daughter, the many times champion FERSARA, is the dam of five champions. This makes a mother-daughter combination not yet equalled. There are other daughters and granddaughters carrying on the BINT SAHARA's family tradition too.

*WADUDDA was invariably referred to as "the famous war mare Wadudda" since she was the favorite war mare of Hashem Bey, but actually all the mares, unless town bred, were war mares—that was their purpose in life. In his catalog, Davenport gave this account:

> WADUDDA, chestnut mare, foaled 1899. Dam a Seglawi-el-Abd, her sire a Dahman Khomais. Wadudda, which means 'affection and love', was the war mare of the great Sheykh of all Sheykhs, Hashem Bey, and was his present to Akmut Haffez, Diplomatic Ruler of the Desert, and a present from Akmut Haffez to Mr. Davenport. She is a rather remarkable individual, having been the favorite war mare of her time of the Ruler of the Anezeh, showing two scars of the lance on her neck. She was ridden from Iskanderoon to Aleppo, to overtake camels that had passed without being checked, a distance of 106 miles, in 11 hours, having, previous to the ride, had her right fore pastern damaged in war.

Plain she may have been, but she was neither coarse nor common; and she was a mare to be proud of. Davenport for some reason never fully described her, aside from such tantalizing but unsatisfactory tidbits as "sparkling eyes," her majestic bearing and high tail carriage. Her descendants, at least in the first few generations, were noted for good tail carriage also.

If *WADUDDA was not well described by Davenport, this was decidedly not the case with the brown stallion *HALEB. In Davenport's entertaining book *My Quest of the Arabian Horse* he spoke of going to see this supposedly fabulous animal so highly esteemed by the Anazeh, which had been given by their supreme sheik to the Governor of Aleppo. He admits that he did not expect the animal to be much, having been disillusioned by "wonder-horses" before. But he was not disappointed this time, saying,

> Right now I want to apologize . . . It did not seem at all probable that the 'Pride of the Desert' would amount to much— but when he was brought to the courtyard I apologized to myself as I am doing to you now. We forgot all about heat and sun reflection. We could only think of the horse. He was of the pure Maneghi Sbeyel strain and what a stocky fellow he was! He was powerful

enough for any purpose, especially for a long killing race where weight was to be carried. There was not a white hair on him, and Akmet Haffez began on his fingers to count the stallion's pedigree through his dams' side, each one of which had been the greatest mare of her time. Other horses were shown, but we remembered only the brown.

*HALEB was a gift from the Governor to Davenport, and this was not well received by the Anazeh sheik, Hashem Bey, who did not take kindly at all to the idea of losing the stallion's services or for a tribal gift to again be given away—and to an infidel at that! In Davenport's farm catalog additional details on the horse are given: "HALEB, brown stallion, foaled 1901. Dam a Maneghi Sbeyel. Sire, a Shueyman Sbah. Bred by the Gomussa tribe of the Sabba Anazeh, and looked upon by the Bedouins of the entire desert as the best stallion in all its tribes, and was a present as 'Pride of the Desert' to the Governor of Aleppo in recognition of his liberal camel tax, and a present from the Governor of Aleppo to Mr. Davenport. His pedigree bears the seal of Hashem Bey, the Sheykh of all Sheykhs and ruler of the Anezeh. More than 200 mares were due to foal to this stallion within a year, between Nejd and Aleppo . . ." The rest of the description is more or less a repeat of that given in Davenport's book except with reference to the stallion's bone, "large and flat;" shoulder "of immense power and slant;" and "He is one of the shortest-backed horses that was ever measured . . ."

A further note in the catalog is of interest:

Knowing well how this horse was fairly worshipped in the Desert by all the tribes, I found that horsemen in America were quick in their firm belief that he was the most remarkable horse they had seen. And when Mr. George Morris, the eminent horse artist, wrote that Haleb was the only horse he ever saw that he could not fault, he seemed to express the general opinion of real horsemen. Mr. Brush, Morgan breeder, wrote of him that he was 'the salvation of the Morgan horse, and if taught to pull could outpull any horse in the world as Justin Morgan did'. And no greater testimonial could be given a stallion that the character of the mares sent to Haleb his first season in America. Among them are the best get of Brown Hal, Allerton Chimes, etc. [Standard-breds]. Though from a country where a horse is never allowed to trot owing to the simple fact that a Bedouin in the Desert rides a saddle without stirrups, still Haleb's action at the trot is quite remarkable when you consider he has never been schooled a day in this line. If he was shown again in the Desert he couldn't be more admired when he was in Vermont, and the older Morgan breeders were most jubilant to see again a horse with the same absolutely perfect disposition as had the Morgans of their earlier recollections.

*HALEB won the Justin Morgan Cup at a show in Vermont, which justi-

43

fies the "compact and powerful" claim, but unfortunately died not long thereafter, having sired but two crops of foals in this country. *HALEB's son LEUCOSIA sired NARKHALEB who carried on the line for a generation or two, but it has died out in tail male. All of *HALEB's descendants are found through the middle of the pedigree with most through his daughters RHUA and SALEEFY, both out of *URFAH.

The original six or eight horses which Davenport hoped to buy in the desert wound up as twenty-seven in all. The stallions in addition to *HALEB were *HOURAN, *MUSON, *HAMRAH, *EL BULAD, *GOMUSA, *AZRA, *DEYR, and *KUSOF.

*HAMRAH, whose purchase as a two-year-old was so well described by Davenport in his book, became the most heavily-used stallion of the whole importation, but his number of foals (54) may be due to his long life, the last foal being registered in 1924. This foal was rather unusual in herself, due to her color, described as "silver roan, with shading light to hindquarters"—she was not a grey, since *HAMRAH was bay, and the foal's dam MELEKY was also bay. Although the color of *HAMRAH's sire is not known, his dam, *URFAH, was a bay; and MELEKY's parents were bay and brown. So this roan must have been a true roan, unexpected though it was. *HAMRAH was a bay, as his name suggests (though it is in feminine form and should have been used for a mare), nicely marked with a narrow strip and three stockings; but he had a very plain head and neck and was steep of croup, as well as having over-angulated hocks. No markings at all can be seen on the only (apparently) published picture of his dam *URFAH, but in his book Davenport says, "there were much the same markings on their white legs, the same general character of hindquarters, and the same very 'racy' appearance throughout." This, by the way, fits the Blunt's description of the Seglawi strain: "The Seglawi-Jedran is powerful and fast but not particularly handsome." The markings of *URFAH (according to the Stud Book) may have been like her son's as far as number of feet were concerned, but they were on the coronets only, not as white legs to knee and hocks, as was the case with her son. This shows how misleading a casual comment can be.

The only Davenport stallion to which a sire line exists with several branches among sires of champions is *DEYR, certainly the least likely candidate for the honor, since he lacked type, quality, or even decent conformation. Luckily his descendants, among the champions, resemble him not at all. Of course if they did, they would not be champions. Normally a sire line in a breed in which type is more important than performance as is the case with the Arabian, will have sons which resemble the sire. In fact that is usually why they carry on a sire line, presuming the line founder was anything worth looking at in the first place. SKOWRONEK is a good example. His son, grandsons, great-grandsons, and so on, generally resemble him, or at least have some of his attributes. To return to *DEYR, it is hard to tell whether he is

44

HARARA (*Deyr-*Haffia)

DEYR D.B.

ANTEZ (Harara-Moliah)

HANAD (*Deyr-Sankirah)

responsible for the coon feet (flat pasterns) so notorious for this line, especially through ANTEZ, or whether it comes from the nick with *WADUDDA, as already mentioned. At any rate this is a very persistant fault, often skipping a generation or two, then cropping up rather un- expectedly but very obviously. The "bulldog muzzle," which is almost as thick (side view) as the jowl is deep, was an early characteristic of the *DEYR line and it too persists at times. HANAD, a son of *DEYR, was used for several years in the Kellogg shows as a high school horse, doing the Spanish Walk and the "rope-jumping trick," in which he jumped a bamboo loop (the "rope") held by his rider. He was a stylish horse, and very trainable. ANTEZ (by Harara, a son of *Deyr), was a golden, irridescent chestnut in contrast to HANAD's chocolate hue, and this beautiful color is characteristic of some of his descendants, as is a flaxen mane and tail. He was sold by Kellogg's to J. M. Dickinson of the Travelers Rest Farm in Tennessee. Among other things, he was tried out in racing, but only against time, since there were no Arabian races

45

in America at that period. He was however also raced against a couple of Thoroughbreds, and as might be expected, he came in third. But at least he was in there trying. This was impressive enough to interest Polish breeders, and as Dickinson was buying some horses from that country, they reciprocated by taking ANTEZ. He was owned by the Arab Horse Breeding Society. He was not a success there however, for according to Dr. Edward Skorkowski, the only one of ANTEZ' get to amount to anything was "out of a Maneghi," and too many of his foals had the flat pasterns of the line. He was quickly sold back to America when a buyer who was looking for a stallion suitable for siring Palominos had been told of ANTEZ. Contrary to some stories, ANTEZ was never raced in Poland; he was an aged horse when sold there.

A previously dead line can come alive merely by a distant descendant siring one or more champions where none had grown before. This is true of the line of *MUSON, who originally had but one line and one champion. The line was resurrected by his great-greatgrandson MUSTAFA and the latter's son KIMFA, through the ORIENTAL branch. *MUSON, the grey stallion ridden by Buffalo Bill Cody in his wild west show in Madison Square Garden, in 1907, and described enthusiastically by him as the most beautiful horse in America, was extremely stylish and high-headed. This high-headedness however exaggerated the bulge under his neck of almost goitre-like degree. So many of the Davenport stallions had this sort of coarse neck that it was known as a Davenport neck. He may have liked it under the misapprehension that it indicated a large windpipe, although surely he should have known enough about anatomy to disbelieve this myth. Actually it is nothing but an upsidedown neck so heavily-muscled it does not appear ewe-necked, which it would be if thin. However the Davenport neck is rare nowadays having been fairly well bred out by use of bloodlines with the right sort of neck. For instance, the necks of KIMFA's offspring are long and arched, totally unlike that of their ancestor *MUSON. There is very little Davenport in KIMFA however, his dam *IORANA being an English import and his sire's dam was by the Crabbet-bred *NASIK.

*HOURAN (not to be confused with the Englishbred *HAURAN) was a golden bay Kehilan Tamri sired by a Hadban Enzihi, and has descendants only through his daughters, notably through HAARANMIN and BINT NIMNARAAH as already detailed under the *NAOMI heading. In the one picture of *HOURAN, in which his markings match those given in the Stud Book, this horse has as underslung a neck as *MUSON; yet two other pictures labelled HOURAN but with the wrong hind foot white, show an upstanding horse of rather racy lines and slim neck.

*KUSOF, a bay Maneghi-Hedruj "with a peculiar dark brown spot on his flank" was purchased at a Circassian village, where *DEYR also was purchased although he had recently been brought from the town of that name on the Euphrates River where *DEYR was bred. *KUSOF's sire was given as a Maneghi-Hedruj in the Stud Book, but as a Jilfan Stam el Bulad in the Davenport catalog. His name, KUSOF, means eclipse. This horse sired only three foals; but his daughter SAMIT had ten, though apparently none are in the pedigrees of modern champions, via tail female.

The chestnut, flaxen-maned brother of *HAMRAH named *EUPHRATES sired only four foals; but there is a line to him through SABOT, dam of SLIPPER and AZREKA of the *BUSHRA family line (from England). The unusual thing about *EUPHRATES is that he was accepted for registration in the Jockey Club, but no others of this importation were since they were not registered in the General Stud Book. Apparently this was a new ruling. Before this, others such as *NEJDME and of course *LEOPARD, had been accepted; and *URFAH, the dam of *EUPHRATES was included to qualify her son, but *HAMRAH, *EUPHRATES' full brother, was unacceptable! The influence of W. R. Brown may have caused the relaxation of the rule, to permit *EUPHRATES' entry on the rolls of the Jockey Club.

*GOMUSA is another stallion enthusiastically described by Davenport in his book as "without a flaw in him," but he also mentions that the horse had a glass eye—"In this country such a thing would be disliked in a horse, but in the desert it is comonly found." It was not the usual human eye—he says plainly that one of the eyeballs was white. In the Davenport catalog he is described as "GOMUSSA, bay colt, foaled 1904. Dam, Maneghi Sbeyel. Sire, Seglawi-Jedran. Bred by the Gomussa tribe of the Sabba Anezeh, who are considered by the Bedouins at large to possess the best horses now to be found in the Arabian desert. This colt's left forefoot is white with a star and white snip, with the underlip tatooed blue after the fashion of the women of the desert. He stands slightly over 15 hands without shoes on; and he is one of the most remarkable horses anyone ever saw, regardless of breed. His back is much shorter than ordinary short-backed horses. He was a present from the Sabba Anezeh to Hickmet Bey (son of the Governor of Aleppo) and a present from Hickmet Bey to Mr. Davenport." The short back eulogy was also given *HALEB of the same strain. In the Stud Book *GOMUSSA is registered as *GOMUSA No. 31 "a chestnut Kehilan-Heyfi, with blaze widening to include part of the nostrils; left foreleg white halfway to knee, left hind pastern white. Sire a Seglawi-Jedran. Foaled 1903." The only thing that matches here is the strain of sire, but SAAIDA No. 66 is credited as a foal by *GOMUSA No. 31 in the Stud Book, and also (to *Gomussa, the bay) in the catalog. Something is awry somewhere, but certainly with the registration, since the catalog and book match, with the foals being by the bay horse—not the mysterious chestnut of the wrong strain and markings. *GOMUSA sired only six foals, all descendants tracing back to him through daughters. As far as is known, none inherited the glass eye.

The grey Seglawi-Obeyran *AZRA was purchased against the wishes of Achmet Haffez, who called him the poorest horse that Davenport bought. Pictures of the horse do not bear out this allegation, so perhaps it was something other than appearance that bothered Haffez. Although *AZRA sired only six foals several lines trace back to him. JOON, a son out of DAHURA (*El Bulad-Nanshan), sired several horses with good trotting action; moreover, he himself was said to be able to hit a smart trot. He is grandsire of the Kellogg stallion COURIER who had excellent action, although not trained "English" until an aged horse having an additional trotting line through his granddam. The credentials of *AZRA seem good enough: "Light gray colt with dark mane, foaled 1903. Dam a Seglawieh Obeyran, Sire, a Keheilan Kroash of the family of Moharib el Hazziz, from the tribe of El Mogathra. Bred by Prince Mesoud el Kashis, and purchased from Sheykh Ali, of the Aba Gomese tribe. His dam one of the present war mares of Hashem Bey, Sheykh of the Anezeh."

*EL BULAD was also well thought of by Davenport:

> EL BULAD, dark bay, foaled 1903. Dam a Jilfah Stam el-Bulad. Sire, Kehilan-Ajuz. Bred by Hassan, the son of Mossia, the son of Hassan Aga. This young horse is one of rare beauty and conformation. Indeed his well-formed body threatens to eclipse even that of Haleb. His lines are extremely pleasant and his bone good and flat. He has shown great ability at the trot though a frictionless galloper. His mother was a war mare of much repute and it took a great deal of influence on the part of Akmut Haffez to persuade the branch of Anezeh near Membij to sell him. He had been in war as a scant two-year-old and as a result will always carry a scar of a war spear on his right jaw. We expect El Bulad to be one of our great sires, as his particular family is very rare. The Jilfans are noted for the peculiar slant of shoulder and hip and this horse is a striking example of that peculiarity.

This horse was a grey however, and should have been turning grey by 1906—possibly the word bay was accidental and should have been dark grey. His daughter DAHURA, out of NANSHAN (*Garaveen-*Nejdme) was a prolific brood matron, producer of seventeen foals four of which were mares that founded branches containing many dams of champions. Possibly the most remarkable was AADAH, a producer of five daughters with their own sub-branches of champion-producing families.

In the opinion of many, the mares of the Davenport importation were much better than the stallions (other than those specifically lauded), because they did not have the peculiar faults of their brethren, (some being uniquely Arabian faults). *WADUDDA has already been mentioned, as has *URFAH to a degree. However the latter mare was the dam of *HAMRAH and *EUPHRATES; and she also founded a strong family with innumerable sub-branches. Her picture, in which she resembles a Standardbred more than an Arabian, shows none of the white

48

mentioned in Davenport's book; but it may fit the Stud Book description since the grass hides her feet, which supposedly were white. She was foaled in 1899, described as "... a bay mare, Dam, a Seglawieh Jedranieh mare owned by the Anezeh. Sire, a Seglawi-el-Abd. This mare was one of remarkable history aside from the details of her purchase. She was known for miles and miles along the Euphrates as the most blood-like individual of her immediate tribe, and was thought by Akmut Haffez to be the best Seglawieh Jedranieh mare in the northern part of the desert.... She is, without question, one of the most spirited animals ever seen." It is through her three daughters that so many champions trace to *URFAH, these being SHERIA (by *Abbeian), RHUA (by *Haleb) and SALEEFY (also by *Haleb). Mares with two or more champions to their credit can be found in all three branches, but the one with the most sub-branches is that of SHERIA, her three daughters all having numerous daughters, but a granddaughter AATIKA (by Tabab) with seven daughters to which champion-producers trace, has some sort of record for daughter-producing. The leading sire IBN HANAD is of the SALEEFY branch of this family, in tail female.

*ABEYAH, a bay mare foaled in 1898, was an Abeyeh-Sherra kieh of the family of Madabh el Hadib, of the Shammar tribe. According to Davenport, "This remarkable mare was taken in war by the Anezeh from the Shammar ... According to Hashem Bey, her head is the rarest of the desert, and in the matter of speed she was looked upon as one of the fleetest." This is the mare ridden by Arthur Moore, who accompanied Davenport on the trip, about whom Davenport often spoke, especially as to his conversion to the Arab admiration society by this mare and her ability to carry him and all tack, plus guns, ammunition, and Turkish gold, to a total of 300 pounds without showing any fatigue, even though the temperature registered 135 degrees. She was a good racer too, as already indicated. Her head had a rather extreme jibbah (bulging forehead) and resultant dish; it was triangular but not at all short, this being true of the majority of superior performance Arabians where sustained heavy breathing is involved. The family does not seem to have survived in tail female, at least in regard to producers of champions. A photograph of *ABEYAH's son, MALIEK, has been used for decades as an example of the classic type, but another photograph of the same horse (who was a good individual) was captioned with the profound message that he was a "poor Davenport because his sire was a Maneghi."

The grey mare *FARHA was another especially described by Davenport in his book: "We were shown other mares of the Anezeh, and bought a white mare, a Manegieh Sbeyel, standing over fifteen hands high... Her eyes were large and very black with brilliant highlights, but at the same time with a soft, kind look." This was another "pure-in-strain mare," being Maneghi of the Ibn Sbeyel substrain by sire and dam. "She was foaled in 1900 and was bred by the Anazeh, her sire bred by Ibn Aga

49

Zidadh of the Gomussa tribe of the Sabba Anezeh." Her daughter KOKHLE had the same large black eyes, but the distinction here is that KOKHLE's son, KOKHLESON, is the sire of RALF, the only stallion of all-Davenport breeding to sire a modern champion. All-Davenport breeding in the sense that it is conceded that *ABBEIAN is Davenport. This seems unlikely however, and he is in the pedigree.

Davenport also imported the desertbred *NEJDRAN, but purchased him in England, not in Syria as the others had been. This horse was a Seglawi-Obeyran (sire's strain not given) imported to England in 1902, and to America two years later. Several lines trace to him through his grandson ALCAZAR, the most successful branch being that of KHALDI. *NEDJRAN was sold to Mrs. Eleanor Gates Tully in California around 1910, who also bought *OBEYRAN and *IBN MAHRUSS from Davenport.

The stallion of which Davenport was most proud was *ABU ZEYD, a son of the famous MESAOUD of Crabbet Park, out for ROSE DIAMOND by AZREK. This bald-faced stocking-legged chestnut so enthused Davenport after his purchase that in a 1911 magazine ad he wrote: "He is the grandest specimen of the Arabian horse I have ever seen and I will give a $100 cup to the owner of any horse that can beat him." Although of all-Crabbet bloodlines *ABU ZEYD (known as Lali-Abdar in England) was not bred by that stud, his breeder being the Hon. George Saville. After the death of Davenport shortly thereafter, *ABU ZEYD became the premier sire of the Maynesboro Stud in Vermont. Many champions trace to this horse, but not in the tail male line.

There is a curious case regarding *ABU ZEYD concerning the color of two of his daughters. He was a red! chestnut, but two of his foals are registered as bay, although out of chestnut mares. Ordinarily chestnut-to-chestnut assures a chestnut foal. But DOMOW, out of *WADUDDA was definitely a bay. She was foaled in the ownership of the Hingham Stock Farm, in 1913. The other bay was RADI, out of *RISALDA, a chestnut, her sire, DAOUD, and dam, RISALA, both chestnut as were the latter's parents. And so were DAOUD's. ROSE DIAMOND however was a bay, but ordinarily the color of a grandparent has no influence when the two parents are chestnut. RADI was foaled in the ownership of W. R. Brown, of the Maynesboro Stud. Both Peter Bradley (Hingham Farm) and Brown were experienced horsemen who could tell a bay foal from a chestnut. If these were isolated cases—with different sires, it could be laid to some sort of mixup with another foal registered at the same time, but the coincidence of two by the same sire, and the only two bays from chestnut parents in the whole Stud Book, then one wonders about the genes in genetics. The marking of *ABU ZEYD follow through to a degree on the foals of DOMOW, the broad blaze with a hooked effect over an eye and four white feet. Unless the mix-up, if any was through two daughters of ABU ZEYD, the unique blaze would be more of a clue than the stockings, as other sires along the line had socks or stockings too, but not that sort of blaze. RADI had no foals and was not the English horse of the same name.

There were other imports in the turn-of-the-century period too, mostly singles. One was *BUSHRA (Azrek-Bozra), a Crabbet mare in foal to MAHRUSS, the importer being a Mr. Eustis, in 1900. Several lines trace back to her from champion-producing mares through her granddaughter SABOT (by *Euphrates). A tail male line traces to her son *IBN MAHRUSS through STAMBUL, a Remount stallion whose sire EL SABOK was the only stallion ever to finish one of the U.S. Official Endurance Rides. As a matter of fact he came in first, but was disqualified for a welt on his back, gained the first day of the ride which had not entirely disappeared by the fifth day. The pedigree of EL SABOK brought in the HAMIDIE lines of *PRIDE, *MANAKEY, and *NEJDME, plus two lines to the Huntington mare *NAOMI and the Davenports *HAMRAH and *EL BULAD, so this was the opposite of the usual case—the top line being Crabbet, the rest of the pedigree American. With the Davenport family lines it is usually the mare line along the bottom of the pedigree the rest American, English or whatever.

One of the most important stallions to be imported in the early days was the dark bay *ASTRALED, a son of MESAOUD and QUEEN OF SHEBA, being the last foal of that famous mare in 1900, bred by Wilfred Blunt. *ASTRALED was imported in 1909, by F. Lothrop Ames, but spent most of his life in Oregon, acquired by the Remount when he was well along in years, then was for some time in Idaho. W. R. Brown, who was a Remount agent, obtained the horse in 1923, getting one crop of foals by him from purebred mares before the horse's death the next year. Just as *ASTRALED was the last foal of his dam, so was GULASTRA the last foal (or in last crop) of his sire. This stallion, out of GULNARE, foaled in 1924, founded the very strong branch of the MESAOUD line in this country. *ASTRALED, by the way, although he sired but the three foals of that last crop, plus two before he had gone out to Oregon, had sired seventeen foals in England, and the majority of Crabbet pedigrees have one or more lines to this son of the QUEEN. So do most Egyptian pedigrees, via his son SOTAMM. His influence in this country can be seen in the Bloodline Charts. Unlike most MESAOUD's, he had little white.

In 1910 F. Lothrop Ames brought over the mare *NARDA II from England, she was a half-sister to *NUREDDIN II and *NASIK, since she was out of NARGHILEH. Her sire was NEJEB. The main claim to fame for this mare is through her son *CRABBET, imported as a yearling, sired by RIJM (sire of *NUREDDIN II and *NASIK), a rather wildly-marked gelding, with bald face, high white on legs, and a big splash of white on one side. But despite the fable about white legs (or rather white feet) being less durable than dark, this tough horse won the

51

1921 U.S. Official Endurance Ride, 300 miles in five days, carrying 245 pounds, over paved roads most of the way. He had finished in the money on two previous rides. His full sister *NOAM was among the finishers of the 1920 Ride; and, weighing only 825 pounds, she carried nearly a third of her own weight in the contest. *CRABBET himself stood 15-2, weighed 925 pounds, and was a full hand taller than his sister. In this he kept the tradition of unusual (for those days) height of the RIJM line (even though his sister didn't) which was also characteristic of his ¾ brother *NUREDDIN II, who was said to be close to 16 hands.

Before bringing in other horses of the Maynesboro Stud, it is of interest to note that a gelding by the Huntington-bred KHALED (*Nimr-*Naomi) out of a Standardbred mare (therefore of that very cross that Huntington designed) made the best time (50 hours, 42 minutes for the 300 miles) in the 1919 test. This was RUSTEM BEY, who always placed high in the Rides, being second in 1920, and although he and *CRABBET finished far ahead of the field in the 1921 test and were the only two horses to gallop freely the next morning, a Thoroughbred was second, with RUSTEM BEY third. Additional oldtime Arabian (i.e. pre-Davenport importation) blood was well represented in these Endurance Rides. The Anglo Arab mare HALCYON (¾ Arabian, a granddaughter of Maidan) won the first of these affairs, a two-breed event of Arabian and Morgans, grades obviously qualifying as Arabians. Weight carried was 180 pounds, the distance was 106 miles in two days, and the time 30 hours, 40 minutes. A Morgan was second, the Arabian stallion YAQUIS (*Garaveen-*Nejdme) was third, and the more well-known stallion *RODAN (Harb-*Rose of Sharon), fourth. The latter made equal time with the winner, but carried only 160 pounds, so was not rated as high. The equally interesting thing about HALCYON is that two days later she won third in the broad jump for officers' chargers at the Madison Square Garden Horse show, the only American horse in the ribbons in a field of thirty-two.

HALCYON was the dam of KINGFISHER, a ⅞ Arabian, sired by *IMAMZADA, and owned by Major Frank Tompkins and ridden by him in the campaign against Pancho Villa in 1916. Major Tompkins was most enthusiastic about KINGFISHER after the horse had gone 219 miles in eleven days. Starting March 31st, on the dash after Villa which ended in the fight at Parral thirteen days later, the horse made the distance of 362 miles, carrying over 200 pounds. "He had never shown any signs of fatigue, never lost courage and was a constant inspiration to his rider. He lost but little flesh, always moved with a quick, springy step with head and tail alertly raised, animated and watchful. In battle, he was fearless, being quite content to keep on the firing line without fuss or objection . . . He went lame only once, due to a thorn in his frog, but did his work just the same. He was never sick, was always ready and $25,000 cannot buy him."

Spencer Borden can take credit for first introducing the Arabian horse to endurance rides in this country, for he and the Morgan owners organized that first event. He was very interested in promoting the Arabian horse for cavalry, one of his books being on that subject, and he gave two horses to cavalry officers, one of these being KINGFISHER. When Borden transferred his interest from Arabian horses to Guernsey cattle, most of his horses were purchased by W. R. Brown, whose Maynesboro Stud interwove the bloodlines of the Huntington and Borden stock with later imports from England and France, making the transition from early to modern times, and contributing immeasurably to the breed from every aspect.

Nearly every horse magazine, as well as the widely-circulated *Country Life* which had a large section devoted to things equine, ran the small advertisement of the Maynesboro Stud with its familiar figure of the flashily-marked and eye-catching *ABU ZEYD. These continued to put Berlin, New Hampshire, on the map, and the Arabian breed in the public eye until the 1930's; while the unrivalled success of the Maynesboro Arabians in the U.S. Army Official Endurance Rides made hardbitten cavalrymen take incredulous note, and led to the eventual recognition and use of Arabian stallions in the Remount.

Although the Maynesboro Stud was founded in 1912, the first foal registered as being bred by W. R. Brown was HAJAR in 1915, by *ABU ZEYD. Apparently *ABU ZEYD had been one of his earliest acquisitions, from the Davenport estate. The first mares were:

No.   9— KHALETTA (Khaled-Nazlina)
No. 161— NAZLET (Khaled-Nazli)
No. 167—*NOAM (Rijm-*Narda II)
No. 51— METOECIA (*Haleb-Nazlina)
No. 16—*SHIBINE (Mesaoud-Shohba)
No. 15— NANDA (*Garaveen-*Nejdme)
No. 168— MATINA (Jahil-Nanda)
No. 132— FAHREDDIN (*Abu Zeyd-*Abeyah)
No. 164—*NARDA II (Rejeb-Narghilieh)
No. 14— ONRUST (*Garaveen-Nonliker)

Obtained from Borden, besides NAZLET, were:

No. 166—*ROSA RUGOSA (*Imamzada-*Rose of Sharon)
No. 165—*RISALDA (Daoud-Risala)
No. 277— GUEMURA (Segario-*Ghazala)
No. 278— GULNARE (*Rodan-*Ghazala)
No. 211—*GHAZALA (Ibn Sherera-Bint Helwa)
No. 222—*NESSA (*Hauran-Raschida)
No. 227— HALMA (*Hauran-Mahal)
No. 162—*ANTIKA (Mesaoud-Asfura)
No. 251—*BUTHEYNA (Seyal-Bereyda)

Premier sire was *ABU ZEYD (Mesaoud-Rose Diamond), followed by

*ASTRALED (Mesaoud-Queen of Sheba)

*BERK (Seyal-Bukra)

RIBAL (*Berk-*Rijma)

*ABU-ZEYD (Mesaoud-Rose Diamond)

*RODAN (Harb-*Rose of Sharon)

REHAL (Sidi-*Ramin)

MAYNESBORO STALLIONS

REHAL (Sidi-*Ramim), and KHALED (*Nimr-*Naomi). *RIZVAN (Ibn Yashmak-*Rijm) and young homebreds were used less extensively, but of course the latter, such as GULASTRA (*Astraled-Gulnare) and RAHAS (Gulastra-Raad) were the important stallions in later years.

As a Remount agent, Brown was able to obtain Arabian stallions owned by the Government, few though they were at the time. The two he stood at stud were *RODAN (Harb-*Rose of Sharon) and *ASTRALED (Mesaoud-Queen of Sheba).

Reference has already been made to both these horses, but due to a fantastic tale that has been told and retold of late, regarding *ASTRALED's journey from Idaho to Vermont, this should be clarified. The story goes that he was ridden, at age 22, that distance, in 21 days! This would have averaged over a hundred miles per day for these three weeks—something no other horse ever did—nor did he. The reason the time and distance was mentioned in the first place was because of the unusual length of time the journey took by train, and the fact that he did not lie down en route. The train must have spent most of the time on sidings, or else it was a wagon train. But no matter what sort of train, it was a slow one. The distance would have been remarkable indeed to be travelled by a horse in the same period.

Brown's gamble on the acquisition of this aged stallion of superior bloodlines was worth while, just in his siring GULASTRA, regardless of others, in that one and last crop of foals. The other Remount stallion, *RODAN, sired twenty-one foals, several of his daughters such as GULNARE, BAZRAH, and FATH founding influential families, through only one son, GHAZI, made a name for himself as a sire.

As well as Maynesboro had done with the American purchases, it was the importation made from England in 1918, that made such an impact on the future of the breed in the United States. Heading this shipment, in 1918, was the magnificent bay stallion *BERK (Seyal-Bukra); who was a champion at halter but known for his bold, free trotting action which he passed on to many of his get. Unfortunately he, like *ASTRALED, died a year after arrival, siring only one crop of foals—those of 1920, only four in all. But he had sired twenty-six in England, and his name appears in most Crabbet pedigrees, especially in horses with plenty of action. One of these was in the same group, *RAMIM, a daughter of the great broodmare RIM. Lady Wentworth, in telling of the problems involved in settling the estate when her mother, Lady Anne Blunt, had died, told of the sale by her father of many Crabbet horses, the lot which went to America among them. She said that "by timely intervention the best stallions were prevented from leaving the country and nothing of irretrievable value except Champion Berk was lost, though a few, including Nureddin at 1,100 pounds had to be repurchased later." His loss after such a short time in America was great, for he could have done as much here as in England in the matter of putting action into the breed. As it was, he did inestimable good through his Englishbred descendants, and to a more limited degree of course, to his last crop. RIBAL (out of *Rijma) did his bit, but even more so did the bold-moving ROSHANA, a flashily-marked bay mare out of *ROKHSA, show her trotting heritage. She was featured in the Kellogg shows in harness, her half sister RABI-YAT, (by Rehal, a grandson of *Berk through *Ramim) who would not tolerate harness, being the three gaited star of those shows and equally impressive. Both mares passed on trotting ability to their descendants.

Besides *BERK, those in the 1918 importation were:

No. 344—*BARAZA (Razaz-Bereyda)
No. 345—*BATTLA (Razaz-Bukra)
No. 346—*RIJMA (Rijm-Risala)
No. 347—*RAMLA (*Astraled-Ridaa)
No. 348—*RAMIM (*Berk-Rim)
No. 349—*RISHRASH (*Naskik-Riyala) (died without produce)
No. 350—*RAJAFAN (Feysul-*Rijma)
No. 351—*ROKHSA (*Nasik-Rokhama)
No. 352—*KASIMA (Narkise-Kasida)
No. 353—*KERBELA (Ibn Yashmak-Kantra) (no produce)
No. 354—*NUEYRA (Daoud-Nefisa)
No. 355—*NUMERA (Sotamm-Nueyra)
No. 356—*NAFIA (Ibn Yashmak-Nessima) stallion
No. 357—*HAZNA (Razaz-Hamasa)
No. 358—*SIMAWA (Rustem-Sarama)
No. 359—*FELESTIN (Ibn Yashmak-Fejr)

In 1921 a stallion and some mares and fillies were imported from France, but the stallion (Bahka) has no get listed. The mares were:

No. 455—*BABEL (Gadban-Balkis II)
—*MAKRINE (Kerro-Makerla)
No. 457—*BALKIS 2nd (El Hassen-Bedadine)
No. 458—*BADINE (Lady Keny-Badoure)

followed a year later by

No. 485—*KOLA (Latif-Destinee) This Latif should not be confused with the *Latif by Antez.

and in 1923 by

No. 509—*HAMIDA (Daoud-Hilmyeh) from England, but bred by S. G. Hough, not Crabbet.

*RAMIM has only two offspring which have descendants today, these being through the stallion REHAL and the mare RAMGHAZA. As the sire of RABIYAT, GHAZAYAT, RAYIK and REHASAFA, to name but a few, he is undeniably on record as a sire of action. The family line from RAMGHAZA is through two daughters by GULASTRA and is well-branched, while one through her champion daughter ANKARA (by Ankar) seems ready to start its own way.

The *RIJMA family is followed through by RAAD (see Kellogg

56

section) which has several champions through its tributaries, but infinitely more representation (not as to family however) through her son RAHAS, a key progenitor of the MESAOUD-*ASTRALED-GULASTRA line, RAHAS being sired by the latter horse. RAAD'S son, DAAREYN, has also done well as a sire, but representing the SKOWRONEK line because of his sire, *RASEYN.

*HAZNA is of the BINT HELWA family (see *Ghazala) and founded a highly important branch of her own, mainly through GHAZAYAT, but also through NAFUD. The former is detailed in the Kellogg section, the latter of note as the dam of ISLAM and BINNI, full brother and sister by GULASTRA. The family line through BINNI has carried on well in quality, if not quantity.

The *SIMAWA family is comparatively small, but this mare's son by GULASTRA, namely KATAR, founded the second strongest branch —so far—of the GULASTRA line with several branches; and his son, KAHAR, is on the Leading Sire List.

*FELESTIN (registered as Falastan in England) is also mentioned in the Kellogg section, as of the same family as *FERDA. Most of the champions tracing to her are through KISHTA (by Akil) and the latter's daughters by FEYD, making these linebred FELUKA mares. Both were excellent producers.

Of the French mares, *KOLA was the one to found a notable family, one line through her daughter FATH (by *Rodan), the other, with more branches, that of FADIH (by Sargon). FATH is the dam of ALYF (a son of Ronek) who was for long a three-gaited and harness performer in the Kellogg shows and one of the chief sires.

HAMIDA too has a number of notable relatives via her feminine descendants all via her daughter GHAZIL (by *Abu Zeyd) and the latter's daughters VALIDA (by Ghawi) and HOWIJA (by Ronek). HOWIJA is the dam of SURRAB (by *Latif) whose sons by ABU FARWA, notably ABU BAHA and SHAHZADA are on the Leading Sire list.

It is easy to trace the family founder and strain of the Crabbet horses from 1890, to fairly recent date. Before 1890, a mare's foals had any sort of names, but thenceforward a system was adopted whereby each mare's foals had names starting with a certain letter. Sometimes the strain dictated this, sometimes the mare's name, if there were several of the same strain. Accordingly RODANIA, a Kehilan-Ajuz of Ibn Rodan, founded the "R" family, mares of this family passing the "R" name to either sons or daughters, but the sons did not give the "R" name to their get. Another founder of an important family was DAJANIA, a Kehilan-Ajuz of the Dajania sub-strain, but in her case it was her daughter NEFISA after whom the names took their initial letter—the "N." The "A" family was comparatively short, since it was founded by the Abeyan-Sherrak mare QUEEN OF SHEBA (the "A" from Abeyan, of

57

course) and she had only one daughter, most of her fame as a broodmare came through her sons AHMAR and *ASTRALED. So all the "A" liners descended from the QUEEN through her daughter ASFURA. The "B" girls trace back to a Seglawi-Jedran mare, BASILISK; so the reason for the "B" is obvious. The "H" family is that of BINT HELWA, (also Seglawi-Jedran) but the American line from *GHAZALA, starts from BINT HELWA's tour of duty in the Blunt's Sheyk Obeyd Stud in Egypt. Her foals after her importation all went to H, so to speak. The "F" line is that of the Maneghi Sbeyel mare FERIDA, and the "S" names trace back to SELMA. All of these families are represented in the Brown importations from Crabbet. Horses bred from these bloodlines by other establishments sometimes held to the same formula, sometimes not. *ABU ZEYD, originally LALI-ABDAR, is an example of one that did not.

One line in the Maynesboro ads that always enlivened the interest of youthful horse lovers as well as those interested principally in the breed, was the offer of a free catalog, and since a new catalog was issued each year, it was the custom to send for the newest editions. This catalog was a dream come true for anyone trying to get solid, factual information on the breed (as well as for kids who were picture happy). Of interest today, aside from pictures of horses to which so many American Arabians trace, are the vital statistics of each horse on the place. Along with date foaled, breeder and so on, were the height and weight, and since this can be pertinent today, here are some of those statistics:

	Hands	Wt.		Hands	Wt.
*ABU ZEYD	15	975	*RIJMA	15	925
*RIZVAN	14-3		NUSARA	14-2	875
REHAL	14-3	910	*ROKHSA	14-2	850
RAHAS	14-3	900	*RAMIM	14-2	850
		(at 3)	BAZRAH	14-3	900
ROSHANA	15	900	GULASTRA	14-2½	900
*KOLA	14-2	975	*HAZNA	14-2½	850
GUEMURA	14-1	800	*HAMIDA	14-2	875
GULNARE	14-2	850	GHAZI	14-2	880
*SIMAWA	14	800	RAAD	15	900
*AZIZA	14-2	875	GHARIFET	14-2	800
RABIYAT	15-0½	975			
*NASR	15	950			

In 1932, Brown imported several Arabians from Egypt, all bred by Prince Mohamed Aly, and all were destined to make their mark in American Arabian bloodlines. They were:

Stallions:

No. 885—*ZARIFE (Ibn Samhan-Mahroussa)
No. 889—*NASR (Rabdan el Azrak-Bint Yamama)

*NASR (Rabdan el Azrak-Bint Yamama)　　*ZARIFE (Ibn Samhan-Mahroussa)

*RODA　　　　　　　　　　　　　H. H. MOHAMED ALI's HAMIDA

Egyptianbreds imported by W.R. Brown

Mares:

    No. 886–*RODA (Mansour-Negma)
    No. 887–*H.H. Mohamed Aly's HAMAMA (Kawkab-Mahroussa)
    No. 890–*H.H. Mohamed Aly's HAMIDA (*Nasr-Mahroussa)
    No. 888–*AZIZA (Jamil-Negma)

BINT YAMAMA was the dam of NEGMA and the latter was the dam of MAHROUSSA, accordingly the relationship through tail female is easily followed. BINT YAMAMA was a Kehilan-Jellabi so of course that is the strain of all the others. It may have been the beautiful pictures of MAHROUSSA in a 1929 issue of Asia magazine that inspired Brown to import her son and daughters as well as relatives, or it may have been from earlier contacts with Prince Mohamed Aly, breeder of these horses, but obviously he was much impressed with MAHROUSSA. Old NEGMA, who lived to be over thirty years old, was very crooked in the hind legs, and this fault was seen in many of her descendants, even the lovely MAHROUSSA showing it to a less extreme degree. However the crooked light hocks, with tied-in bone was usually most noticeable through intense inbreeding to animals of the NEGMA family.

    *NASR was a fine race horse in Egypt, and who both Poland and Spain had tried to purchase, according to General Dickinson. He was

59

successful at various distances, but his best record was at six furlongs (1:18 3/5ths, 124 lbs.), and he retired sound and unblemished. *NASR was shown in the 1933 National Arabian Show in Nashville, winning Reserve Championship, as he did the following year in the ownership of General Dickinson's Travelers Rest Farm.

*ZARIFE, like *NASR, was also sold to Travelers Rest, and in 1939, was purchased by the Van Vleet Arabian Ranch in Colorado, where for years he was featured in the exhibitions at the ranch and as a working cow horse in the high Rockies.

A number of champions trace to *NASR and *ZARIFE in tail male, but JULEP, a son of GULASTRA and *AZIZA, is on the Leading Sire list.

Others on this list tracing to Maynesboro stock are:

FADJUR (through Ghazi, Gharifet, Ribal)

GA'ZI (Rahas, Rabiyat, Gulastra, *Kola, *Abu Zeyd, Bazrah, *Rizvan, Gulnare)

YATEZ (*Abu Zeyd, Raad)

GARAFF (*Rodan, *Kola)

IMARAFF (Ribal)

ABU BAHA (Rahas, Rabiyat, *Abu Zeyd, *Hamida)

AL-MARAH RADAMES (*Abu Zeyd, Bazrah, Gharifet)

FERZON (Ghazi, Gharifet, Ribal, *Abu Zeyd)

AARAF (Ribal, Gulnare, *Rizvan, Nusara)

AARIEF (Ribal, Gulnare, *Rizvan, Nusara)

ABU FARWA (Rahas, Rabiyat)

SYNBAD (Gulastra, *Aziza, Ghazayat)

AL-MARAH ERKA (*Roda, Gulastra)

AL-MARAH SAFIR (Gulastra)

GAZON (*Abu Zeyd)

ROYAL SON (Ghazi, Gharifet, Ribal)

ZITEZ (Rehal, Gulastra, Rabiyat)

ANTEZEYN SKOWRONEK (Rahas, Rabiyat, *Abu Zeyd)

SHAHZADA (Rahas, Rabiyat, *Abu Zeyd, *Hamida)

HANRAFF (*Abu Zeyd)

KAHAR (Gulastra, *Simawa, *Rodan, Larkspur)

HALLANY MISTANNY (*Zarife, *Roda)

LUTAF (*Rodan, *Kola, Rahas, Bazrah)

The "Brown horses" were competitors in all available horse shows as well as in the more unusual affairs—the Endurance Tests. RABIYAT, in the sales list at the dispersal of Maynesboro horses, was noted as "Played on the Andover Polo Team 2 years;" ROSHANA "Took firsts in the show ring" (these were always open shows at that time) and all four stallions on the list (Rehal, Gulastra, Ghazi and Rahas) were annotated "Ride and drive," with RAHAS having an additional notation "A proven sire of big, able well built foals (kept this horse as superior to Champion Bazleyd)." The latter horse was twice "National Champion" by virtue of winning the stallion class at the National Arabian show in Nashville, Tennessee, in 1933 and 1934. This was not a national show such as held today, but merely an all-Arabian show title national. It was the first effort to hold such an event.

W. R. Brown was president of the Arabian Horse Club from 1918 to 1939, and at the time of his resignation the Club made the following tribute:

> "It is appropriate at this time to acknowledge the extraordinary contribution of Mr. Brown to this organization and to record his unparalled service to Arabian horse breeding in the United States. At a time when the most prominent early breeders were passing out of the picture and affairs of this organization were at a low ebb, Mr. Brown undertook the presidency of the Club.
>
> Mr. Brown assembled by purchase at home and abroad foundation stock of unsurpassed quality. He developed a stud of international importance that will be a strong influence in Arab horse breeding in the United States for all time.
>
> By careful judgment and thorough preparation he competed in the United States Army Endurance Tests with such success as to re-establish the peerless reputation of the Arabian horse for endurance.
>
> It is to Mr. Brown's sterling qualities of foresight, tenacity, and loyalty to his ideals, that the members of the Arabian Horse Club pay their respects."

The first president of the Arabian Horse Club (the "Registry" had not yet been added to the name) was James A. Lawrence; the second, elected in 1917 was Peter Bradley (of the Hingham Stock Farm, and partner of Homer Davenport). After his death his horses were obtained by John J. Winant, Governor of New Hampshire; C. D. Clarke of Indio and F. E. Lewis of the Diamond Bar Ranch, Spadra—both these last being in California. W. K. Kellogg eventually bought these Clarke and Lewis horses, the first ones he obtained.

Albert W. Harris of Chicago was the fourth president of the club and was one of the earliest breeders. His first horses were NEJDRAN JR. (*Nejdran-Sheba), RHUA (*Haleb-*Urfah), SAIDA (*Gomusa-*Hadba), MORFDA (*Hamrah-Dahura) and ONRUST (*Garaveen-Nonliker). In 1924, he imported from England the grey stallion *NURI PASHA (*Nureddin II-Ruth Kesia), a plain-headed, plain-necked, cat-hammed horse whose beauty was in his character and performance. He was the favorite horse of Harris throughout his life. *NURI PASHA's get were easy to recognise, usually having his same head and other points. Imported at the same time was *ANA (Dwarka D.B.-Amida). If the usually-published picture of DWARKA is typical of that horse, he was coarse-headed and stunted (in appearance but not necessarily size) with light quarters. This horse was owned by the Prince of Wales, and was

61

written up in most glowing terms—so warm in fact that it did not seem possible the picture was of the horse described. He had been a good race horse in India, making it even more impossible to believe the picture was of DWARKA, even though it was supposedly taken in his old age. AMIDA (IBN YASHMAK-AJRAMIEH) was of the QUEEN OF SHEBA family as her name indicates, AJRAMIEH being by MESAOUD out of the QUEEN. *ANA was a full sister of *ALDEBAR, imported later. The sire of *NURI PASHA was hailed for his size (nearly 16 hands, according to the tallest tales) and was Crabbet Park's best broodmare sire, giving them size and scope, but not beauty of head or neck. RUTH KESIA was a granddaughter of AZREK, the desertbred Seglawi-Jedran stallion of trotting fame, through her sire BEN AZREK. Her dam BORAK was by BOANERGES out of KESIA II, the latter out of the desertbred KESIA.

In 1931, Harris imported four mares from Arabia from the King's stables, one of which died without progeny. The remaining three were *TAIRAH, a Seglawi-Jedran; *NUFOUD, a Kehilan-Ajuz; and *SAMIRAH, a Hamdani-Simri. *SUNSHINE, a chestnut stallion sired by "a desertbred Hadban-Hamdani" (presumably a stallion by a Hadban out of a Hamdani) was an en-utero import from *TAIRAH. He, NEJDRAN JR., and *NURI PASHA were the main sires of the Harris breeding program. *SUNSHINE was another plain horse, even coarse, with this battery of stallions, the product of this establishment naturally would not be known for type or beauty, but the Harris horses were strong on performance—not because they were plain, but because they were *used*. The same would have been true if he had placed more emphasis on type and quality.

The beautiful stallion KATAR is listed as being bred by A. W. Harris, but since he was sired by GULASTRA and his dam was purchased from the Maynesboro Stud, where GULASTRA stood; apparently W. R. Brown was the breeder. In those days the owner of the mare at the time of foaling was the breeder. KATAR was undoubtedly the best of the Harris stallions, Arabian type, well-conformed, and a good sire. He was one of the Harris donations to the Remount, along with three mares. KATAR founded a several-branched line with many champions to its credit, mainly through KAHAR and his sons. The *NURI PASHA line has a few champion descendants also, but rarely of more than one champion per sire. The *SUNSHINE line is not represented by sires of champions.

Albert W. Harris was an imposing figure and looked in his element on horseback, resembling portraits of General Robert E. Lee. He was an avid enthusiast of endurance testing, and won the first U.S. Official Endurance Ride on the Brown mare *RAMLA (*Astraled-Ridaa) an import from the Crabbet Stud, which never had a foal but made a name for herself and the breed in this event. The Harris horses were kept at both Lake Geneva, Wisconsin, and Chino, California; the latter is geographically close to the Kellogg Arabian Horse Ranch and in the Chino

Valley, locale of many Arabian ranches today as well as Thoroughbred and other horse-breeding establishments. The Harris horses in California, often competed against the Kellogg Arabians; and honors would see-saw between them in certain classes at fairs and horse shows.

This brings the first quarter-century of Arabian breeding in America to not an end but a milestone, for the results of these importations and breeding programs merged imperceptibly into the next era.

As already noted, the Arabian Horse Club of America was founded in 1908, and was the first all-Arabian registry in the world. Before this date Arabians were listed as Oriental horses and sometimes as Arabians, in the various Thoroughbred registries of the world, (in those which would include them at all). When the Jockey Club would not accept the Davenport importations from the desert (because of not being first registered in the G.S.B.), and because of the stepped-up interest engendered in the breed because of that importation, the idea of a separate registry was conceived and put in force. The first Stud Book, published in 1909, listed 71 Arabians, the second edition ended with No. 74. This one was more of a revision than an actual new addition, however; the third was issued in 1913, and entitled Volume I of the Arabian National Stud Book, with 127 horses included. Up to this time Spencer Borden had not registered his horses (already in the American Stud Book of the Jockey Club), having been embroiled in a quarrel with the Club over the Davenport horses, which for some inexpicable reason he did not consider acceptable. This delay accounted for the higher numbers assigned the Borden horses even though they were older or imported earlier than most of those previously registered. The next Stud Book was published in 1918, this being Volume II; and in 1927, Volume III was issued. In it, the total number of horses registered from 1908 to 1927 amounted to 639. The Annual Report in 1923 gave a breakdown of the growth of the Club as follows:

	1920	1921	1922	1923
Stallions	29	11	20	16
Mares	25	9	25	12
Total	54	20	45	28

It is interesting to note that the 1969 average was well over a hundred times the 1920 number of yearly registrations. And the number compounds annually.

III

THE MIDDLE YEARS

The star of the Arabian breed was in ascendence beyond all doubt in the second quarter of the breed's domain in the New World, as indicated by the growing number of importations from abroad.

The first in this period, and one of the most important, was that of W. K. Kellogg, in 1926, from the Crabbet Park Stud of England. This was nearly a decade after the Brown importations from the same stud, which was then in litigation after the death of Lady Anne Blunt. Except for the older individuals, the Kellogg horses had been bred by the Blunt's daughter, Lady Wentworth, author of *The Authentic Arabian* and the massive yet intensely interesting tome *Thoroughbred Racing Stock* as well as other books mostly on Arabians and their relatives. The Arabians in the 1926 shipment to the W. K. Kellogg Arabian Horse Ranch in Pomona, California were:

Stallions and colts:

> No. 597—*RASEYN, grey, (Skowronek-Rayya) 3 years
> No. 604—*NASIK, bay, (Rijm-Narghileh) 18 years
> No. 599—*RIMAL, bay, (Hazzam-Rim) 1 year—sold, and gelded
> No. 607—*RASWAN, grey, (Skowronek-Rim) 5 years
> No. 613—*FERDIN, chestnut, (*Nureddin II *Ferda) imported en utero
> No. 612—*RAZAM, chestnut, (Hazzam-*Rasima) imported en utero

Mares and fillies:

> No. 595—*FERDISIA, bay, (Rafeef-*Ferda) imported as foal
> No. 596—*FERDA, bay, (Rustem-Feluka) 13 years
> No. 615—*FARASIN, bay, (Rasim-*Ferda) 6 years
> No. 598—*ROSSANA, grey, (Skowronek-Rose of Hind) 5 years
> No. 600—*RAIDA, grey, (Nadir or Skowronek-Rabla) 4 years
> No. 601—*RIFLA, chestnut, (Rasim-Rim) 6 years
> No. 602—*RASAFA, chestnut, (Rafeef-*Rasima) imported as foal
> No. 603—*BAHREYN, brown, (*Rizvan-*Battla) 2 years
> No. 605—*RIFDA, chestnut, (*Nureddin II-**Rifla) imported as foal
> No. 606—*RASIMA, chestnut, (Daoud-Rose of Hind) 9 years
> No. 608—*BINT, bay, (Shareer-*Farasin) imported as foal

Except for *BINT, the imported foals named in this country (i.e. not by Crabbet) held to the customary designations—the "F" names going back to the desertbred FERIDA, the "R"s to RODANIA, and so on, therefore by referring back to the Maynesboro importation, the strains of each can readily be determined.

This importation was made when the Kellogg Ranch was only a year old. It had been founded in 1925, by W. K. Kellogg, of Battle Creek, Michigan—the Kellogg of breakfast cereal fame. The first horses had been purchased in group lots, and might be called the Lewis and Clarke horses, though hardly dating back to the Northwest explorations. One lot was from James E. Lewis's Diamond-Bar Ranch in Spadra, a couple of miles from Kellogg's, the other from C. D. Clarke of Indio, near Palm Springs; and all the horses were of Davenport or with a line to Hamidie breeding. These were of course registered only in the Arabian Horse Club, the Crabbet importations and the later acquisitions from W. R. Brown being double-registered (Jockey Club as well as A.H.C.). Only rarely were the mares of the latter ever bred to the single registered stallions, although the opposite case—that of Davenport mares being bred to Crabbet or Maynesboro stallions was customary. The plain mare *RIFDA was one of those exceptions, having been bred to HANAD on several occasions; and *RAIDA had several foals by JADAAN.

Volume IV of the Stud Book gives the sire of *RAIDA as NADIR, but the General Stud Book lists "NADIR or SKOWRONEK," the last-used stallion always being the last in G.S.B. rules. All stallions to which a mare is bred over a period of weeks, or months, if the first horse was sold, injured, died, or if the mare did not "catch" to him, or for whatever reason (even just the changing of mind of the owner or by an accident), must be named. It is generally conceded that the last one was the sire of the foal, assuming dates to be correct. In this case there was no doubt. SKOWRONEK sired only greys, *RAIDA was a grey, her dam was bay. NADIR too was bay, so the sire had to be a grey, namely SKOWRONEK. But at the time this factor regarding grey inheritance either was not known or was ignored. The Kellogg manager, H. H. Reese, not being certain SKOWRONEK was the sire (especially with Nadir given as sire in the Stud Book) did not hold this mare in the same regard as he did *ROSSANA, who was always acclaimed as "the first mare by Skowronek to be imported to America." So the holding to the double registry in this breeding was ignored. Also *ROSSANA had the typical SKOWRONEK head, while *RAIDA's was more rectangular, accordingly, the former was the most photographed as well. *RAIDA was sold after producing the JADAAN foals and one by KAABA, thereafter being bred only to her new owner's stallion, a Davenport horse.

*NASIK wa the patriarch of the importation, and Lady Wentworth's description of him as "A magnificent horse of the type liked best by the Bedouins, having style and quality to a superlative degree" was most

65

FARANA (°Nasik-°Farasin)

°FERDIN (°Nureddin II-°Ferda)

RIJM

°NUREDDIN

MAHRUSS

°NASIK

ONE LINE OF MAHRUSS

apropos. He was gentle as the proverbial kitten, but full of fire and will to go. His head was beautiful, though not the exaggerated type; and his eyes were large and expressive. At Kellogg's his mane was always kept clipped (which I thought was rather awful, for most Arabians don't look good without a foretop), the idea being to make his neck look longer, which it did; but he still would have looked much better with full mane, and long forelock. *NASIK was quite low in the back at age eighteen, but none of his foals was low-backed and practically all were very short-backed—FARANA being a good example. *NASIK had extreme lay-back of shoulder, probably accentuated by the lowering of his back; his withers were high and his croup level. A brilliant golden bay (which however darkened with age) with his black points intensified by short stockings and with a neat strip in the face, *NASIK was a handsome horse—all-Arabian in appearance and temperament. His back had become very low by the time he was thirty years of age, but he was still vigorous and full of *joi de vivre*. However Reese said he was tired of looking at that low back and ordered *NASIK destroyed; the veterinarian and the grooms who helped with the job said that they never saw a horse who tried so hard to cling to life as poor old *NASIK did after that lethal dose. The desertbred *DEYR was destroyed for a somewhat similar reason as soon as Reese saw the horse, after becoming manager of the ranch in 1927. It was not *DEYR's back, but his over-all bad conformation and lack of quality that caused his death sentence. He too though comparatively young (23 to *Nasik's 30) was in good condition. An ugly mare or one with a low back, or sickle hocks or any similar blight to the eye can be hidden in a back pasture, but not a stallion, and thus the eventual fate of these two, utterly different though they were. *DEYR's skeleton was given to the Los Angeles County Museum of Natural History, and is still on exhibition there. In the book *The Kellogg Arabians* it is stated that *DEYR has five lumbar vertebrae, but this is in error—he has six, but the lateral wings of two of them had fused, making it appear to be five instead of six. A count of the vertical processes shows the six vertebrae. It's unfortunate that *NASIK's skeleton was not similarly saved. The skeleton of the Arabian in the American Museum of Natural History is the Maneghi horse *NIMR, showing five lumbar vertebrae.

The *NASIK line did not approach that of *RASEYN in the champion-siring race, but then few lines did, or do, except through other sons of SKOWRONEK or *ASTRALED. Nevertheless the line is breeding on well, through the branches founded by FARANA, RIFNAS, and SIKIN especially, while that of NAJUR (a half brother of Bint Sedjur) had a representative in ALICANTE's GHAZAL, sire of four champions. The Sire Line charts show the branches but do not show the broodmare sires, of which FARANA has turned out to be one of the best. Admired originally for his catlike agility and speed as an exhibition stockhorse, he was expected to put this trait in his get, which he did. His excellent shoulder and withers, short back, and level croup were among his assets, wonderful for counteracting the deficiencies of the SKOWRONEK line as to shoulder, and for other lines as to back and croup. His neck could definitely have been longer, and while his profile was straight (which is perfectly acceptable in the Standard) it would look dished when he was in action—his nostrils flaring and big eyes popping as he put every ounce of energy into his work. FARANA won several stockhorse classes and a lightweight stockhorse championship at the Coronado National Horse Show but probably, like other stockhorses of the time, he would have bolted at the sight of a cow in the ring. However he did what was required then and was spectacular in sliding stops from a dead run, and he did spins so fast that once in a while he left his rider still up in the air, also spinning before an ignominious landing. He was a fast backer, almost trotting backward, as he made his exit—in reverse gear—from the Kellogg arena; and of course he backed fast and straight in the process of the stockhorse rituals. If *NASIK had never sired another foal, he would be well remembered because of this sensational worker. FARANA performed every Sunday, twice a day, for over ten years along with regular works and other shows. He was never cooled out even when brought in sopping wet on a hot day and panting from his all-out exertions; he was just run into the stall and tied up. It is a wonder he didn't stiffen up or get unsound. Some stockhorse judges condemned him for too-light bone (it was fine, but not tied in nor too light), but he remained clean-legged through the years. He was much too stylish—with too-high neck (though the head-carriage was good) and "fancy" high-carried tail—to be a proper cow horse, but he did not have good enough action at the trot for English performance. Moreover, he bucked whenever it was attempted to put a flat saddle on him. He did do the Spanish walk in harness, however, before taking up his specialty, which he engineered himself by his constant refusal to accept an English saddle without active protest. His full brother SIKIN was usually shown in "costume" at a gallop; and although having somewhat better action than FARANA, he still did not have enough flexion to qualify him as a three-gaited horse or for harness. He, in contrast to his brother and exemplifying the vagaries of genetics, had a long, arched neck, and a pretty head, fairly well dished. Several champions trace to SIKIN in tail male as well as through his daughters.

*RASEYN is of course the star of the Kellogg stallions, though he was not so considered at first. He was a beautiful horse, nearly black at three years, but dappling out nicely and holding the dappling for a fairly long time. However, throughout the series of ownerships of the ranch, it was always hoped to get a son of *RASEYN with a longer neck and cleaner, better-sloped shoulder with high withers. He himself was mutton-withered. This fault became more evident as he matured (he actually had indication of withers when young and seemed fairly short-

*RASEYN (Skowronek-Rayya)   *CRABBET SURA (Skowronek-Sardhana)

backed as well). His back was low in his medium and old age; the low withers and comparatively straight shoulders (compared to *Ferdin and Farana, that is) causing the back to seem longer as it became "easy ." Straight shoulders without withers always make a horse longer in the back than good layback with withers that also blend well in to the back. *RASEYN's croup was long and level; he was much better than his rival, *RAFFLES, in levelness of croup and straightness of hind legs. His bone was excellent, but he was a little over in the knees due to his having been used as a jumper when young. SKOWRONEK too was just a smidgen over at the knees, a benevolent fault compared to its opposite condition, calf-knees. *RASEYN's head was not quite as dry and clean-cut as was that of his son FERSEYN (and neither one had any jibbah), nor were his eyes quite as large and prominent as those of FERSEYN.

*RASEYN too was used for years in the Sunday shows, practically all his life through various ownerships of the ranch. The major part of the time he was used as a five-gaited horse. He had a fairly good trot as a three-gaited horse, but when the other two gaits were added, he relaxed to a pleasure trot, putting all his steam and action into the rack and slow gait.

*RASEYN never sired a chestnut, his foals being either grey, bay or brown with little or no white. This made them rather hard to sell as foals, compared to the sparkling chestnuts with their satiny coats and white markings. The *Raseyn foals were furry compared to the foals by other stallions until they shed off to the new coat. As a matter of fact, the drabness of the dull browns and bays without white to relieve the monotony was one of the exasperating things about *RASEYN. At that time most of the Kellogg horses were sold as young foals, and the chunky little fluff-balls simply did not compare to the elegant sleekness and cheerful markings of chestnuts and bright bays. But usually they did have pretty heads. Most of the time FARANA was dominant for bay

69

or brown, with sometimes a grey mare taking precedence in color of the foal. This was a drawback as many people wanted a "chestnut *Raseyn" or "chestnut Farana," but definitely not a grey or bay, or even less saleable when young, a brown. Through the years color preferences have fluctuated, but sires dominant for one color have their drawbacks on this account.

The temperament of *RASEYN was not as kindly as that of the other stallions. He was nippy, this having been accentuated by an effort to make a trick horse of him at three or four, so it wasn't a good idea to turn your back on him. He took the coat off the back of his trainer. Once he bit through the hat and ear of a groom which was quite a feat, for old Juan never took his hat off even when he was sick in bed according to reports. Maybe *RASEYN was trying to see if it *could* be taken off.

FERSEYN, out of *FERDA, was the leading sire of champions for many years, and also leads in the number of branches his sons founded in regard to sires of champions. He is seconded by SUREYN, out of the SKOWRONEK mare *CRABBET SURA (therefore closely inbred). This horse was for many years a Remount stallion and only salvaged for purebred breeding after he was well along in years. RONEK is another founder of a many-branched line, this horse being out of *BAHREYN (*Rizvan-*Battla) which accounts for his action and ability to pass it on, because *BATTLA has an AZREK line, and *RIZVAN himself had a good trot. RONEK was a five-gaited horse, like his sire. He was sold as a youngster to the Travelers Rest Farm in Tennessee, where he was trained as a gaited horse. According to the Dickinson catalog he was "Champion stallion and first prize Arab under saddle Illinois State Fair 1937. A show horse of brilliant action." He was the sire of the Kellogg stallion ALYF, for long the senior sire at that ranch, who was naturally five-gaited but who was deliberately trained away from the rack and slow gait to perfect him as a three-gaited and harness horse, since RABIYAS was at the time the five-gaited horse of the Kellogg shows.

Several *RASEYN sons were sent out as Remount stallions when the Army owned the ranch. Besides SUREYN, others included were GAMHURI, RASAKKLA and RALET. RALET was featured for many years as a "liberty jumper" (without rider) in the Sunday shows. Flying around the ring taking the jumps effortlessly, then coming to a rearing stop in front of his trainer, this rich bay stallion was a pleasure to watch. His full brother, SHEREYN, won the lightweight stockhorse class at the Cow Palace open show among additional open-show wins, and before that had been a real working ranch-horse. SHEREYN was also a successful competitor on trail rides.

Of the stallions in the 1926 importation, *RASWAN was considered to be superior to *RASEYN. However Lady Wentworth is said to have given him as a bonus to Carl Schmidt, who was manager of the Ranch for a few months and had gone to England to obtain these horses, just as the aged *NASIK had been given to Mr. Kellogg. After all a stiff price had been paid for the group—around $82,000 at a time when a dollar was worth a hundred cents, not just a dime. No one ever knew what Kellogg thought, at any time, but everyone found out his reaction to this—the gift of a handsome young stallion, the best of the lot, to his employee, while the bonus given to him, the buyer, was an eighteen-year-old stallion naturally considered to be well past his prime. In the resultant flap, the ownership must have been transferred to Kellogg, despite recently-published material to the contrary (that transfer was requested, but not definitely given). The horse is registered as being imported and owned by W. K. Kellogg. His registration certificate, still in existence, gives Kellogg as the owner. Therefore when Schmidt rode the horse off the ranch, contrary to orders, *RASWAN was not his property. The cause of the accident resulting in the death of the horse, as told at Kellogg's, was that he had been tied to a fence at a ranch house in the Spadra hills and broke loose to fraternize with a team of mules, stepping into the harrow or cultivator to which they were hitched. It was due to this he received the deep cut under the fetlock, which could not be healed because of its location, and he had to be destroyed. By contrast, Schmidt's version was that Kellogg had a groom deliberately "hamstring" the horse in order "to collect the $10,000 or $15,000 insurance." That a multi-millionnaire, who had just gone to considerable expense to buy the best Arabians available, would kill the best of the lot for insurance money is too ridiculous to even consider. Especially since the horse was registered in Kellogg's name and was legally his at the time. Needless to say, Schmidt was no longer an employee of Kellogg after this incident, but nevertheless he decided to memorialize the horse by changing his name from Carl Schmidt to Carl Raswan when he, a German, became a naturalized citizen.

Since this may be the first case of a man naming himself after a horse, rather than the more usual opposite instance, it is of interest, but especially so since Raswan became a prolific writer on the subject of Arabian horses and his name is therefore well known. He is also responsible for the three-strain theory in which the *type* of Arabian horses allegedly conforms only to the strain of the dam, thus disallowing any influence of the sire whatsoever. If it had been a three-type argument (since there are even more types than that in the breed) there would be no cause to disagree, but he insisted on its following a strain *name*. But enough of that.

*RASWAN sired no foals in this country but lives on through the three he sired in England, namely STAR OF THE HILLS, *ROSE OF FRANCE and FERHAN. The first, a mare, was sold to Russia, where she produced KRONA, dam of TAKTIKA, whose son PIETUSZOK was a fine race horse (all Arabs are raced in Russia) and after being sold to Poland became a leading sire of race winners for several years. He

71

has halter champions to his credit also, namely *GAYPOLKA and *BAJ-RAM. *ROSE OF FRANCE will be noted later, as a Selby import. FERHAN (out of Fejr, a half sister of *Ferda), as the sire of INDIAN GOLD, is in the pedigree of *ROSANTHUS, *SERAFIX, SILFINA and SILVER GILT. With a record like that from only three foals, what could *RASWAN have done here with the opportunity given *RASEYN? Or at least half that, since they would have had to share what few mares there were then.

The hide of this unlucky horse covered a table in the reception room of the ranch office and showed that he was a cinnamon-grey, not the black-dappled grey of *RASEYN; yet he photographed distinctly dappled. Years after his death, the desiccated hind leg of a horse was found far back in a closet in the main stable building, and it turned out to be that of *RASWAN, evidently kept to show where the cut had been. It was just below the fetlock, on the back of the pastern, so the horse most certainly had not been hamstrung, the deep cut substantiating the version of his wound as told by ranch employees, not that of Schmidt.

Of the remaining imported males, the yearling colt *RIMAL was eventually gelded. The two en utero imports were both colts, one being *RAZAM who has no registered get; the other was *FERDIN. This half brother of FERSEYN was as much representative of the RIJM line as the former was of SKOWRONEK, *FERDIN being by *NUREDDIN II. He was good in his way to overcome the shoulder shortcomings of the SKOWRONEK descendants as was his close relative FARANA, and had excellent conformation throughout with a marvelous set of legs, but his head was characteristic of his sire and grandsire, being plain (but not coarse). He had two attributes said to be much admired by the Bedouins but greeted with less enthusiasm here—the "human eye," showing too much white, and the side-carried tail. This last was also characteristic of *NUREDDIN II and RIJM. *FERDIN is represented by champions in tail male through ROSSDIN, but more numerously through daughters, in the middle of the pedigree.

Of the mares of the 1926 importation, the old mare *FERDA is by long odds the best represented by champion descendants, both in tail female mares of her family, and of course through her sons and grandsons. FERSEYN has already been noted, also *FERDIN. *FARASIN, as the dam of FARANA and SIKIN is worthy of note on that alone, but her daughters—full sisters of those horses—were also prepotent, especially NARASA. To this mare trace in tail female, the champions RONARA, IBN HANRAH, LA BAHIA, ROHANNA, BINT RONARA, PULQUE and TONDELAYO, through the NARLET branch; and via NAFA, ORTEZ, NAFATEZ, NITEZ, NAFASON, BLACK MAGIC, BOLERO, NATEZ and TANGO, among others. Through other daughters of *FERDA (Danas, Ferdeyna, Ferdika and *Ferdisia), there were still more branches; that of *FERDISIA had the most branches (next to that of *Farasin).

*FERDA was from a distinguished family—her half sister FEJR (by Rijm) being the dam of *FELESTIN, imported by Brown in 1918. This mare (by Ibn Yashmak) was the dam of KISHTA (by Akil), whose two daughters FEYN and MILANNE (both by Feyd, a son of Farana) produced five and four champions respectively. The former's included several Top Tens and a Canadian National Champion. Another daughter of FEJR was sold to Poland, this being FASILA (by Rasim), whose son *SULEJMAN by the great racer FETYSZ is on the Leading Sire list.

*FERDA was called "one of the top mares of England" by Jack Humphreys, manager of the Maynesboro Stud, who had made a trip to England just after the purchase of the Kellogg group. The old mare was of correct conformation throughout, having none of the faults peculiar to the breed; but neither was her head typical, though it was breedy and clean-cut. She was an "incubator mare" in respect to heads, her foals usually inheriting the type of head from the sire (but usually improved in chiselling, as in the case of Ferseyn compared to his sire). Not only in the passive atmosphere of the halter classes, but in the performance arena or field, the descendants of *FERDA have proven their worth.

*RIFLA was a beautiful mare, winner of championships in the early shows and fairs, and was the dam of RIFNAS and SHEMSEH, the latter the founder of the main branches of this family, featured by mares with three champions each to their credit. She had a couple of white patches under the body, but she had only short socks (to fetlocks) on three legs, in contradiction to the idea that a body spot always accompanies high white. She was blaze-faced. Her son RIFNAS had no body spot, and only a narrow strip, but the white on all four legs was high above the knees on the forelegs, though only to the hocks behind. *RIFDA, without the class of her dam, was usually bred to HANAD, but she was also dam of RIFDAH (by *Rahal), an exceedingly plain mare without much to recommend her, (no wonder, her sire and dam were both by *Nurrendin II); but she did make history of a sort by producing the first set of twins at Kellogg's.

*RASIMA is represented best through the produce of her daughter JALILA and Selby imports, but her daughter *RASAFA is tail-female ancestress of several champion producers, one through REHASASFA (by Rehal) and another through FERAFA (by *Ferdin). Another line via ANTAFA (by Antez) resulted in several branches, but mostly singles.

*BAHREYN was a hot-tempered little mare whose ears nearly touched at the tips, supporting the old-wives' tale that such horses had this sort of temperament, whether or not it was usually true. As the dam of RONEK, this mare is worthy of note, but she also has tail-female descendants which produced champions, one through FEREYN (by *Ferdin), the other through BAHDINA, also by *FERDIN.

Other groups of horses were acquired by the Kellogg Ranch in its

73

early attempt to build up a large herd of broodmares, as well as an occasional new stallion. Most of these were of course Davenport breeding plus some Borden-Huntington, these being the majority of American bloodlines at the time, aside from the select group of Maynesboro horses which had been bred to a certain standard and improved with the best imported animals then obtainable. Accordingly when the Maynesboro Stud went out of business, its horses were quickly bought up by the Kellogg Ranch, J. M. Dickinson, and the then-new Hearst Ranch. The mares obtained by Kellogg's, and known thereafter as "the Brown mares" (to the confusion of anyone thinking this meant their color) were: RAAB, RAAD, RABIYAT, ROSHANA, RAYIK, GHAZAYAT, BAZIKH, BAKMAL and NUSARA. Although not imports as such, their influence had such an impact on the breeding stock of Kellogg's they are worth a few words on their own.

RABIYAT and ROSHANA, half sisters out of *ROKHSA and by a grandson of *BERK and *BERK himself, respectively, were bold, free-moving trotters, RABIYAT as a three-gaited (park) mare and ROSHANA in harness. RABIYAT is the dam of the five-gaited stallion RABIYAS (by Rahas), whose son ABU FARWA is the chief progenitor of the MESAOUD line in this country through the *ASTRALED branch. This can be traced through the Sire Line charts. Several lines of champion-producing mares trace to RABIYAT in tail female, but a great many more to ROSHANA, whose daughters RAJIH, RAYIM, RAZI, RAYIK, RABBANI and ROSEYNA all have such producers to their credit, most through several branches. It must be admitted however that most of these were from her Maynesboro-bred daughters, since she was an aged mare when obtained by Kellogg's. An exception is ROSEYNA by *RASEYN. The only mare of non-Maynesboro, Crabbet or Egyptian breeding still at Kellogg's when it was turned over to the Army was SHEHERZADE, (a daughter of Rayik sired by Joon). Since this mare had the action of the ROSHANA family she was used as a three-gaited mare in the Sunday shows. She passed on this ability to her son COURIER as well. RAYIK was sold to the Hearst Ranch about a year after her arrival, and so the Kellogg Ranch lost a good mare in that way (Sheherzade being bred by Hearst).

BAZIKH was remarkable for her extreme jibbah. In her own way she managed to bring to life still another old belief—that a bulging forhead indicated an ornery or stubborn disposition. She may not have been stubborn, but she was hardly a sweet-tempered mare either, nor was her daughter RAHIKA, a mare with a really beautiful head and neck. RAHIKA, was foaled in pasture, it took half a day to catch her and old BAZIKH; and the filly was spooky thereafter . . . which had nothing to do with the accidental birthplace, but rather her temperament. She too had a prominent forehead, as her skull shows so well on the skeleton still seen at Cal Poly—(as Kellogg's is known today). Both BAZIKH and

RAHIKA were excellent mares otherwise. As a matter of fact, the old mare had been a good saddle animal, though it may be significant that the wording "good safe ride" was not used regarding her on the sales list —just the ambiguous "ridden some." A good number of champions descend from BAZIKH, including EL NATTALL (Pacific Coast Champion Stallion) who was out of NATTA (Farana-Rahika); NATTA also founded a many-branched family of champion-producing mares. From BAZIKH's daughter SETANA (by Farana) are the lines to which the good brood-matrons TAHIR and BARQ trace. The BAZRAH family has five main branches and innumerable sub-branches, but at Kellogg's the line came only through BAZIKH and BAKMAL (the former by *Abu Zeyd, the latter by Rahas). A beautiful neck was characteristic of most mares of this family, along with good over-all conformation.

NUSARA was an aged mare when purchased, and consequently did not have many foals at Kellogg's. Of the four branches tracing to her, two are from her Kellogg produce. However one branch (of the Maynesboro lines) was an important one indeed, for this is the family founded by NADIRAT (by *Rizvan), whose daughter AARAH is the dam of the fine sires AARAF and AARIEF, both being excellent three-gaited horses, as was their full sister AARAFA, a mare that was in the class of RABIYAT when it came to a bold, balanced and high trot. AARAFA is the dam of LEWISFIELD SUN GOD, among others while her brothers are both on the Leading Sire list with ten champions each. Old NUSARA herself was no beauty, her neck being heavy underneath, practically upside-down; so the quality of this family cannot be claimed by that mare herself. Subsequent crosses of *RIZVAN, GHADAF and *RAFFLES have made the change for the better—much better.

GHAZAYAT was of the BINT HELWA family via the latter's daughter *HAZNA, who was also dam of NAFUD, to which BINNI traces. GHAZAYAT was by REHAL (Sidi-*Ramim) already mentioned as a fine sire of real performance horses, especially as to trotting ability, one of his daughters being that all-time great, RABIYAT. There are five lines of champion-producers founded by GHAZAYAT, one being that of YATANA (full sister of the stallion El Kumait) already mentioned regarding her sire FARANA. There are eight branches of the YATANA family, nearly all with their own sub-branches, and most in multiples of champions. Her daughters were by a variety of sires—*SULEJMAN, a Polish import (but out of an "F" mare of Crabbet), the Egyptian import *FADL; a *RAFFLES son, IMARAFF; and a *FADL son, ABOU. The FARANA nick with GHAZAYAT was better than that with *RASEYN, RABIYAS or RIFNAS, though these lines did produce some champions. Her daughter GHAZEYNA was the dam of GEZAN, a rather big-headed (possibly stunted) horse by ANTEZ, a rather compressed type for the GHAZAYAT family, but sire of two champions. GHAZAYAT had a good but not extreme head, a long and nicely-arched neck, excellent conformation throughout, and was a very good riding horse. Quite a number of the "Brown" mares had assorted types of skin trouble, and GHAZAYAT was no exception. The hair at first just came off in small patches, but one year her whole forehand—head, neck, shoulder—had no hair at all. Oddly enough, that seemed to be the climax—for with her next coat and thereafter she had no more such problems. RAAB was another—in her case she was dotted with small, round hairless spots. BAKMAL had a more common problem—the loss of pigmentation around eyes and muzzle, though she was a chestnut, and this was an affliction seen more often on greys.

RAAD was by SIDI out of *RIJMA, quite a nice mare with good neck and level croup. SIDI was a neatly-marked chestnut by the Huntington stallion KHALED out of *ROSA RUGOSA, who did not inherit the blaze and stockings of his dam and granddam. RAAD herself was a red chestnut with only a star and one white coronet, who would have been handsomer with a little more white, but in conformation she was an excellent riding type. Her neck was not as nicely arched as some, but good enough, and her head was plain. She was the dam of RAHAS, who certainly had enough white and was inclined to pass on a bit too much at times of a broad blaze and sometimes the typical Arabian body-spot which is seen in the MESAOUD line, which he represented. He was by GULASTRA. The tail-female representatives (as to champions) of RAAD are through her daughter RAAB (by *Abu Zeyd), a real saddle-horse in conformation though she had (as did many other Arabs) a prominent "jumping bump" on the croup and not quite as long of croup as desirable. YATEZ, by *WITEZ II, a Leading Sire with 18 champions to his credit, is of the RAAB family line.

But to return to imports—in 1936 another group was brought over, only three individuals but important ones they became. They were the mares *INCORONATA, *RISSLETTA, and *SURA, the latter having her name changed to "CRABBET SURA" because the former name had already been used in the Stud Book. *INCORONATA was by SKOWRONEK out of NISREEN, the "I" name marking the first change from the "N" of the NEFISA family. She was a half sister of *INDAIA, dam of INDRAFF. Tail female descendants of *INCORONATA are through SONATA (by Sikin) and EL ADALON (by Rossdin), both multi-champion producing lines. *RISSLETTA has already been mentioned in regard to ABU FARWA, but her daughter JOANNA also by RABIYAS, was a champion of the Southern California show, and a couple of other branches trace to her. *RISSLETTA had the most beautiful head and neck of any of the Kellogg horses, imported or not, and usually passed these attributes on to her foals. The third mare *CRABBET SURA has but one tail female line to her (through a daughter by Farana) but she has made history through her son SUREYN, already mentioned under the heading of *RASEYN. *CRABBET SURA was a pretty mare, beautifully dappled when first imported, but as she gradually lost her dapples, black roan patches showed up on her barrel, haunches, shoulder and neck. Apparently this odd coloration is not strongly inheritable, for it has not shown up among her son SUREYN's get to any extent, if at all.

The Egyptian imports *KING JOHN and *MALOUMA were not imported by Kellogg's but by Herman Frank and later purchased from him. The stallion had been a good race horse in Cairo, and before that was a polo pony. One of his three race wins was at a mile and a half. He was shown in the Sunday exhibitions as a three-gaited horse, having a high and very airy way of going. *KING JOHN was used in several movies—in "The Scarlet Empress" he was the mount of Marlene Deitrich. He was inclined to lop his ears, a very unusual trait among Arabian horses; also, he had a speckled skin rather than black, visible on his muzzle at all times, and on his body when wet. He was said to be desertbred.

*MALOUMA was bred in Cairo, by MALOUM out of SHEHA, and was seen in the races by Mr. Frank who so admired the mare that he bought her then and there. She had a short head (in contrast to the long, narrow one of *King John), but the muzzle was blocky and thick compared to the SKOWRONEK type of neat muzzle. She had such spring of rib that the saddle always worked forward on her shoulder to the extent it was impossible to prevent girth sores in back of her elbows. Higher withers would have helped keep the saddle in place. Her neck was short, in keeping with her compact build.

Three daughters carry on the *MALOUMA family—two by FARANA —namely FARLOUMA and POMONA AVESTA, and one by *RASEYN, RALOUMA. Besides her daughter's contribution, FARLOUMA is the dam of FARLOWA (by Abu Farwa), for many years a senior sire at Cal Poly and sire of several champions, one of which, FARLO, sired FAROLITO, winner of many championships. A sister of RALOUMA, RASOULMA, is the dam of ROAYAS, sire of two champions.

The W. K. Kellogg Arabian Horse Ranch was given to the University of California in 1932, after which it was known as the W. K. Kellogg Institute, which sounded like an asylum. During the war it was taken back by Mr. Kellogg—or at least taken away from the University—and donated to the War Department as a Remount depot, in October 1943. The University kept the $600,000 grant which had been given along with the original gift of ranch and horses, but the total value of the property, buildings and horses was set at approximately three million dollars. Ninety-four horses were a good part of this evaluation. The ranch's name was again changed, this time to the W. K. Kellogg Quartermaster Depot (Remount), always a nuisance to write with the "Remount" always seeming to be sort of an apologetic afterthought. At the same time twenty-four purebreds from Fort Robinson were shipped to the ranch.

These were the horses donated by several breeders in the interest of promoting the Arabian horse for the Remount program, in which stallions were placed with agents throughout the country, for use on grade mares at around ten dollars a head. The idea was to upgrade potential cavalry stock. However after the war it was obvious that cavalry was "going metal," so the Remount was disbanded. Many of the Remount Arabians were sold, although a few were kept at Kellogg's (all of whose horses had also been put on the block, but saved by public outcry). More of this later in its own time and place.

In 1928 Ameen Rihani of New York imported *NOURA, a bay Maneghi-Hedruj mare and her foal *MUHA sired by a Seglawi, also a bay Hamdani-Simri stallion, SAOUD, sire desertbred, and no strain, as was the case of the mare's sire. They were bred "at King Ibn Saoud's Stables, Ar-Riyadh, Nejd." No champions trace to the stallion in tail male, but there are two lines from *MUHA to which champion-producing mares trace and the Leading Sire TSALI is one of this family.

In 1929, K. A. Bistany of Buffalo, New York imported *SAADA, a grey mare registered as a "Jalfa Sattam-el-Boulad; sire El Kamar, d.b.; Dam Salma, d.b.; Bred by Najib Bey Souliman. Baalbeck, Syria." The strain is of course Jilfan. One champion traces to *SAADA through tail female.

The year 1928 was noteworthy to the Arabian horse world in that it marked the first importations from England by Roger Selby for his Selby Stud in Portsmouth, Ohio. This stud was to become a major force in the industry, with the majority of its imports having great influence. The first group was followed by others in 1930, 1932 and 1933. They were:

1928:

    No. 808—*MIRZAM (Rafeef-Marhaba) ch.st.
    No. 811—*KAREYMA (Naseem-Julnar) gr.f.
    No. 813—*INDAIA (Raseem-Nisreen) b.f.
    No. 815—*RIFALA (Skowronek-Rissla) gr.m.

1930:

    *MIRAGE (by a d.b. Kehilan-Ajuz ex a d.b. Seglawi-Jedran) gr.st.
    No. 809—*KIYAMA (Rafeef-Julnar) ch.m.
    No. 810—*HILWE (Najib-Hafra) b.m.
    No. 812—*SELMNAB (Nawab-Simrieh) b.m.
    No. 814—*RASELMA (Raseem-Salmnab) b.f.
    No. 819—*JERAMA (Jeruan-*Kiyama) ch.f.
    No. 855—*NAMILLA (*Nureddin II-Nejma) gr.f.
    No. 856—*RASMINA (Shareer-Jalila) ch.f.
    No. 857—*ROSE OF FRANCE (*Raswan-Jalila) gr.m.

RAFFLES (Skowronek-*Rifala)   MIRAGE D.B.
   1932:

     No. 950–*RAHAL (*Nureddin II-Rim) ch.st.
     No. 951–*SELMIAN (Naseem-Selima) gr. st.
     No. 952–*RAFFLES (Skowronek-*Rifala) gr.st.
     No. 953–*MENZIL (*Nureddin II Marhaba) b.c.
     No. 954–*RISHAFIEH (Jeruan-Rishafa) ch.f.

   1933:

     No. 973–*RIMINI (Skowronek-Rim) gr.m.
     No. 974–*NUREDDIN II (Rijm-Narghileh) ch.st.

The Crabbet naming system (for families) works on most of these, but takes a strange jog on some others. For instance JALILA is by SKOW-RONEK out of RASIMA, so should be an "R" mare (as her daughters are). A new initial is the "M" of the Seglawi-Obeyran desertbred MESHURA whose sire was a Maneghi-Hedruj of Ibn Sbeyel. She is represented by MARHABA (Daoud-Mabruka). MABRUKA was by AZREK out of MESHURA. HAFRA, dam of *HILWE, was by *BERK out of HILMYEH; this was of the "H" family of BINT HELWA, with *HAFRA's pedigree of interest due to the double line to AZREK, since HILMYEH's sire is AHMAR, a son of AZREK and grandsire of *BERK. *MIRAGE is not an "M" family horse, probably having been named before importation to England.

Of the Selby stallions, there is no doubt as to which turned out to be the most influential, but they will be taken in order of arrival:

*MIRZAM leaves no tail-male representatives among present champions, but a grandson, RAFMIRZ, a highly successful show horse and sire, is out of a daughter of *MIRZAM. MIRZAIA was one of the mares donated to the Remount, and was at Kellogg's during the time of its Remount ownership. *MIRZAM's name is in the pedigree of other high-going park and harness show horses also, through his son MUDIR, his daughter RIPPLES, and through a daughter of MIRZAIA, TALEH. *MIRZAM himself won the three-gaited (as park classes were then called) championship at the Nashville National in 1934. He is said to

79

have possessed unusual fire and energy, which he could have inherited from his grandsire *NASIK.

The desertbred *MIRAGE was a stylish grey, 14-2 foaled in 1909, and therefore he was twenty-one years old when imported. Bred by the Sebaa Anazeh, he was a Seglawi-Jedran sired by a Kehilan-Ajuz. *MIRAGE had been selected to head the stud of King Faisal of Iraq, who paid $2,500 for him as a young horse. He was eventually acquired by Lady Wentworth but she did not use him at stud to any degree, if at all. Although she said she was waiting until she received a guaranteed proof of breeding from the king, it is possible that the action of the General Stud Book in closing its pages to all but descendants of stock already registered therein had something to do with it. However the horse could have been registered with the Arab Horse Society of England. *MIRAGE was champion at the Richmond show, England, in 1926, which is remarkable enough at the age of seventeen, but even more so was his championship at the 1934 Nashville National when he was twenty-five. Although his head was narrow and not at all gazelle like, it was breedy with large expressive eyes. This stallion's main fault was crooked hind legs, but his good points were numerous enough to minimize this in his overall appraisal. A few years ago a writer took exception to this horse's hind legs having been called crooked, but since they are obviously over-angulated in every picture, they certainly were not straight, in the usual connotation of that term.

The *MIRAGE line is a popular one. It descends through several sons, but most sub-branches by far trace back through IMAGE (out of *Rifala), a nick that would tend to produce crooked hocks, since the RISALA–RISSLA–*RIFALA family is hardly noted for straight-dropped hind legs. The IMAGE line has many segments, as can be seen in the Sire Line charts. Although his full brother RIFAGE does not have as many branches tracing to him, he himself sired more champions than did IMAGE. The Selby catalog states that IMAGE had a "proud, springy, strutting trot, with lots of bloom and animation," and indeed a good number of "action" horses do trace to IMAGE, though not necessarily through tail male. Similarly so do a number of such performance horses trace to RIFAGE.

*RAHAL has no sires of champions tracing directly to him in tail male, but a number of champions do acknowledge his influence through the middle of the pedigree. For instance he is the maternal grandsire of HANRAH, the sire of IBN HANRAH. He was helpful in giving size and scope to his descendants, as did his sire, but care had to be taken not to mate plain-headed mares to him, or the result was less than pleasing, to understate the case. An example is the inexplicable combination of *RAHAL and *RIFDA, when both were sired by *NUREDDIN II, and the result, RIFDAH, was "intensified plain," as would be expected. *RAHAL had a breedy, clean-cut head with neat ears and large eyes, but it was not exactly Arabic; his neck was long and well-arched, but his croup was extremely short—a heritage from his dam. He carried his tail to one side, as did his sire and grandsire. A wry tail was one of the pet hates of H. H. Reese, who had leased *RAHAL for the Kellogg Ranch, so he decided to help nature a bit by having the tail "cut" (an operation on the tendons) on one side to straighten its carriage. Alas, the operation was a success, but the patient carried his tail on the opposite side thereafter. *RAHAL was 15-3, but since he was a leggy horse, much of that height was via the wrong place—his cannons—which were too long. He was a beautiful mover—his trot was extremely bold and airy, although not especially high. His size and impressive presence made him a worthy addition to the Kellogg shows.

*SELMIAN, foaled in 1929, was a pretty horse, seemingly small, but his comparatively high withers brought his height to 15 hands. He too was five-gaited, for in those days no one was afraid to train for five gaits, as they are now (the fear being of imitating the Saddlebred). *SELMIAN has only one son carrying on the line (with champions), but his daughters have done right well for him. Two are out of *RISHAFIEH, another line is through SELFRA, a daughter of *ROSE OF FRANCE, and a third via SELMIANA, who is out of the *NUREDDIN II mare NURSELMA.

*RAFFLES, foaled in 1926, needs no introduction, for his fame has nearly outlived that of the Selby Stud itself. He was a pony in size, standing 13-3 and weighing 850 pounds, but if he had had withers of average elevation he would have measured two inches taller. Actually this 13-3 *is* two inches higher than the figure given in other descriptions of *RAFFLES, 13-1, and even a long toe would hardly have made that much differences—unless of Shetland or Hackney pony dimensions. Whatever his actual height, *RAFFLES sired foals which generally matured to the average height. Most of the *RAFFLES get are noted for beauty of head and neck, though some had the "Raffles bump" on the nose, giving an effect of dish that was really a rise from the plane of the head to the nasal bump. As with *RASEYN, he was inclined to sire horses too low in the withers, even mutton-withered in many of his intensely inbred descendants, but when care was taken to overcome this, the forehand of his progeny was very good. On the average, the *RAFFLES horses had a reachier neck than did the *RASEYNs, but then he himself had a longer rein than did the latter. *RAFFLES had a somewhat more Arabian head than did *RASEYN, with more chiselling, but *RASEYN had the advantage of excellent hindquarters with straight-dropped hind legs and superior bone below the hock. Then too, *RASEYN's get was restricted to grey or various shades of bay, but *RAFFLES could also sire chestnuts, a definite asset, since a good segment of the nation's horsemen prefer this color, or at least don't like to be restricted to one or two colors. The opinion that a horse which sires "pure grey" (grey only), is some sort of deluxe transmitter of all desirable points because of this one particular dominance, may be true for a very few color related attributes, but not at all in most cases.

It has been said that *RAFFLES was deliberately incest-bred by Lady Wentworth to produce a stallion for use in crossing on Welsh ponies. This may or may not be true, since she may have found from previous experience that inbreeding to SKOWRONEK could produce dwarfism is some instances. However the dam of *RAFFLES was herself pony size, only 13-2 (a full hand below the dividing-line between ponies and horses) so returning her to her sire, no big horse himself, would have at least an outside chance of producing a "pony." At Kellogg's the mating of *RASEYN to *ROSSANA, both by SKOWRONEK, produced even smaller ponies on two different occasions, and this experiment was abruptly stopped. The first one died young, the second matured around twelve hands, and was totally unlike *RAFFLES in that he was a horse in minature, while *RAFFLES has a decided Welsh look, stocky of body and broad of head. The *ROSSANA colt was very fine-boned, narrow, with a "horse" head in keeping with the type of body, and rather Roman-nosed. His ears were long, fine and incurved, nearly touching at the tips. He was gelded, which was rather a shame, for although he had no virtue for Arabian breeding, he would have been good as a pony sire.

While the *ROSSANA nick was disastrous with *RASEYN, the same type of cross turned out well with another SKOWRONEK mare, *CRAB-BET SURA, and produced, among others, the great sire SUREYN. Possibly the fact that this mare owned *NUREDDIN II as a grandsire prevented the trend to miniaturization.

*RAFFLES and *RASEYN were long-time rivals in the matter of sire lines of American champions, and they were close on other statistics too. *RAFFLES was the younger by three years, but had not been used at stud as early as *RASEYN. On the other hand *RASEYN had become sterile when his adversary was still siring foals. Strangely enough, these two, whose records were so similar—to a point, lived out their old age in adjoining paddocks at Alice Payne's Asil Ranch in Chino, California. She had purchased *RAFFLES shortly after he had recovered from a broken leg, around 1950, and he continued to sire foals until his death in 1953. *RASEYN had been given to Mrs. Payne when it was obvious he would no longer be useful as a sire, and the Payne care of old horses was well known.

*RASEYN had sired 135 foals, all but a couple from Kellogg or Remount mares. Of these 26 were colts and eventually used at stud in siring purebreds. Other sons had been assigned to Remount agents and except for a few "rescues" (of which Sureyn was one) they were lost to purebred breeding. *RAFFLES sired 122 foals, of which 43 were colts ultimately siring registered get. A compilation of the comparative statistics on the result, in regard to winning bloodlines versus total sired (1953-1967) is this:

	*RAFFLES	*RASEYN
Number of sons at stud	43	26
Number of champions sired by sons, grandsons, etc. (direct tail male only)	365	240
Number of sons, grandsons, etc. at stud (tail male only)	184	120
Number of foals sired by horses of these male lines	4425	2348
Percentage of champions to number of foals sired by stallions of these male lines	.8%	.10%

Of the 25,569 entries in the Stud Books from 1950 to end of 1965 (giving foals of 1965 time to be of championship-competitive age), 6,773, or around one-fourth, of all the foals registered were of the *RAFFLES-*RASEYN bloodlines. Of the sires of ten or more champions, slightly more than one-half are of one or the other of these two lines, with FERSEYN (by *Raseyn) being the leading sire in the country for many years, displaced in 1968 by *SERAFIX, a horse also of the SKOWRONEK male line, but through NASEEM. When it is remembered that this number represents only the tail-male tracing (the top line of the pedigree) and absolutely ignores the several other crosses to SKOWRONEK elsewhere in the pedigree, then the influence of SKOWRONEK in American Arabs can be nothing less than overwhelming. In addition further representation through tail male, that of NASEEM, is not only reflected through *SERAFIX, but also the Russian-bred *NABORR (Naseem having been sold to Russia along with several other Arabians, just as had Mesaoud been sold there earlier) and his sire NEGATIW, now in Poland.

Before leaving *RAFFLES, it should be pointed out that he won the three-gaited championship at the Nashville National in 1933. The Selby catalog stated that "His natural action is exceptionally high" (and Selby knew action when he saw it, as he exhibited Saddlebreds too); and George Ford Morris, the horse artist, agreed with this. He said: "To my mind Raffles is not only one of the greatest individuals of the Arab breed that has ever come under my observation but he possesses one outstanding characteristic that I have never seen in any other Arabian stallion and which is of utmost importance to American breeders in adapting the Arabian to our tastes and demands in horseflesh; that is a square, true, free and fast trot. I do not know whether or not he transmits this with any degree of uniformity to his get but if he does he should make a name for himself in the annals of Arab horse breeding as illustrous as Messenger in the history of the trotter." *RAFFLES passed on this desirable trait to a degree, especially when in the course of his inevitable inbreeding, the nick was "double *Rifala" rather than just "double

Skowronek." It was the line to *BERK through *RIFALA that brought in trotting blood, not SKOWRONEK, who was not an especially good mover. The action was brought out best by the intensification of AZREK blood, whether through *BERK or not, outcross or not.

*MENZIL has no registered foals to his credit but may have been used for cross-breeding, which was tried at Selby's, as witness the case of *RIFALA. *KAREYMA too had produced a half Arab foal, this one by a five-gaited pony; and the foal matured larger than either of its parents. While nothing is lost by crossing Arabians with stallions of other breeds, it does seem a shame to lose a year or so from two of the best mares of the importations.

*NUREDDIN II, a chestnut foaled in 1911, standing 15-3. Large size would be expected from this sire line (though his full brother *NASIK was only 15-1) since his sire RIJM stood 15-3¾ths, and RIJM's grandsire MAHRUSS, a horse bred by Ali Pasha Sherif of Egypt from of Abbas Pasha stock, stood 15-2. The latter horse was of very good conformation throughout, though his neck was a bit thick. His head was typy with slightly upturned profile, not straight or inclined to be convex, as was the case of RIJM, *NUREDDIN II, and *NURI PASHA; his topline was level, the tailset high, and legs seemingly perfect. MAHRUSS founded the second sire line from ZOBEYNI (being by Wazir, a son of that horse) MESAOUD of course being the other. The maternal grand-dam of MAHRUSS was FARAS SAOUDA (the mare of Saoud), one of the eleven parti-color mares purchased by Abbas Pasha in the desert. Wilfrid Blunt called MAHRUSS one of the most beautiful Arabs he had ever seen, and doubtless this was one of the reasons for using his blood-lines so often. FARAS SAOUDA was a Wadnah Hursan, her sire was a Shueyman Sbah, so MAHRUSS was of course a Wadnan Hursan. *NUREDDIN II and *NASIK were Kehilan-Dajania, and coincidentally the granddams (*Rose of Sharon and Nefisa) in their pedigree are both by the desertbred HADBAN, while these mares are out of the foundation mares, both desertbred, RODANIA and DAJANIA. The grandsires are both Egyptian bred, MESAOUD and MAHRUSS II. The pedigree of *NUREDDIN II is typical of early Crabbet breeding. An amusing sidelight is that, because of his height and plain head, *NUREDDIN was pronounced by certain "authorities" here as being obviously "sired by a thoroughbred." Yet the horse is a ringer for his sire (though better in many respects), having the same head and neck, and even the same side-carried tail sported by RIJM. It would take considerable time to find a Thoroughbred identical to RIJM in these characteristics including the non-Thoroughbred but very Arabian trait of the wry tail. If *NURED-DIN II had been sired by a good Thoroughbred, he would have certainly been even better in the forehand and longer of croup, since the hunters which he is accused of resembling (conformation hunters) are superior to him in elegance of neck, length of shoulder and croup. Many even

84

have less slope of croup than do some champion Arabians. And no one ever claimed the desertbred SHERIFA, (so admired by everyone who saw her in the Blunt's desert travels, for the beauty of her head) to be half Thoroughbred, yet they described her as being built like a hunter, "head apart."

The plainness of the *NUREDDIN II head has been hard to elminate in bloodlines originally plain to start with and mixed with his, but he turned out to be a useful cross on refined lines that needed more scope and size; and he became one of Crabbet's best broodmare sires. It happened that every time *NUREDDIN II and SKOWRONEK competed against each other, the former always won. Aside from the fact that the judges may have preferred his size—and that he had withers—it may also have been that when on parade he looked more typically Arabian than he appears in his photographs—which was certainly true of his son *FERDIN and his nephew FARANA. Lady Wentworth, in acknowledging his worth as a broodmare sire, said she was disappointed that he had sired no really outstanding sons. Nevertheless he did sire FARIS (out of Fejr) and SHAREER (out of Selima), both of which appear to have surpassed their sire in unretouched beauty (Lady Wentworth was prone to roughly retouch most photographs, almost ruining them). FARIS sired RIFARI and RISSALIX; the latter was founder of the line to which *COUNT DORSAZ belongs, and both are represented by champions here, especially the COUNT.

Others are through *FERDIN and *NURI PASHA. The English sire RISSALIX is a full brother of the beautiful RIFARI (both out of Rissla) and is the sire of SUVOROV, BLUE DOMINO, and MIKENO, among others, as well as the *COUNT. So it would not seem that *NUREDDIN's sire line was such a loss after all. The FARIS nick was similar to that which served the RIJM line best at Kellogg's—in other words the Maneghi family of FELUKA (by Mesaoud) in England through FEJR and here through *FERDA or her daughter *FARASIN. By the way, did you ever wonder who was the first NUREDDIN? He was a half brother, sired by DAOUD, foaled in 1903. It would have been interesting to see how he compared with his namesake, but he must have died young.

The record of the first three mares imported by the Selby Stud would be hard to equal anywhere at any time, as this first group included *KAREYMA, *INDAIA, and *RIFALA.

*KAREYMA, a tiny mare, standing only 13-3, was a grey and foaled in 1927. She and *ROSE OF FRANCE were five-gaited; and although several Arabian stallions have been trained to five gaits, I can't remember any other Arabian mares similarly educated, except in South Africa where five-gaited Arabians (including Crabbet-breds) are customary. She won a first under saddle and at halter at the Ohio State Fair in 1932, and she was second in the National Five-Gaited Arab Championship in 1934. This daughter of SKOWRONEK made a name for herself through the tail female line with champion-producing mares, as well as in the family line of the Leading Sires. In the latter, GALIMAR, GEYM, RAFFEY and SKORAGE all belong to the *KAREYMA family. In the broodmare catagory, the two branches trace back to her through RAGEYMA (by *Mirage) and RAFEYMA (by *Raffles), the former having more branches, including that of a leading broodmatron GAJALA (by *Raffles), dam of five champions.

The "K" names trace back to KIBLA, though the two Selby imports of that family are by the inexplicably-named JULNAR (by Abu Zeyd) whose dam was KABILA (by Feysul), she a daughter of KIBLA who was by MESAOUD. This line traces farther back (through MAKBULA II, etc.) to the well-publicized Kehilet-Jellabiet of Feysul, otherwise known as the Jellabiet Feysul, for which Abbas Pasha is said to have paid 7,000 pounds. KIBLA, who certainly appears to have been short-coupled, nevertheless had 18 pairs of ribs and 6 lumbar vertebrae.

*INDAIA was a bay mare, foaled in 1927, and standing 14-3. She was one of the early transfers of the "N" names to the "I"s, so of course traces to NEFISA. *INDAIA is of course most noted as the dam of INDRAFF and INDY, but she also founded a family of champion-producing mares, through seven daughters and their produce. Her daughter MIRZAIA was the dam of RAFMIRZ. MIRZAIA was for several years at Kellogg's as one of the Remount mares. She was of fair size, with good length of rein, but rough-coupled. Through INDRAFF, who was for many years close to the top on the Leading Sire list, the blood lines of *INDAIA have been widely diffused. For that matter so has that of *NUREDDIN II through the same source, since he was the maternal grandsire of *INDAIA. INDRAFF was the first and most famous son of *RAFFLES, although there are other sons of the latter which are rapidly catching up on the INDRAFF total. *INDAIA's daughter RAFLA is the dam of RAPTURE, sire of 19 champions. RAFLA is a sister of INDRAFF.

By all odds the most influential of the Selby mares was *RIFALA, who was only 13-2. It is not too surprising that her incest-bred son, *RAFFLES, should be as small. She was the winner of the Gold Medal at the Royal Show in 1922; first prize, Horsham, 1923; and a silver cup at the Sussex County Show the same year. In America she was Champion mare at the Nashville National in 1933. Her dam RISSLA was by *BERK, both of these having been cited by Lady Wentworth as having "brilliant action" at the trot. Her first foal in America was RIFBO, sired by a Saddlebred, who resembled her next son IMAGE enough to revive the belief in telegony. But RIFBO had the calf knees characteristic of the Saddlebred. *RIFALA did not have much chance in regard to broodmares tracing to her in tail female, since she had only one daughter—RAGALA by *MIRAGE. However RAGALA founded a four-branched family of champion-producing mares, though they average only one per mare.

MARES OF THE SELBY STUD

Left to right: SLIPPER (Yima-Sabot), °RIMINI (Skowronek-Rim), °ROSE OF FRANCE (°Raswan-Jalila), °NAMILLA (°Nureddin II-Nejmia), °RIFALA (Skowronek-Rissla) and °KAREYMA (Naseem-Julnar).

Whatever she lost in family lines however, °RIFALA more than made up in sons, these being °RAFFLES, IMAGE, RIFAGE and PHANTOM. The latter was by her son IMAGE so was incest-bred to her, rather than to SKOWRONEK, which was the case of °RAFFLES. RIFAGE has turned out to be the most champion-siring line after °RAFFLES, with IMAGE next. PHANTOM was younger and having had less time, sired only half the number of champions credited to RIFAGE. It is impossible to estimate how many modern Arabians carry the °RIFALA bloodline, but it has to be an astronomical number, distributing the °MIRAGE line along with it, or else double SKOWRONEK. As might be expected from the °MIRAGE-°RIFALA nick, IMAGE was quite crooked of hock and RIFAGE even more so. When due attention was paid to this fault, it was possible to breed away from it, as the straight-legged descendants of this blood attest. It must be admitted however that crooked hocks or straight legs can be found on horses of identical breeding (not both at once, though), including full brothers or sisters, so it pays to have Lady Luck in the pedigree—close up.

°KIYAMA was a chestnut mare, foaled in 1926, 14-3 hands high. She was of the KIBLA family, as was °KAREYMA. In tail female, only one line seems to trace to this mare, as far as production of champions is concerned, and that was not through the daughter imported with her, °JERAMA.

87

*HILWE, was a dark baymare, 14-2, foaled in 1920. Although having only one line in tail female to produce a champion, her son AGWE (by *Mirage) is the sire of JASPRE, a handsome stallion with three champions to his credit. *HILWE is of the HAFRA (by *Berk) branch of the BINT HELWA family, the other branch being that of *HAMIDA (by Daoud) of the Brown importation.

*SELMNAB, was a bay, 14 hands, foaled in 1920. The Selby catalog describes her as having "the wildest desert appearing eye of the group of brood mares." Just what a "desert appearing eye" may be is not easy to figure, but may mean the human eye so often stated by writers to be admired in the desert. She certainly shows the white of her eye in her picture. Her sire is comparatively unknown—this mare being his only foal. He was a son of *ASTRALED and NEFISA, foaled in 1905. *SELMNAB seems to have been a really good mare, and one of the few of the time to have straight hind legs. Her family is that of SELMA I, down through SOBHA (by Wazir), who is represented by two branches— one through SIWA by AHMAR, the other through SIWA's full sister SELMA II. The latter's daughter SIMRIEH (by Seyal) is the dam of *SELMNAB, to whom three champion-producing lines trace, some of the mares therein being dams of two or more such winners. Her sons, NABRAFF (by Raffles) and IDOL (by *Mirage) and SELMAGE (by Image), have sired champions. *SELMNAB was accompanied to America by her foal *RASELMA, a daughter of RASEEM, but apparently she died —at least she had no produce.

*NAMILLA was sold early and is represented by one champion. Although an "N" mare, she is not of the NEFISA (Dajania) family. *RASMINA, was a chestnut, 14-2, and was foaled in 1928. This is a half sister of *ROSE OF FRANCE, *RASMINA being sired by SHAREER while the ROSE was by *RASWAN. Through her two daughters she founded a good family, but as yet not a long one. She was the dam of RASRAFF (by *Raffles) whose name is found in many Payne-bred horses but who sired no champions; of IBN RAFFLES, ditto as to champions; and RASAGE (by *Mirage), who sired one.

*ROSE OF FRANCE, a grey, was foaled in 1926, 14-3 hands high. As noted above, this mare is of the same family as *RASMINA. Their dam is inexplicably a "J" name (Jalila), though out of *RASIMA of the "R" family. The ROSE was a beautiful-fronted mare, but she was very odd in back of the saddle, so to speak. Her back was long, her croup peaked, her tail set on low, and her hind legs were straight of stifle and overbent of hock. Apparently she did not pass on these unlovely features (which were similar to those of Naseem who also had a beautiful head and neck); and her inbreeding to SKOWRONEK should not have allowed it in the first place. Her dam was by that horse while she was by *RASWAN, a son of that famous sire. About all of SKOWRONEK that showed, other than color, was the forehand. The mare had better withers. This is another mare said to have been five gaited. The lines back to *ROSE OF FRANCE are many, through daughters sired by GULASTRA, RONEK, *MIRZAM, *SELMIAN and *MIRAGE. The branches therefrom are very often represented by producers of at least three champions, while two of the daughters themselves (Rose of Luzon and Bride Rose) are in this category.

*RISHAFIEH, chestnut, 15-1, was foaled in 1930. This mare was plain-headed as her double-*Nureddin breeding would indicate, but apparently she had been bred as a performer, specifically a jumper. Her sire JERUAN (*Nureddin II-Rose of Persia) was a winner of several jumping prizes and her maternal granddam, RISH, was a mare that was very good in the hunting field. RISH, like her greatgrandsire JEROBOAM, had a glass eye, but apparently she herself did not pass it on, any more than did the Davenport horse *GOMUSA with a similar blue eye; yet BAZRAH, a mare with both eyes of natural color, has several descendants with this glass feature. By the way this is *not* a defect (the eye being perfectly good) but admittedly it does not beautify a horse's face. *RISHAFIEH's daughters, two by *SELMIAN and one by *RAFFLES, founded the branches of this family. One of the former (Ishmia) is the dam of three champions, while a couple in the latter sub-branches have two each. As *RISHAFIEH and the two daughters mentioned (the other's name being Raffieh) were sold to the Van Vleet Ranch in Colorado, the winners in this line were produced there. Most were by RIFAGE and *ZARIFE.

*RIMINI was the last of the mares imported by the Selby Stud. She was a 14-3 grey, foaled in 1925, and is listed in the Selby catalog as being a "half-sister of *RIFALA," which she most certainly was not, being merely by the same sire. A half sister would have been out of the same dam (not by the *same sire*), the dam in this case was the fine "trotting" mare RISSLA, contributor of much of *RIFALA's excellence. This is of course contrary to human usage of the term, but is correct in horse language. *RIMINI is however, a half sister of *RIFLA, *RAHAL, RASEEM, *RAMIM and RISSAM, among others, and a full sister to *RASWAN. This is a distinguished collection, but they lack the added zip of AZREK supplied by the RISSLA family (except through their own sires) and important to anyone wanting a horse that might be able to trot. Half brothers and sisters of *RIFALA include, among others: RISSLINA, IREX, RISSALMA, RISSALIX and *RISSILETTA, with IREX being a three-quarter brother, actually. RISSLINA is the dam of *RISSLETTA (not the same as *Rissiletta), dam of ABU FARWA. It can be seen that the various "halves" are completely different, one set having a quality the other does not, though both are composed of noteworthy individuals. *RIMINI produced no fillies, but more than made up for that with her son NAHARIN, by GULASTRA, sire of seven champions. She also produced ROMBLON by *CZUBUTHAN, sire of one champion. A full brother to NAHARIN, MACASSAR, was sold to Guatemala, which can only be regarded as a loss to this country, as his picture shows he was as fine a colt as his breeding indicates.

The descendants of the Selby Stud practically founded the industry in the East and Midwest, and those areas are still known as "Raffles Country." The influence of the Selby horses cannot be underestimated. In 1959, after the Stud had more or less gone out of business, its horses were sold to Mrs. William Hewitt's Friendship Farm, East Moline, Illinois. There were nineteen in the group, of which the stallions were GEYM (*Raffles-Rageyma) and IMAGINATION (Image-Rafina). GEYM became a Leading Sire thereafter, with six champions. IMAGINATION has two. One of the mares, NABIMA, founded the leading producing branch of the *SELMNAB family, and most of the others also have done well in the show world ever since.

The Selby catalog is one of the most beautiful ever issued for an Arabian stud farm, packed with pictures and information. There are a few errors in some of the material quoted, such as that regarding color, wherein it was said that "they are never parti-colored," but ever since the publication of the Abbas Pasha records in Prince Mohamed Aly's book *Breeding of Pure Bred Arab Horses* (1936) the suspicion that pinto was once an Arabian color was emphatically confirmed. A collector's item, this catalog has been reprinted by the Arabian Horse Owners' Association.

In 1932 Henry B. Babson of Chicago, Illinois made an importation that was to prove influential in regard to Egyptian bloodlines. They were brought in the same time as those of W. R. Brown, and were:

No. 892—*BINT BINT DURRA (Ibn Radban-Bint Durra) ch. m.
    Kehilan-Ajuz
No. 893—*BINT SAADA (Ibn Samhan-Saada) ch. m.
    Seglawi-Jedran
No. 894—*BINT BINT SABBAH (Bayyad-Bint Sabbah) b. m.
    Kehilan-Dahman
No. 895—*MAAROUFA (Ibn Radban-Mahroussa) gr. m.
    Kehilan-Jellabi
No. 896—*FADL (Ibn Radban-Mahroussa) gr. st. Kehilan-Jellabi
No. 897—*BINT SERRA I (Sotamm-Serra) b. m. Seglawi-Jedran

In 1938, along with a group imported by J. M. Dickinson, he brought in five horses from Poland, several of which were to have lasting influence as well:

No. 1541—*KOSTRZEWA (Koheilan I-Dziewanna) ch.m.
    Seglawi-Jedran
No. 1542—*KASZTELANKA (Koheilan I-Bialogrodka) Hadban
    Enzehi b.m.
No. 1543—*AZJA IV (Landsknecht-Asra) b.m. Seglawi-Jedran
No. 1544—*RYBITWA (Almanzor-Jaskolka II ch.m. Kehilan-Ajuz

No. 1545—*SULEJMAN (Fetysz-Fasila) gr.st. Maneghi Ibn-Sbeyel and two foaled after arrival:

No. 1681—*ZEWA (Kaszmir-*Kostrzewa) gr.f.

No. 1682—*WARSAW (Ofir-*Kasztelanka) b.c.

The grey stallion *FADL, foaled in 1930, was a handsome horse with a somewhat shorter head than most of the mares of the importation. He was a full brother to *MAAROUFA and a half brother (in some instance three-quarter) to the Egyptianbreds imported by W. R. Brown. *FADL, like many others of the Babson horses, was trained with versatility in view, in his case as a polo pony, and also as a competitor in a hundred-mile endurance ride. Although his hind legs were comparatively straight, there were enough animals with crooked hocks in his ancestry to cause the tendency toward this fault to become fixed or at least very evident when he was used at a target for inbreeding, or even when the same ancestors' influence was intensified by this same inbreeding. All too often the hock was also very small or light, and the bone below the hock was tied-in. However not all the horses of this breeding had crooked hind legs, indeed some had as fine underpinning as could be desired, but the percentage of undesirables was high enough to give, rather unfairly, all Egyptian horses a bad name in this respect. The "new Egyptians" bred since the 1950s, reflect the remedial effect of a new breeding program in Egypt, due to the management's own awareness of the prevalence of this fault in its stock.

The most successful branch of the *FADL sire line by far is that of FADHEILAN, this horse being the result of a complete outcross, he being out of the Polish mare *KASZTELANKA. When FADHEILAN in turn was mated to the all-time champion producer of champions, BINT

*KASZTELANKA (Koheilan I-Bialogrodka)   *FADL (Ibn -Rabdan-Mahroussa)

91

SAHARA, this was another completely "cold" cross, resulting in the very popular stallion FADJUR, sire of 27 champions to the end of 1968. His closest rivals in the *FADL sire line are DISAAN and ZAB, both with six champions. The former is all Egyptian, inbred to *FADL; while ZAB, though also inbred to *FADL, has the English import *ALDEBAR as one grandsire.

The dark chestnut IBN RABDAN was said by Prince Mohamed Aly to always sire dark chestnuts ... "no matter what the colour of the mares. This will go on until he covers a mare who produces the form and type of her own strain; if she is the better bred she will dominate in the formation and colouring of the foal." In the case of MAHROUSSA, she must have been better bred, for her son and daughter by that horse are her own color, grey. In an article in the May, 1927 *The Arab Horse* (England), IBN RABDAN is referred to, along with another much-admired sire, BALANCE. The place mentioned, Kafr Farouk, is still the main breeding farm for the Egyptian Agricultural Organization:

> The average of breeding at Kafr Farouk is about 20 foals yearly, and of those over 70 per cent prove successful either as stallions or mares. Never before have they managed to obtain such a magnificent specimen of the Arab as BALANCE, and the Committee is already studying ways and means whereby it may be possible to produce others of this type. IBN RABDAN has been responsible for some good horses and ponies, but they have fallen far short of the standard set by BALANCE. Two of IBN RABDAN's stock on the race courses at present are REALL and RABDAN.

BALANCE, Egypt's best racer and sire of good performers, is represented in today's pedigrees, one being that of *TALAL, a recent import as an aged horse, who had been in 44 races but retired sound, and who is now a multi-champion in America. IBN RABDAN's name is also in this pedigree. So IBN RABDAN and BALANCE, contemporaries so often compared, and even photographed together, are now brothers in blood in some of the "new Egyptian" horses.

The mares of this importation seem to have all been of fine riding type, with clean shoulders, well laid back and with high withers. A few were rather plain headed by today's standards, and some had crooked hind legs, which is not surprising when their ancestry is known. The chestnut daughter of IBN RABDAN, *BINT BINT DURRA, imported as a two-year-old (as were most of the others) resembled her sire. Although she seems to have no champions tracing to her in direct tail female, her son FA RABDAN sired one. Another chestnut, *BINT SAADA, who also foaled in 1930, has a similar record. Her son on the chart was FADDAN, two of whose sons have sired one champion each.

*BINT BINT SABBAH, a bay, 1930, earned a write-up in a 1936 article on the Arabian show of that year, in connection with which a three day test of sorts was held, open to all Arabians and to any other breed 15-3 or under. A total of 26 horses were entered, of which 15 were Arabs, two were Tennessee Walking Horses, two were Standardbreds, and one was part-Saddlebred—the latter winning the event. A distance of 15-20 miles a day over three different routes was covered. Jumping, as well as a handiness test, was held the last day in the arena. The article stated: "The third prize winner, the Arab mare BINT BINT SABBAH, emerged a heroine. Weighing little more than 800 pounds, she carried 189 pounds, finishing half the distance in 1 hour 15 minutes in the mud, and walking the second lap so as not to finish ahead of the three hour minimum. Her head and tail were always up and she never took a deep breath." This mare established a many-faceted family, having four daughters which produced a champion each and two granddaughters with and two respectively. Her sons FABAH and KHEBIR, her granddaughter's son ZAB, and her daughter's son DISAAN founded branches of the *FADL sire line.

*MAAROUFA, grey, foaled 1931, quite similar to her photogenic mother, was the dam of seventeen foals, twelve of them by FAY EL DINE, her "nephew," and of course therefore closely inbred. Through three daughters of this breeding her family is carried on. As far as present champions are concerned (tail female tracing), all branches end in singles except in the case of GAY-NEGMA, with three. This mare (Gay-Negma) is the product of a complete outcross. The branch with most sub-branches is that of BINT MAAROUFA, produced when *MAAROUFA was twenty-two years old (she had two more foals after that). Her son BAAROUF sired six champions, and apparently is the only one aside from ALHAAMED to make a dent in the sire-line picture. He is by the English bred *ALDEBAR who was a greatgrandson of AZREK, so it is not too surprising that many of his son's descendants showed bold and airy trotting action, such as that featured by the champion three gaited performer ROUF. The other son of *MAAROUFA to make an impression as a sire was ALHAAMED, by ALCAZAR, also a "cold" cross, he being combined Davenport and Hamidie lines.

*BINT SERRA I, a bay foaled in 1923, was a granddaughter of *ASTRALED. Her sire SOTAMM (bred by Crabbet) was by that noted stallion, so this segment of her pedigree is familiar to Americans. SOTAMM actually was double Queen of Sheba in that her name is twice in his pedigree, once as dam of *ASTRALED, and again as dam of AHMAR, sire of SOTAMM's dam SELMA II. SOTAMM is also greatgrandsire of *BINT BINT SABBAH. Further relationship to American lines is through *BINT SERRA's greatgranddam, who is none other than the great mare *GHAZALA. And BINT carried on in a manner worthy of her ancestors, two of her four sons becoming the premier sires of the Babson farm, namely FAY-EL-DINE and *FA-SERR, both by *FADL. This was outcross breeding, though Egyptian, for even without the Crabbet line, there is no close-up relationship. The FAY-EL-DINE line is second to FAD-

HEILAN's (in the *Fadl list) with the much younger FA-SERR being fourth (Fa-el-Gemar is third). As to the family affair, *BINT SERRA's daughters who carried on in a champion producing capacity (or through *their* daughters, etc.) were three, namely FAZALA, FA-DEENE and FA GHAGAHA.

As the Egyptian imports had been brought over in conjunction with the shipment to W. R. Brown, so also was the importation from Poland a cooperative affair, this time with General J. M. Dickinson, who had previously brought in a group from that country. Heading the lot was *SULEJMAN, another foreigner whose breeding was at least in part familiar, for his dam, FASILA, was sold to Poland by Lady Wentworth along with NITLA, SARDHANA (dam of *Crabbet Sura), RAMAYANA and the champion stallion RASIM (sire of Fasila). RASIM had a highly successful career in the show ring in England, both at halter and under saddle, trading top spots at times in the former events with SKOWRONEK (when *Nureddin II wasn't the winner). In the 1923 London Show, the results were: (1) RASIM; (2) SKOWRONEK; (3) MUSTAFA KAMIL; and (4) *ALDEBARAN, a horse later imported by Henry Babson. In Poland, RASIM and the mares of this importation were owned by Baron W. Bicker. RASIM sired many fine horses in his new country. The circle made a full turn when the "artists' dream" mare CELINA, exported to England, won the English championship in tough competition in 1961, and this mare was inbred to RASIM. To return to *SULEJMAN (Polish for Suleiman), he was raced as a three-year-old, as all Arabians in Poland are tested on the track. He was second three times; third, four times; and once he was out of the money with a fourth. The shortest distance for three-year-olds is 1600 meters, a few yards short of a mile (Arabs are not raced in Poland until age three). However, he also competed in races up to 2000 meters. His sire FETYSZ was a great winner and sire of winners on the track. FETYSZ was by BAKSZYSZ and called the Raffles of Poland. *SULEJMAN was imported as a three-year-old at the end of the racing season, and was only shown once. This was at the 1937 Illinois State Fair where he won his class. *SULEJMAN, in Babson tradition, was trained to jump. He also was trained for polo, but whether or not these polo-trained stallions of the Babson Stud (*Fadl, *Sulejman, etc.) actually were used in polo matches I don't know. *SULEJMAN was an alert and fiery stallion, but he was an ideal riding horse—which is not surprising considering his conformation and training. There is really hardly anything to be said in faulting him, for he had no outstanding or dominant fault. Photographs of his sire, FETYSZ all show that horse to have straight, almost too-straight hind legs, yet a painting of FETYSZ grafts on him as crooked a pair of sickle hocks as ever seen. This can be blamed on the artist, not the horse. *SULEJMAN sired six champions out of a total of thirty-nine foals, giving him a respectable percentage of fifteen per cent. His most famous son was TOBRUK (out of

Fa Zala), a real performing horse who became the leading sire among the *SULEJMAN descendants, with five champions and a dual branched line via his grandson ZABAD. Two of TOBRUK's well-known daughters are the champions ROSEBRUK and BAY MAGIC. The latter gained fame initially as the highest-priced mare sold at auction to that time, the amount coinciding with her registration number 10,000—ten thousand dollars.

*KOSTRZEWA was a chestnut foaled in 1929, bred by the Janow-Podlaski State Stud of Poland. Her markings make interesting reading since in addition to the usual white markings, if any, the brands on these Polish imports (those over two years old) were recorded: "Brand of crown on right side of back, 83 on left side of back, with crown on left stifle with J under crown." *KASZTELANKA was similarly branded, but her number was 82. *KOSTRZEWA's sire KOHEILAN I was bred by the Bablona Stud of Hungary and was an admirably-conformed grey who founded a distinguished line in Poland. The dam of *KOSTRZEWA was DZIEWANNA, "liberated" by the Russians at the beginning of World War II; and she became an exceptional ancestress of speedy horses in that country through two of her sons foaled in Poland—PIOLUN and SKRZYP. The latter was the sire of SPUTNIK who holds two speed records, and six of the seven record-holders have PIOLUN in the pedigree as grandsire, either through his son PRIBOJ or through the daughters PIRAMIDA or PARFUMERIYA. This line (Piolun) nicked especially well with the RISSLA family of Crabbet stock. PRIBOJ is the sire of PIETUSZOK (sire of four American champions at halter) who has often been the leading sire of race winners in Poland. One of his sons is *BAJRAM, a Top Ten winner here, and a leading money-winner of his 3-year-old year in Polish races, before importation to America. *KOSTRZEWA founded a family with several branches, through the all Polish *ZEWA and the half Egyptian GA-GAZAL. She was a celebrated race mare. Being undefeated in two years of competition, and she was leading money-winner and winner of the Oaks in 1933. The influence of DZIEWANNA in the production of runners is little less than remarkable.

*KASZTELANKA was a bay, foaled in 1929, by the same sire as *KOSTRZEWA, while her dam traces back to the desertbred ELSISSA I, imported to Poland by Prince Sanguszko in 1874. *KASZTELANKA was a moderately successful race mare, starting only four times yet never unplaced. Although she has no daughters that maintained a champion producing family for her, *KASZTELANKA is well remembered as the dam of the fiery FADHEILAN. Since the same presence and animated style is not the trademark of the other *FADL sons, some of it must be attributed to *KASZTELANKA, with FADHEILAN passing it on to FADJUR, and he in turn to most of his get.

*AZJA IV was also a bay, and foaled in 1935. Her sire, LANDSKNECHT, was a rather Thoroughbred-like son of KOHEILAN IV, bred by the Weil Stud of Germany, and he too was a very successful race-horse. *AZJA's dam was bred in Yugoslavia by the Inocenzdvor Stud, established in Ilok, in 1894, with stock tracing to the King of Wurtemburg's Weil stud in Germany. *AZJA was of course too young to have raced, as was *RYBITWA. Although she had only two daughters, they established a two-branched family of champion-producers, but it is through her son AZRAFF that this mare makes history. AZRAFF, bred by Walter Ross of Kansas City was of course by *RAFFLES, but two other of her sons sired a champion or two. In fact only one of *AZJA's produce failed to contribute to the championship rolls.

The last mare of this group, *RYBITWA, was a chestnut foaled in 1935, who apparently had only four foals, none of which are represented by champions in tail female.

Two en utero imports were *ZEWA, by the highly successful racer KASZMIR (the horse disastrously considered by bettors to be too beautiful to run), a grey filly later donated to the Remount; and *WARSAW, a colt by OFIR (sire of *WITEZ II) and out of *KASZTELANKA. It was unfortunate that this son of the internationally renowned OFIR was sold to Colombia, where he was lost to the breed. He seems to have been a top individual. A few foals were sired by *WARSAW before he left, but no son has carried on for him.

As already detailed under the information on the Harris import *ANA, the chestnut stallion *ALDEBAR was a full brother to that mare, and was of the QUEEN OF SHEBA family line. His sire was the desertbred horse DWARKA who raced in India, owned or leased in his old age by the Prince of Wales in 1917; and destroyed when he was 29, in 1921. *ALDEBAR was bred by H.R.H. The Prince of Wales, foaled in 1919, and is the sire of five foals in England. These include the fine sire ALGOL, whose daughters were influential in the pedigree of the great champion DARGEE, one (Aatika) producing his sire MANASSEH, the other being MYOLA, DARGEE's dam. *ALDEBAR was originally—in England—ALDEBARAN, but his name was shortened for registration in America, since there was already a horse of that name in the A.H.C.R. stud book. This caused some confusion, both as to the identity of an "Aldebar" from the English point of view, and in mistaking "Aldebaran" for the first-named ALDEBARAN No. 778 (Stambul-*Baraza). The import is *ALDEBAR No. 1864. Further confusion can be caused regarding DARGEE's pedigree, for the AATIKA therein should not be mistaken for the mare of the same name in this country. *ALDEBAR was imported by Babson in 1940.

The final Babson import was *NIMROD, a bay stallion foaled in 1952, bred by H. V. M. Clark in England, and brought to this country in 1958. His sire was CHAMPURRADO, a very handsome son of the beautiful fronted (but sickle hocked) IREX. The head and neck of IREX, like those of his sire NASEEM, are practically artists' ideals. *NIMROD's dam is NAUTCH GIRL, impeccably bred, by SAINFOIN (Rasim-Safarjal) out of NASIRA (Nadir-Nasra). *NIMROD has two champions to his credit.

The Babson horses have made a great contribution to American Arabians, both through the Egyptian and Polish importations, but the English stallions have done well too. These horses were not cream puff, pudgy, stall-fed do-nothings, but were worked at some phase of performance, including polo, jumping, and trail (endurance) rides, as well as the usual horse show events.

The influence of J. M. Dickinson, of Franklin, Tennessee and later Santa Barbara, California, cannot be overestimated. Not only did he import great horses and buy many imported by others, he also obtained Americanbreds, all of which he used at a variety of things. He also started the first all Arabian shows as well. His yearly catalogs were—and are—of great value to those who want to get down to the bare facts and to heck with the fluffy fantasies and romance (another word for congealed fibs, or tall tales which have been transferred from legend to "fact"). The businesslike, almost computerized, system of sorting out these facts is unequalled. The lists of horses, together with their breeding, breeder, age, color, strain and history in a concisely composed list is worth the value of these collectors' items. General Dickinson was one of those dedicated scholars—like W. R. Brown, Randolph Huntington and Spencer Borden—who knew not only the Arabian, but the horse. No matter how well-informed a person may be about one breed, he cannot be a true scholar and have a fully rounded education and an evaluation of even that one breed unless he also knows and appreciates the others.

Traveler's Rest Farm, in Franklin, was originally known for its Saddlebreds, but it wasn't long until the fame of its Arabians spread around the world. By noting the destinations of some of the horses pictured in the catalogs they soon followed to all parts of the world as well. In fact, American exports have been at a standstill now, in comparison to the worldwide trade established by Dickinson.

Among his first purchases were the Egyptian imports of the Maynesboro Stud as well as several of its homebreds and the French import *KOLA. The stallion ANTEZ was obtained from the Kellogg Ranch in 1930 and used at Travelers Rest for thre years before his sale to Europe.

The very first importation ever made direct from Poland was that of General Dickinson in 1937, consisting of six mares:

    No. 1309—*PRZEPIORKA, chestnut, (Almanzor-Jaskolka II)
        1930 Kehilan-Ajuz
    No. 1310—*LASSA, chestnut, (Koheilan I-Zulejma) 1930
        Kehilan-Moradi
    No. 1311—*LILIANA, grey, (Linkoln-Cazpla) 1930 Kehilan-Ajuz
    No. 1312—*MATTARIA, grey (Kafifan-Koncha) 1926
        Seglawi-Jedran

No. 1313—*NIWKA, grey, (Fetysz-Dziwa) 1932 Kehilan-Moradi

No. 1314—*NORA, chestnut, (Hardy-Dora) 1932 Kehilan-Moradi

Except for *LILIANA and *MATTARIA, all were bred by the Janow-Podlaski State Stud, the other two being bred by the estate of Jana Kleniew and the Behen Stud of Counts Roman and Jozef Potocki, respectively.

*PRZEPIORKA was out of JASKOLKA II, and the latter has been claimed as the dam of SKOWRONEK by some owners of horses of this family, but this mare is no relation at all to JASKOLKA (Yaskolka), SKOWRONEK's dam, the only similarity being the name. They are not even of the same family. JASKOLKA II is a daughter of the super matron GAZELLA II, who was also dam, among others, of ELEGANTKA (dam of Lowelas, Opal, Wielki Szlem, etc.), FRYGA II (dam of Ofirka), HARDY (great racer), MAKATA (dam of Witraz), NAJADA (dam of *Naganka, the dam of the champion Mikado) and TARASZCZA, dam of NEGATIW (sire of *Naborr). GAZELLA II was captured by the Russians in 1939 when she was twenty-five, but she had no foals thereafter and died at thirty years of age. The champion mare *ARWILGA is of the GAZELLA II family through ARWILA, also out of JASKOLKA II. The Army import *WIERNA traces to GAZELLA II through her dam KAMEA who is a daughter of ELEGANTKA. The sire of *PRZEPIORKA was ALMANZOR, descended from one of the three famous mares imported in 1945, direct from the desert by Count Dzieduszycki (as was the tail female foundation mare of the Gazella II family, the original Gazella.) ALMANZOR was the third highest sire of Arabian money-winners in 1938. Champions trace back to *PRZEPIORKA in three lines, the leading producer therein being SHAMARA.

*LASSA, like the foregoing mare, was beautifully conformed, with excellent shoulder and withers, lightly arched neck and a clean-cut, breedy head. She was champion mare, and fourth-placed Arab under saddle at the 1937 Illinois State Fair, in a class of thirteen (the three placing ahead of her were stallions). Moreover she was ridden in this class by General Dickinson's daughter Maxi, then only ten years old. Her colt by ANTEZ, imported en utero, *LATIF, founded a sire line through two sons. He resembled his sire exactly as to head, and his neck was very thick and underslung. In tail female, champions trace to *LASSA through two daughters by *CZUBUTHAN.

*MATTARIA's sire was the Egyptian bred KAFIFAN, a horse of the NEGMA family. Her dam was one of Count Potocki's best broodmares; but the nick with KAFIFAN was certainly not a successful one if good looks was the object, for this was a very plain mare, her head especially so. Apparently no champions trace to her in tail female, but her son MAHRI, by GULASTRA was champion (before 1953) and sired one champion. He was later destroyed because of a broken leg.

*LILIANA, though of good type and with a pretty head, also seems to be unrepresented by any champions via her daughters. Her sire was of the BAKSZYSZ line, and dam was sired by MASSAD, an Egyptian bred of the Ali Pasha Sherif stables, purchased at the dispersal sale in 1896.

*NIWKA was a half sister to the great stallion OFIR, memorable as the sire of *WITEZ II, WITRAZ and WIELKI SZLEM among others. He was victim of the Russian version of the blitz, being taken to Russia where he continued as a successful sire. The sire of *NIWKA also sired *SULEJMAN, and this horse (Fetysz) was sold in 1936 as a leading stallion in the German State Stud at Trakehnen. *NIWKA raced in Poland, but evidently without spectacular success. Since these races are considered as trials, and proof of sound constitution and temperament rather than speed, she passed her tests, as it is termed. A son of this mare was sold to Colombia, a daughter to Mexico, and another to Hawaii. This was rather typical of the Dickinson exports, but also a reason why some mares have little representation today. *NIWKA is one with that fate, as far as champions are concerned.

*NORA's sire HARDY was an undefeated race horse, the Derby being among his wins; but he was plain headed, and unlike most Polish horses (good racers or not) was rather steep of croup. But he had superior legs and a beautiful shoulder. HARDY's record of 2:50 for 2400 meters (nearly 1½ miles) was not broken until 1939, when the aptly-named URGENCE, a chestnut filly of French breeding equalled this mark. The best time (in Poland) for this distance now is 2:49, held by PIEN, carrying 130 pounds. *NORA too passed her efficiency test but was apparently unplaced. She was one of the more handsome mares of Traveler's Rest, and her head was lean and chiseled with a lot of breed character though comparatively long. One champion is credited to her account. One of her sons was sent to Nicaragua and a daughter to Hawaii.

The second importation was that which was combined with the Babson group from Poland, in 1938. The grey stallion *CZUBUTHAN was head man, the rest of the five imports being mares. He was a good race horse, although he didn't look like one. He did not have the long, well-sloped shoulder usually associated with successful runners and the resultant depth of heart. Nor was he especially Arabian type, but he certainly must have been the General's favorite stallion by all odds. He had raced two seasons, winning six of his seventeen starts, placing second, eight times; third, three times; and never going unplaced. He was the second highest money-winner and beat the Derby winner in a 3200 meter race (around two miles). *CZUBUTHAN's grandsire HERMIT was a desertbred, purchased in Bombay, in 1910. He was the sire of KASZMIR's dam, that celebrated stallion who won at all distances, and his record for the mile in Poland still stands—1:47½. This was beaten only by the Russian SPUTNIK (who was actually half Polish), by a half-second. KASZMIR, it will be remembered, was the horse that lost thousands of zlotys for bettors because they could not believe he could beat the racier-looking horses, because he was too beautiful. With *CZUBUTHAN the case was somewhat different, he was not especially beautiful, but neither did he look racy at all. He was far from ugly however. In fact he was a good-looking horse, but he lacked class and refinement. It might be added that although *CZUBUTHAN did not give the impression of good heart girth, he measured 73 inches, while KOLASTRA was the same, but *CZUBUTHAN stood only 15 hands and KOLASTRA was 15-2½. *NASR, who was the same height as *CZUBUTHAN, measured only 70 inches girth, but he was quite narrow fronted, which explains part of it.

The summary of horses in this importation, including *CZUBUTHAN, is:

No. 1499—*CZUBUTHAN, grey, (Dzingishan III-Ryfka)
1933 Kehilan-Ajuz
No. 1500—*BA-IDA, chestnut, (Flisak-Pomponia II) 1932
Kehilan-Dajania
No. 1501—*AENIZA, grey, (Dzingishan III-Fanfara) 1931
Kehilan-Dajania
No. 1502—*UGRA, chestnut, (Kuhailan Kruszan-Sahara) 1935
Hadban Enzehi
No. 1498—*BABOLNA, chestnut, (Durbar-Bona) 1935
Kehilan-Mimrih

*BA-IDA (spelled Baida in Poland) was a truly fine mare in every respect and was a strong competitor on the race course. In eleven starts in 1937, she won three races; she was second four times, and third, once. *BA-IDA was never defeated at a mile and an eighth and was one of the five fastest Arabian mares to that date. She was a full sister to CEMIRA, a leading money-winner in 1936-37. She was by the same sire as BAKHTIARI, leading money-winner in 1938. Her sire FLISAK was a great racer, winning the Derby in a total of nine out of eleven races. He was a typy, beautifully conformed horse.   His Daughter, MOKKA, was the dam of *LOTNIK. *BA-IDA's dam also produced the stallion EL-HAIFI, by the same sire as the celebrated OFIR; and among others, he sired *CARMENCITA EL HAIFI. EL-HAIFI was one of the many horses confiscated by the Germans, and he was sent to Debica. Luckily both the Germans and Russians appreciated the Polish Arabians, for in every case, captured animals of this breed were used in their own or Polish Arabian breeding programs. *BA-IDA is the dam of BATAAN (by *Czubuthan), who was one of the stallions donated to the Remount. She is of the family of MLECHA, one of the famed three Kehilans imported from the desert in 1845—the others being SAHARA and GAZELLA.

*AENIZA is of the same family as *BA-IDA. In fact, her dam (Fanfara 1914) was also the dam of POMPONIA II. FANFARA was a well-conformed mare; and *AENIZA was much like her, except for crooked hind legs and a short, rather steep croup. Neither of these faults was seen on FANFARA—that mare had an unusually long croup for an Arabian, and it was also quite level. This family has even more branches. Another of POMPONIA II's is that of ATFA, dam of MUFTA, whose son *MUZULMANIN is a many time halter champion and National Champion Pleasure Horse (and is also an ex-race horse, competing for two years, before importation). A third line is that of *BA-IDA's sister CEMIRA whose daughter CEREKIEW is dam of *CZESTER, another Scottsdale champion (as is *Muzulmanin). *AENIZA was raced with moderate success as a three-year-old. She is by the same sire as *CZUBU-THAN, so she was never bred to him. She had three foals by KENUR, an exceedingly plain horse, but who was considered exceptional by Dickinson, according to his catalog. KENUR was from desertbred parents imported by A. W. Harris. All of *AENIZA's foals by GULASTRA (two of them fillies) wound up with descendants producing champions, two in tail female, the other through the son, BANCORAN. A third daughter by IBN HANAD, SUNNY ACRES GABY has produced a champion. *AENIZA herself set the style by having two to her credit.

UGRA was by the desertbred KUHAILAN-KRUSZAN, imported in 1927 by Prince Roman Sanguszko. He was the sire of many successful racers including SAGAR, winner of the Derby and Oaks in 1937. SAGAR is the dam of GRAND, himself a fine race horse and sire of winners. The Dickinson catalog calls *UGRA a sister of SAGAR, but their dams are not even related. *UGRA too was raced as a three-year-old. One daughter has continued the line (championwise) for *UGRA.

The fourth mare was *BABOLNA, whose sire was a son of the celebrated HERMIT. Her dam BONA was out of POMPONIA 1902 who was also the dam of the distinguished broodmatron ZULEJMA. ZULEJMA includes DZIWA and FERJA among her daughters as well as *LASSA. *BABOLNA was donated to the Remount, and was sent with other donated Arabians to the Kellogg Ranch (then known as the Pomona Quartermaster Depot, Remount). She is the dam of a champion as is one of her daughters and a granddaughter. She was a smooth bodied mare, and her head was good enough but marred by lop ears. This is supposedly a sign of good temper, but on an Arabian it is simply a sign of lop ears. She did not seem to transmit this trait.

*KASMIRA was foaled in 1939, the year following her dam's arrival in America. She was by the fabulous KASZMIR out of *BA-IDA, and she was a grey.

A number of mares were obtained from other sources as well. One was *AIRE, bred by Guilherme Echenique, Jr., in Brazil. This bay mare was by ALI out of RAIRA, the former described as being by HAURRAM II out of ARRAHMA, "a chestnut Maneghi Hedruj stallion. Won 1st at 'Palermo' (Buenos Aires) 1926, a strong and beautiful horse with very refined head." In turn his sire HAURRAM II was by RACID out of HAYDE—"chestnut Kehilan Ajuz stallion. As a three-year-old, and four

101

in subsequent years he was adjudged grand champion stallion at Palermo, the great South American show. In the show ring he defeated, among others, Ajman, Rukham and Risfan, imported from England. He was never defeated, and was called the 'faultless horse'." RACID (Hadi-Rakeb) was "A golden chestnut Maneghi Hedruj stallion reputed to have been a model of symmetry and standing over 15-1." RACID's sire was a desert-bred "Chestnut Seglawi Jedran stallion, imported Argentina 1898, by Hernan Ayerza." As to the ladies, "ALI's dam was by AJMAN out of SIFRIYA, "a chestnut Managhieh Hedruj mare foaled in Argentina." Her sire is of familiar breeding for he was bred in England, by FEYSUL out of AJRAMIEH and accordingly, of the QUEEN OF SHEBA family. SIFRIYA was by SAEKAT out of DARBUCA, her sire being "a red chestnut desertbred stallion Seglawi Jedran imported Argentina 1898 by Ayerza in whose stud he became leading stallion." DARBUCA was by DEYMAN out of MEKKA, and DEYMAN was "a red bay Maneghi Hedruj st. imp. Argentina by Herman Ayerza." MECCA (Gailan-Maana-qui) was "said to be the best daughter of Maanaqui" and was a red bay. MAANAQUI was a desertbred foaled in 1884: "A grey Maneghieh Hedruj mare, sired by a Seglawi Jedran, imported Argentina 1894, by Herman Ayerza, where she was an important mare in his stud, and is reputed to be tap-root mare of his best Maneghi horses." Going way back to *AIRE's dam, this mare (Raira) was "a red bay Seglawieh Jedran mare of Marighiyah strain. Exported 1929 to Brazil, where she became one of the principal mares of Mr. Echenique's Haras Er Rasul." She was by RUST-NAR out of MELIHAH, and certainly the breeding of the former is familiar enough, for he was by RUSTEM out of NARGHILEH, and of course bred by Crabbet. MELIHAH was bred by Ayerza and was "A bay Segla-wieh Jedran mare. Exported Brazil at age 20 when a large price was paid for her." She was by MEBRUK out of RAHAT, the former being by RICHAM out of MEKKA, already mentioned. RICHAM was a desertbred "A dark bay Kehilan Korisham stallion sired by a Seglawi Jedran, imported Argentina 1898 by Ayerza." RAHAT (Racid-Mohareb) was by the same sire as that of HAURRAM II, while her dam was by MARHUM out of KARIBAN. MARHUM was a desertbred, a Kehilan-Ajuz also imported by Ayerez. KARIBAN also was a desertbred. Her description is "Blood chest-nut Seglawieh Jedran mare of Marighiyah strain, bred by Cherebet Pacha. Imported Argentina, 1898, by Hernan Ayerza in whose Cabana, 'El Aduar,' she became an important foundation mare." All of this is given in detail because the bloodlines are unfamiliar here until traced back a way.

   *AIRE was shipped to America in the summer of 1934 for exhibition in the second National Arabian Horse Show at Nashville. Unfortunately the six-weeks journey by sea and rail caused her to lose so much weight that she could not be shown.   However, in 1935 she won a saddle class. As a two-year-old she had won a championship for Arabians at Porto Alegre,

*AENIZA (Dzinhishan III-Fanfara)   *LASSA (Koheilan I-Zulejma)

*PRZEPIORKA (Almanzor-Jaskolka II)   *CZUBUTHAN (Dzingishan III-Ryfka)

including a gold medal and silver cup, in 1931. She was a well built mare, possibly lacking class, but certainly she would be hard to beat as to body. One line traces back to her through a granddaughter, INDAIRE, producing three champions. A note regarding the Aduar Stud may be in order: "It was founded in 1892 by Hernan Ayerza, and he imported ten stallions and ten mares from Arabia by special permission of the Sultan of Turkey. He made importations of twenty stallions and ten mares from 1894 to 1931, about half of them coming from Arabia, a few from England, and more from France and Hungary.... It has produced two hundred purebred Arabs."

Another import acquired by Dickinson was *EXOCHORDA, chestnut Seglawi-Jedran mare foaled in 1924, imported in 1930 by Henry Herbermann, and was bred in Cairo, Egypt. He brought over at the same time *IBN NAFA (Ibn Rabdan-Nafa). *EXOCHORDA was by AIGLON "a D.B. Seglawi Jedran stallion. Imported Egypt by Ahmed Ibiah. A winner of 12 races." Her dam was LEILA, a desertbred imported to Egypt in 1920 by Captain W. R. Owen. Two lines trace to *EXOCHORDA through her daughter SULEIKA by *IBN NAFA. As in all other cases, there are of course other lines, but these refer to ones which end up with dams of champions.

Dickinson purchasd several of the Babson imports, including *RIMINI and *ROSE OF FRANCE, of the Crabbet groups, and *KASZTELANKA and KOSTRZEWA of the Polish lot. These have already been dealt with under their respective headings.

103

A couple of imports were made in 1939 by Dickinson, one being from England, the other from Brazil. *KADIRA (Joseph-Karaka) although tracing to RODANIA, was not entirely of Crabbet blood. No champions trace to this mare in direct tail female.

*NAHRAWANA (Nahrawan-Haliah II) was a bay who foaled in 1936, and was imported as a three-year-old. She traces to the Kehilet Ajuz (of Mohamed Haddal) mare HAYDEE, who was foaled in 1891 and imported to Argentina by Hernan Ayerza. NAHRAWAN was by SKOWRONEK out of NESSIMA, so that line is familiar enough. *NAH-RAWANA's dam was by HAURRAM II (paternal grandsire of *Aire) out of RACBAR (Rustnar-Havilah). RUSTNAR is another English horse, already mentioned (re *Aire), while HAVILAH is by HADI out of MAALEK. HADI was a chestnut Abeyan sired by a Seglawi, desertbred and imported by Ayerza in 1898. MAALEK was imported to Argentina en utero, her dam being HAYDEE, her sire MARUM. HAYDEE was sired by a Seglawi-Jedran, and was described as the best Arabian mare ever imported to South America. *NAHRAWANA, shortly before leaving for the United States, was first prize Arabian filly and also winner of the Sociedade Agricola De Pelotas for best Arabian in the show, at the 1938 Livestock show, held at Pelotas, Brazil. Her daughter HORADABA is the dam of a champion in British Columbia.

The number of famous sires and broodmatrons, as well as performance horses, bred at Travelers Rest is astronomical, and the more influential of these will be noted in due course. General Dickinson went out of business around 1950, but the Travelers Rest Farm is being continued from a basis of descendants of the original stock in Columbia, Tennessee by his daughter, Mrs. Margaret Dickinson Fleming.

The Crabbetbred stallion *ROSANTHUS and mares *CROWN OF INDIA and *INDIAN DAWN were imported in 1940 by Frederick L. Wehr, Ruxton, Maryland. *ROSANTHUS is by INDIAN GOLD out of the "trotting mare" RISSLINA. *CROWN OF INDIA is by RIX out of INDIAN CROWN; the other mare is by RISSAM out of NEZMA, and therefore a full sister to *NIZZAM. Although *ROSANTHUS himself sired but one champion, four of his sons have come to his aid, HAZEM BEY leading with four. *CROWN OF INDIA (a half sister of Indian Magic) is the dam of a champion, and so is a daughter of *INDIAN DAWN.

In 1941, Donald S. Hopkins of Spokane, Washington imported two mares bred by Mrs. H. V. M. Clark, England, but only one, *BALIS (Sainfoin-Bekr) had any foals. This mare, a bay foaled in 1936, is founder of one line to date. BEKR is by NIMR (not the American import of that name) out of BELKA.

A unique importation was made in 1934 from a country which hitherto had not supplied us with Arabian horses. The horses were brought here from Spain by Mr. and Mrs. J. E. Draper of Richmond, California;

104

*NAKKLA (Fondak-*Menfis)

and this importation too was to prove influential within the breed, few though its numbers may have been. The animals were:

No. 1218—*BARAKAT (Fondak-*Meca) Gr.m. 1932
    Seglawi-al-Abd
No. 1219—*MECA (Ursus-Siria) Ch.m. 1923 Seglawi-al-Abd
No. 1217—*MENFIS (Egipto-Siria) Gr.m. 1927 Seglawi-al-Abd
No. 1915—*NAKKLA (Fondak-*Menfis) Gr. 1932 Seglawi-al-Abd
No. 1216—*RAS-EL-AYN (Axdir-*Meca) Gr.st. 1933
    Seglawi-al-Abd

An article by Mrs. Draper in *The Western Horseman* in the 1930's gives her impression of some of the horses and the main studs:

> On the *finca* of Jose M. Ybarra (owner of the Ybarra Steamship lines), a group of mares with foals was brought in for our inspection. At this *finca* they were using as their No. 1 stallion, the magnificent URSUS, at that time 24 years of age. He came into the patio like a three-year-old—head and tail carried high. One could never guess his age from his gait an appearance. URSUS was imported from Russia by the Spanish Government, and sired many champions as well as some of the fastest Arabians of Spain.
>
> The Ex-Duke of Veragua, Christopher Columbus (Cristobal Colon, the only living descendant of the original Christopher

Columbus) treated us to a truly gorgeous show of trained Arabians. His stud was composed of animals from Arabia, England, Poland, and France, as well as Spain. One of his most highly prized was a son of the above mentioned URSUS—SIRIO III by name, Grand Champion Arabian Stallion of Spain in 1930. At that time Cristobal Colon was offered 150,000 pesetas (approximately $15,000) for SIRIO III.

The Ex-Marquis of Demecq, perhaps the largest breeder of Arabians in Spain, and from whom we subsequently made our purchases, brought them out in splendid array. For many years, the eminent horseman, Senior Don Pedro of Domecq and Rivero, (the Ex-Marquis of Domecq) has been most instrumental in improving the Arabian horse in Spain. He influenced the importation of many fine horses, including ORNIS in 1912, foaled in Russia in 1909. ORNIS is a three-quarter brother of the famous SKOWRONEK of England, being sired by IBRAHIM, out of SIKORA. The dam of SIKORA was YASKOULKA, also the dam of SKOWRONEK. Proof of the keen selection lies in the fact that SKOWRONEK did not go to England for some time after ORNIS had be imported to Spain. (ORNIS, however, was only ⅞ths Arabian.)

The Drapers encountered the usual unexpected problems when trying to export their prizes from Spain. Aside from the fact that this was only a short time after the overthrow of the monarchy, which occasioned enough dilemmas in itself, the horses were practically on the dock when the Drapers were informed that it was illegal to export Arabian horses from Spain, due to the great expense the government had taken to obtain breeding stock in the first place with the object of improving local stock. However with due process of string-pulling and red-tape unravelling, the first importation of Spanish Arabians was on its way to America.

Both *MECA and *MENFIS founded strong families. *NAKKLA was sold to the Kellogg Ranch, where she produced several fine foals by *RASEYN, one of which (the last, in fact, hence his name) was PO-MONA AMEN. Another was RASAKKLA. The other families are prolifically represented by the champions sired by SUREYN, a son of *RASEYN, so obviously the Spanish breeding nicked well with the SKOWRONEK line. Fifteen of SUREYN's twenty-three champions were from mares of the SIRIA family as represented by *MECA and *MENFIS through their female descendants.

K. A. Bistany of Buffalo, New York, imported a mare and a stallion in 1933. These were the grey Maneghi-Sbeyli mare *ALYLA, foaled 1929, and the grey Hamdani-Simri stallion *AL-MASHOOR, foaled 1928. The mare was bred by Chickrallah Abdallah, Jebel, while *AL-MASHOOR was bred by Abdallah Azaar, Damascus, Syria. This horse was of excellent conformation according to his pictures, except for a quite thick neck. A caption under one of his photographs states that he "is a direct descendant of the celebrated war horse Hamdany Samry which carried the

106

Prophet Mohamed from Mecca on his flight to Medina in the year 622." This shows how gullible people can be, for Mohamed rode a camel, a quite famous one incidently, on that historic flight. The name "Hamdany Samry" was not that of a war horse of the time but is a strain. As a matter of fact this strain apparently had its origin at least ten centuries later.

A number of winners trace to these horses, but not in direct tail male or tail female. *AL-MASHOOR was grand champion of the Nashville all Arabian show in 1935.

In 1947 the largest importation straight from the Near East since that of Homer Davenport forty-one years previously, was made by the Hearst Ranch of San Simeon, California. This ranch had been founded on Kellogg and Maynesboro stock and its head stallions at this time were RAHAS, REHAL, GHAZI and GULASTRA.

This expedition consisted of the ranch manager, Preston Dyer; Dr. Pulling, the veterinarian; and John Williamson (W. K. Kellogg's grandson), official photographer. The trip took five and a half months, encompassing points in North Africa as well as the Near Eastern countries. Near Damascus they were entertained by the Rualla clan of the Anazeh tribe, dining in the greasy-handed Arab style with Emir Fawaz Shalaan and his son Emir M'Hitaab Ibn Shalaan. They were shown many horses there (which the Emirs had trouble identifying without the help of onlookers) but none elicited any enthusiasm. This was not due to the customary emaciated condition of the animals, but simply because of the utter lack of Arabian type and quality, along with poor conformation and a conglomeration of unsoundnesses. This same problem was encountered among the horses of the lesser tribes as well. A published story to the effect that a "fine mare' was discovered among one of the important horse-breeding tribes and ridden post haste to a place where horses were being gathered, has been called erroneous (though not by that exact word) by John Williamson. He states flatly that all the horses were obtained in Lebanon, from the stables of Henri Pharoan, Foreign Minister of that country. Pharoan's racing stables are said to be the largest in the world, with 250 horses in training. He not only maintains his own stud farms, but sends emissaries to all the tribes in search of likely candidates for racing, and this may account for the lack of good horses remaining for other buyers. Another reason for lack of horses in any number among the tribes was the ban placed on raiding in the 1920's. Raiding was one of the most lucrative and pleasure-filled occupations of the camel-breeding tribes (and others), and it was these which had bred the best and most horses in the past. The outlawing of outlawry, so to speak, practically eliminated the use for horses in the economy of the desert-dwellers, for horses were an essential part of raiding—as well as protection from being raided. It also made even more poverty-stricken an already poor nomad people, so horses were sold off—and the day of the war mare was gone. King Ibn Saoud is said to have bought any horse his desperate subjects took to him, in order to ease their situation at least temporarily. This may account for the wide variety of type and quality found among the horses in his stables, but on the other hand they were probably kept separate from the ones which had been bred by him for several generations.

Many of the horses obtained in Lebanon were in training, and some had already been raced. *ARKANE, a twelve year old bay stallion had won every one of his seventeen starts over a two year period, and was a gift from Pharoan. Some of the horses were desertbred, others had been bred by Pharoan. They have the usual strain names although these are not listed in the Stud Book due to the Registry's stand on such matters. *ARKANE is the sire of ADMARKA, dam of ZELAMAT, and *MOUN-WER sired the dam of RAHMOUN. *ZAMAL, a typy grey, won several prizes in California shows, and he too is represented by champions. *MOUNWER did fairly well in the same shows, but although he had a beautiful shoulder and high withers, plus other attributes and lots of style, he also had very crooked hind legs and this fault may have lessened his appeal with judges.

The importation included:

Stallions: Foaled

Stallions	Foaled
No. 4205—*SNOUNOU, grey	1942
No. 4207—*BOURHANE, grey	1941
No. 4210—*MOUNWER, chestnut	1943
No. 4212—*ARKANE, bay	1936
No. 4216—*ZAMAL, grey	1944
No. 4217—*GHAMIL, chestnut	1944

Mares	
No. 4206—*NAJWA, grey	1944
No. 4208—*LAYYA, grey	1943
No. 4209—*KOUHAILANE, grey	1943
No. 4211—*LEBNANIAH, grey	1943
No. 4213—*MANSOURAH, grey	1944
No. 4214—*RAJWA, grey	1938
No. 4215—*BINT RAJWA, grey	1945
No. 4218—*NOUWAYRA, grey	1941

*BINT RAJWA, *KOUHAILANE, and *LEBNANIAH have all either produced a champion or two, or their daughters have.

In this same year other desertbreds were imported. These were from the stables of H.R.H. Amir Saud Ibn Abdul Aziz Al Saud—in other words the King of Saudi Arabia. The spelling here is that given at time of importation and it is interesting to note that in about ten importations from the same source there are about that many different ways of either spelling the names or the inclusion of various titles. At any rate the horses came from the King's main stables in the oasis town of Riyadh, and while such animals may not have lived the free (when not shackled) life of the desert, no one can disagree with the fact that this central area of Nejd is *in* the desert. These imports were *MUNIFAN, a stocking-legged, blaze-faced chestnut, and *MUNIFEH a bay mare. The stallion was quite a stylish horse, with many good points to recommend him although he was also low-backed and crooked-hocked. The mare had a very short croup, extremely light bone, and sickle hocks. They were imported by George O'Brien of Los Angeles.

A unique import was *MOURAD No. 4515 (Quari-Nadra), a grey stallion foaled in 1944 and brought here by Paul Valty Ray. The unusual feature here is that *MOURAD was bred by the Jumenterie de Meknes, in Meknes, Morocco. This name gives the impression it is one of the many French Remount depots in that country. In these depots, Arabian stallions, usually desertbreds, are used at stud along with the more plentiful Barbs and Arab-Barbs. There is no reason to believe that an Arabian from Morocco is a Barb any more than an Arabian from America is a mustang, Morgan, American Saddlebred or any other native breed, assuming the Arabian's credentials are in order. Apparently he sired only two foals, and those were in Canada; but his daughter BONNIE ANNIE LAURIE, is the dam of a champion. This is quite an international affair. The horse was foaled in North Africa in a French Remount station (presumably); he was apparently shipped to Canada, and his Canadian daughter is Scottish by name, his son has an Arabic name, and all are registered in the Arabian Horse Registry of America.

The year 1947 was a good one for desertbreds. Admiral R. L. Conolly of La Jolla, Califorina imported *AL HAMDANIEH from Saudi Arabia in that year, but nothing more specific is given. She was a grey seven-year-old. A line to her is kept alive by a granddaughter, dam of a champion.

Due to late registration the well publicized importation by the Remount department of the Army in 1945 was not included with listings of that year, but instead with the records of both 1946 and 1947. Before going into details regarding the horses themselves, an explanation is in order as to why the Army was so anxious to acquire these Arabians and the other horses they imported. The Remount is often mentioned in the history of Arabian horses in the United States, so a quotation from the booklet *Parade of Horses Recently Imported From Europe* is pertinent:

> Although its activities had been a Quartermaster Corps responsibility for many years, the Army Remount Service was not officially established as such until 5 October 1917. Its purpose at that time was to purchase, process, train and issue horses and mules required by the military establishment. Three permanent depots were in operation for that purpose: Fort Reno, Oklahoma, Fort Keogh, Montana; and Front Royal, Virginia. In 1919, the Depot at Fort Keogh was turned over to the Department of Agriculture for use as an experimental farm, and the activities transferred to Fort

109

Robinson, Nebraska, an old frontier post which was first established in 1874.

During World War I, thirty odd auxiliary Remount Depots of varying capacities were set up at the principal Army cantonments throughout the United States, and an Officers' Candidate School for Remount officers was established at Camp Joseph E. Johnston, Florida. To meet the animal needs of the A.E.F., 135,914 horses and mules were purchased in France; 18,462 in Spain; 21,238 in Great Britain; and 306,321 in the United States. In the course of purchasing a large number of horses in the United States, it developed that there was an alarming lack of good riding horses.

In 1919, the War Department established the Remount Board, consisting of prominent civilian horsemen and Army officers, for the purpose of considering, reporting and making recommendations to the Chief of Staff upon all matters pertaining to the supervision and regulation of breeding operations for public animals for the War Department.

As it takes six or seven years to turn out a horse for use in war, and as the supply of horses could not be put into forced production, as is possible with other miltiary supplies, it was recognized that a long-range plan should be put into effect to improve the breed of horses in the United States, so that in the event of any future emergency, there would be a reservoir of good horses upon which the Army could draw. The Department of Agriculture was conducting a minor horse-breeding program with a small annual appropriation. The Remount Board, after a thorough study of the matter, recommended that the Army conduct all activities designed to improve the breed. The Department of Agriculture concurred heartily in this proposal and operations began in 1920.

The Army Remount Service, over the period of years between 1921 and 1945, has increased the holding of its stallions from 165 to a top of over 700, by purchase, by donations, and by breeding activities at the various Remount Depots, where bands of good broodmares are maintained. These stallions are placed with civilian agents without expense to the government. In this way, the Army has insured that good stallions are available to all horsemen generally and has created a reservoir of good animals available to the Army in time of emergency. In addition, many depot foals have been raised and issued.

The Army Remount Service was well established and ready for expansion when the emergency was declared in 1940. The Remount Depots were set up to receive, condition and issue the animals, and the Remount Areas were established and ready to purchase and ship them. The results of the breeding plan were very apparent in the type of animals available.

In 1943, the Kellogg Arabian Stud Farm (operated by the University of California was donated to the Government and became the Pomona QM Depot (Remount). It was a property

110

of very considerable value, and its work is devoted to the breeding of purebred Arabian horses and the placing of Arabian stallions throughout the far West.

During the war period; the Army Remount Service purchased 25,619 riding horses; 1,333 draft horses; and 30,290 pack mules. Considerable aid was given the U.S.Coast Guard in equipping; training, and supervising the operation of their mounted Beach Patrols throughout the United States.

Regarding the horses described in the booklet, the following foreword was given:

Listed herein are brief pedigrees of horses imported from Europe by the U.S. Army Remount Service during the Fall of 1945.

There are 63 Thoroughbreds; 18 pure Arabs; 16 Grade Arabs; 9 Lippizzaners; and 37 Half-breds.

Most of these animals were captured from the German Wehrmacht by The American Army of Invasion. A few were requisitioned from German citizens by our Army of Occupation. Still others were requisitioned from the ex-German government (other than the Wehrmacht). All of those requisitioned were appraised and entered for subsequent inter-allied reparations settlement . . .

It is felt that these horses are a most valuable addition to our Remount blood stock. These, together with others that may be shipped from Europe later, represent some of the finest bloodlines in the world. Furthermore, many of them are the result of selective breeding on the part of governmental agencies in continental Europe; with selection guided by possible military use of the horses produced.

With characteristic German thoroughness, these horses have been bred for temperament, durability and thriftness for generations. Thoroughbreds and grades alike have been thoroughly tried in many ways and only those with exceptional performance records were sent to the governmental nurseries for breeding.

This system of selective breeding is exactly in accordance with the objectives of the American Remount Service. Of course, our Remount has been in operation but twenty-five years; theirs' for centuries. They have benefited from continuity of policy through life-long assignment of those in charge and from strong governmental support.

We feel that we can advance our Army Breeding Plan many years through adapting to our own Remount Program the experience of Europeans and the results obtained by them.

The Arabian horses captured from the Germans were mostly those originally captured by the Germans from the Poles after the first blitz into Poland that fateful September of 1939. The Russians, attacking from the east, captured the great stud of Janow-Podlaski and carefully collected the Arabian purebreds (all identifiable by brands and records, as well as by captured personnel) and shipped them off to the Tersk stud farm in the Caucasus. At this and other studs the Poles tried to save their horses by hurrying them off to safety, but many were lost en route or placed with farmers. The Germans, methodical always, took note of the brands of the various stud farms, publishing the list in the German magazine *Sankt Georg* so that all horsemen could be on the lookout for horses so branded. In this manner many horses were retrieved, including *WITEZ II. Others, such as *LOTNIK, were commandeered at the racetrack, and many of the horses in training continued to race for the benefit of their captors. A carefully chosen group of stallions and mares was shipped to a German stud in Czechoslovakia, and these animals were the ones from which the Remount officers made their selection for shipment to America. The whole story of their capture by General Patton's troops in the closing days of World War II is thrilling enough for a novel, and in fact the parallel history of the Lippizzaners as told in a Disney movie gives a fair impression of the adventure. If General Patton had not been a cavalryman who appreciated good horses, the appeal to him to save these animals from the oncoming (hungry) Russian forces might not have been answered. Thus war changed the course of Arabian horse history in the United States. The impact made by these Polish imports has been enormous, especially in view of their having been vedettes scouting the way for the new invasions of Polishbreds in the 1960s.

The stallions were:

No. 3932—*LOTNIK (Opal-Mokka) Grey, 1938, 15
No. 3933—*WITEZ II (Ofir-Federacja) bay, 1938, 15-0½
No. 4006—*WISOK (*Witez II-Sokora) bay, 1944, 14-2 (at 2 yrs.)
No. 4005—*PILOT (Trypolis-Zalotna) grey, 1943, 14-2 (at 3 yrs.)
No. 4051—*LARTUR-4 (Lartur-10 Koheilan IV) grey, 1932
No. 6603—*TARNIK (*Lotnik-*Tarnina) grey, 1946,
     imp. en utero

Mares:

No. 3934—*CHLOE (Lirnik-Malaga) grey, 1938, 14
No. 4003—*STOLA (Trypolis-Sokora) grey, 1943, 14-3½ (at 3 yrs.)
No. 4002—*243 MERSUCH III-3 (Mersuch III-205 Ajeeb)
     grey, 1940, 14-3½
No. 4007—*ZALMA (Miecznik-Zalotna) bay, 1944, 14-0½ (at 2 yrs.)
No. 4116—*240 KEHILAN VIII-5 (Koheilan VIII-2 Mersuch I)
     grey, 1940
No. 6752—*KABA (Koheilan IV-3 - Kasba) grey, 1932, 14-2
No. 6796—*KOBYLA (*Lotnik-*Kaba) grey, 1946, imp. en utero
No. 10906—*NIKOLE (*Lotnik-*Chloe) grey, 1946, imp. en utero
No. 3935—*WIERNA (Ofir-Kamea) bay, 1938, 14-2½
No. 4687—*SIGLEILAN (Siglavy-Bagdady V-*240 Koheilan
     VIII-5) grey, 1946, imp. en utero

No. 3937—*WIERKA (Miecznik-*Wierna) bay, 1944, 14-0½
  (at 2 yrs.)
No. 4004—*WERRA (Trypolis-*Wierna) grey, 1943, 14-3¾
  (at 3 yrs.)
No. 4001—*231 KUHAYLAN-ZAID 8
  (Kuhaylan-Zaid - 2 Mersuch 1) grey, 1937, 14-3¾
No. 3935—*IWONKA III (Ibn Mohamet-Lysa) chestnut, 1936 15
No. 3936—*TARNINA (Lowelas-Limba) grey, 14-3
No. 6779—*HABANERA (Witraz-Hedshra) bay, 1943, 14
  (at 3 yrs.)

The horses were shipped to Fort Robinson, then to Pomona, after their acclimatization at Front Royal. Earlier, in 1941, the Directors of the Arabian Horse Club of America had donated at least one horse each to the Remount, as detailed in the following report:

The Directors of the Arabian Horse Club of America have made possible the formation of an Arabian Horse Stud by the United States Remount of the War Department. One or more horses were given by each Director, and these were horses of unquestioned quality, horses not for sale, and which could not be purchased. The foundation stock of this Stud as founded and their donors are listed as follows:

ZEWA No. 1681 ....Henry B. Babson
BABOLNA No. 1498, and her 1941 foal ......J. M. Dickinson
NIHT No. 578 ....Albert W. Harris
HORMA No. 636 ....Albert W. Harris
KEHEFE No. 768 ....Albert W. Harris
KATAR No. 724 ....Albert W. Harris
SURANA No. 1356 ....W. K. Kellogg
RIFNETTA No. 1660 ....W. K. Kellogg
SONATA No. 1661 ....W. K. Kellogg
MIRZAIA No. 1010 ....Roger A. Selby
RAGIA No. 1375 ....L. W. Van Vleet

These horses were maintained at Fort Robinson for a few years, and when the group was shipped to the Army's newly acquired Pomona

*LOTNIK (Opal-Mokka)   *WITEZ II (Ofir-Federacja)

113

Quartermaster Depot (Remount) in 1944, the number had increased to twenty-four. Another stallion and twelve yearlings and weanlings accounted for the additional stock.

To the horses of The Arabian Horse Stud were added all those of the Kellogg Ranch, and finally those of the Army importation, but by that time of course the whole operation had become that of the Remount.

Unfortunately for the Remount Service, the Army had decided the horse was obsolete in modern warfare, and the Remount was transferred to the Department of Agriculture, then phased out in 1949. The Kellogg ranch was actually put on the Army surplus list, along with all the Remount horses. The reaction to the public was instantaneous and effective, with Senator Richard Nixon helping in the fight to save the ranch and the Arabian horses. Kellogg himself was understandably hurt and dismayed by the government's action, for this three-million-dollar ranch and its stock were given to the Army with the understanding it would promote not only the Remount, but especially the Arabian breed. The Arabian Horse Association of Southern California was the first organization to start the ball rolling in saving the ranch and through its efforts the various politicians and others with authority halted the sale of the ranch, but not of the horses. Some were sold at auction at Kellogg's, while others were shipped back to Fort Robinson for auction with the other breeds owned by the Remount. Some of the Remount agents were allowed to buy the stallions which were stationed with them at the time.

The Polish imports had attracted great attention while at Kellogg's, but some stallion owners who depended on much of their income from stud fees were antagonistic to all Remount stallions, especially the imports, due to the wide publicity they had received. All kinds of silly stories were circulated to discourage use of the Remount stallions, who stood at the low fee of Remount stallions everywhere, ($10 to $20) and were therefore a menace to the earning capacity of homegrown stallions. The joke of this is that one of the perpetrators of the most vicious stories against Polish Arabians eventually imported some Polish horses himself. Although the grey *LOTNIK was the most admired by horsemen in general (he was widely publicized as "the German Super Horse"), it was the bay *WITEZ II who turned out to be the super sire. Because of his more clean cut head, he was the one generally favored by Arabian owners. Of course there was more to his qualities than the head—he was well built throughout. His only noticeable fault was that his neck was slightly plain, in that it was somewhat heavy underneath. His hind legs were not as straight as *LOTNIK's but they were nevertheless excellent and strong.

*LOTNIK was almost impossible to fault, except for his head, which was Arabic enough but not as classically-carved as that of *WITEZ II. It is no wonder that opinions varied as to which was the superior horse.

114

One of the admirers of *WITEZ II was E. E. Hurlbutt, then of Calabasas, California. When he found that this stallion was to sold at auction in Nebraska, he flew there, determined to buy the horse if it were at all possible. *WITEZ II sold for $8100 and the winning bidder was Hurlbutt, in cooperation with Fred Arth, from whom Hurlbutt soon bought his interest. The horse was inseparable from the Hurlbutts ever after, except for a lease of a couple of years late in his life to the Betts Ranch in Colorado.

The auction in Fort Reno was held May 25, 1949. Details released by the Department of Agriculture were:

> A total of 54 animals was sold, consisting of 81 Thoroughbreds, 12 unregistered Thoroughbreds (European), 12 Arabians, 36 Half-breds and 1 Lippizzaner, the average price of the lot being $850.97. The average price of the Thoroughbreds was $7750.00; the Arabians, $1,467.70, the Half-breds $660.41.

At this time the usual price for a yearling filly was around $600, and this is reflected in the averages of the auction at Kellogg's:

> The United States Department of Agriculture held a sale by sealed bids on the surplus Arabians at the Kellogg Ranch, Pomona, California. The following summary gives the prices paid for the Arabians:

		Average
Six Broodmares	$9,681.50	$1,613.58
Seven Two and Three year old Fillies	4.516.00	645.14
Eight Yearling Fillies	4,764.32	595.54
Eleven Two to Four year old Stallions ..	4,867.11	442.46
Ten Yearling Colts	2,513.00	351.30

Of the Arabians sold at Fort Robinson, the lot included, besides *WITEZ II, several other imports as well Americanbreds: *240 KOHEILAN VIII-5, *231 KUHAYLAN-ZAID 8, *243 MERSUCH III-3, RIFNETTA, SONATA, *WERRA, *WIERKA, *WIERNA, TIARA and *ZEWA and several others. At Pomona some of the better known animals were *CHLOE, *HABANERA, *IWONKA III, KEHEFE, MIRZAIA, *STOLA, *TARNINA, *WONTEZ, TARNIK, RABOL, NATAF, CELONESE, NIKOLE, and RIFTEZ. *LOTNIK apparently was not in this sale, and had been with a Remount agent at the time. The foregoing horses were surplus as stated, but a good number had been retained by the Kellogg Ranch which, after its salvaging from a fate worse than death—possible sale for subdivision—was donated to the California State Polytechnic College. It is now known as the Kellogg Campus of that college, or more familiarly as Cal Poly.

The success of *WITEZ as a sire is shown in the Sire Line charts. Among his winners were Pacific Coast Champions ZITEZ and NATEZ (the latter twice winner of this honor as well as a reserve, also Top

115

Ten in the Nationals); BOLERO, three times a Top Ten winner; and NAFATEZ, Reserve Pacific Coast Champion. Other top ten winners are YATEZ, FERTEZZA, MITEZ, HIRZAN and WITEZAR. Also the Canadian Top Tens: BLACK MAGIC, BOLERO, TANGO (twice), HIRZAN (twice), WITEZAR, WITEZYM and YATEZ. in the working division *WITEZ II was the sire of Legion Merit winner AMATEZ (Reserve Pacific Coast Champion g); ZIKEZ, Pacific Coast English Pleasure Champion; and RONTEZA winner of the $1000 Reined Cow Horse Stake at the San Francisco Cow Palace against fifty national contenders of all breeds. In addition, his son OFIR (named after the sire of *WITEZ II) was the winner of three of the 2½ mile races of 1959-60 and was second in another. Besides the feats of his sons and daughters, *WITEZ himself was twice Grand Champion (when that award was given) of the Southern California All-Arabian show and was Pacific Coast Champion in 1953, on which occasion his son ZITEZ was reserve. The 1968 National Champion ZARABO is by BOLERO, and other second, third and fourth-generation descendants of *WITEZ II continue to make their presence felt in not only the ever-present halter classes but in all types of performance as well, including jumping. The remarkable record of *WITEZ II and his descendants was indirectly influential in the 1961 and onward importations from Poland.

*WITEZ II was one of the celebrated triumvirate of stallions of the "W" names, the other two being WIELKI SZLEM (Grand Slam) and WITRAZ (Stained Glass). All of these were foals of 1938, sired by OFIR, a son of the desertbred KUHAILAN-HAIFI.

*LOTNIK had been sold to a rancher and remained in the back hills for many years. After his owner's death he was sold to the Desert Arabian Ranch of Robert Aste in Scottsdale, Arizona, where he sired a couple of crops of foals before his death. He was a gentle horse and a beautiful one, but he was not the sire that *WITEZ II was. His name meant "flyer."

*PILOT was of the TRYPOLIS line, and five other sons of TRYPOLIS are represented by American champions as is *PILOT. He was not kept at Kellogg's as a depot sire but was issued early, along with many of the Kellogg bred colts and stallions. *PILOT is the sire of a champion and of a Top Ten Western Pleasure horse.

*LARTUR-4 was not brought to Kellogg's and may have been issued as a Remount sire direct from Fort Robinson. At any rate he apparently has no purebred foals.

*WISOK was injured in the train trip to Pomona and was almost slated for death because of the seriousness of the injury. However he was saved and issued to a Remount agent. Until 1960 he had sired many halfbreds but only one purebred, and had been used as a roping horse, cutting horse, pleasure horse, child's horse, and parade horse, which is "a lot of horse." His offspring had a reputation for being fast walkers (which is also true of Rahas get). Under new ownership this stallion has sired a number of purebred foals, but only in the last few years.

Several of the Remount mares founded good producing families. Among the most notable are those of *CHLOE and *WIERNA. The former has a two-branched line, through LITTLE BIT and CHLOEYN; the latter has two Top Ten mares among her champions, with one of them going on to the National Championship. The *WIERNA family also has a National Champion to its credit. This is the promising sire BAY-ABI, whose dam ANGYL is a daughter of *WIERNA. Both CHLOEYN and ANGYL are sired by *RASEYN. The. other two *WIERKA branches are through TIARA and *WIERKA.

The family of *IWONKA III is international in its relationships. In Poland the line is carried on through her daughter BALALAJKA, whose two daughters BANDOLA and ARFA were among the most valuable in that country as producers of high quality Arabians. These mares are full sisters of the U.S. National Champion Stallion *BASK; ARFA is the dam of the National Champion Mare *ARWISTAWA, while BANDOLA produced the Top Ten stallion *BAJRAM and a younger champion, *BARYSZ. An Americanbred daughter of *IWONKA III, namely WIWONKA, is the dam of the Great Plains Champion KANEYN. Of the other Army imports *HABANERA, *TARNINA, *231 KUHAYLAN-ZAID 8, *KABA and *243 MERSUCH III-3 are all producers of one or two champions. The mares with the numbered names are those bred by the famous Babolna Stud of Hungary. They are always given their sire's name (and sometimes he is a No. I, II, III or higher in Roman numerals) prefixed by their own foal number and suffixed by the number assigned to them after they are put in the broodmare band. So 231 KUHAYLAN-ZAID-8 is the 231st foal by that horse, and the eighth of them to become classified as a broodmare.

Canada had its own imports in this period as well. The chestnut stallion *VICTORY DAY II No. 4347 was imported to Toronto by R. M. Sketch in 1946. He was by the sixteen hand RIFFAL and out of SHA-BRYEH, and was bred by T. C. Armitage. This is of the *ASTRALED sire line through SOTAMM, and *VICTORY DAY II is the sire of one champion. *ROSHEBA (Shihab-Roxana) No. 4228, and *KURRAH (Gharbi-Gara) No. 4229, both grey mares, were imported by P. J. Smith of Meadowvale, Ontario, in 1947.

At this point the Arabian Horse Club Registry was slightly over forty years of age; and at the end of 1949 it had registered 5864 horses, which were owned by about 1500 persons. At that time a forecast was made that by the year 1958, when the Registry was fifty years old, 10,000 horses would have been registered. This projection was not far wrong, the actual number was 14,277, which is quite an increase over the original 71 horses.

Prior to Volume V of the *Arabian Stud Book*, the format of the Stud books included the strains of each animal's sire and dam, the markings,

117

*CHLOE (Lirnik-Malaga)

*STOLA (Trypolis-Sokora)

*WIERKA (Miecznik-*Wierna)

*WERRA (Trypolis-*Wierna)

*TARNINA (Lowelas-Limba)

*IWONKA III (Ibn Mohamet-Lysa)

POLISH MARES IMPORTED BY THE U.S. ARMY

118

and the produce of mares and the get of stallions of those animals old enough to have any offspring. Supplements were issued every year. The last of these was of course Volume IV, which in some instances was bound with the supplement for the year 1939. With Volume V only the bare facts are published, the colors and sex are abbreviated, and in all it contains much information in small compass. One problem however is that in the list of colors, black, very rare in the Arabian breed, is included while brown is not. In fact, the majority of Arabians called black are actually brown by definition if they show any tan around muzzle or flank. There are many brown Arabians, but true blacks are unique, though they do exist. Two other colors, one extremely rare, the other so far apparently non-existent, are roan and white. Both are forms of grey in the incorrect sense, but true roan has a dark head (usually) and never changes color once the foal has acquired its permanent coat. By contrast, grey goes through various shades until it can become either white or fleabitten. But white as a color of foal is unknown, as of absolute record, in the Arabian breed. To register a mature animal (as in the case of an import) as "white" when it is an aged grey, immediately invokes images of so-called albinos, which are true whites of that color from birth but with pink skin. Aged greys, though white, have black skin except under white markings. Accordingly, it is strange to find the three rare or (in the case of white) never-never colors in the breed included, but the fairly common brown is excluded. Moreover, the abbreviation for grey is given as "G" which is the universal abbreviation for a gelding. While it is true that geldings are rarely registered (most registrations being of foals) and in any case are not numerous in this breed, surely the directors should have known of their existence and of the abbreviation used for them. It may not be so bad in the stud books, though it does cause momentary pause when one reads "gelding" automatically for a "G" (grey) mare, but occasionally this original error is pick up by show programs; and then it does make for some peculiar reading.

The system used by the present books has been widely praised as to format, and it does make for comparably easy reference, providing you have all of the set from Volume V (which lists all registered in previous books) up to the present. This constitutes quite a library, for these books are now issued yearly. Moreover some names of horses have been changed, and to date no list of such changes has been printed; Consequently there is no way to locate the registration of that animal if its name is all that is known. In searching for the progeny of any particular animal through the years one must first know its number, for the foals are listed by their registration number under the number of their sire and also of their dam. Since no names are given in the progeny section of the stud books, it is impossible to know which list of numbers belong to what horse; for unless the animal is a recent import with offspring imported with him or her, his name is not listed in the same book. The only way

119

to discover the name of the progenitor in question is to look up the data on the foal, and of course it will be given there, as sire or dam as the case may be. Naturally it would be easier on those concerned if names of sires and dams could be included with their numbers, but the Registry has enough problems as it is, and this would involve more typesetting and expense. It is to be hoped that sometime in the future a supplement will be issued listing all stallions and mares which have registered progeny, cross-filed both by number and alphabetically.

Family strains have been indicated whenever possible, to this point, for they are of interest to anyone intrigued by this ancient system of tracing at least part of a horse's lineage. The strains were throughly mixed as early as 1840, according to the Abbas Pasha pedigrees; and certainly they were equally homogenized in more recent decades, as witness the breeding of horses imported or desertbred thereafter. The Registry discontinued the recording of strain names in 1940 as noted in a report of that year:

> The next matter to receive serious consideration was whether or not the registry should drop the Arabic family names. Nobody seemed to know why this practice of continuing the archaic method of identification used by the Arabs was carried over into our registry, as it was not of a real sign of breeding. It was just a method of identification carried down from the matriarchate and still used by the Tuaregs of the Sahara. The child was given the name of its mother to identify it, as the identity of the mother was always known, whether that of the father was or not. In checking up on the progress of horses of different families, it was found they had little of any specific family blood, if any, from an ancestral standpoint. This was authenticated by several well-versed breeders of Arabian horses. As the Arabian Horse Club registry certificate is authenticated proof of pure blood, it was decided that family names would not be used in the future. If some breeders think it advisable to sell horses on the strength of their family names, the purchaser led to make selections on such a family basis would rightly lose faith in a certificate indicating a family only partially existent in the blood of his horse. Whether such purchaser, when he had discovered this, would have redress on the breeder who sold the horse on the basis of family blood might be debatable. However, as a result of this decision, stud books and registration certificates have not carried any reference to Arabic families since this time.

IV

IMPORTATIONS IN THE FIFTIES

By this time the reader might be wondering if there had been no Americanbred Arabians worthy of mention since practically all reference has been made to imported horses. As a matter of fact there were hundreds of worthy Arabians bred in this country in the same period, but importations are included first for the simple fact that every Arabian horse in this country either descended from imported stock or is itself an import. Therefore if all foreign bred horses are listed (minus the usual misses and errors) every owner can find a relative of his horse somewhere down the line. Moreover it is useful to be able to locate such references without having to thumb through all the stud books. The influential Americanbreds will be dealt with in due course.

When it comes to the two decades after World War II, the imports were so numerous that I found that if it was not actually a case of biting off more than one can chew it was at least more than it was possible to digest. Accordingly the reader will have to do some of his own digesting from the data presented, and I will merely touch on the highlights, or on stud farms founded by these importations. Although it may seem that there are a great number of imported horses, it is in fact minuscule by proportion to the Americanbreds. Take 1966 for example: There were 52 imports, which is quite a few. *But* there were 5339 registrations in that year, which means that there were 5287 Americanbreds foaled in the same period. Therefore the ratio would be .0009 per cent imported stock—the proverbial grain of sand (or is it a drop in a bucket?), yet despite this unfavorable ratio the imported horses have made noticeable inroads into show and performance statistics.

One of the early immigrants in the 1950s was the Egyptianbred *MOFTAKHAR who did not acquire his present status as a sire until acquired by Douglas Marshall of Texas. While this horse has sired some halter champions he is best remembered as the sire of race horses, especially EL GOHARI and EL GABAL. The former won several of the mile-and-a-half races (under the pari-mutuel betting system) including the 1968 Arabian Classic at Evangeline Downs in Louisiana. The comparatively new EL GABAL won the first of the short races for Arabians at Turf Paradise in Phoenix, Arizona. *MOFTAKHAR is a son of ENZAHI who in turn was a son of NABRAS, described as "a powerfully built race horse of Mahmoud El Itribi Pasha, which, like most of

121

its sons, has won several races." The picture of NABRAS indicates anything but a powerfully built horse, in fact he is quite otherwise, at least by our standards. Nevertheless NABRAS must have helped the perfor· mance factor of the sons of *MOFTAKHAR, although Egyptian Arabians in general have speed.

Of the Ross horses, several have left their mark on American stock and also by their own performance (or appearance at halter) in the show ring. *RITHAN has five champions to his credit and a son who has also made a start in that capacity. *SHAMADAN, a three-gaited winner (park) in stakes and regular classes has also done well as a sire. Of the mares, *ASHAN, *SENGA and *SHAYBA have all become producers of champions and founders of families with similar capacities. The last two are full sisters to the Rogers import *SILVER CRYSTAL.

I have a program of the 1948 Arab Horse Society Summer Show held at Roehampton in which Lady Wentworth wrote comments on several of the horses. Some of the remarks are rather pungent, as was her way. However she wrote of *RITHAN: "A beautiful horse, champion at two shows this year." In the class for Arabs (they are usually not called Arabians in England) under saddle, *RITHAN was "restive; could not be mounted and was sent out." Indeed the whole class must have been

*SERAFIX

122

in the nature of a refined rodeo, for "BOAZ was unmanageble—threw his rider and was sent out;" INDIAN JEWEL "attacks other horses and should never win" (he didn't); HAJI was "riotous and badly ridden" while STAR DIAMOND "stood first but got upset and was sent out." Presumably "upset" is not to be taken literally, but considering the actions of the other horses, who knows? Classes for Arabs under saddle needless to say have vastly improved, in England, since that date. By the way, the American Stud Book gives William Hay as breeder of *RITHAN, but this program and the A.H.S. Stud Book give Lady Wentworth as his breeder. Lady Wentworth termed *SENGA "a lovely mare", but she was less enthusiastic about a mare of rather conglomerate breeding: "lovely head, awful hocks and quarters." At this show RAKTHA was champion stallion, GRAND ROYAL reserve, while the mare winners were GREY ROYAL, champion, and CROWN ROYAL, reserve.

This period marked the founding of the Rogers Arabian Stud, in Walnut Creek, California which has become one of the most formidable in the nation. The first mares were obtained in Arabia. John Rogers had spent many years in Arabia, and in the course of events he was able to closely observe 800 of the approximately 1200 purebred horses remaining in Saudi Arabia, as well as many in Iraq, Syria and Egypt. The grey *SUBAIHA was the favorite. The booklet on the Rogers Stud states:

> Something of Subaiha's background is of interest. In 1944 we were the first privileged to visit the Royal Stables in the oasis of Hofuf. The featured mare was Hamdaniya, a 27 year old mashusha (rose-speckled grey, not fleabitten). The attendants proudly told us that the great King Ibn Saoud had ridden this mare in the last wars in the 1920's. Next, the 4 year old Subaiha was brought out to how the old mare had looked in her youth. Both horses, although quite thin, made a lifetime impression because of their spirit, conformation, obvious intelligence and over-all balance. Three years later the writer was indeed fortunate to be requested to name what he considered one of the best mares in the Royal Stables. It took only a moment to recall a few of the best and settle on Subaiha.

Her name means "the youthful one," indicating it was merely descriptive compared to "the old one," her dam. However she remained youthful in spirit. As Rogers said, "She is still as fast as the finest horses of the breed and light and collected under saddle. She was winner of a blue ribbon in the Cow Palace her first time in a ring or near a crowd."

*BAKHAITAH (fortunate) and *MUNEERAH (possessor of light) were desertbred in every sense of the word. They were first seen in a caravan, the mare* BAKHAITAH was one of four tied to racing camels, while the filly frollicked around them. Naturally the sight of horses was enough to induce Rogers to move in for a closer look. He was riding in a pickup truck with a guide and an interpreter and hoped to talk to

*SUBAIHA D.B. at 27 years   THORAYYAH D.B.

the owner of the mare and filly, but the dust kicked up by a bullet across their bow, so to speak, (almost into it), made them decide on a diplomatic course, so they didn't try to penetrate the "lead curtain." However a tracer was put on the owner of the horses and several months later the Bedouins, through various contacts, discovered the identity of the caravan owner. This turned out to be Amir Ajran al Ajran, paramount shiekh of the Bani Khalid tribe, and from him *BAKHAITAH was eventually purchased. It was a bit more difficult to buy the filly however, as she was owned by the Amir and two of his brothers; and it was necessary to obtain their consent before she could be sold, but the fact that she and her dam were to be used for breeding purposes influenced them enough to close the deal. *MUNEERAH and a daughter have both produced champions.

*THORAYYAH was bred by Shaikh Kahifah bin Mohamed Alkhalifeh of Bahrain and was a noted race mare. The fact that her head has a straight, almost convex profile is of interest because this feature ties in with comments made by several writers who happened to mention the Arabian horses of Bahrain (Bahreyn). One was H. R. P. Dickson in *The Arab of the Desert* who said, "The shaikhs of Bahrain similarly keep the Roman-nosed Shawaf (Kuhailan) breed, and yet again Al Duwish, Shaikh of the Mutair tribe, used in the past to keep the equally famous Krush strain . . ." *THORAYYAH's face is not exactly Roman-nosed but it isn't dished either. She is the dam of three champion sons, all uniformly beautifully conformed, and all by *SERAFIX. One of them, METEOR, owned by Mr. and Mrs. Stanley Kubela of Palacios, Texas, is as versatile as the Arabian is claimed to be but usually isn't. His talents range from racing, to various show-ring performances, and he was also twice a Top Ten winner at halter, and once in western pleasure. His full brother HATHFAN, owned by the Circle J. Ranch in Big Stone, Alberta, Canada, is a Canadian Top Ten champion along with receiving highest honors at several open as well as all Arabian shows. HATHFAN is a working ranch horse, also an adept performer and ribbon-winner in gymkhana events.

124

Desertbreds are usually at a disadvantage compared to Arabians which have been bred to a certain standard in western countries for several generations. It is not surprising therefore that the English mares, and later the Polish, had a better producing record as far as show winners are concerned. By long odds the best of these has been the grey mare *SILVER CRYSTAL: dam of the National Champion stallion MUJAHID; of the Reserve National Champion mare SILVER DAWN (also twice Pacific Coast Champion and once Reserve); SERAJ, a Top Ten stallion and Pacific Coast Champion; of SILFIX, a Top Ten stallion and Pacific Slope Champion (also twice Reserve); of the imported *SILWA, also a champion; of the broodmatron *ROYAL SILVER, dam of the Top Tens ROYAL MAGIC and ROYAL JEWEL (the latter also Pacific Coast Champion), and of the champion ROYAL GOLD. Both *SILWA and her daughter *SILWARA are also notable producers. Since this just touches on the wins of this family it can be seen that *SILVER CRYSTAL was a good investment.

*SERAFIRE first flashed onto the show horizons as a free-moving, high-going park mare, with many stake wins on her list. However in her short life she also made her mark as a producer; for she is the dam of the mare STARFIRE who was a Top Ten winner but unfortunately died later due to an accident, and INDIAN GENII, a National Champion mare.

In 1954 John Rogers purchased the champion stallion *SERAFIX from Lady Wentworth. He had seen other horses on several occasions but thought the price too high—moreover, the price went up each year. His wife persuaded him to consider the purchase of such a fine stallion as an investment, and it didn't really take much persuasion of this sort to convince Rogers that "now was the hour." *SERAFIX proved an even better investment than *SILVER CRYSTAL. This magnificent chestnut is now the leading sire of champions in this country, with forty-six champions of Class A shows to his credit along with innumerable winners of performance events. *SERAFIX himself was several times champion in California shows, but after receiving an injury in the trailer, he was kept home thereafter. He had a fine way of moving, with plenty of action and dynamic presence, but he was never shown in park class, due to the trailer incident. This stallion stands at fifteen hands and is extremely refined; his neck is naturally arched (no phony photographic tricks needed for him), and his tail carriage is high.

Although the harem of *SERAFIX was restricted to the Rogers' mares for many years, that does not mean that the bloodlines were not varied. The imports already listed show some of the variety, and Americanbreds and later imports added to it. Rogers does not believe in close inbreeding, and certainly the success of *SERAFIX bears out the value of this opinion. To date he has sired only 142 foals, and the percentage of champions to all these is 33 per cent. It goes even higher when the percentage is based only on those two years of age or older, that is, old enough to compete for championships. The percentage then leaps to 39 per cent. *SERAFIX had the unique distinction in 1962 of being the sire of five Top Ten winners, four of them mares, of which two went on to become National Champion and Reserve. It will take some time to equal this.

The bay stallion NATEZ, a son of *WITEZ II, assists in the breeding program. He was twice Pacific Coast Champion and once Reserve, and was also a Top Ten stallion. His sire was Pacific Coast Champion at the age of fourteen. Among the four champions sired by NATEZ is the National Champion mare INDIAN GENII, already mentioned under the heading of *SERAFIRE.

In 1961 several mares were imported from Poland as well as one from England. Of these *MUSZKATELA has produced the most champions to date, with MUSKATEER at present having the most wins, including Great Plains Championship and a Canadian Top Ten win. *CALIOPE is the dam of two champions, and she herself won such honors. Her son *GAYPOLKA, sired by PIETUSZOK and imported en utero, includes a Top Ten, a Canadian Breeders' championship and a Reserve Pacific Northwest championship among his successes. CARINOSA, a daughter of *CALIOPE by *SERAFIX (as are the sons of *Muszkatela), has won innumerable English (and western) pleasure championships and is a Top Ten winner in the former category. She is also a halter champion.

*CHIMENA is the dam of SERJ, a champion and talented park performer with plenty of action and speed. *BLUE RAFIA is the English representative; her son *BLUE DANUBE, however, was sired in England by Patricia Lindsay's Polish stallion *GERWAZY. *BLUE DANUBE is now a champion and winner in park events. At the Rogers auction in 1967, he brought the highest price ever paid (at auction) for an Arabian stallion up to that date.

In 1963 another Polish mare was imported by Rogers, namely *CAROCHA, and in 1965 a mare and filly from Spain were added to the broodmare band. These were *DINORAH III and *YAMINA. The most recent addition to the stud was the grey colt *KARADJORDJE, another son of the eye-catching dappled grey GERWAZY, a former race horse who has won several combined training events as well as jumping and under-saddle classes. The unpronounceable and unspellable name *KARADJORDJE means "Black George" in combination of Turkish and Serbian languages, and the colt was named after a legendary hero of that name.

In the catalog of the 1967 auction, Rogers states that "We emphasize breeding horses and winning at halter because it gets too complicated to include performance champions. Needless to say, ours are 'Doing Horses,' having won a National Performance Class—many top 10 ribbons —finished first in the 100 mile One Day Ride and winners in every kind

126

of event Arabians are trained for, including a 2½ mile race and Legion of Merit." This sums up the situation nicely. It could be added that Rogers has backed almost every Arabian activity in which real utility is emphasised. He has ridden in competitive trail rides himself and was one of the founders of the Arabian Horse Racing Association, under whose rules pari-mutuel racing for Arabians has been conducted at several tracks since 1966. He had also been chairman of an earlier association which conducted two and a half mile races on an exhibition basis, and he was one of the most hard working presidents of the International Arabian Horse Association, during the years 1964 and 1965.

Of the three Englishbreds imported by Mrs. Anne McCormick of Scottsdale, Arizona, *RIFILLA may have produced one champion more than did *IORANA, but the latter's son KIMFA has started out with remarkable success as a sire, with seven champions so far. It is not the number of these, but the ratio of all foals versus champions that is surprising. For KIMFA sired only twelve foals up to and including 1965, then because the quality of his foals was evident, there was a resultant jump to twenty sired the following year. *IORANA is the dam of the champion ESARE. She is a granddaughter of the lovely SHAMNAR, dam of *COUNT DORSAZ and is of the RIYALA branch of the RO-DANIA family. *SUN ROYAL sired one champion although he had little opportunity at stud compared to the senior sire of the McCormick Ranch, MUSTAFA. In 1963 Mrs. McCormick imported the great sire *NABORR (Nabor) from Poland in a group imported by other breeders, mostly in the Scottsdale area. Although then thirteen years old, *NA-BORR stood the tumultuous ocean crossing much better than did his younger shipmates. He remained comparatively fat, while the majority of the others were little less than battered skeletons. This stallion had been obtained from Russia by the Polish State Studs and was permitted to leave only after his sire NEGATIW (Naseem-Taraczcza) had in turn been purchased from the Russian stud farm, Tersk, in the Caucasus. *NABORR is the sire of ten champions, all but one of them bred in Poland; because he has not been at public stud since 1964 his opportunity here, as to number of foals, has been extremely limited. It was because of the closing of his book to outside mares that buyers flocked to Poland for his get and returned with the animals which quickly attained their crown. These included winners of the National Championship and Canadian National Championship (*Dornaba) and many Top Ten and regional winners. They will be noted in due course. While the majority of *NABORRs are not too fast; some, notably those out of mares noted for their speedy offspring, did well on the track in Poland. One of these is the Derby winner *MIRZAZ (Mirza), now a Top Ten park horse. That gorgeous grey, *GWALIOR, winner of innumerable park stakes as well as harness and combination, and of course many halter championships including Top Ten wins, is also a son of *NABORR; he too is an ex-racehorse. It is unfortunate that the services of *NABORR are not available to the public, but at least now there are plenty of good sons in this country.

In 1950 Alex Hindi and Sons of Duran, New Mexico brought in three Lebanonbred horses, bred by their relatives in that country. *DAHAM, a classy dappled grey, had been a successful race horse in Beirut, and he was a champion in America; moreover he is the sire of two champions. His stablemate *BINT ATTEBE is a very smoothly made mare whose length and levelness of croup have rarely been equalled by other champions. Among her wins was a Top Ten placement. She and *DAHAM, combined to produce ANTAR IBN DAHAM, a handsome grey whose championship career was cut short by a serious leg injury. All of the Hindi horses are used for ranch work, none are pampered in the least. Several have been taken right off the range, so to speak, and have won in the informal races held in connection with shows. Not to forget *DALAL—this mare also is the dam of a champion.

*ELECTRIC STORM, imported by Nancy Magro of Montgomery, Ohio has been a winner in performance classes. He is the sire of one champion. *RISSILLETTA, who should not be confused with *RIS-SLETTA (dam of Abu Farwa, Joanna, etc.) is the dam of *RIFILLA who was imported by Mrs. McCormick, but apparently she produced no champions here herself. Highlight of 1957 was the shipload of horses from the Crabbet Park and Hanstead Studs of England, made possible by the death of the owners of these studs, Lady Wentworth and Lady Yule, respectively. The importation was made by Bazy Tankersley whose farm was then in Washington, D.C. This, the Al-Marah Arabian Horse Farm, is the largest in the country; and up to that point it had featured the bloodlines of INDRAFF and his sire *RAFFLES, the former of all Crabbet breeding, the latter bred at that establishment. The Al-Marah farm has now been moved to Barnesville, Maryland. The most successful sire of champions in this group was *ROYAL DIAMOND with ten, and he had been featured for some time as a main sire of that farm. *ROYAL CONSTELLATION was sold at one of the Al-Marah auctions and became a highly-successful performer in harness, combination and park classes, who is also the sire of two champions. He, like *ROYAL DIA-MOND, has a beautiful reach of neck, but is smoother of body. *CRYS-TAL VOYAGER also sired a champion, while *LITTLE OWL (sold at the auction, as were most of the colts and stallions of this importation), has won in a variety of performance classes. Although usually shown English, this horse is more western in type and action.

Several of the mares and fillies were also sold at the aforementioned auction, but those which have produced champions, or whose daughters have done so, are *CROWN OF DESTINY (2), *SALINAS (3), *SILWA (2), and *SILWARA. The latter is the dam of the Top Ten mare COUNTESS OF LASMA. While this does not seem a proportionate number of champions from such a group of wellbred mares, many are well represented instead in the field of performance, which of course is also true of most bloodlines.

In 1959 the fine performance stallion *COUNT DORSAZ, was imported by Al-Marah on lease. As is often the result, the horse was eventually purchased outright. He had won the Arab Riding Class at the International Horse Show (England) four times, and in addition he was winner of the Winston Churchill Cup for the Supreme Champion Riding Horse (all breeds) once, and he was Reserve for this honor on two other occasions. In America he quickly became a popular sire who can claim twenty halter champions, including COUNT BAZY, National Champion stallion of 1967; COUNTESS OF LASMA (Top Ten), and FOUR WINDS MAJA (Top Ten). Two of his sons have sired champions, while a grandson, *THE COUNT OF AL-MARAH, has sired three.

Mrs. Tankersley is another Arabian breeder who believes the breed can shine in performance, and she has entered horses in the various racing projects, in cattle working trials, and many endurance rides, often riding in the latter herself. She has encouraged youngsters in the use of prospective ownership of Arabians. In general she has been much more than just the nation's largest breeder of Arabians.

This same year, 1959, was notable in that it featured two importations from Egypt of more than the usual one or two individual horses. Actually the first was brought over in 1958, but was not included in the Stud Book of that year, so is considered here as of 1959. This group of horses was imported by Richard G. Pritzlaff of Sapello, New Mexico. They repre-

*COUNT DORSAZ (Rissalix-Shamnar)

129

sent some of the best blood of Egypt but as yet are not represented by champions—one reason being they apparently have never been shown.

It was the importation of three grey yearlings in 1959 that proved to be the spark that ignited the enthusiasm for the new Egyptian horses however. This was the group personally selected in Egypt by Mr. and Mrs. Donald Forbis of Chickasha, Oklahoma who have lived many years in the Near East and thoroughly know the Oriental horse in all its variations. One of these yearlings was *ANSATA IBN HALIMA+, winner of many halter championships, including The Region 5 (Southwest) championship and two Top Ten placements. He is a horse with excellent action (as have so many Egyptian imports), and he has won several park classes. *ANSATA IBN HALIMA+ is the sire of two champions—one from each of his stablemates. In 1965 the grey mare *ANSATA BINT BUKRA was added, and she in turn added the filly *ANSATA BINT MISR the following year. These were owned in partnership with Mr. and Mrs. William L. Ferni. The Forbises have written many interesting and informative articles on the horses of Persia, Syria, Turkey, Mesopotamia and so on, but it was their report of the Egyptian horses, along with excellent photographs of previously poorly-pictured breeding stock that revitalized interest in Egyptian Arabians.

IMPORTATIONS
1950 - 1952

A.H.C.R. NUMBER	NAME	SIRE AND DAM	COLOR	SEX	DATE FOALED	BREEDER

Imported by R. G. Follis, San Francisco, California

6599　*AL MISINNAH (Abayan DB-Al Misinnah DB) Bay m. 1947. Amyr Saud Liluwi, Saudi Arabia

Imported by F. E. Mars, The Plains, Virginia

6780　*EL ABIAD (Karawane DB-*Rajwa) Gr. st. 1946 Henri Pharoan, Lebanon

Imported by Esther Ames, M.D.

5947　*MAHRAA DB, Bay m. 1943. Amir Saud Ibn Abdullah Ibn Jiluwi, Hassa, Saudi Arabia

Imported by Esther Ames, M.D.

5946　*MUHAIRA (DB-*Mahraa) Bay m. 1948. Esther B. Ames, M.D.; Dhahran, Saudi Arabia

Imported by Chares H. Votey, Jr., Braintree, Massachusetts

6835　*MOFTAKHAR (Enzahi-Kateefa) Gr. st. 1946. Royal Agricultural Society, Cairo, Egypt.

Imported by the Queen Mother of Egypt

6712　*SAEMA (Gazel el Din-Bint-Dalal) Gr. m. 1945. R.A.S. Cairo, Egypt

Imported by Walter W. Ross and Co., Kansas City, Missouri:

6994　*AMANDA (Raktha-Ghezala) Bay m. 1941. Lady Wentworth, Eng.

6993　*ASHAN (Rix-*Senga) Ch. m. 1941. William Hay, England

7836	°KALAM (°Rithan-°Ashan) Ch. st. 1952 William Hay, Imp. en utero					
7835	°KALLAL (°Rithan-°Ringlet) Ch. st. 1952. William Hay, Imp. en utero					
7836	°RANGOON (°Rithan-°Shayba) Gr. st. 1952. William Hay, Imp. en utero					
6995	°RINGLET (Astralis-Rudeyna) Ch. m. 1932. Mrs. E. M. Carroll, Eng.					
7275	°RITHAN (Raktha-Rishna) Ch. st. 1951. Lady Wentworth, England					
6992	°SENGA (Rangoon-Somara) Gr. m. 1936. William Hay, England					
7276	°SHAMADAN (°Rithan-Somara) Ch. st. 1947. William Hay, England					
6991	°SHAYBA (Rangoon-Somara) Gr. m. 1941. William Hay, England					

(Two Rangoons are named here, the original was a son of Skowronek, the other is the one imported en utero and named as a foal in this country.)

Imported by John Rogers, Walnut Creek, California:

5944	°BAKHAITAH Desertbred Gr. m. 1943. Saud Ibn Abdullah Jiluwi, Saudi Arabia
5945	°MUNEERAH (DB stallion-°Bakhaitah) Gr. m. 1947. Amir Ajran Bin Hamad Al Ajran, Saudi Arabia
7417	°ROYAL SILVER (Grand Royal-°Silver Crystal) Gr. m. 1952. Lady Wentworth, England. Imp. en utero
7426	°SERAFIRE (Indian Magic-Grey Royal) Gr. m. 1950. Lady Wentworth, England
7183	°SILVER CRYSTAL (Rangoon-Somara) Gr. m. 1937. William Hay, England
5942	°SUBAIHA Desertbred. Gr. m. 1940. Saud Ibn Abdullah Jiluwi, Saudi Arabia
5943	°TAFFEL (DB stallion-°Subaiha) Gr. m. 1948. Saud Ibn Abdullah Jiluwi, Saudi Arabia
5941	°THORAYYAH Desertbred. Bay m. 1940. Shaikh Khalifah Bin Mohamed Al Khalifah, Bahrain, Arabia

IMPORTATIONS
1953 - 1956

Imported by T. Cremer, New York, N.Y., 1953:

8415	°CHADIGA (Edh Dhahab-°Ritla) Bay m. 1952. Dr. H.C.E.M. Houtappel, Holland
8410	°FAIKA (Edh Dhahab-°Latifaa) Bay m. 1950. Dr. H.C.E.M. Houtappel, Holland
8416	°FATIMAA (°Nizzam-°2Mishka) Ch. m. 1949. Dr. H.C.E.M. Houtappel, Holland
8412	°HAJEEL (Edh Dhahab-°Mishka) Ch. st. 1951. Dr. H.C.E.M. Houtappel, Holland
8413	°KEBIR (Edh Dhahab-Mish-Mash) Bay st. 1952. Dr. H.C.E.M. Houtappel, Holland

8414 *RITLA (Rythal-Mish-Mash) Bay m. 1939. Dr. H.C.E.M. Houtappel, Holland

8418 *LEILA NAKHLA (*Nizzam-*Latifaa) Bay m. 1952. Dr. H.C.E.M. Houtappel, Holland

8411 *MISHKA (Karusen-Mish Mash) Ch. m. 1943. Dr. H.C.E.M. Houtappel, Holland

Imported by Mrs. Anne McCormick, Scottsdale, Arizona, 1953:

8565 *IORANA (Radi-Namilla) Bay m. 1942. Lady Yule, England

8567 *RIFILLA (Oran-*Rissilletta) Ch. m. 1951. Wentworth, Crabbet Park and Burton Studs, England

8566 *SUN ROYAL (Indian Gold-Sharima) Ch. st. 1946. Wentworth, Crabbet Park and Burton Studs, England

Imported by Alex Hindi and Sons, Duran, N.M., 1950:

10851 *BINT ATTEBE (Attebe-Yumna) Gr. m. 1946. Sabhi Hindi, Rayak, Lebanon

8205 *DAHAM (Shaje El Arab-Moonah) Gr. st. 1947. Soubhe Hindi, Rayak, Lebanon

9822 *DALAL (Kuhaylan-Sada) Gr. m. 1947. Soubhe Hindi, Rayak, Lebanon

Imported by Nancy Magro, Montgomery, Ohio, 1956:

11515 *ELECTRIC STORM (Indian Magic-Silfina) Gr. st. 1952. Crabbet Park Stud, England

11513 *RISSILLETTA (Indian Gold-Rissla) Ch. 1943 Crabbet Park Stud, England

12947 *SEA MOON (Royal Crystal-*Rissilletta) Gr. st. 1957. Imp. en utero. Crabbet Park Stud, England

Individual importations:

Imported by Dr. and Mrs. Alfred Godward, San Francisco, California, 1952

11234 *IBN FARHAN (Dahman-El Obeya) Bl. st. 1947. Ragheb Mohamed El Halaby, Egypt

Imported by W. E. Bermingham, Rye, N.Y., 1954

9825 *SHAMREEN (Oran-Sharima) Ch. st. 1950. Wentworth, Crabbet Park and Burton Studs, England

Imported by John Rogers, Walnut Creek, California, 1953

8955 *SERAFIX (Raktha-*Serafina) Ch. st. 1949. the Rt. Hon. Lady Wentworth, England

IMPORTATIONS
1957 - 1958

A.H.C.R. NUMBER	NAME	SIRE AND DAM	COLOR	SEX	DATE FOALED	BREEDER

Imported from England by Bazy Tankersley, Washington, D.C. in 1957:

12884 *ALICIA (Iridos-*Salinas) Gr. m. 1957. Miss G. M. Yule

12905 *BLUE MILLET (Blue Domino-Namilla) Ch. m. 1954. Miss G. M. Yule

12911   *BRIGHT DIAMOND (Bright Shadow-*Silver Diamond) Ch. st. 1957. Wentworth, Crabbet Park and Burton Studs

12904   *CROWN OF DESTINY (Oran-Grey Royal) Ch. m. 1951. Wentworth, Crabbet Park and Burton Studs.

12910   *CRYSTAL SPECIAL (Royal Crystal-Extra Special) Ch. st. 1957. Wentworth, Crabbet Park and Burton Studs

12885   *CRYSTAL VOYAGER (Royal Crystal-Nerina) Ch. st. 1957. Wentworth, Crabbet Park and Burton Studs

12903   *GREY STELLA (Grey Owl-Umatella) Gr. m. 1953. Miss G. M. Yule

12902   *INDIAN DIAMOND (Oran-Indian Flower) Ch. m. 1946. Wentworth, Crabbet Park and Burton Studs

12900   *KABARA (Rissalix-Shamnar) Ch. m. 1949. Miss G. M. Yule

12901   *LITTLE OWL (Grey Owl-*Kabara) Gr. st. 1954. Miss. G. M. Yule

12913   *LUCRETIA (Count Orlando-*Minta) Ch. m. 1957. Miss G. M. Yule

12899   *MINTA (Rasham-Wardi) Ch. m. 1948. Mrs. E. M. Carroll, Ireland

12907   *NADEYRIA (*Count Dorsaz-*Radeyra) Ch. m. 1955. Mrs. B. Dixon

12912   *ORSINO (Count Orlando-Rafeena) Gr. st. 1957. Miss G. M. Yule This horse was re-named *THE COUNT OF AL-MARAH

12898   *RADEYRA (Radi-Niseyra) Ch. m. 1948. Miss. G. M. Yule

12897   *REENEXA (Irex-Rafeena) Gr. m. 1950. Mrs. G. Armstrong-Jones

12896   *ROSSALISSA (Grey Owl-Rosalina) Ch. m. 1953. Miss M. C. E. Lyon

12887   *ROYAL CONSTELLATION (Grand Royal-*Serafina) Ch. st. 1955. Wentworth, Crabbet Park and Burton Studs

12906   *ROYAL DIAMOND (Oran-Grey Royal) Gr. st. 1948 Wentworth, Crabbet Park and Burton Studs

12883   *SALINAS (Grey Owl-Shamnar) Gr. m. 1947. Miss G. M. Yule

12889   *SILVER DIAMOND (Grand Royal-Silver Gilt) Ch. m. 1952. Wentworth, Crabbet Park and Burton Studs

12908   *SILVER GLORY (*Silver Vanity-Silfina) Ch. m. 1956. Wentworth, Crabbet Park and Burton Studs

12888   *SILVER GRAND (Grand Royal-Silver Gilt) Gr. m. 1951. Wentworth, Crabbet Park and Burton Studs

12890   *SHADES OF NIGHT (Rissam-Sharfina) Ch. m. 1946. Wentworth, Crabbet Park and Burton Studs

12909   *SILWA (Raktah-*Silver Crystal) Gr. m. 1960. Wentworth, Crabbet Park and Burton Studs.

12886   *SILWARA (Dargee-*Silwa) Gr. m. 1955. Wentworth, Crabbet Park and Burton Studs

12895   *SIYAMA (Grand Royal-*Serafina) Ch. m. 1953. Wentworth, Crabbet Park and Burton Studs.

12894   *TAHEKI (Grey Owl-Rikitea Ch. m. 1953. Miss G. M. Yule

12893   *THORA GRANT (General Grant-*Thorayya) Ch. m. 1956. Miss G. M. Yule

12892   *THORAYYA (Rissalix-Samsie) Bay m. 1949. Miss G. M. Yule

12891   *ZULIMA (Rissalix-Queen Zenobia) Bay m. 1952. Miss G. M. Yule

These were purchased from the estates of Lady Wentworth and Miss Yule, both of which had died in 1957. This may account for the fact that only one mare was in foal. This was °SALINAS, whose foal was registered later.

A.H.C.R. NUMBER   NAME   SIRE AND DAM   COLOR   SEX   DATE FOALED   BREEDER

13847   °BLUE SAL (Blue Domino-°Salinas) Ch. m. 1958. Imp. en utuero. Estate of Miss G. M. Yule

Imported from England by Mrs. J. G. Hudson, Oakville, Ontario, Canada:
12666   °MANOLA (General Grant-°Manolita) Bay st. 1956. Mr. and Mrs. W. E. Dinsdale
12665   °MANOLITA (Manasseh-Myola) Bay m. 1949. G. H. Buxton
12667 *MINARETTA (Alexus-Myoletta) Ch. m. 1954. Mr. and Mrs. W.E. Dinsdale.

Horses imported from England by Charles Kee, Toronto, Canada:
12531   °RISSALIRA (Rissalix-Risara) Gr. m. 1947. Mrs. E. M. Murray
12530   °SHAREINE (Shahim-Josepha) Bay m. 1946. Miss M. Burrows
Other importations:

Imported by Annie E. Riggs, Wilton, Conneticut
12008   °KATINA (Naseel-Wardi) Bay m. 1951. Mrs. E. M. Carroll, Ireland
Imported by Mrs. Frederick Winthrop, Ipswich, Massachusetts
13687   °ZAKII (Shihab-Zahra) Ch. st. 1946. Thriplow Farms, Ltd., England

IMPORTATIONS
1959

Importations from Egypt by Richard G. Pritzlaff, Sapello, New Mexico, 1958. These were not registered until 1959, so are included in Vol. X (1959) of the Stud Book:

A.H.C.R. NUMBER   NAME   SIRE AND DAM   COLOR   SEX   DATE FOALED   BREEDER

14457   °BINT DAHMA (El Sareei-Dahma) Ch. m. 1956. Egyptian Agricultural Society
14454   °BINT EL BATAA (Nazeer-El Bataa) Bl. m. 1955. Egyptian Agricultural Society
14455   °BINT MONIET EL NEFOUS (Nazeer-Moniet El Nefous) Egyptian Agricultural Society
14456   °BINT NEFISA (El Sareei-Nefisa) Bay m. 1957. Egyptian Agricultural Society

The dam of this mare should not be confused with the much earlier mare of the Crabbet Stud. The Egyptian NEFISA is by BALANCE out of HELWA.

14453   °RASHAD IBN NAZEER (Nazeer-Yashmak) Bay st. 1955. Egyptian Agricultural Society

Again, names might be confused. This YASHMAK is not the same as an earlier one.

Importations from Egypt by Mr. and Mrs. Donald L. Forbis, Chickasha, Okla.:
15898   °ANSATA BINT MABROUKA (Nazeer-Mabrouka) Gr. m. 1958. Egyptian Agricultural Society

134

15896   °ANSATA BINT ZAAFARANA (Nazeer-Zaafarana) Gr. m. 1958.
Egyptian Agricultural Society

15897   °ANSATA IBN HALIMA (Nazeer-Halima) Gr. st. 1958. Egyptian
Agricultural Society

Other importations:

Imported 1950 by S. G. Bennett, Georgetown, Ontario, Canada

15479   °MIHRIMA (Riffal-Namilla) Bay m. 1946. Miss G. M. Yule, England

Dam imported by S. G. Bennett

15480   °SENAB (Grey Owl-°Mihrama) Gr. st. 1951. Imp. en utero.
Miss G. M. Yule, England

Imported by B. T. Jones, Jr. Cortland, N.Y. 1958

14380   °ALDOURIE (Manasseh-Algoletta) Ch. st. 1949. George Ruxton, Eng.

Imported by Bazy Tankersley, Washington, D.C.

14388   °COUNT DORSAZ (Rissalix-Shamnar) Ch. st. 1945. Lady Yule, Eng.

15997   °CHAZWAANE (Souci-Salome) Gr. m. 1953. Mrs. De Moussac,
Sidi Bou Hadid, Tunisia

15998   °NURAH (Hamdani DB-Obay DB) Ch. m. 1954. Mrs. J. H. Gildea,
Dammam, Saudi Arabia

Imported by F. M. Hunter, Jr., Summerville, South Carolina

14390   °PRINCE OF BRAY (Blue Domino-Shayba Thania) Gr. st. 1955.
B. Dixon, England

Imported by A. E. Langford, Fairless Hills, Pa.

14389   °SHY KISS (Shihab-Karaka) Gr. m. 1947. C. D. Hough, England

Imported by Mr. and Mrs. J. L. Simpson, Calgary, Alberta, Canada:

14741   °SILFARINA (°Silver Vanity-Serafina) Gr. m. 1957. Lady

14740   °RAZIRI (Indian Magic-Rosinella) Gr. st. 1955. Lady Wentworth,
England

°ANSATA IBN HALIMA (Nazeer-Halima)   °EL MUDIR (Wielki Szlem-Munira)

V

IMPORTATIONS IN THE SIXTIES

The importation of Arabians became so popular in the 1960s that the Registry tried several means by which to slow down the trend. This comprised a heavy "import duty" as it might be called, at one time as high as $1500; later this was rescinded and reduced to $500, which was nevertheless a lot of money to be added to the purchase price and transportation costs. Besides this, the horses had to pass inspection and prove to be of exceptional quality, and this too was a rather harsh measure in regard to breeding stock desired for a certain feature. Often the imports are aged mares, long past their prime, and these do not usually qualify for beauty contests. Performance too was often the desired attribute, and the best "doers" are not always the best "lookers" (and vice-versa), so the haunting worry of whether or not a horse or mare might pass inspection was a problem of importers. Many a high-class mare was turned down because of fear her head might not appeal to "head-hunters," if any should be among the Registry inspectors. However despite everything, the inspectors proved to be much less narrow minded than the machinations of the Registry had given cause for importers to believe; and few, if any, of the horses from approved countries (Poland, England, Egypt, etc.) were turned down. The same was not always true of imports from the Near East, including Saudi Arabia. At least the maneuvers of the Registry made importers be very selective in their choices.

A 1960 importation was that of Robert O Anderson of Roswell, New Mexico. These were all from the stud of H.V.M. Clark in England, ordinarily an almost impossible source from which to obtain horses. It is not that Clark hasn't plenty of horses, and good ones at that—it's just that he won't sell them. Apparently these were not shown often, nor have their offspring either, as no winners (of championships) are credited to this source. The same is true of several of the other immigrants of this year.

The horses imported from England by W. C. Miller of Dallas, Texas did go to the shows however. *SHARAFA is the dam of two champions, one of which is the son of DARGEE, *GEORGE WASHINGTON.

A notable mare was imported to Canada in 1960; none other than the famous *SERAFINA, dam of *SERAFIX, *SILVER DRIFT, *ROYAL CONSTELLATION, *SILFARINA, and *ORAN VAN CRABBET as well as the en utero import *BRIGHT GOLD. She was brought over by S. G. Bennett of Toronto.

The most notable import of 1960 is undoubtably the photogenic Hollander *NIZZAM, who was bred by Lady Wentworth but had been owned by Dr. H.C.E.M. Houtappel of Laren, Holland for several years, and who was the chief sire of his Rodania Stud. *NIZZAM is a beautiful and typy horse who quickly engendered the enthusiasm of breeders in America even before they had seen him, due to the excellent pictures taken of him in Holland, as well as those of his foals which were equally appealing. He is a good example of the loss that could have occured to the breed if horses with body spots are avoided in breeding; for both his sire and dam have such a spot, but *NIZZAM doesn't, nor apparently do his foals. This stallion too was at first leased and then purchased by Mr. and Mrs. Hewitt in partnership with James F. Lewis, Jr. of Charlottesville, Virginia and divided his time between the two establishments. *NIZZAM is the sire of fourteen champions; among them with the Lewisfield prefix —NIZZORO (Top 5 East Coast), NIZZOR+ (Champion Region 7) and NIZZABA (Top Ten and East Coast Champion). LEWISFIELD NIZ-ZOR was also a Top Ten Western Pleasure Horse and has acquired the Legion of Merit as well. Several of the *NIZZAM horses have had success in action classes as well, especially the stakes-winning NIZZORO. *NIZZAM was seventeen years old when imported, so his record at stud is especially good in view of this fact. He was, and still is, a picture horse, the artists' ideal of the Arabian.

The year 1961 might be called the Polish Renaissance, for in that period two importations were made from Poland, the first made by private citizens since 1938, and the first since Poland had been entrapped behind the Iron Curtain. It was not until I read an article by Patricia Lindsay in the English *Arab Horse News* that I knew Arabians were still bred in Poland, but now it was shown that not only were there fine individuals of the breed in that country but that it was also possible to buy them, since some had already been exported to England. One of these was Miss Lindsay's spectacular grey mare KARRAMBA, another was the beautiful bay broodmare CELINA, which had been immediately pur-chased at dockside by that connoisseur of Arabian horses, H. V. M. Clark. CELINA was later grand champion of England, and KARRAMBA also won high honors on several occasions. A grey colt, GERWAZY, also had been imported by Miss Lindsay and he later became the hero of combined training events, cross-country and show ring jumping, and also won in the more static halter classes. He was of course an ex-racehorse.

It was through the aid of Miss Lindsay that the first post-war Polish importations were made. It was in fact because of an article she wrote for the *Arab Horse Society News* in England that I became intrigued with these horses in the first place, then H. H. Reese decided some new blood could be of use and asked me to contact Miss Lindsay regarding the possibility of obtaining a good stallion from Poland. To come to the point, she took pictures and notes of the various horses, recommending *ARDA-

HAN and ARGOS as having the best pedigrees and conformation, along with good action. *ARDAHAN was selected, but he happened to also be the most expensive, so two other buyers formed a syndicate of sorts with Reese. These were Raymond Ashton and Charles Doner. In the meantime I had interested several other people in the Polish horses from pictures sent by Animex and Miss Lindsay, and the first to buy mares was Frisco Mari of La Puente, who decided on *SZARZA and *SABAA. The former is the dam of the Reserve National Champion AMERIGO and the Canadian and American Top Ten mare REGINAA.

None of us knew how to import horses, so John Rogers, an old hand at this sort of thing, was contacted by telephone. He not only was of great help, but wanted to know what was up. When told, he too was interested in obtaining a mare. I sent him pictures and he chose *SAKWA, mainly from the performance angle, since she was a full sister of *SABEL-LINA, a Derby winner and dam of two Derby winners. Later he contacted Miss Lindsay directly and purchased *CALIOPE on her recommendation. This mare is a champion herself and is the dam of two—the Top Ten stallion GAYPOLKA, and CARINOSA, the latter also a noted performance mare. Ashton decided he wanted a mare in addition to a "piece" of *ARDAHAN, so ordered *BIKA from Poland, and then added a filly of Miss Lindsay's, out of her great mare KARRAMBA. This was *KOCHANA, whose name means sweetheart in Polish. Doner too became infected with the buy-more disease and wanted a mare as a Christmas present for his wife. Miss Lindsay told him of one of the earlier imports to England which was owned by Miss Lyon and might be purchased. This was *CARMENCITA, whose name was suffixed with EL HAIFI after importation here. In addition another stallion *MO-HACZ, was purchased along with *ARDAHAN. It was his high and airy way of going that induced his purchase, and Miss Lindsay had recommended him on that account only.

The Polish horses had been purchased by Miss Lindsay for her clients and, since political forces were in a bit of an upheaval at the time, they were shipped to England rather than directly to America. There they were joined by the two others and shipped to the United States by different routes—part went directly to New York and were vanned across the country, the others took the scenic route through the Panama Canal up to the Port of Los Angeles. All arrived in fine fettle and excellent shape, which is more than can be said for a number of later sea voyages.

So well pleased were several of the importers that they decided to buy some more, and in addition a number of others joined in on the adventure. This time we dealt directly with Poland, through the export agency Animex (Animal Export) in Warsaw. This agency handles all animal exports both live and dead, the latter meaning meat, but also including slaughter horses for those European countries that indulge in that taste. Even fish (canned) is included, so the business transacted

FETYSZ (Bakszysz-Siglavy Bagdady)

MIECZNIK (Fetysz-Koalicja)

*SULEJMAN (Fetysz-Fasila)

DOKTRYNER (Miecznik-Blaga)

GERWAZY (Doktryner-Gwara)

*MUZULMANIN (Doktryner-Mufta)

THE FETYSZ LINE

139

by this one small office is tremendous and accounts for the long, long delays so often encountered by even the most eager and affluent buyers, not to mention the casual inquirers. It was comparatively easy, as Animex has all the forms to sign and knows the ropes so to speak. Another reason for going direct was the real flap that had developed over the papers of the horses purchased by Miss Lindsay for some of the buyers, for as far as Animex was concerned they had sold these animals to England, not to the United States. This was eventually straightened out, but not until after it had thrown a scare into the buyers, for the horses were already here . . . but could not be registered until the transfer had been made. Thereafter the direct approach was taken, and it was of course best, despite the highly annoying delays in getting response from Animex. American buyers "want what they want when they want it" and are inclined to either get so anxious they flit over to Europe to get the job done, or lose interest entirely.

Although the horses had been purchased in October 1960, they did not arrive until January 1961. The next group was in the same year, but in December. Five were those of Robert Aste, *CYTRYS, *ARWILGA, *DOLA, *JAWITA, and *MUZAA; two went to Rogers—*CHIMENA and *MUSZKATELA; while Janice Rust bought *EL MUDIR, *EGERIA, and *FORTUNKA; and Charles Doner bought two more stallions *MIRZAZ (Mirza) and *MUZULMANIN+. It was due to the 1961 importations, plus the success of *WITEZ II and other Army imports, not to forget also that SKOWRONEK was bred in Poland, that the flood of Polish imports continued to pour into America. Nor was the contribution of earlier imports forgotten.

Due to the heart attack suffered by Raymond Ashton a couple of years thereafter, and the death of H. H. Reese, the two stallions of the syndicate became the property of Charles Doner.

*ARDAHAN has been champion on several occasions, including two of California's largest shows, and he is also the sire of four champions. He is one of the few Polish horses that was not raced, having been part of an experiment in training Arabian colts for military training, similar to the Olympic Three-Day Event, involving dressage, cross-country and show-ring jumping, but in this case, a long drive in harness as the final phase of the test.

*MOHACZ, one of the better race horses in Poland, won two of the Del Mar show races, with *MIRZAZ a fast-closing second, the rest of the field far back each time. Although *MOHACZ had shown beautiful action when first imported, he lost it about a year thereafter, especially when shod, and thenceforward became a "bean-shooter," with no flexion at all. However he is the sire of DIZANNE, a champion mare with extravagant action which always elicits oohs and ahs from the ringside. She is also a park stakes winner. *MUZULMANIN+ won his first championship at Scottsdale, in fact it was his first show, I believe. He started something too, in that he so impressed Dr. E. E. La Croix that that astute horseman was inclined to wonder "are there any more at home like you" and dashed off to Poland to see if such was the case. The results of that and subsequent trips are history. *MUZULMANIN+ was champion at the big Santa Barbara show, among other wins, and topped his career by winning the National English Pleasure Championship. *MIRZAZ had won the Derby after his purchase by Doner, and although he had been in only three races as a four-year-old in 1961 he was nevertheless the second-highest money winner. This was due mostly to his Derby winnings but he had won another race and was second in the other. As a three-year-old he had won three out of seven starts, evidently preferring distance, for his successes were in the longer events. He was second from the top in that year also in money won. His time for the Derby (3:41 for the 3000 meters) was the fastest in recent time, but has now been equalled by the phenomenal mare ORLA (full sister of *Orzel). *MIRZAZ, a beautiful mover, has won several park classes and climaxed his career in this high-falutin' type of performance by becoming a National Top Ten Park Horse. He is one of the few *NA-BORRs which have a superior race record. This can be credited to his dam, MIRA, as most of her foals have been very "quick." She is the dam of another Derby winner, MIR SAID, who now is siring fast runners. Two of *MIRZAZ's sons have shown great aptitude for racing, namely ELSINORE CAMIR and ELSINORE MIRZAN.

*MUZULMANIN+ had been raced for two years with mild success and one win, but his placid disposition did not inspire him to try too hard. He is the sire of one champion to date, and most of his get have the same beautiful neck as well as his long and level croup.

In Scottsdale, the horses of the Aste importation made an instant impression, with *ARWILGA becoming Reserve Champion at the Scottsdale show on her first outing. Later *CYTRYS won an English Pleasure stake and he also placed well in halter classes. He had been a rival of *MIRZAZ in the races in Poland and had beaten him once. Following his sale at the Aste auction, *CYTRYS has won halter championships in the east and has continued to win or place in English pleasure competition. He is the sire of one champion to date. All of the imported mares brought high prices at the auction after Mr. Aste's death in 1968. The game little race mare *JAWITA brought $10,000 and *ARWILGA brought $14,100 in that sale, the latter the highest price paid up to that time for an Arabian at auction. It has since been eclipsed by the $21,000 paid for a three year old filly by *BASK at an eastern auction. Aste had imported several other mares in 1963 in the group that had such a rough sea voyage. As a result of the heavy seas the best mare of the lot died of complications encountered through foaling en route. The foal of course also died. The other mares in this shipment were *ANDALUZJA,

141

*ARDAHAN (Trypolis-Adis Abeba)   *SZARZA (Ali Said-Salwa)

*ANTWERPIA, and *EGINA. They too brought high prices, as did *CYTRYS.

The two mares and filly brought in by the Mari family were quickly augmented by two colts, *CORSAIR and *CENTAUR. It is the grey mare *SZARZA who has turned out to be the star of the group, as she has already produced the Reserve National Champion stallion AMERIGO and the Canadian and American Top Ten mare REGINAA. AMERIGO is already the sire of a champion. *SABA unfortunately died recently but at least a daughter was kept to carry on for this well-bred mare.

The Ashton mare *BIKA produced a foal almost as soon as the van slowed down for the final stop. The filly *KOCHANA was a daughter of KARRAMBA. She was showing beautiful action in harness with good prospects in the shows, when her career was cut short by the severe heart attack of Mr. Ashton, which eventually resulted in the sale of his horses

*BACHANTKA had a good show career and was a producer of one champion among several winners for the Varians, while *OSTROGA is the dam of the champion THE ARISTOCRAT, a son of *ARDAHAN. *NAGANKA, a real mover, is the dam of the sensational grey stallion MIKADO, who is now capitalizing on that inheritance by wins in park classes, but it has also been to his advantage in the way he could trot out in halter classes as well. This champion is sired by the Varian's National Champion BAY-ABI.

Janice Rust did well on her selections too. *EL MUDIR (without the "El" in Poland),is a magnificent horse under saddle, with a beautiful, fluid, and high action—a real pleasure to watch. He is another ex-race horse (and he had a fine record) who has gone on to win in park classes, topping his wins with a Top Ten placement. *EGERIA was followed in 1964 by her daughter *EGRETA, the dam of two champions, namely *EMAUS and HALALI ENCHANTED, by *NABORR and COMET respectively. *EGERIA is also the dam of the Polish stallion EGO, who sired the 1968 National Champion Park Horse, *PROWIZJA, whose dam was a fine

142

race mare who dead-heated with BRANIBOR in winning the 1962 Derby.

For the McBrides, *GAWRA produced a colt shortly after arrival, this being *DOKHAILAN, who later was a Top Ten Western Pleasure Horse. He also did well at halter. The grey mare *MORTISSA was supposed to have come along with *GAWRA but was delayed until she was proven in foal. She was therefore shipped alone, and took matters her own way by deciding to foal in the van. She and the foal were left in a Midwestern lean-to for a few days until the colt was strong enough to complete the trip. This colt, *CZORTAN, has been sold back to the same general locale, but he had sired such a good foal from *GAWRA that she was sent way back to be re-bred to him—a rather unusual affair.

The buyers of *CZORTAN were Paul and Sandra Loeber of Palatine, Illinois, and they had imported in 1962 the grey stallion *DALIH (the "ox" after a German Arabian's name merely indicates it is purebred, so this horse is not *DALIH OX as registered here, but *DALIH). At the same time the beautiful mare *SANACHT was imported, also from Germany. *DALIH is the sire of AMURATH ROXANA, a Region I champion mare.

The importation of the Sir William Farm was made with the purpose of resale and apparently all were sold fairly soon, except the very high-priced *FAROAN+ (Pharoah) who was purchased the following year by E. J. Tweed. *FAROAN+ won many championships, and he is a Canadian Top Ten winner. His dam FORTA is one of the best known broodmatrons of Poland, her sons including EQUIFOR (whose Derby record is still unmatched) and the great racehorse and sire CZORT. The mare *KOCHA-NAS was required to alter her name from its original KOCHANA, because of the Ashton filly's importation a year earlier. She had been a good race mare and is the dam of two imports. One of them, *TRYNCZA, is the dam of one of the most handsome colts in Poland, TINIAN.

*COUNT ORLANDO, imported in 1961, has already been mentioned. *ORAN VAN CRABBET has been a consistent winner in park classes climaxed in 1966 by the Park National Championships. The Egyptian horse *GHALII unfortunately died young, but he did sire a champion. His registration is upside down in the Stud Book, with NAZEER given as his dam rather than his sire, the reason being that the Egyptian pedigrees place the dam's name at the top. Ordinarily the Registry catches such variations from the norm and makes the necessary corrections. The other two individual imports, *AANASEH and *DIAMOND SPARKLE both have a champion to their credit, though these champions are geldings, rather stopping those lines for the present.

The five horses brought in by Lewis Payne included England's top riding class winner, *ASTRAN. He too (like *Count Dorsaz) won the Winston Churchill Cup in all breed competition, but he won more than once. A very typy horse with huge eyes and tiny muzzle, arched crest and gaily carried tail, *ASTRAN always made a favorable impression. Even in American shows this was true, where higher action is expected (in park classes) than is usual in England where judging is along hack lines (similar to English pleasure) he won well. He was high-placed in several stakes and won stallion park classes. He has a beautiful way of moving, very free-flowing, with sufficient lift to make him a real park horse. Although he has yet sired no champions, ROBERT-E-LEE won one of the races in Albuquerque and has done well in others. Since Payne is rarely home (his work taking him throughout the world), his horses have not been shown recently, other than *ASTRAN who was on lease to the Elsinore Stud. The produce of his mares has not been to the shows, but they represent fine English bloodlines, while *HAMRA JOHARA was bred by the king of Saudi Arabia and is more of an Arabian type mare than the usual desertbred.

In 1962 Douglas Marshall made the first of a series of importations from Egypt. His business entails many trips to Egypt and the Near East, and he was well acquainted with the management of the Egyptian Agricultural Association and its horses. If the horses of these importations which have so far been exhibited or at least pictured are any criteria, his knowledge of the breed, as well as the right connections, enabled him to select the very best available, possibly some that were not available as far as the ordinary horse buyer from abroad is concerned. Already the owner of fine Americanbreds, Marshal showed both for a few years, then decided to sell his Americanbreds, which included many champions at both halter and performance, and concentrate on the new Egyptians. It is not the easiest thing in the world to import horses from the Near East, especially in these days of turmoil. So the "Marshall Plan" is to concentrate representatives of Egypt's best bloodlines at his Gleannloch Farms in Spring, Texas, enabling Americans (or others) to see the cream of Egyptian Arabians under the best possible conditions. It is not possible to see them in what Americans consider good flesh in Egypt, nor are they shown to advantage by Egyptian grooms, or rather, handlers. Also Egyptian yearlings and two-year-olds are very narrow and thin according to American opinion, and this early feeding method naturally results in rather narrow-built horses. The Egyptians (and Arabs) prefer them to be slim, and pictures of American champions leave them not only cold, but contemptuous, in the customary "we ride our horses, we do not eat them" reaction. Nevertheless American tastes must be catered to, and Egyptian horses either foaled here or imported as foals, quickly acquire additional substance. Some even are too wide by riding horse standards.

In view of the unsettled conditions that often make a visit to Egypt a somewhat adventurous affair and the exportation of a horse from there very tricky indeed for the average person, this oasis of Egyptian blood-lines is manna from the heavens, or at least an allah-send. What should be one of its greatest advantages, aside from the superb selection of founda-

*BINT MAISA EL SAGHIRA (Nazeer-Maisa)   *MORAFIC (Nazeer-Mabrouka)

tion stock, is that there is enough variety of bloodlines that close inbreeding need not be resorted to, in keeping with the custom in Egypt where inbreeding, close or not, is avoided. There is an emphasis on the NAZEER sire line, and judging by the extremely offset knees of a closely inbred horse of this line, and the same but less extreme degree of this fault on a NAZEER son, one wonders if this is characteristic of NAZEER. While this stallion has crooked hocks, the majority of the Marshall imports by him (as well as the Ansata horses) have had straight hind legs, and if it were not for the fact that other importers had been less selective in this regard, one might have believed that all his get avoided this over-angulation. So possibly there are two dangers in close inbreeding to this horse, but his near ethereal beauty and other good qualities are inclined to make most everyone overlook any fault whatsoever. This is true of all eye-catching horses.

The first show horse to bring the new imports into the news was *BINT MAISA EL SAGHIRA+, a beautiful bay mare who won her Legion of Merit award by virtue of many halter championships from coast to coast and in addition several English pleasure and park stakes. She was Top Ten at halter and in English pleasure. She had a light and airy trot with plenty of action, as is so often the case of Egyptian horses as well as Polish (i.e. from countries where Arabian horses are raced, and are "athletes", not pudgy blobs). A mare from the largest group of Egyptian imports (1965), *NAHLAH+, was reserve National Champion and a pleasure class stakes winner; while *FAWKIA (a 1966 import) was Top Ten, as was the stallion *SABA EL ZAHRAA+, a very heavy boned horse, representing the 1963 group, who is in addition a Legion of Merit horse. The pride of "Little Egypt" as Spring, Texas might be known, is the chief stallion *MORAFIC, also a champion and a winner in performance. This stallion, like many others of the E.A.O. young stock, had been placed in training for racing, but could not be rated, to put it mildly. In fact he simply ran away each time he went on the track, according to

145

one report. So he was retired to stud instead. In Poland such a temperament would have ruled a horse *out* of the stud instead of into it, but Egypt does not select breeding stock in the same way. The E.A.O. horses were simply tested for speed and stamina. Everyone talks about *MORAFIC's head, though not always to the same point, for its extreme dish sends some "head hunters" into lyrical transports of joy, while to others its exaggeration is a defect. So to each his own. Like the majority of the Marshall imports, this stallion has a beautiful long shoulder and high withers, something Arabian horses in this country can use to more advantage than the extremely dished face. It will be interesting to see whether or not the slim and elegant, very dry quality of the Egyptian Arabians will remain that way after generations of good living on American feed. If they do become gross, thick headed, bull necked and mutton withered, then we can assume that conditions in Egypt may have had more to do with their airy-fairy quality than did any such virtue in their ancestry.

A stallion imported from England in 1962 was destined to leave his mark on Arabian society. This was the classy grey *SILVER VANITY, a Crabbet-bred who had been a great winner in English shows. He was a combined investment of Bazy Tankersley and Charles Prange, and has paid out well, since he has already become the sire of six champions.

In 1963 the "great Polish invasion," or rather the first of several, took place in Scottsdale, Arizona. Dr. E. E. LaCroix, as already hinted, had wondered "are there any more at home like you" when he looked over the 1962 Scottsdale champion, *MUZULMANIN+. So he went to Poland to see for himself. What he saw evidently pleased him, for he purchased off the track and in racing condition, the future National Champion *BASK+; the future Top Ten, Great Plains Champion, Pacific Northwest Champion and Canadian National Champion *BAJRAM; the future Reserve National Champion mare *BOLTONKA+ and other winners too

*BASK (Witraz-Balalajka)   *BOLTONKA (Arax-Bulgotka)

146

numerous to include here. *BASK+ was then seven years old, a veteran of four years racing, while *BOLTONKA+, at five had twenty races behind her in two years of such contests. Both were absolutely sound, as was the juvenile whiz, the grey colt *BAJRAM (pronounced as if the j were an i=Bairam) who was the second-highest money-winner of his age group, the three-year-olds. Not every breeder of show horses, accustomed to their plump outlines, can see a horse either in training or emaciated. These of course were the former, in hard flesh, not in the least thin, nor yet graciously curved. However in one fell swoop Doctor LaCroix selected the winners of America's greatest beauty prizes. Moreover both *BASK+ and *BOLTONKA+ were spectacular under saddle, the former equally sensational in harness, and he won the National Championship in park, and the Reserve in harness and combination as well, which makes him a truly *great* stallion in the breed, where that adjective is liberally applied to horses who do nothing more than sire several champions, indeed seldom leaving their home corral. To top off his performance career, *BASK+ bids fair to make another record, this time as a sire, for already he has eleven champions to his credit despite his relatively short time in this country. Others of the importation which won highest honors are *GDYNIA+, National English Pleasure Champion of 1966 and *WIRGINIA, winner of the same title in 1968.

The foregoing horses were brought over in two groups—one arriving in March, the other in May. The unfortunate members of the first lot came by sea, in what turned out to the worst weather in decades. The ship went ten days at full throttle, yet made no headway to speak of, so great were the seas roiled up by the storms. To make things worse, it had put in at a French port for hay, but all that was obtained was straw, and that constituted the feed of the horses for the rest of the voyage. It is no wonder that most of the animals were a horrifying collection of battered bones on arrival. *BASK+ and *BAJRAM were among them, and as already told, so was the complacent *NABORR, to whom poor feed and shifty footing seemed no problem at all. After this lesson, most importers flew plane loads of horses over, rather than go through such misery (mental, if not actual) again.

In 1966 Doctor LaCroix returned to Poland to see if the then-three-year-old colt he had seen the previous year had developed as he had expected. This was *GWALIOR+ and the results of this second look are now history, for *GWALIOR+ has won many championships at halter, in park classes, combination and under saddle; he was twice Top Ten and twice champion at the prestigious Scottsdale show, among others. He too had been purchased off the track, but like most NABORRs, he was not too enthusiastic a runner. However he more than makes up for that by his park performance here, where he has style and action to spare. *GWALIOR's foals are not yet old enough to compete for championships but they have shown their potential in their junior wins.

147

The importation made in 1963 by E. J. Tweed was a very large one, though mostly of mares and fillies, few of which have ever been shown. However it was a different case with the stallions. *GWIAZDOR, a full brother of *GWALIOR had acquired a Canadian Top Ten placing among other wins and was just rounding into his best form as a performance horse when he died from an intestinal ailment on the eve of the annual Scottsdale show. His stablemate *CZESTER+ was champion at this venue a couple of days later and went on from there to collect a series of championships throughout the country, gaining two U. S. Top Tens and one in Canada as well as a reserve in Region 5. The Tweed importation of 1967 included some sensational horses from widely differing types of performance. One was *ORZEL, a magnificent red chestnut who, like *MIRZAZ, was second-highest of his age group as a three-year-old in 1966. He was a full brother of the great race mare ORLA, winner of the Derby and Oaks and highest money-winner among the four-year-olds, with 112,500 zlotys compared to the next highest (Sala) with 58,500. ORLA's Derby time equalled that of *MIRZAZ with 3:41 for the 3000 meters (1⅞ miles). *ORZEL lived up to expectations by winning every race in which he was entered for the 1½ mile events under pari-mutuel betting, with the exception of one, in which he was second to EL GOHARI. However he had beaten that horse previously and wound up the season by winning the Championship Stakes at Phoenix, beating KONTIKI, who up to that time had been undefeated, and who had included EL GOHARI among his victims. All three of the horses shouldered heavy imposts in their races, *ORZEL with 142 pounds and KONTIKI with 140 in the Championship Stakes, for which the time was 2:49 4/5ths. After retirement he tried his luck as a show horse and promptly won a championship.

An equally sensational performer was *PROWIZJA, who had been sold to Leo Knight of Lafayette, Louisiana by the Brusally Ranch, as Tweed's establishment is known. This mare had been taken to Lasma's to be bred to *BASK, and so impressed Doctor LaCroix with her action that he offered to show her for a few months. As is now well known, those few months included a trip to the National show at Albuquerque. There this high-flying mare won the National Park Championship, and moreover all three judges placed her first, the only one of the National Champions in any class to receive this distinction. That it was popular was indicated by the applause that followed along with the mare around the ring, reaching a roaring crescendo when her name was announced as winner. At this show the top contenders were worked out together, making an exciting and real horse show in this class. Her sire is a dappled brown son of COMET while her dam PROWARDA dead-heated with the black horse BRANIBOR for the 1962 Derby. PROWARDA was bred in Russia, as was PIETUSZOK, sire of *BAJRAM and *ORZEL, and as was also *NABORR and his sire NEGATIW.

A third import of note was the bay *SALINAA (Salina in Poland), a beautiful headed mare with a neck of profoundly graceful contouring, reachy and arched. Once in the United States, she quickly won a championship and was honored with a "most classic" Arabian prize. Then, along with two other COMET's, *SALINAA helped capture the get-of-sire class for COMET in the 1968 Scottsdale competition. In Poland she had been sold over the protestations of the stud manager and others who valued her highly, but the price offered eventually pried her loose from her covert and all who had come to cherish her. As if to soothe the loss, *SALINAA's foal, then just four months old, was not to be sold for any price. However, sadness, clad in irony, was to dampen the accolades so quickly accorded this notable importation. Following the 1968 Scottsdale show *SALINAA became the victim of a skin malady which persisted and spread to the eyes, possibly as a threat to her sight. She was subsequently retired as a brood mare.

*ZBRUCZ, a brilliant bay son of COMET, is the latest star of the Tweed constellation to come to the front, making his start in Scottsdale in 1968 where he won his age class, and the following year he won the stallion park event, and was second only to the old master, *EL MUDIR, in the stake. Like *ETER, another newly imported son of COMET, *ZBRUCZ is exceptionally level of topline and has a beautiful reach of neck.

A truly select group of horses was imported in 1963 by Dr. Howard Kale of Seattle, Washington. These were the Polish mares *DORNABA and *ESKADRA and the twelve year old stallion *SILVER DRIFT from England's Crabbet Park Stud. The latter is a full brother of America's leading sire *SERAFIX. Among the multiple wins of the mares are for *DORNABA: Pacific Northwest Champion, Reserve National Champion 1965; the following year, Canadian Top Ten, Pacific Northwest Champion, Region 6 (Midwest) Champion, Canadian National Champion and U.S. National Champion. Also Reserve National Champion English Pleasure Horse in 1966 to another Polish import, Lasma's *GDYNIA. In the meantime, *ESKADRA was not idle. Along with several show championships she was Top Ten in both Canada and the United States in 1966 and the next year was Reserve Pacific Northwest Champion. Among her performance wins was a Top Ten placement in park. *DORNABA's career was cut short in 1969 when she died foaling which was a great loss to the breed as well as to her owner.

Shortly before his death, A. M. Work of Portland, Oregon had purchased the grey mare *CISSA and her colt *CYPR. The mare is also the dam of *CYTRYS and another champion CYRUSS. *CYPR has done well in various events, ranging from cutting to racing. *CISSA too was unlucky and died a couple of years later.

A pair of Englishbreds was imported by Mrs. George Whitcomb of Riverside, California on different occasions in 1963. These were *BLUE MANTLE and *PRINCE ZAIM, both of which became top performers

149

in park and English pleasure respectively, each gaining a Top Ten place-ment in their categories. Both are unusually striking horses under saddle although *BLUE MANTLE is inclined to throw his feet (goose step) when forced beyond his optimum speed at the trot. *PRINCE ZAIM has won regional English pleasure classes among his other conquests.

Among the several individual importations of this year was the typy grey Russianbred, *NABORR, already mentioned. Another was the bay mare *BANDERA, imported by Arlyne and Hal Clay of Scottsdale, and this mare is responsible for the later, and large, importation made by the Clays in cooperation with their partner in racing interests, Mr. Struck. *BANDERA was herself a good race mare but her forte in her new home was at halter and in any class featuring action, for she could trot on like a Standardbred. Among her championships was a Top Ten in 1965. Her sire ROZMARYN was a leading sire of race winners a few years ago, a place later taken by PIETUSZOK. In 1967 the Clay & Struck Ranches imported a plane-load of Polish Arabians. One of them I had first seen in Poland on the race track, and at the Scottsdale show there he was all prim and proper, winner of an English pleasure class. This was *MECZET, a veteran of four years' racing, so it speaks well of his temper-ament that he was so quickly converted to pleasure placidity. *KLUSZYN too was a good racehorse. He was converted here to park work, while *MARZANNA, another veteran of the racing wars, having had three years' experience before importation was kept in training another year for the Phoenix races, of which she won one of the mile and a half events. She had won five races as a three and a four-year-old but couldn't get closer than second at five, only to be revitalized at six to win her first race of the season in 1967, just before her sale to America.

James F. Lewis, Jr. of Charlottesville, Virginia added to his extensive hoard of fine Arabians in 1964 by an importation from England, mostly broodmares and fillies, but headed by the well bred and accomplished stallion *TOUCH OF MAGIC. With a name like that he should have been able to do anything, and in fact he was used as a hunter by Lady Russell, his former owner. Not only did he hunt regularly but also he competed successfully in dressage, combined training events and one day horse trials, the latter two types of events already mentioned in regard to Miss Lindsay's imported stallion GERWAZY in England. *TOUCH OF MAGIC was a beautifully dappled grey at the time of importation and sported an even more spectacular stage of dappling when he was just another hunter in the field. He is of fair size, standing 15-1, and as might be expected of a good hunter he has a reachy neck and sound conformation. Moreover he is a typy Arabian as well. None of these horses have been here long enough to have foals eligible for championship com-petition, but an en utero import, *LEWISFIELD MAGIC, has attained champion status. This group was augmented in 1965 by four more mares,

150

three of them in foal, subsequent produce accounting for the additional names on the list. This group also was from England.

An importation from Poland to Canada in 1964 had considerable impact in the United States as well, for one of its members was the classically beautiful and extremely ¹reedy mare *ARWISTAWA. The importer was P. B. Williamson of Kelowna, British Columbia. *ARWIST-AWA was a mare with an outstanding race record and until 1968 was co-holder of the Polish record (for Arabs) of 3:08 for 2600 meters (1¾ miles). In that year DUNAJEC (a son of Branibor) clipped a tenth of a second off this time. *ARWISTAWA, in one year of showing, was Reserve to *DORNABA+ for the Pacific Northwest Championship but then went on to take the Canadian and United States National Championships, automatically stopping her further halter competition by these wins. In the U.S. win, she turned the tables on *DORNABA+ who had to be content with Reserve until the following year when she too was National Champion. The rivalry continued into performance as well, and in English pleasure classes *DORNABA+ usually won over all competitors, but in one instance *ARWISTAWA was reserve champion to that dazzling silver beauty. *ARWISTAWA also placed in park classes before retirement to the broodmare band.

The stallion *BARYSZ has a Canadian Top Ten among his wins, and was a good race horse at three and four years of age, with a total of five firsts. The other horse, *KIRKOR, was only three at time of importation and had been in only one race. A third import is also among the stallions of Williamson's Double U Ranch, but this is the Top Ten champion

*DORNABA (Naborr-Darda)   *ARWISTAWA (Geyran-Arfa) at the track at Warsaw

*GAYPOLKA, imported en utero by John Rogers in 1961, and it was this stallion which inspired the purchase of additional Polish horses and the eventual changeover to all Polish breeding stock for the ranch.

A good number of other importations were made in 1964, from Poland, England, and Arabia, in addition to those listed under previous importations of their owners, but space does not allow inclusion of all.

In 1965 there were several importations but again they were additions to others, in the most part. An exception is the mare and colt brought over from Egypt by Jay Stream, whose address then was in Illinois but is now in California. The colt, now stallion, is the grey *IBN MONIET EL NEFOUS, and the mare *NAGAT. Apparently neither has been shown.

The invasions from Europe were headed by representatives from a new source in 1966. These were from Spain and occasioned great interest. Unfortunately due to assorted problems, the Steen Ranch, which had purchased them in Spain was forced to discontinue all livestock operations a year later, and the horses were sold at auction, except for reserves which were sold thereafter. They have been in this country too short a time to have had records as progenitors of show winners. Several had done well in the shows before the sale, however.

This same year marked the importation of three mares, a foal, and a stallion from Poland by Denise Borg's Four Winds Farm of Delavan, Wisconsin. Leader of this group was the stallion *WIRAZ, a breedy Arabian with excellent action, which, in view of the interlocking effects of racing and trotting action, is not too surprising. *WIRAZ had a fine record on the track, with nine wins in four years. Since he was fifth highest money winner at three, and third highest at four, ditto at five, and fourth at six, he obviously placed in the money on most other occasions as well. Incidentally it is interesting to note that two of those above him on the three-year-olds' list became American imports—*ANDALUZJA and *BAJRAM (2nd and 3rd respectively), the former an Aste mare, the latter a Lasma stallion. Actually *ANDALUZJA is now owned by Lasma too as she was purchased from the Aste estate. This mare was a real race horse although in training for only one year. From six starts she won two and was second three times. To return to *WIRAZ—this stallion has already won championships and has been widely admired both for his conformation and his stylish, bold action. That he was still absolutely clean-legged after four years of racing which included 41 starts is in itself an acomplishment, and in this he parallelled the record of *BASK on his pre-show career. The grey mare *KASKADA was like the majority of *NABORRs is a race, she was not a young lady in a hurry. But at least she ran in six races, managing to come in fourth in one, and that is more than the average Arabian seems to do in this country . . . that is, many can't even stand training, let alone racing. When it came to stand-

ca (if it wins consistently), *KASKADA came into her own. Among the

152

championships charmed into being by this beautiful mare was the Reserve of the Region 6 area (Midwest).

Most of the other imports of this year have been covered previously, if they have made history of note, with the exception af *MADRYGAL, imported by Halberg Arabians, Iron, Minnesota. His racing record was also typically *NABORR, but he did win one race out of 19 starts. Again it should be stressed that just being able to keep in training and race during three seasons is an accomplishment in itself, especially when the horse retires clean-legged enough to win halter championships. *MADRY-GAL has not only made such wins but one of them was unique in that the judge became so enamored of the horse that he later bought *MA-DRYGAL, after the memory of the stallion would not leave his mind. He was already owner of another handsome stallion with an excellent show and sire record, so the impression made by this *NABORR son must have been a case of love at both first and second sights, or more properly, second thoughts.

The veteran Arabian breeder Robert B. Field of Leavenworth, Washington was another who died within a short time after importing a horse or horses. He had purchased the bay mare *CARISSIMA, a veteran herself at seventeen years of age, and her foal *CARUSO. Apparently *CARISSIMA was acquired thereafter by the Lasma Stud, for the registration of her 1967 foal, imported en utero gives that stud as its importer. This colt, by NEGATIW, has been given the logical name *POSITIW (the Polish W is pronounced as a V). Which reminds me of the grey mare CAMERA, purchased in Poland by Patricia Lindsay, and which previously had a foal by NEGATIW. Now there was an opportunity for a name! Unfortunately the foal died, the mare was exported and now that chance is gone. The Poles incidently, saw no such intriguing name linkage, for to them it wasn't "camera" but simply a name, pronounced with the accent on the center syllable—Ca-MER-a.

The importations of 1967 have mostly been incorporated into previous groups involving other lots. However there are exceptions and one was the group brought in by Leon Rubin of New York. The stallion was the dappled grey *CARRADOR, while the four mares included the golden bay *TRYNCZA, a really beautiful mare with classic head but rather cresty neck. Her son TINIAN by NEGATIW was a good race horse and looks like an ultra-refined version of the horses of the Parthenon. The fiery chestnut KANIA was a successful race mare, with two wins out of five starts placing her fifth highest of the thirty-one three-year-olds of her year. *CERT won one out of six races, while *DIMATRA is an aged broodmare whose daughter *DAMIETTA had been imported in 1964 together with *CARMENN, by Frank Smathers of Miami Beach, Florida. *DAMIETTA has won a championship at halter while *CARMENN (nee Carmen) has won well in English pleasure competition.

Of the remaining imports of 1967 the one to make news is the grey

*SANACHT (Hadban Enzahi-Hathor)   *TALAL (Nazeer-Zaafarana)

Egyptian stallion *TALAL. This son of NAZEER is a veteran of forty-four races and has several wins, and, like the Polish ex-racers which became champions, his legs remain absolutely clean. His importers are given as R. D. and S. F. Loken, who owned him in Egypt, but thereafter his owners have been listed as Mr. and Mrs. Jim Kline of Whittier, California. Certainly he has been in California ever since he arrived and has been the particular pride and joy of the Klines, who already had several other fine show horses including the immortal park mare MALIFA. *TALAL is a typical NAZEER of the desert type, not the heavier American-fed version. Like many other Egyptianbreds, he has been criticized as being narrow, which he is. But as already stated, that is the way the Egyptians prefer their horses. It is also the result of near starvation (according to American views) feeding methods of weanlings, yearling and two-year-olds. Actually the best-fed and roundest horses in Egypt are the race horses, for they pay their way and it is only good sense to keep them well fed all their early lives. Not *over* fed however. *TALAL was an instant success from his first appearance in the show ring, even though he was eleven years old at the time. He, like *GWALIOR and others of this same ethereal, extremely classic quality, seems to make the average stallion look coarse and dumpy. But it is his trot that makes the ringside go wild over him, for it is high, springy, and utterly his—not man-made. The stallion has now won several championships and was reserve to *GWALIOR at the 1969 "little National," the Scottsdale show.

A group imported in 1967 but registered in 1968 was that of Frank Y. Smith of Chatsworth, California. It was headed by the bay stallion *ETER and included two mares also direct from Poland. *FARMACJA and *GIELDA, and also the Polishbred *ALMAVIVA, obtained in England from Patricia Lindsay. *ALMAVIVA was a durable race mare with many wins to her credit, and she was second in the Oaks. In England she had won well in halter competition.

154

IMPORTATIONS
1960

Imported by Robert O. Anderson, Roswell, New Mexico:

16269   °BASHOM (Champurrado-Baranova) Bay st. 1949. H. V. Musgrave Clark, England

16270   °FEYSUL II (Sainfoin-Fantasia) Bay st. 1948. H. V. Musgrave Clark, England

16268   °FITNAH (Rashid-Farida) Bay m. 1955. H. V. Musgrave Clark, England

16271   °NERO (Champurrado-Nejiba) Bay st. 1953. H. V. Musgrave Clark, England

16266   °RANJI (Barak-Ruth II) Bay st. 1952. Duke of Marlborough, England

16267   °SALOTE (Champurrado-Selma II) Ch. m. 1954. H. V. M. Clark, Eng.

The NEJIBA and SELMA II in these pedigrees are not the earlier ones of the same names registered in the General Stud Book by the Crabbet Stud. Many of the Clark horses were named after famous horses of Crabbet Park, but in the stud books of the Arab Horse Society, not the G.S.B., which of course the latter would not allow.

Imported by S. J. Roach, Graham, Texas:

18028   °AMIRAA (Masud DB-°Halwaaji) Gr. m. 1959. Saud Ibn Abd Al Aziz, Riyadh, Saudi Arabia

18027   °HALWAAJI (Sari DB-Idah DB) Ch. m. 1954. Saud Ibn Abd Al Aziz. Riyadh, Saudi Arabia

18025   °RUDAAN (Mashur DB-Sitah DB) Ch. m. 1951. Saud Ibn Abd Al Aziz, Riyadh, Saudi Arabia

18026   °TAAMRI (Balam DB-Ubayd DB) Ch. st. 1948. Saud Ibn Abd Al Aziz, Riyadh, Saudi Arabia

Imported by Robert Am Ende, Vernon, Connecticut:

16216   °ASTREELIA (Jaleel-Astrab) Ch. m. 1948. Bernard Dixon, England

16216   °FIONA (Aaron-Fayella) Bay m. 1948. Mrs. N. E. Elms, England

16214   °GOLDEN HAZE (°Count Dorsaz-Shallufah) Ch. m. 1954. Mrs. E. M. Murray, England

Imported en utero, from two of the foregoing mares:

17223   °FIREXA (°Ibn Irex-°Fiona) Bay m. 1960. Pamela M. Bowen, Eng.

16671   °GOLDEN ZEHARIF (Rifiari-°Golden Haze) Ch. m. 1960. Margaret Murray, England

Imported by Eleanor Lee Gilbert:

16085   °KIRSEMSA (Al Kurus-17th Kirsema) Ch. m. 1955. Konya Stud Farm, Konya, Turkey

16086   °LV. YILDIZ (Alceylan 1st-Colciegi) Ch. st. 1955. Osman Deniz, Urfa Suruc, Turkey

Imported by W. C. Miller, Dallas, Texas:

16647   °DANCING DUST (Dargee-Dancing Diamond) Ch. m. 1959. Crabbet Arabian Stud, England

155

16646   *SHARAFA (*Silver Vanity-Sharfina) Gr. m. 1957. Crabbet Arabian
         Stud, England

18164   *GEORGE WASHINGTON (Dargee-*Sharafa) Gr. st. 1961.
         Imp. en utero. Crabbet Arabian Stud, England

Individual imports, including in-foal mares and their subsequent produce:
Imported by Queen Mother Nazli of Egypt
16054   *FADELL (Kheir-Bint Radia) Gr. st. 1938. Royal Agricultural Society,
         Egypt

Imported by George A. and Marietta D. Whitcomb, Riverside California
16069   *BAYARD (Greatheart-Teresita) Ch. st. 1958. Miss Margaret Greely,
         England

Imported by Mary L. Simpson, Calgary, Alberta, Canada
17130   *IBN IREX (Irex-Rosheiya) Ch. st. 1954. Miss M. J. Stevens, England

Imported by George W. and Holly P. Decker, Morris, N.Y.
16183   *MORAEA (Irex-Manzana) Bay m. 1950. Mrs. E. M. Murray, Eng.

Dam imported by George and Holly Decker
16869   *SHADEL IREX (Rifari-*Moraea) Bay st. 1960. Imp. en utero.
         Miss P. Moltens, Scotland

Imported by William A. and Patricia Hewitt, East Moline, Ill.
16070   *NIZZAM (Rissam-Nezma) Bay st. 1943. Lady Wentworth, England

Imported by S. G. Bennett, Toronto, Ontario, Canada.
17129   *SERAFINA (Indian Gold-Sharfina) Ch. m. 1945. Wentworth,
         Crabbet and Burton Studs, England

18936   *BRIGHT GOLD (Bright Shadow-*Serafina) Ch. m. 1961.
         Imp. en utero. Crabbet Arabian Stud

Imported by Merle J. and Ronald H. Dow, Perham, Maine
16734   *SHORANA (Oran-Shalina) Ch. m. 1957. Wentworth, Crabbet Park
         and Burton Studs

Imported by Mr. and Mrs. Thel Horn, Davison, Michigan
17870   *XANADU'S VOLTAGE   *(Greatheart-Teresita) Ch. st. 1959.
         Miss. M. Greely, England

The Crabbet Arabian Stud, 1959 and thereafter, is that of C. G. Covey, who
carries on the Crabbet bloodlines with many of the Wentworth horses.

IMPORTATIONS
1961

Imported by Raymond Ashton, Kaysville, Utah:
18401   *BIKA (Wielki Szlem-Panika) Gr. m. 1948. Albigowa State Stud,
         Poland

18402   *BIKOMET (Comet-*Bika) Ch. st. 1961. Imp. en utero. Nowy Dwor
         State Stud, Poland

18400   *KOCHANA (Faher-Karramba) Gr. m. 1959. Albigowa State Stud,
         Poland. Dam exported to England, *KOCHANA foaled there.

Imported from Poland by Robert L. Aste, Scottsdale, Arizona:

19659   *ARWILGA (Wielki-Szlem-Arwila) Gr. m. 1957. Albigowa State Stud

19660   *CYTRYS (Trypolis-*Cissa) Bay st. 1957 Nowy Dowr State Stud

19658   *DOLA (Comet-Diara Mokka) Bay m. 1959. Nowy Dwor State Stud

19657   *JAWITA (Wielki Szlem Jaffa) Gr. m. 1955. Nowy Dwor State Stud

19656   *MUZAA (Comet-Musailima) Ch. m. 1959. Nowy Dwor State Stud

23278   *WIELKI (Czort-*Jawita) Gr. st. 1962. Imp. en utero.
Nowy Dwor State Stud

Imported by John Rogers, Walnut Creek, California:

18675   *CALIOPE (Witraz-Canaria) Bay m. 1953. Albigowa Stud, Poland

18676   *GAYPOLKA (Pietuszok-*Caliope) Ch. st. 1961. Albigowa Stud,
Poland

20341   *CHIMENA (Ali Said-Carmen) Gr. m. 1956. Nowy Dwor State Stud,
Poland

20886   *CHIMENKA(Czort-*Chimena) Gr. m. 1962. Imp. en utero.

20887   *ELEGANTHKA (Aquinor-*Muszkatela))Gr. m. 1962. Imp. en
utero. Janow State Stud, Poland

18674   *IBN CZORT (Czort-*Sakwa) Ch. g. 1961. Imp. en utero.
Nowy Dwor State Stud, Poland

20342   *MUSZKATELA (Witraz-Musailima) Bay m. 1951. Albigowa State
Stud, Poland

18673   *SAKWA (Abu Afas-Sabda) Ch. m. 1953. Nowy Dwor State Stud,
Poland

20466   *BLUE RAFFIA (Blue Domino-Rafeena) Ch. m. 1956. Miss G. M.
Yule, England

20888   *BLUE DANUBE (Gerwazy-*Blue Raffia) Bay st. 1962. Miss P. M.
Lindsay, England

Imported by Lewis A. Payne, Stillwater, Oklahoma:

20423   *ASTRAN (*Rithan-Astrab) Ch. st. 1951. Bernard Dixon, England

20427   *HAMRA JOHARA (Kabir Ahmar DB-Rajabah DB) Ch. m. 1952.
King Abu Al-Aziz Ibn Saud, Saudi Arabia

20425   *MELLAWIEH (Indian Magic-Mifaria) Ch. m. 1951. Lady Anne
Lytton, England

20424   *MICAH BINT MIKENO (Mikeno-Myoletta) Ch. m. 1959.
Mrs. H. Linney, England

20426   *QASUMAH (Oran-Sirella) Ch. m. 1961. C. G. Covey, Crabbet Stud,
England

23148   *QUATIFAH (Manto-*Mellawieh) Ch. m. 1962. Imp. en utero.
Lady Anne Lytton, England

Imported by Frisco Mari, La Puente, California:

18274   *CENTAUR (Comet-*Sabaa) Gr. st. 1961. Imp. en utero.

18276   *CORSAIR (Comet-*Szarza) Gr. st. 1961. Imp. en utero.
Nowy Dwor State Stud, Poland

18272   *SABAA (Wielki Szlem-Sabda) Bay m. 1951. Nowy Dwor State Stud,
Poland

18273   *SABARIA (Comet-*Sabaa) Bay m. 1961. Nowy Dwor State Stud,
Poland

18275   *SZARZA (Ali Said-Salwa) Gr. m. 1956. Nowy Dwor State Stud,
Poland

(*Sabaa originally Saba, in Poland)

Imported by Mrs. Francis Rust, Evans, Georgia:

19913   *EL MUDIR (Wielki Szlem-Munira) Bay st. 1955. Nowy Dwor State
Stud, Poland

19914   *EGERIA (Witraz-*Enorme) Bay m. 1951. Albigowa State Stud,
Poland

19915   *FORTUNKA (Amurath Sahib-Forta) Bay m. 1953. Michalow
State Stud, Poland

22057   *HALALI FALENE (*El Mudir-Egeria) Bay m. 1962. Imp. en utero.
Nowy Dwor State Stud, Poland

20567   *HALALI SKYLARK (Grand-*Fortunka) Bay m. 1962. Imp. en utero.
Michalow State Stud, Poland

(*El Mudir originally Mudir, in Poland)

Imported by Varian Arabians, Halcyon, California:

20339   *BACHANTKA (Wiekli Szlem-Balalajka) Gr. m. 1957. Albigowa
State Stud, Poland

20338   *NAGANKA (Bad Afas-Najada) Gr. m. 1952. Nwy Dwor State Stud,
Poland

20340   *OSTROGA (Duch-Orda) Bay m. 1956. Michalow State Stud, Poland

Imported by Inez M. Doner, and Charles H. Doner, Elsinore, California:

18315   *CARMECITA EL HAIFI (El Haifi-Carmen) Gr. m. 1949.
Nowy Dwor State Stud, Poland

(Originally Carmencita, in Poland. Sold to England, imported from there.)

18316   *EASTER HOPE (Sole Hope-*Carmencita el Haifi) B/gr. m. 1961.
Imp. en utero. Miss M. C. E. Lyon, England

20464   *MIRZAZ (*Naborr-Mira) Gr. st. 1957. Albigowa State Stud, Poland

(Originally Mirza, in Poland)

20465   *MUZULMANIN (Doktryner-Mufta) Ch. st. 1957. Michalow
State Stud, Poland

Imported by Raymond J. Aston, Charles H. Doner and H. H. Reese, of
Kaysville, Utah, Elsinore, California and Pomona, California respectively:

18278   *ARDAHAN (Trypolis-Adis Abeda) Gr. st. 1954. Michalow State
Stud, Poland

18277   *MOHACZ (Trypolis-Mimonka) Gr. st. 1955. Nowy Dwor State Stud,
Poland

Horses imported by Frank Smathers, Jr., Miami Beach, Florida:

19916   *MAGIC RIBBON (Indian Magic-Blue Raffia) Gr. m. 1960.
Miss P. M. Lindsay, England

19917   *SILVER PEARL (*Silver Vanity-Perle d'Or) Gr. m. 1960.
Margaret Greely, England

Other imports:

Imp. en utero by John Cusack, Erindale, Ontario, Canada

19912　*AANASSEH (Manasseh-*Diamond Sparkle) Ch. st. 1959.
Mrs. S. Bomford, England

Imported by John Cusack, Erindale, Ontario, Canada

19911　*DIAMOND SPARKLE (Bright Shadow-*Indian Diamond) Ch. m.
1953. Lady Wentworth, England

Imported by Robert A. AmEnde, Vernon, Connecticut

18313　*COUNT ORLANDO (*Count Dorsaz-Umatella) Ch. st. 1951.
Miss G. M. Yule, England

Imported by James E. McBride, Covina, California

20428　*GAWRA (Doktryner-Gwara) Ch. m. 1957. Michalow State Stud,
Poland

Imported en utero by James E. McBride, Covina, California

20826　*DOKHAILAN (Grand-*Gawra) Ch. st. 1962. Michalow State Stud,
Poland

Imported by the U. S. Dept. of Agriculture, Washington, D.C.

18271　*GHALII (Nazeer-Galila) Gr. st. 1957. Egyptian Agricultural Society,
Egypt

Imported by Merle J. and Ronald H. Dow, Perham, Maine

18314　*ORAN VAN CRABBET (Oran-*Serafina) Ch. st. 1960. Wentworth,
Carbbet Park and Burton Studs, England

IMPORTATIONS
1962

Horses imported by Douglas B. Marshall, Houston, Texas:

23222　*BINT BINT KATEEFA (Antar-Bint Kateefa) Ch. m. 1960.
Egyptian Agricultural Organization, Cairo, Egypt

23221　*BINT MAISA (Nazeer-Maisa) Bay m. 1959. Egyptian Agricultural
Organization, Cairo, Egypt

23220　*BINT MAISA EL SAGHIRA (Nazeer-Maisa) Bay m. 1958.
Egyptian Agricultural Organization, Cairo, Egypt

23223　*BINT NEFISAA (Nazeer-Nefisa) Gr. m. 1959. Egyptian
Agricultural Organization, Cairo, Egypt

Horses imported by Sir William Farm, Hillsdale, New York and Shearbrook
Farms, Clayton, Ohio:

22551　*AMBARA (Wielki-Szlem-Alhambra) Gr. m. 1951. Nowy Dwor State
Stud, Poland

22554　*FAROAN (*Naborr-Forta) Gr. st. 1958. Michalow State Stud,
Poland

22553　*KOCHANAS (Wielki Szlem-Kaszma) Bay m. 1952. Nowy Dwor
State Stud, Poland

(Originally Kochana, in Poland)

22552 *SATYRA (Trypolis-*Sabaa) Gr. m. 1957. Nowy Dwor State Stud, Poland

24163 *SCHARA (Ferrum-*Kohanas) Bay m. 1963. Imp. en utero. Janow State Stud, Poland

Also:

24568 *IBN NEGATIW (Negatiw-*Satyra) Gr. st. Imp. en utero. Janow State Stud. Registered in name of John R. Graney, Leroy, N.Y. as importer

Imported by James E. McBride, Covina, California:

23198 *MORTISSA (Trypolis-Mordzana) Gr. m. 1957. Nowy Dwor State Stud, Poland

23216 *CZORTAN (Czort-*Mortissa) Gr. st. 1962. Nowy Dwor State Stud, Poland

Imported by Paul and Sandra Loeber, Palatine, Illinois:

21257 *DALIH (Hadban Enzehi-Halisa) Gr. st. 1959. Wurttemburg Landgestut, Marbach, Germany

21258 *SANACHT (Hadban Enzehi-Hathor) Gr. m. 1960. Wyrttemburg Landgestut, Marbach, Germany.

Imported by Rodney Tetrault, Eaton, Indiana:

24245 *DORMINO (Blue Domino-*Dorseema) Ch. st. 1963. Imp. en utero. Rodney Tetrault

22549 *BINT DORSEEMA (General Grant-*Dorseema) Ch. m. 1962. Rodney Tetrault

22550 *DORSEEMA (*Count Dorsaz-Reema) Ch. m. 1958. T. W. I. Hedly, England

Imported by Don C. Chandler or Dr. H. F. Kale, Fairbanks, Alk. and Seattle, Wn

23582 *CHUKRAN (Gerwazy-Czantoria) Gr. st. 1961. Miss P. M. Lindsay, England

Imported by Queen Nazli of Egypt, 1950

20678 *EL AKHRANI (Nabras-Bint Rustem) Bl. st. 1937. Royal Agricultural Society, Egypt

Imported by Jane Sadoff, Cazenovia, N.Y.

20677 *NIZREEN (Naseel-Raxina) Gr. m. 1958. Mrs. S. A. Nicholson, Eire

Imported by Bazy Tankersley, Washington, D.C. and Charles H. Prange, New Hope, Pa.

22555 *SILVER VANITY (Oran-Silver Gilt) Gr. st. 1950. Lady Wentworth, England

Imported by Merle J. and Ronald H. Dow, Perham, Maine

20703 *WENTWORTH SILVER SHADOW (Bright Shadow-Wentworth Golden Shadow) Gr. st. 1961. Crabbet Arabian Stud, England

IMPORTATIONS
1963

Imported by the Lasma Arabian Stud, Scottsdale, Arizona:

25461 *BAJRAM (Pietuszok-Bandola) Gr. st. 1959. Albigowa State Stud, Poland

25460   *BASK (Witraz-Balalajka) Bay st. 1956. Albigowa State Stud, Poland

25457   *BOLTONKA (Arax-Bulgotka) Bay m. 1958. Albigowa State Stud, Poland

25725   *CHAZARA (Chazar-*Mesalina) Gr. m. 1963. Imp. en utero. Janow State Stud, Poland

25458   *COSMOSA (Witraz-Canaria) Bay m. 1950. Albigowa State Stud, Poland

26164   *COZMOS (Branibor-*Cosmosa) Bay st. 1963. Imp. en utero. Michalow State Stud, Poland

25455   *DZISNA (*Naborr-Dyska) Gr. m. 1960. Michalow State Stud, Poland

25453   *GDYNIA (Comet-*Gwozdawa) Gr. m. 1952. Michalow State Stud, Poland

25450   *GWADIANA (Amurath Sahib-Gwara) Gr. m. 1952. Michalow State Stud, Poland

25451   *GWAR (Comet-*Gwardiana) Gr. st. 1963. Michalow State Stud, Poland

25452   *GWOZDAWA (*Naborr-*Gwadiana) Gr. m. 1958. Michalow State Stud, Poland

25462   *GWYN (Comet-*Gwadiana) Gr. m. 1963. Imp en utero. Michalow State Stud, Poland

25456   *MESALINA (Geyran-Musailima) Gr. m. 1958. Nowy Dwor State Stud, Poland

25459   *PORTULAKA (Faher-Porfira) Bay m. 1960. Michalow State Stud, Poland

25454   *WIRGINIA (*Naborr-Werbena) Gr. m. 1961. Michalow State Stud, Poland

Imported by E. J. Tweed, Scottsdale, Arizona:

25446   *ABHAZJA (Omar II-Arfa) Bay m. 1956. Albigowa State Stud, Poland

25449   *ALGORINA (Ali Said-Alga) Gr. m. 1957. Nowy Dwor State Stud, Poland

25440   *ALMERIAA (Faher-*Ambara) Gr. m. 1959. (Originally Almeria) Albigowa State Stud, Poland

25441   *BASTA (Comet-Bajdara) Gr. m. 1959. Nowy Dwor State Stud, Poland

25447   *CHLOSTA (Faher-*Carissima) Gr. m. 1960. Albigowa State Stud, Poland

25437   *CZESTER (Comet-Cerekiew) Gr. st. 1960. Nowy Dwor State Stud, Poland

25444   *DASZENKA (Trypolis-Daszma) Bay m. 1956. Nowy Dwor State Stud, Poland

25448   *GENUA (Grand-Gwara) Bay m. 1960. Michalow State Stud, Poland

25445   *GONTYNA (Doktryner-Gazella) Gr. m. 1956. Michalow State Stud, Poland

25436   *GWIAZDOR (*Naborr-*Gwadiana) Gr. st. 1959. Michalow State Stud, Poland

25438   *MIROLUBA (Faher-Mira) Gr. m. 1960. Albigowa State Stud, Poland

25443   °NAWOJKA (Wielki Szlem-Najada) Gr. m. 1956. Nowy Dwor State Stud, Poland

25439   °RIFATA (Faher-Rasima) Bay m. 1959. Albigowa State Stud, Poland

25442   °WARNA (°Naborr-Wielki Zorza) Gr. m. 1957. Albigowa State Stud, Poland

27673   *BRUSALLY BRANABAR (Branibor-*Gontuna) Bl. st. 1964. Imp. en utero, Michalow State Stud, Poland.

27672   °BRUSALLY CHAZAN (Chazar-°Nawojka) Bay st. 1964. Imp. en utero. Janow State Stud, Poland

27674   °BRUSALLY CZORTA (Czort-°Abhazja) Ch. m. 1964. Imp. en utero. Janow State Stud, Poland

Imported by Robert L. Aste, Scottsdale, Arizona:

25446   °ANDALUZJA (Grand-°Antwerpia) Bay m. 1959. Michalow State Stud, Poland

25467   °ANTWERPIA (Werset-Adis Abeba) Ch. m. 1953. Michalow State Stud, Poland

25467   °EGINA (Laur-°Enorme) Ch. m. 1959. Janow State Stud, Poland

25726   °WERBOR (°Naborr-°Antwerpia) Gr. st. Imp. en utero. Michalow State Stud, Poland

Imported by Guy Stillman, Scottsdale, Arizona:

25470   °ANGOLA (°Naborr-Adis Abeba) Gr. m. 1960. Michalow State Stud, Poland

25469   °MIMIKA (Ali Said-Mimonka) Gr. m. 1956. Nowy Dwor State Stud, Poland

28943   °CHAZMINKA (Chazar-°Miminka) Gı. m. 1964. Imp en utero. Janow State Stud, Poland

Imported by Dr. H. F. Kale, Seattle, Washington:

25464   °DORNABA (°Naborr-Darda) Gr. m. 1960. Michalow State Stud, Poland

25465   °ESKADRA (°Naborr-Ela) Gr. m. 1959. Michalow State Stud, Poland

23494   °SILVER DRIFT (Raktha-°Serafina) Gr. st. 1951. Lady Wentworth, England

Imported by A. M. Work, Portland, Oregon:

25473   °CISSA (Wielki Szlem-Larissa) Gr. m. 1949. Nowy Dwor State Stud, Poland

25474   °CYPR (Pietuszok-°Cissa) Bay st. 1963. Janow State Stud, Poland

Imported by Douglas B. Marshall, Spring, Texas:

26696   °EL ZUBI (Al Wishaw DB-Alia DB) Gr. st. 1957. H.H. El Sharif Nassir Bin Jamil, Jordan

26509   °SABA EL ZAHRAA (°Morafic-°Salomy) Gr. st. 1963. Imp. en utero. Egyptian Agricultural Organization, Egypt

23583   °SALOMY (El Sareei-Malaka) Gr. m. 1957. Egyptian Agricultural Organization, Egypt

Imported by Marietta D. Whitcomb, Riverside, California:

23460   °BLUE MANTLE (Blue Domino-°Princess Zia) Ch. st. 1962. Miss M. Greely, England

25722   *PRINCE ZAIM (Greatheart-*Princess Zia) Ch. st. 1961.
Miss M. Greely, England

Imported by Rodney Tetrault, Eaton, Indiana:

23718   *BINT NEGATIW (Negatiw-*Enorme) Gr. m. 1963. Imp. en utero.
Janow State Stud, Poland

23717   *ENORME (Trypolis-Norma) Gr. m. 1944. Janow State Stud, Poland

Individual importations:

Imported by H. E. or Arlyne M. Clay, Scottsdale, Arizona

25475   *BANDERA (Rozmaryn-Bajadera) Bay m. 1955. Michalow State
Stud, Poland

Imported by John M. Rogers, Walnut Creek, California

23796   *CAROCHA (Arcus-Carmen) Gr. m. 1958. Michalow State Stud,
Poland

Imported by Howard F. Kale, Jr., Seattle, Washington and E. M. Arndt, Aloha,
Oregon.

25463   *ELBA (Pietuszok-Ellora) Bay m. 1962. Janow State Stud, Poland

Imported by Mr. and Mrs. W. W. Walton, Jr., Helotes, Texas

26163   *GOLDEN DOMINO (Blue Domino-Crystal Dew) Ch. st. 1962.
Mrs. I. Scott, England

Imported by Mike Nichols, New York, N.Y.

24725   *MAHEYL (Bright Shadow-Myolanda) Ch. st. 1961. Crabbet Arabian
Stud, England

Imported by Anne McCormick, Scottsdale, Arizona

25472   *NABORR (Negatiw-Lagodna) Gr. st. 1950. Tiersk Stud, Soviet Union
(Originally Nabor. Sold to Poland 1955)

Imported by Anne S. Davison, Hinton, Alberta, Canada

25471   *PALLADA (Comet-Pandora) Gr. m. 1959. Nowy Dwor State Stud,
Poland

IMPORTATIONS
1964

Imported by James F. Lewis, Jr., Charlottesville, Virginia:

28000   *BLUE TANGO (Blue Magic-Shaybet) Ch. st. 1964. Imp. en utero.
Mrs. N. Theobold, England

27092   *DORO (Dargee- Rasana) Ch. m. 1962. Mrs. E. M. Thomas, England

27095   *FLYING STORM (Indian Magic-Taima) Gr. m. 1954. Miss M.C.E.
Lyon, England

27096   *FIRE OPAL (Dargee-Wentworth Golden Shadow) Gr. m. 1963.
Mrs. S. Bomford, England

27094   *GOLDEN FAIRY (My Man-Sugar Plum Fairy) Ch. m. 1963.
Mrs. S. Bomford, England

28001   *LEWISFIELD MAGIC (Indian Magic-*Michelia) Ch. st. 1964.
Imp. en utero. Mrs. E. M. Thomas, England

27098 °MICHELIA (°Count Orlando-Rissalma) Ch. m. 1959. Mrs. E. M. Thomas, England

27093 °SHAYBET (Blue Domino-Shayba Thania) Bay m. 1953. Bernard Dixon, England

27097 °SILVER BELLE (Raktha-°Silver Crystal) Gr. m. 1946. Lady Wentworth, England

27091 °SOLANGE (Sole Hope-Yanni) Bay m. 1962. Miss M. C. E. Lyon, England

30310 °TOUCH OF MAGIC (Indian Magic-Indian Diamond) Gr. st. 1957. Lady Wentworth, England

27090 °ZILLA (Indian Magic-Silent Wings) Gr. m. 1960. C. G. Covey, England

Imported by P. B. Williamson, Kelowna, B.C., Canada:

30378 °ARNIKA (Faher-Arwila) Gr. m. 1960. Albigowa State Stud, England

30376 °ARWISTAWA (Geyran-Arfa) Gr. m. 1958. Albigowa State Stud, Poland

30379 °BARYSZ (Faher-Bandola) Gr. st. 1960. Albigowa State Stud, Poland

30372 °EDYCJA (°Naborr-Estokada) Gr. m. 1962. Michalow State Stud, Poland

30373 °ESTERKA (Anarchista-Estokada) Ch. m. 1959. Michalow State Stud, Poland

30371 °GORCZYCA (°Naborr-Gwara) Gr. m. 1961. Michalow State Stud, Poland

30375 °HARDA (Pietuszok-Harfa) Ch. m. 1963. Janow State Stud, Poland

30374 °HARPIA (Pietuszok-Harfa) Ch. m. 1962. Janow State Stud, Poland

30370 °KIRKOR (Gwarny-Carmen) Gr. st. 1961. Michalow State Stud, Poland

30377 °RUSALKAA (Czort-Rusznika) Bay m. 1960. Nowy Dwor State Stud, Poland

(Originally Rusalka, in Poland)

Imported by Douglas B. Marshall, Spring, Texas:

30262 °BINT MONA (Nazeer-Mona) Gr. m. 1958. Egyptian Agricultural Organization, Egypt

30264 °IBN ANTAR (Antar-°Bint Mona) Gr. st. 1964. Egyptian Agricultural Organization, Egypt

27100 °SAMMARA (°Morafic-Samira) Gr. m. 1960. Egyptian Agricultural Organization, Egypt

30265 °SANAAA (Sid Abouhom-Yashmak) Gr. m. 1961. Egyptian Agricultural Organization, Egypt

Imported by Mrs. Francis Rust, Evans, Georgia:

27118 °EGRETA (Doktryner-°Egeria) Gr. m. 1956. Michalow State Stud, Poland

27119 °EMAUS (°Naborr-°Egreta) Gr. st. 1963. Michalow State Stud, Poland

28951 °HALALI ENCHANTED (Comet-°Egreta) Bay m. 1964. Imp. en utero. Michalow State Stud, Poland

164

Imported by Frank Smathers, Jr., Miami Beach, Florida:

27088 °CARMENN (Pietuszok-Celina) Bay m. 1959. Polish Government. Foaled in England. Dam owned by H. V. M. Clark, England

27089 °DAMIETTA (Trypolis-Dimatra) Ch. m. 1957. Bred by Nowy Dwor State Stud, Poland

30262 °KAHLUA (Gerwazy-°Damietta) Bay m. 1964. Imp. en utero. Patricia Lindsay, England

Imported by R. Edwin Fischer, Canton, Ontario, Canada:

27009 °KASZTEL (Wielki Szlem-Kaszma) Bay st. 1951. Nowy Dwor State Stud, Poland

27010 °MOCZARKA (°Laur-Mira) Bay m. 1956. Albigowa State Stud, Poland

Individual importations:

Imported by Ella N. Chastain, El Cajon, California

27762 °AL-OBAYYAH (parents DB) Gr. m. 1957. Royal Stables of Al-Sa'ud, Riyadh, Saudi Arabia

Imported by Elizabeth A. Esson, Birchrunville, Pa.

27087 °BALQUIS (Mikeno-Roshara) Gr. m. 1962. Mrs. G. M. Lancaster, England

Imported by S. G. Bennett, Georgetown, Ontario, Canada

27086 °NARIMM (Bright Shadow-Nerinora) Ch. st. 1961. Crabbet Arabian Stud, England

Imported by Susan Rae and Sharon Dee Woll, Corona, California

27773 °PHAROS (Argos-Perle D'or) Gr. st. 1963. Miss M. Greely, England

Imported by William A. or Patricia Hewitt, East Moline, Illinois

28703 °SARAHA (Bahram-Selma II) Ch. m. 1959. H. V. M. Clark, England

IMPORTATIONS
1965

Imported by Douglas B. Marshall, Spring, Texas:

32267 °BINT BINTE EL BATAA (Eman-°Binte El Batta) Gr. m. 1964. Egyptian Agricultural Organization

32266 °BINTE EL BATAA (Nazeer-El Bataa) Gr. m. 1958. Egyptian Agricultural Organization

32273 °DAWLAT (Antar-Sheherezada) Ch. m. 1961. Egyptian Agricultural Organization

32268 °FAHIDD (Antar-Helwa) Ch. st. 1961. Egyptian Agricultural Organization

32271 °GHAZALAHH (Mashour-Bint Farida) Gr. m. 1951. Egyptian Agricultural Organization

32269 °HEKMAT (Antar-Samia) Ch. m. 1961. Egyptian Agricultural Organization

32263   *HOYEDA (*Morafic-Mona) Ch. m. 1963. Egyptian Agricultural Organization

35260   *IBN SAMEH (Sameh-*Nabilahh) Bay st. 1966. Imp. en utero. Douglas Marshall

33412   *IBN WANIS (Mozzafar-*Binte El Bataa) Gr. st. Imp. en utero. Douglas Marshall

32265   *KHOFO (*Morafic-*Nabilahh) Ch. st. 1965. Egyptian Agricultural Organization

32261   *MORAFIC (Nazeer-Mabrouka) Gr. st. 1956. Egyptian Agricultural Organization

32264   *NABILAHH (Antar-Frashah) Gr. m. 1960. Egyptian Agricultural Organization

32262   *NAHLAH (*Morafic-Mohgah) Gr. m. 1962. Egyptian Agricultural Organization

32272   *SAFAA (Sameh-Lubna) Ch. m. 1962. Egyptian Agricultural Organization

32270   *SHAMAH (Sameh-Rafica) Bay m. 1961. Egyptian Agricultural Organization

Imported by James F. Lewis, Jr., Charlottesville, Virginia:

31945   *CHERAN (Rakan-Simiha) Ch. m. 1959. W. L. Sword, Scotland

31946   *DRAGONESSE (*Count Orlando-Dragonfly) Bay m. 1960. Mrs. N. MacLean, England

31943   *SIRIKIT   *Alexus-Rexeena) Ch. m. 1961. Mr. and Mrs. W. E. Dinsdale, England

31944   *SNOWFIRE (Kami-Castanea) Ch. m. 1963. Miss M. Evans, England

36192   *LEWISFIELD DRAGON (Iridos-*Dragonesse) Bay st. 1966. Imp. en utero. Jas. F. Lewis

36194   *LEWISFIELD IRAX (Iridos-*Sirikit) Ch. st. 1966. Imp. en utero. Jas. F. Lewis, Jr.

36193   *LEWISFIELD IREXA (Iridos-*Cheran) Ch. m. 1966. Imp. en utero. Jas. F. Lewis, Jr.

Imported by James M. Kline, Whittier, California:

34989   *HODA (Alaa El Dean-Fathia) Gr. m. 1963. Egyptian Agricultural Organization

34988   *LEBLEBA (Gassir-Samira) Gr. m. 1963. Egyptian Agricultural Organization

Imported by John M. Rogers, Walnut Creek, California:

34409   *DINORAH III (Uad-Martin - Kirat) Gr. m. 1960. Luis Ybarra e Ybarra, Spain

35195   *DON SEVILLE (Corinto-*Dinorah III) Gr. st. 1966. Imp. en utero. Luis Ybarra e Ybarra, Spain

34408   *YAMINA (Zurich-Brussa II) Gr. m. 1963. Luis G. Afan de Ribera, Spain

Imported by Jay Stream, Wheaton, Illinois:

33488   *IBN MONIET EL NEFOUS (*Morafic-Moniet El Nefous) Gr. st. 1964. Egyptian Agricultural Organization

33489   °NAGAT (Antar-Abla) Gr. m. 1960. Egyptian Agricultural
Organization

Imported by Bazy Tankersley, Washington, D.C.:
34986   °PRINCESS ZIA (°Count Dorsaz-Queen Zenobia) Ch. m. 1954.
Miss G. M. Yule, England

(on lease)
34987   °ROYAL DOMINION (Blue Domino-°Princess Zia) Ch. st. 1964.
M. Greely, England

Imported by Mr. and Mrs. William L. Freni and Mr. and Mrs. Donald L.
Forbis, Chickasha, Oklahoma:
33487   °ANSATA BINT BUKRA (Nazeer-Bukra) Gr. m. 1959. Egyptian
Agricultural Association, Egypt
36452   °ANSATA BINT MISR (Sameh-°Ansata Bint Bukra) 1966.
Imp. en utero. Egyptian Agricultural Association, Egypt

Imported by Patricia Lee, Blaine, Tennessee:
30791   °NUALEXA (Champurrado-Alexa) Ch. m. 1957. Lady May
Abel-Smith, England

IMPORTATIONS
1966

Imported by the Steen Ranches, Reno, Nevada:
35205   °ALDEBARAN II (Malvito-Halconera) Bay m. 1957. Jose De Ybarra,
Spain
35203   °AGATA III (Malvito-Famula) Bay m. 1961. Yeguada Military, Spain
35206   °BARICH DE WASHOE (Zurich-°Aldebaran II) Gr. st. 1965.
Imp. en utero. Luis De Ybarra, Spain
35207   °BRUSSA II (Uad El Kebir-Lakme) Gr. m. 1958. Luis M. Ybarra,
Y. Gomez, Spain
35218   °LIATA DE WASHOE (Tabal-°Talia III) Ch. m. 1965. Don Miguel
Osuna Escalera, Spain
35209   °PALABRITA (Barquillo-Hacienda) Gr. m. 1952. Yeguada Military,
Spain
35208   °PAGANA III (Damasco III-Escala) Gr. m. 1952. Yeguada Military,
Spain
36086   °OROMANA (Maquillo-°Sauce II) Gr. m. 1960. Louis Domeq
Rivero, Spain
35210   °RABADILLA (Damasco III-Beni Amer) Gr. m. 1953. Yeguada ,
Military, Spain
35211   °RABIETA (Damasco III-Yaima) Gr. m. 1953. Yeguada Military,
Spain
35212   °RABIOSA (Barquillo-Labrada) Gr. m. 1953. Yeguada Military,
Spain
35212   °RAPAZA (Barquillo-Gauta) Gr. m. 1953. Yeguada Military, Spain
35214   °SABIDURIA (Maquillo-Habladuria) Ch. m. 1954. Don Miguel
Osuna Escalera, Spain

36084 °SACUDIDA (Aboukir-Bandera) Gr. m. 1954. Yeguada Military, Spain

35216 °SALINA (Aboukir-Famula) Gr. m. 1954. Yeguada Military, Spain

36085 °SAUCE II (Barquillo-Farina) Gr. m. 1954. Yeguada Military, Spain

35249 °TABALIA DE WASHOE (Tabal-°Talia III) Ch. st. 1966. Imp en utero. Miguel Osuna Escalera, Spain

35215 °TADURIA DE WASHOE (Tabal-°Sabiduria) Gr. m. 1965. Miguel Osuna Escalera, Spain

36088 °TAFAL DE WASHOE (Tabal-°Tafia II) Gr. m. 1965. Don Miguel Osuna, Spain

36087 °TAIFA II (Dante-Katiuska) Gr. m. 1953. Josepha Reina Carvajal, Spain

35204 °TAGATA DE WASHOE (Tabal-°Agata III) Ch. m. 1965. Don Miguel Osuna Escalera, Spain

35217 °TALIA III (Dante-Dinorah II) Bay m. 1953. Josepha Reina Carvajal, Spain

35219 °VENTOLINA (Congo-Kafira) Gr. m. 1954. Jose M. De Ybarra, Spain

35220 °YAMA (Fabuloso-Neyma II) Gr. m. 1955 Jose M. De Ybarra, Spain

35221 °YOKOHAMA (Fabuloso-Nubia II) Gr. m. 1955. Jose M. De Ybarra, Spain

35222 °ZURHAMA DE WASHOE (Zurich-°Yokohama) Gr. st. 1965. Jose M. De Ybarra, Spain

Imported by H. E. or Arlyne M. Clay, Scottsdale, Arizona:

36270 °AMFIBIA (Sedziwoj-°Ambara) Gr. m. 1961. Albigowa State Stud, Poland

36271 °AMPLA (Czort-°Amfiibia) Bay m. 1966. Janow State Stud, Poland

36269 °BIHAR (Negatiw-°Bigotka) Gr. st. 1966. Janow State Stud, Poland

36268 °BIGOTKA (Arcus-Bint Munira) Bay m. 1958. Nowy Dwor State Stud, Poland

42086 °NEGAM (Negatiw-°Amfiibia) Gr. st. 1966. Imp. en utero. Janow State Stud, Poland

42087 °NEGOTKA (Negatiw-°Bigotka) Gr. m. 1967. Imp. en utero. Janow State Stud, Poland

Imported by Douglas B. Marshall, Spring, Texas:

38939 °BERLANTY (Sid Abouhom-Maysona) Gr. m. 1960. Egyptian Agricultural Organization

38938 °EMAN (Antar-Abla) Gr. m. 1963. Egyptian Agricultural Organization

38940 °FAWKIA (Sameh-Mamlouka) Gr. m. 1965. Egyptian Agricultural Organization

38936 °ROMANAA II (Sameh-Nazeera) Ch. m. 1963. Egyptian Agricultural Organization

38937 °SOMAIA (Antar-Abla) Gr. m. 1965. Egyptian Agricultural Organization

38935 °THABIT (Alaa Eldin-Kaydahom) Gr. st. 1964. Egyptian Agricultural Organization

Imported by Four Winds Farm, Delavan, Wisconsin:

35793 °BRYZEIDA (Comet-Bint Munira) Bay m. 1959. Nowy Dwor State Stud, Poland

35794 °KASKADA (°Naborr-Karmen II) Gr. m. 1959. Michalow State Stud, Poland

35796 °ROKIET (Czort-°Rokitka) Ch. st. 1966. Janow State Stud, Poland

35795 °ROKITKA (Arax-Rokiczana) Bay m. 1958. Janow State Stud, Poland

35792 °WIRAZ (Comet-Wikeli Zorza) Gr. st. 1959. Nowy Dwor State Stud, Poland

Imported by Constance L. Cobb, and Bonnie J. Cobb, Reeds, Missouri:

37774 °FURTHA SHELALL (Ragus DB-Malika DB) Gr. st. 1960. Khalid Al-Dossary, Saudi Arabia

37775 °HABITI (desertbred) Bay m. 1952. Mansur Ibn Ahmad Ibn Abbas, Saudi Arabia

36944 °JALAM AL UBAYAN (desertbred) Ch. st. 1949. Amir Saud Ibn Abdaullah Ibn Jiluwi, Saudi Arabia

37776 °JALAM FAIRLIE (°Jalam Al-Ubayan - °Habiti) Bay st. 1966. Imp. en utero. Bonnie J. Cobb, Reeds, Missouri

Imported by Robert B. Field, Leavenworth, Washington:

36266 °CARISSIMA (Witraz-Musailima) Bay m. 1949. Albigowa State Stud, Poland

36267 °CARUSO (Negatiw-°Carissima) Gr. st. 1966. Janow State Stud, Poland

Individual importations:

Imported by Don C. Chandler, Fairbanks, Alaska

36299 °LAWINA (°Naborr-Lawenda) Gr. m. 1962. Michalow State Stud, Poland

Imported by John M. Rogers, Walnut Creek, California

38066 °KARADJORDJE (Gerwazy-Karramba) Gr. st. 1965. Patricia M. Lindsay, England

Imported by Lasma Arabian Stud, Scottdale, Arizona

36089 °GWALIOR (°Naborr-°Gwadiana) Gr. st. 1961. Michalow State Stud, Poland

Imported by Halberg Arabians, Iron, Minnesota

35618 °MADRYGAL (°Naborr-Madiara) Gr. st. 1960. Michalow State Stud, Poland

Imported by W. C. Andrews, Lamar, South Carolina

36945 °SHERI (°Jalam Al Ubayan-Sabiha DB) Ch. m. 1963. W. C. Andrews, Lamar, South Carolina

IMPORTATIONS
1967

Imported by Clay and Struck Arabian Ranches, Scottsdale, Arizona:

24011 °ARROW (Ariel-Bint Badaria) Bay st. 1967. Michalow State Stud, Poland

42006   °BINT BADARIA (Wielki Szlem-Badiara) Bay m. 1958. Michalow
        State Stud, Poland
42013   °CZARTAWA (Mir Said-Czaruta) Bay m. 1963. Michalow State Stud,
        Poland
42013   °DAR (Comet-Darda) Gr. st. 1963. Michalow State Stud, Poland
42015   °FLIS (Comet-Forta) Gr. st. 1963. Michalow State Stud, Poland
42008   °GALBOR (°Naborr-Galopada) Gr. st. 1964. Michalow State Stud,
        Poland
42003   °GALICJA (Grand-Galopada) Bay m. 1961. Michalow State Stud,
        Poland
42007   °GULDEN (Comet-Galopada) Gr. st. 1963. Michalow State Stud,
        Poland
42010   °KLUSZYN (Sedziwoj-°Kochanas) Bay st. 1961. Albigowa State Stud,
        Poland
42012   °MAKO (Kord-°Mafia) Bay st. 1967. Michalow State Stud, Poland
42017   °MARZANNA (Grand-Madiara) Bay m. 1961. Michalow State Stud,
        Poland
42009   °MECZET (Comet-°Mimika) Gr. st. 1961. Janow State Stud, Poland
42004   °MAFIA (El Trypoli-Madiara) Bay m. 1962. Michalow State Stud,
        Poland
42016   °RUSZT (Czort-Rusznica) Ch. st. 1962. Janow State Stud, Poland
42005   °TRYGUZA (Trypolis-°Ambara) Bay m. 1958. Michalow State Stud,
        Poland

Imported by E. J. Tweed, Scottsdale, Arizona:
41022   °BULAWA (Laur-Bulgotka) Bay m. 1959. Janow State Stud, Poland
41026   °CERERA (Ferrum-Cerekiew) Bay m. 1963. Janow State Stud,
        Poland
41020   °LAURA (Ariel-°Lawenda) Bay m. 1967. Janow State Stud, Poland
41023   °LAWENDA (Doktryner-Laguna) Gr. m. 1955. Michalow State Stud,
        Poland
41024   °MANNA (°Naborr-Manilla) Gr. m. 1963. Michalow State Stud,
        Poland
41019   °ORZEL (Pietuszok-Ofirka) Ch. st. 1963. Janow State Stud, Poland
40933   °PALETA (Comet-Planeta) Gr. m. 1964. Michalow State Stud, Poland
41018   °PROWIZJA (Ego-Prowarda) Bay m. 1964. Janow State Stud, Poland
41021   °SALINAA (Comet-Salwa) Bay m. 1960. Janow State Stud, Poland
41025   °WISLICA (Branibor-Wataha) Bay m. 1964. Michalow State Stud,
        Poland
41027   °ZBRUCZ (Comet-Znachorka) Bay st. 1963. Michalow State Stud,
        Poland

Imported by Leon Rubin, New York, N.Y.:
44989   °CARRADOR (Comet-Czaruta) Gr. st. 1960. Janow State Stud,
        Poland
44993   °CERTA (Pietuszok-Cerozja) Bay m. 1962. Janow State Stud, Poland
44990   °DIMATRA (Wielki Szlem-Imatra) Gr. m. 1950. Janow State Stud,
        Poland
44991   °KANIAA (Czort-Kassala) Ch. m. 1962. Janow State Stud, Poland

44992 °TRYNCZA (Trypolis-°Kochanas) Bay m. 1958. Janow State Stud, Poland

(The °Kochanas listed as the dam of two of the foregoing imports is Kochana—without the final "s" in Poland. The earlier import named °Kochana was foaled in England although bred in Poland, and is much younger than re-named mare °Kochanas. Also the original name of °Kaniaa is Kania, and the same addition of a final "a" is used for °Salinaa, whose name was originally Salina. Previous use of names is the reason for alteration of names on imports).

Imported by Dr. and Mrs. William A. McCrea, Alliance, Ohio:

42019 °KANOSSA (Czort-Canberra) Ch. m. 1961. Janow State Stud, Poland

42018 °LESZCYNA (Comet-°Lawenda) Gr. m. 1963. Michalow State Stud, Poland

Imported by Elizabeth Ann Carrothers, Byran, Texas:

43906 °IBN IRIDOS (Iridos-°Ruzica) Gr. st. 1967. Patricia Lindsay, Eng.

45332 °ROYAL IRIDOS (Iridos-°Ruzica) Gr. st. 1968. Imp en utero. Patricia Lindsay, England

43905 °RUZICA (Gerwazy-Rosjanka) Gr. m. 1961. Patricia Lindsay, Eng.

Imported by Sidney Z. Rehka, Burbank, California:

43308 °ANWARR (°Morafic-Ghazah) Gr. st. 1963. Egyptian Agricultural Society, Egypt

43309 °BINT GAZELLA (Sid Abouhom-Gazella) Gr. m. 1959. Egyptian Agricultural Society, Egypt

Imported by R. D. and S. F. Loken, Hartsdale, New York:

45330 °FAKHER EL DIN (Nazeer-Moniet el Nefous) Ch. st. 1960. Egyptian Agricultural Society, Egypt

45329 °TALAL (Nazeer-Zaafarana) Gr. st. 1957. Egyptian Agricultural Association, Egypt

Imported by Mercedes Erin Barthes, Silver Spring, Maryland:

45331 °CARACOLA (Jaecero-Saffana) Gr. m. 1961. Antonia Egea Delgado, Spain

Horses imported late in 1967, but not registered until 1968:

Imported by Frank Y. Smith & Co., Chatsworth, California:

46769 °ETER (Comet-Estokada) Bay st. 1963. Michalow State Stud, Poland

46770 °FARMACJA (El Trypoli-Forta) Ch. m. 1962. Michalow State Stud, Poland

46771 °GIELDA (°Naborr-°Gontyna) Gr. m. 1962. Michalow State Stud, Poland

50934 °ALMAVIVA (Wielki Szlem-Alhambra) Bay m. 1956. Nowy Dwor State Stud, Poland

53309 °ALONDRAA (Grojec-°Almaviva) Bay m. 1968. Imp. un utero.

53310 °GALIA (Chazar-°Gielda) Gr. m. 1968. Imp. un utero. Michalow

There were large importations in 1968, both from Egypt and Poland, with the usual smaller groups as well from other countries. However the Stud Book information was not yet published on these, as of July 1969.

171

VI

THE CULT OF THE CHAMPION

Throughout this time the emphasis has been on championships of horses shown in hand rather than on performance. This is because the National Championship at halter, for instance, is considered the ultimate in achievement in the breed, and as long as this is so it is necessary to cater to that taste. Nevertheless performance is gradually assuming more importance. Because of the self-destructive effects of champion worship, the International Arabian Horse Association initiated the Legion of Merit awards, which can be earned by winning points at both halter and performance. Since its inception in 1960, out of thousands of Arabians shown, only 163 have qualified for this award up to 1969.

Before continuing, a word on certain terminology used in American horse shows might be helpful to foreign readers. One of the most confusing is the English pleasure class, creating strange mental visions of assorted pleasures indulged in by the English. However this is merely a type of class for horses used for pleasure riding, which in this instance are ridden with English tack in contrast to those equipped with western saddle and bridle. Riders of course wear corresponding attire. The English pleasure horse is similar in performance, to a degree, to a hack, but not a hunter hack, and the gaits are the walk, trot and canter, with two phases of the trot and a hand gallop in addition to the canter. The English horse (although often horses are shown in both classes) is ideally an animal with longer neck, more scope and action than the western horse, which has only a scuffling jog as its trot, while its version of the canter is the low-going lope, and it carries the head low. The western horse, to appear "western" is normally a chunkier individual than its English cousin. In England, the class designated "ridden" is essentially the same as our English pleasure to a degree, but here the judge does not ride the horses. With often as many as sixty entries per class, it can be seen that this old English custom could not be carried out in American shows.

The park horses are much more collected and full of fire than the pleasure animals, with decidely more life and impulsion in their trot. Or, to put it succinctly, they have more action, and action is defined in horse husbandry books as "having flexion of knees and hocks." The formal driving horse also has maximum action and presence, with a proud and bold way of going. Cutting may confuse anyone not familiar with the term, but a cutting horse is simply one used for cutting an individual cow from the herd and preventing it from returning immediately to its mates. There are many more types of classes in American shows which are unknown in other countries but the foregoing are the titles that cause the most confusion.

The various pleasure classes are the most heavily filled, often to the point of causing their divison into two sections of around thirty entries each. Since the pleasure class is for horses which are supposedly safe for any rider (as safe as a horse can be considered) and are perfectly trained, one way to lower the number of entries would be to exclude professional trainers from these affairs. After all, a pleasure horse is for the average amateur who either can't do anything more than cruise around the nice safe ring without disastrous result, or who doesn't care about any more adventurous course. Or it is for the horse which has no talent for anything better—the horse with no action or presence which is needed for park; no ability to jump, for hunter or jumping classes; no cow-sense for cutting, nor agility for reining. Actually, many of the horses destined for the eternal dreary rounds of pleasure plodding, are capable of much higher things but they simply are never given the chance. Many of them have excellent conformation, making them appear to be worthy prospects for racing (where honest, sound basic conformation really counts) or jumping. Consequently it is frustrating to see all those good horses more or less going to waste so to speak, when other classes, requiring higher education—or more ability, are sparsely filled. Yet the pleasure classes continue to overflow. They are so over filled indeed that many a good horse is lost in the crowd, and never given a real chance to show his worth. If professionals were banned from pleasure classes they would perforce have to train for other events, and this would be an advancement all around.

At present, with nearly a hundred all-Arabian shows held yearly in North America, it is almost impossible to visualize a time when there were no Arabian classes in horse shows, and such a thing as an all-Arabian show was not even the most optimistic dream. Only fairs at first, and then occasional horse shows condescended to include classes for Arabians, either in hand or performance. The Arabian may be the oldest breed of horse in existence, but it is a newcomer to the horse show world. It was the last to engage in formal horse show competition. All the regular classes were designed for other breeds, so there was nothing left for the Arabian which would not be a duplication of work performed by other breeds. There was an exception, the so-called native costume class in which the costumes are more native to Hollywood or the stage than to any native of Arabia. Otherwise there was nothing to do but "copy" the other breeds. The park horse is a diluted version of the Saddlebred three-gaited horse; the stockhorse classes of all sorts are the battlefield of the Quarter Horse and various partbreds; the harness classes are the forte of the Standardbred, Saddlebred, and the various heavy-harness

173

horses and ponies; the jumping classes allow all breeds but Thorough-breds prevail. How could the Arabian fit in here? Obviously it would be accused of copying another breed no matter what its course, except when buried under the "native tassels." This was the situation in 1945 when the first all-Arabian show was held in Flintridge, California.

It will be remembered that a show for Arabians only had been held on two or three occasions in Tennessee and lastly in Ohio, and these were termed National shows, as was the Stallion Show in Waterloo, Ohio and a number of classes held in conjunction with the Cheyenne, Wyoming show several years later. But none of these were held on a continuing basis in the way the California show and its satellites were, nor were they of the same stature.

But this is getting ahead of the story, for as yet the first Arabian horse association has not been mentioned and only a fleeting reference has been made of the progenitor of the modern all-Arabian horse show, American style.

The first association of Arabian horse owners to organize for the purpose of promoting and exhibiting this breed was The Arabian Horse Breeders Society of Southern California, founded December 12, 1944, at a meeting held in the home of Mr. and Mrs. Warren Phillips in Glendale. Mrs. Joanna Phillips was elected the first president of the embryo association which was destined to grow at such a rate that it soon had to be divided by areas, or rather California came to be represented by several clubs, rather than one. The original name was eventually changed to its present one of the Arabian Horse Association of Southern California, although it wasn't long before Southern California too was represented by several more associations. California then had the highest concentration of Arabian owners, and still does. As of March 1969 the Registry reported that state as having 8,853 registered living Arabian horses, the next highest being Ohio with 2,299 Arabians. It is not surprising therefore, that there should be such an abundance of energetic Arabian horse associations in the Golden State, all of which stage their own shows.

The initial show of the ancestral California society was held in 1945 on the oak-studded grounds of the Flintridge Hunt Club. As Joanna Phillips was a long-time exhibitor of dogs (Chow Chows) she suggested one of the dog game's most respected judges, William Meyers Jones, to be judge for this show. It is not at all surprising that a dog judge, especially a terrier specialist such as Jones, should know horses equally well. In fact much of the Fox Terrier standard on conformation is based on the standard of excellence for a hunter, as the wording indicates. At any rate the judging of the show was professionally done and progressed without a hitch. Champion stallion was DISEYN and reserve was SHAMEYN, the former by FERSEYN, the latter by a son of FERSEYN, so this sire got off to an early start on his champion-siring career. Neither of these early winners is credited to the account of any sire however, as

174

this was well before the Yearbook statistics were started. The reserve champion was only a yearling, for at that time no rule prevented yearlings or even weanlings from earning a championship. He placed over a couple of colts that were later to become well-known—FERNEYN and EL NATTALL (second and third respectively, with EL NATTALL a few years later gaining the first Pacific Coast Championship. There were sixty-three entries in the seventeen classes. Only four were performance events, one each for English and western pleasure, and two for trail and rein horses respectively. There was no championship class for mares, for some reason, and this sort of thing was also the case in Oregon shows for a while. Evidently the idea was to promote stallions, not mares. The champion stallion died young, but he had sired a mare that made his name live on. This was DIZA, an almost unbeatable mare in harness and combination classes. Her daughter DIZANNE has already been mentioned in regard to her (Dizanne's) sire *MOHACZ.

The second show was similar to the first but with many more entries. It too was staged at Flintridge. Breeding classes were judged by Professor C. E. Howell, a professor of animal husbandry at Davis, and formerly a manager of the Kellogg Ranch. MUSTAFA, a smooth made chestnut was champion stallion, with ROAYAS reserve. The former is the sire of five champions, but his sire line is carried on by KIMFA. ROAYAS too has made a name for himself as a sire, and it is interesting to note that the mare which placed fifth in the class won by the immortal broodmatron BINT SAHARA, was NARLET. This mare is the dam of RONARA, producer of four champions including IBN HANRAH. RONARA (by Roayas) herself placed third in the foal sweepstakes. It was at the first show, incidently, where the idiotic term "underyearling" was used in place of foal (or weanling, but some were sucklings) and naturally this non-word has been picked up by other organizations and incorporated into their class specifications along with everything else started by the California group. I remember rebelling against the term when I made out the program for the 1947 show, but thought surely someone would wake up eventually and make the correction. So far no one has. The foal sweepstakes just mentioned were termed the Underyearling Sweepstakes, but no sweepstakes were held for "under two-year-olds" (yearlings) and so on, up to "under mares" (for 3-year-old fillies). This merely indicates how silly the original—the underyearling word—is. At this show male yearlings (and foals) were properly termed colts, but were called "stallions" at two. Yet fillies were correctly called "fillies" until four years of age. Needless to say, the show committee needed educating. This show featured a Grand Entry, with prizes for about everything. A rather funny one was an award not only for the best silver saddle, but also one for the best copper (copper-mounted) saddle, when the only one in existence in this locale, or possibly anywhere else, was the one owned by the Phillips. It was a beautiful outfit though. There were again the four performance classes as before, plus one for harness horses. This last was won by ALYF, from the Pomona Quartermaster Depot, which had also won first and second in stock horses with SERIFH and KATORMA.

The third show was the beginning of greater things for not only Southern California all-Arabian shows, but those elsewhere. The Flintridge grounds were no longer available so a hurried search had to be made for another locale. Devonshire Downs in the San Fernando Valley was finally chosen, and then a publicity program unprecedented in Arabian show history was initiated, resulting in newspaper stories at least once a week and then every day, as show time approached. Ward Wells was prevailed upon to bring his dressage Arabian SHARIK down to San Fernando Valley for an exhibition, and one of the many sons of King Ibn Saoud of Arabia was on hand to present trophies. The resultant entry was the greatest ever recorded for an all-Arabian show to that date, 1947, with 167 horses, plus many which were post-entered. The judge was the eminent Egyptian authority on Arabian horses, Dr. Ameen Zahir, now Undersecretary of State, Ministry of Agriculture in Cairo. He shocked American sensibilities somewhat by turning down all the horses that he considered to be too fat. At that time the horses had not reached that state of rotundity which now is the custom (or was for a while), so what he would think of our still more plump show horses of a later date can be well imagined. The champion of this show was the two year old colt RAMAH (Raafrah-Rasoulma) with Reserve to FERSEYN, winner of the stallion class which had the respectable entry—for those days—of twenty-six horses plus post entries. Champion mare was SKOLMA a three-year-old full sister of the champion stallion, so although RAMAH's win was not a popular one (and he has been heard from since, in show history), at least the judging was remarkably consistent in the selection of siblings for top honors. Less so was the choice for the reserve spots, where a ten year old stallion was contrasted in the feminine division with a three-month-old suckling filly. This was DUR-RAH (Roayas-Shantah), who apparently either died or had no foals, for she was unheard of thereafter, as far as I know. Mr. and Mrs. H. H. Reese had sponsored the trophy for the stallion class, so Mrs. Reese had the unique honor of awarding it to her own horse. The mare class had fifteen entries and was won by ROANIGA (Roabrah-Ghanigat). ROAYAS won the stockhorse class and also the special class for any Arab two years or over with "Best Head of Classic Type." Again there was consistency, for ROAYAS was a half brother to the two champions, his dam being RASOULMA (*Raseyn-*Malouma), but his sire was ROABRAH while theirs was RAAFRAH.

Since there was a race track at Devonshire Downs (as the name indicates), a couple of races were added. One was the usual sprint—the other was less common—a walking race. The 300-yard dash was won by ZIYADI, a tough, hard-muscled ranch horse sired by ALLA AMAR-

176

WARD, and he repeated this breeze in the quarter-mile race in 1948 at Pomona. The walking race was won by DINAZI, a son of GHAZI.

The classes for this show, were still rather informal, and championships could be won by the first place winner of any class, from foal on up. But the reserve champion also had to be selected from the remaining blue ribbon winners, not as at present where the second place horse from the class won by the eventual champion can also compete for reserve.

Since my husband was chairman of the show committee for the 1947 extravaganza, I naturally had to do much of the paper work, including the planning of the program. This last item was right up my alley so to speak, in that I could set it up the way I wanted—along the lines of the programs of large national shows, but adding information that seemed desirable in a one breed show. This included the breeding (sire and dam, plus the sire of the dam, color, age, sex, etc.), of each animal, not only in the index of entries, but in the breeding classes as well. Following the custom of the big open shows, I listed the color, age, and sex of each animal in the performance classes. Thus it was possible to have pertinent information at a glance, without having to flip back to the index for it. Following the usual horse show custom, height was also listed, and while probably of no great value, it is interesting to check back on those entries and find the height of any of the horses. This format, with some deletions, was continued through the years and has now become standard. Many improvements have been made in the interim and other clubs have used the same format, and the Scottsdale program, a pet project of the late Robert Aste, is doubtless the best of the lot. The design for the Southern California club's program, designed by Charles Bracker is unique and especially applicable to the theme of versatility in all Arabian shows.

I had judged several Arabian shows in this period and found it very frustrating to be forced to select the reserve champion from the remaining first place winners, instead of having the choice of taking the reserve from the second place horse of the class from which the champion came. It often happens that one class will have a number of top animals, while other classes will consist of uniformly mediocre specimens. This is less the case now than it was in the early days, but it still happens. In such an event the really good horse which was just edged out by a whisker, more or less, by the eventual champion, certainly qualified for the reserve championship to a greater degree than would any less admirable but nevertheless blue ribbon winner from another class. Needless to say I wanted some changes made in the rules.

As an exhibitor of Airedale Terriers, I had had plenty of experience in dog shows, wherein the second-place dog of the class from which the Winners Dog came (that's the title, equivalent to champion in a horse show) was qualified to compete for reserve, against the first place winners of the other classes in that sex. Guy Williams, who later became chair- of the show committee, was an exhibitor of Doberman Pinschers, and he used to rage against the horse show situation in this regard. Whether it was his influence or whether it was the fact that the National Stallion show already had such a system, the fact remains that in 1953 (or possibly a year earlier) the rules were changed to the present custom of allowing the second place animal to compete for reserve if the horse which had won over it in the same class won the championship. So now all first and second place winners, two years or over, are brought into the ring for the championship judging. Also the age limit had been changed as indicated, permitting only the two-year-olds and over to compete for the championship, thus effectively stopping the practice of awarding a championship or reserve to a cute roly-poly foal over mature horses.

In 1947 the president of the Society was Oliver R. Jones, while Joanna Phillips was secretary, and Alice Bracker was in charge of public relations, later to become secretary over a long period of years. The 1948 president was Major Cecil Edwards, who had initiated so many innovations the previous year as show chairman. He had been the Executive Officer of the Pomona Q.M. Depot (Remount), and of course was well acquainted with the Arabian horse owners of the area. His father was one of the first Remount agents in Oregon, standing such horses as STAMBUL, JEDRAN and RIFNAS as well as the Thoroughbred LAWRENCE M. Edwards was a Registered A.H.S.A. judge for several breeds and had been on the Horse Buying Board of the Remount, so in view of his experience and qualifications it is not surprising that he initiated so many new programs in the still young Arabian organization. One of the most important ideas he promoted was that of the Society's joining the American Horse Shows Association. This in turn involved drawing up a set of rules for the Arabian division of the A.H.S.A. Rule Book. Up to this point there had been no uniformity of rules for judging Arabian horses, either at halter or in performance—in fact in many cases there were no rules at all, of any specific nature.

The chairman of the show committee for 1948 was Guy Williams, as aggressive and determined as the Dobermans he bred, so it is no surprise that the show that year transcended the success of the "Spectacular" of the previous occasion. It drew an even larger entry and as many spectators, although it was a two day event, while the Devonshire Downs classic had quite a few non-paying, non-counted members of the gallery who slid in seemingly by the hundreds, through unguarded openings in the fence. Sad though this may have been from a monetary point of view, the idea that an all Arabian horse show could engender this much public interest is something to reflect upon in itself.

This fourth show was held at the Pomona fairgrounds, on the track in front of the grandstand, not in the Carnation Stables ring where so many shows have been held recently. Since the stands are relatively far away from the horses, and high—giving a bird's eye view—it was not too satisfactory from the avid exhibitors' point of view, many of whom prefer to cluster at ringside and eagle-eye each horse, fault-by-fault or virtue-by-virtue, depending on whether the animals were rivals or those in which they have an interest. This show, like its predecessor, had been widely and profusely publicised. Adding to the lure were two gate prizes, a chestnut colt donated by H. H. Reese and a bay colt donated by E. E. Hurlbutt. Books of tickets on these gate prizes were sold in advance, as well as the daily admission tickets. There were assorted special events, such as an exhibition of Reese's ALLA AMARWARD and fifty of his get; the desertbred *MUNIFAN and *MUNIFAH and their filly; a tent-pegging competition ("pig-sticking") made popular by British troops in India a century or so ago; and three types of races. There was the quarter-mile running race, won by ZIYADI, as already noted, and AUL-ANI (Rifnas-Follyat) won the trotting event. These two horses were half brothers, since they were both out of FOLLYAT, rather a coincidence in this sort of an event compared to look-alike halter wins. FOLLYAT (Babyat-Fenzileh) is of the tail female line of *BALKIS II, a French import. In addition to these faster races was a walking race of an eighth of a mile, won by a ten year old gelding, GHAZAN. He was a working ranch horse, like ZIYADI, and was a full brother of FARAWI, sire of BINT SAHARA, foundation mare of the highly successful establishment of Mr. and Mrs. Frank McCoy. The trotting and walking races are the most difficult for an Arabian, since its natural inclination is to shift to a faster gear when maximum speed at the lower gait is achieved, so holding gait was more of a deciding issue than actual speed at the trot or walk in many instances. There was another exhibition at this show, of the justly famous MONEYNA. It was billed thus: "Mr. Harvey Ellis and his celebrated Arabian mare Moneyna, demonstrate on command, without use of bridle, all of the gaits and movements required of the Western stock horse. Moneyna responds instantly to her trainer's commands either in the show ring or on the trail."

Colonel F. W. Koester, former Commanding Officer of the Pomona Quartermaster Depot (Remount), judged this show. He had plenty of opportunity to admire MONEYNA, and made her not only the champion mare, but also Grand Champion of the show. She is by *RASEYN out of MONICA, and her son FERNEYN is on the Leading Sire List with twelve champions to his credit while his younger brother NEYSEYN has two. Reserve to MONEYNA was JOANNA, a full sister of ABU FARWA who went on to take the championship the following year. The get of ABU FARWA won three classes here, with BARQ taking the Yearling Futurity; ABU BAHA (now sire of 15 champions) won over a group of seventeen colt foals at the age of five months; and ALLABU was first among yearling colts. FERSARA, second in the Yearling Futurity (filly division) soon got even with BARQ, for this daughter of BINT SAHARA was undefeated thereafter and won the Kellogg Perpetual Trophy through achieving grand champion of this show three times in later years. BARQ

179

is presently the dam of three champions, while FERSARA had five, although she died comparatively young.

The champion stallion was a two-year-old, JEDRAZAL, sired by the Remount stallion JEDRAN, but which horse he did not resemble to any notable degree. He was also reserve champion stallion in 1951 to *WITEZ II, who was grand champion of the show. Reserve to JEDRAZAL at this 1948 show however was MUSTAFA, a previous champion of Flintridge days.

Whoever made up the program for this show did not correct any of the boners made by exhibitors, so a strange assortment of sexes and ages was found listed in the younger classes. Not only were there such things as "two-month-old stallions" in the foal classes, along with the properly classified "colts," but one half Arabian listing in a filly class is a "chestnut colt," which by its name most certainly was female. But to anyone thinking a foal was called a colt regardless of sex, this would not have been astounding. This is one reason why members of the program committee have to know at least rudimentary horse terminology, as used in horse shows. Novice exhibitors have an excuse, officials of a show do not.

The Southern California shows continued to set records for entries in succeeding years, and to list them any further would take too much space. The first five had set the example however and on this account alone deserved somewhat detailed history. Other associations were founded and held their first shows in the late forties and early fifties.

A big factor in homogenizing Arabian interests in this early period was the publication of the first all Arabian magazine, the *Arabian Horse News*.

FERSARA (Ferseyn-Bint Sahara)

Its editor was Anna Best Joder of Cheyenne, Wyoming (later of Boulder, Colorado) and not only did she initiate the first publication of an Arabian magazine, but she also was in part responsible for the formation of the West Central States Arabian Horse Association. This club held its first show in Cheyenne in 1949. It had 137 entries, including half Arabs, from twelve different states. Champion stallion was RAFAZ, a son of RIFAGE. Apparently no mare championship was offered, but the *RASEYN mare, ATABI, won the twelve entry mare class. Ward Wells was the judge, and he also gave an exhibition of dressage with his chestnut stallion Sharik. Quarter-mile running races and a walking race were among the more unusual features of this show.

The next year this event went national with classes for national championship competition, although not at all along the same lines of today's Nationals. The *RAFFLES mare CASSANDRA won the rather grandiose title of Grand National Champion Mare, with MIRAZ gaining the equivalent for stallions. This stallion is a three-quarter brother of the fine sire AZRAFF, as he is out of *AZJA IV and by IMAGE. Reserves at this show to the "Grand" titles were MONEYNA and BACARAM, the latter by ALLA AMARWARD. A three judge system was used here for the first time. They were James Dean, Dr. Gordon Stocking and Charlie B. Team. There were 157 entries, including half Arabians, but very few of the purebreds were in the national classes—the majority were entered in the regular show categories. Entries came in from fifteen states.

While I do not have the dates of the first shows of the majority of Arabian associations across the country, I do have one in the Midwest which may serve as an indication of the rise in number of all Arabian shows by area. This is the Illinois show, in 1951, a four day affair with nearly a hundred entries. This is less than at some other shows, but these were purebred only—no half breds. Here a dressage exhibition was also the featured special; the grey stallion KAMLAH (Kemah-Kama) was ridden by Professor Arthur Konyot, a graduate of the Spanish Riding School in Vienna. Champion stallion was AL-MARAH EL HEZZEZ by INDRAFF, with reserve going to RUFFLES, a son of *RAFFLES. Champion mare was RAGUTAYA, by GULASTRA; and ALINTHA, sired by KALAT, was reserve. The mare and foal class was labeled "mare and colt" by which we could assume fillies were barred, but again it's a case of people not knowing that word "foal." Another dilly is a class for "horse colts," a farmer's term for just plain "colts," that is, males. But the howler of the lot was the class for hermaphrodites, apparently, since it was labeled "filly colts." To be equally colloquial, "them animals just ain't."

Before there were all Arabian shows in the East, the big event was the National Stallion Show in Waterloo, Iowa, which included halter classes for colts and stallions, and at first only a costume class for Arabians. Several entered and won well in parade classes however. In fact in 1948, the first three placements went to Arabian stallions, although twelve

181

stallions of other breeds also competed. The halter competition was hardly numerous at this 1948 affair, with only six in the stallion class and a total of ten in the younger classifications. That year's winner was INDRAFF. Consequently having won at the National Stallion Show's Arabian class, he was "National Champion." In 1949 entries were stronger, and RAFMIRZ was champion. This time there were twelve entries in the under-four divisions and a formidible fourteen in the stallion class, which included many champions from other shows. An interesting sidelight is that INDRAFF and RAFMIRZ are three-quarter brothers, both by *RAFFLES but the former is out of *INDAIA while RAFMIRZ is out of a daughter of that mare. SELMAGE like these other two, bred by the Selby Stud, had been winner of the 1947 show; but no other record seems to be available. In the 1949 event he won the costume class as well as the reserve championship to RAFMIRZ. High point of the show however, from the propaganda standpoint, was having an Arabian win the open stock horse class with 28 entries. This whiz was the great little performer ARRAF, also by *RAFFLES, who continued to win in these or cutting events thereafter. Also KARELIAN won the English pleasure class of 25 entries, with all other Arabs entered also placing. KARELIAN is a son of KAHAR. While this show was undoubtedly a good one, and it afforded a better opportunity for publicizing the Arabian and its ability than do the all Arabian shows, it nevertheless lacked something—mares. It might be called discrimination against the fair sex. They and geldings were permitted in some performance classes, but naturally not in halter classes in a show of this name. Therefore it is not surprising that the need for a show of their own was felt in the Midwest, and the Illinois event was a start in that direction.

The Midwest Arabian Horse Owners' association had been organized for a couple of years before it held its first show, having previously confined its efforts to obtaining Arabian classes at open horse shows. Its first show was held in St. Louis, in 1952, with an entry of 122 horses, judged by Ward Wells. Dan Gainey's horses had dominated the Midwest scene for several years, and it was the same here, with GALIMAR going champion stallion and GALIROSE champion mare. They were sire and daughter, and GALIMAR was a son of GAYSAR.

This same year another first took place. There were so many shows on the Pacific Coast that the idea was conceived to hold a Pacific Coast Championship, and thus was started the soon to be snowballing concept of regional shows throughout the country. Dr. William Munson judged this event, placing EL NATTALL champion and ZITEZ reserve in stallions; and FERSARA topped the mares, placing over the first National Champion mare (of the Cheyenne show) CASSANDRA.

The Arabian Horse Club of Oregon should have been mentioned before this as it is the second oldest on the west coast, I believe. Its first show was held in 1947. In 1949 it moved from the Gresham showgrounds to the Portland International Livestock Exposiiton arena. Unfortunately I have no further data on this club and its shows, other than that Ward Wells was its President and/or Show Manager for several years.

By 1950 there were so many Arabian associations that it was felt that a central organization should be formed to harmonize the activities of the local groups. This was the reason for the founding of the International Arabian Horse Association that year in Salt Lake City. Represented at the conference were the Arabian Horse Association of Southern California, The Arabian Horse Association of Northern California, The Arabian Horse Breeders Association of Oregon, the Intermountain Arabian Horse Association and the West Central Arabian Horse Association. It will be noted that the original names had been changed somewhat and by 1950 the California group had already expanded into two, with the resultant regional name changes. In a few months short of twenty years this original five has become ninety, with a total membership of 10,000 people.

The first president was E. E. Hurlbutt of California, and he put in many hours, days and years of hard work on behalf of the International which helped form the structure of the great organization it is today. Succeeding presidents have been Warren Buckley, Illinois; Roy Flippen, Nevada; W. C. Miller, Texas; Joseph H. Buchanan, Iowa; Burr Betts, Colorado; Ivan E. Rowe, Oklahoma; John Rogers, California; Richard Newman, Colorado; Dr. John L. Thomas, Pennsylvania, and as of this writing, Jay Stream of California. Much of the work of the International is carried on through committees numbering something over thirty, covering all internal machinery of the organization and also everything pertaining to the interest and promotion of the Arabian horse, including racing and ranch horse trials. Research and youth activities are two quite different areas also covered. As a sideline the International registers half Arabians, which is quite an industry in itself. The Executive Secretary of the International is Ralph E. Goodall, with offices in Burbank, California.

One aspect of the International that should be mentioned is its score-keeping on show wins and for Legion of Merit. It publishes the beautiful and picture-packed Yearbooks from which the statistics used here are taken. These books were first initiated by Larry and Murl Duff, and the work was eventually taken over by the International. The series of booklets known as The Golden Books are published by this organization also, concerned with all aspects of showing horses.

In 1958 the *Arabian Horse Journal* was born, only to be challenged two years later by stiff competition in the form of *Arabian Horse World*. The latter, with its profuse use of color throughout was, at the time, a new idea in Arabian magazines. The International bought the *Journal* in 1963, and it became *The International Arabian Horse*. Then, in 1965, it was sold to the *Arabian Horse News*, which became the official organ of the International. The *News* is now owned by the Tom Funstons, the

World by the Jay Shulers. Each has whopping issues of about 300 pages with abundant color photos. Noteworthy among the monthly newsstand publications is *Horse & Rider* magazine which devotes considerable attention to the Arabian in each issue. These magazines keep up with all the news, constantly informing the reader of show results, latest techniques and, in general, provide an excellent overall view of the Arabian in America.

FADJUR (Fadheilan-Bint Sahara)   FADHEILAN (*Fadl-*Kasztelanka)

LEADING SIRES OF CHAMPIONS 1953-1970 INCLUSIVE
(Reserve Champions included, but not Junior, Class A shows only)

NAME	NUMBER OF CHAMPIONS	SIRE LINE	MAIN BRANCH. (Not necessarily sire, but main branching of line.)
°Serafix	48	Skowronek (Poland)	Naseem (England)
Ferseyn	38	Skowronek	°Raseyn (England)
Fadjur	35	°Fadl (Egypt)	Fadheilan
Indraff	30	Skowronek	°Raffles (England)
Ga'Zi	29	°Astraled (England)	Abu Farwa
°Witez II	29	Ofir (Poland)	
°Bask	25	Ofir	Witraz (Poland)
°Count Dorsaz	25	°Nureddin II	Rissalix (England)
Sureyn	25	Skowronek	°Raseyn
Ferzon	22	Skowronek	°Raseyn
°Silver Drift	22	Skowronek	Naseem
Azraff	21	Skowronek	°Raffles
Yatez	20	Ofir	°Witez II (Poland)
Rapture	20	Skowronek	°Raffles
Rifraff	19	Skowronek	°Raffles
°Nizzam	18	Skowronek	Naseem
Garaff	18	Skowronek	°Raffles
Al-Marah Radames	17	Skowronek	°Raffles
Ferneyn	17	Skowronek	°Raseyn
Imaraff	17	Skowronek	°Raffles
Abu Baha	15	°Astraled	Abu Farwa
°Naborr	14	Skowronek	Naseem (England, Russia)
Rifage	14	°Mirage DB	
Seneyn	14	Skowronek	°Raseyn
Hanraff	13	Skowronek	°Raffles
Ibn Hanrah	13	°Deyr	Hanad
Synbad	13	°Astraled	Julep
Handeyraff	12	Skowronek	°Raffles
Gazon	11	°Raseyn	Ferseyn
Hallany-Mistanny	11	Ibn Samhan (Egypt)	°Zarife (Egypt)
Julep	11	°Astraled	Gulastra
°Morafic	11	Nazeer (Egypt)	
Rafmirz	11	Skowronek	°Raffles
Aaraf	10	Skowronek	°Raffles
Aarief	10	Skowronek	°Raffles
Abu Farwa	10	°Astraled	Gulastra
Comet (Poland)	10	Kuhailan Afas DB	Abu Afas (Poland)
Geym	10	Skowronek	°Raffles
Kimfa	10	°Muson DB	Mustafa
Naharin	10	°Astraled	Gulastra
Nitez	10	Ofir	°Witez II
Radamason	10	°Raffles	Indraff
°Royal Diamond	10	°Astraled	Oran (England)
The Real McCoy	10	°Raffles	Aarief

SIRES OF 5 TO 9 CHAMPIONS

6— Aahdin	8— Galimar	7— Rafgar
6— Abu Alla	6— Habu	6— Raminage
7— Al-Marah Erka	6— Ibn Hanad	7—°Raseyn
6— Al-Marah Indraff	5— Ibn Mraff	6—°Rithan
7— Al-Marah Safir	7— Image	5— Roayas
8—°Ansata Ibn Halmia	9— Indy	5— Ronek
6— Antezeyn Skowronek	7— Kahar	5— Royal Son
6— Baarouf	7— Lutaf	6— Safinat Afnas
9— Bamby	6— Mishma	6— Shahzada
8— Bay-Abi	8— Mraff	7— Shalimar Gillette
8— Bu-Zahr	7— Mujahid	6— Sharrik
5— Carlani	5— Mustafa	6—°Silver Vanity
9— Cedardell Heritage	5— Nazeer (Egypt)	8— Skorage
7— Courier	6— Phantom	6— Sotep
8— Daareyn	5— Pietuszok (Poland)	6—°Sulejman
6— Disaan	8— Pomona Ahmen	9— Surf
5— Durral	8— Pulque	5— Saneyn
6— El Nahar	8— Rafden	5— Tobruk
9— El Sirocco	7— Raffey	9— Tsali
9— Fadi	6— Raffi	7— Witezar
5— Farlowa	9—°Raffles	6— Zab
		5— Zitez

PERCENTAGE OF CHAMPIONS TO FOALS SIRED

NAME	NO. OF CHAMPIONS	NO. OF FOALS	%	NAME	NO. OF CHAMPIONS	NO. OF FOALS	%
°Serafix	48	130	36%	Rapture	20	139	14%
Ferseyn	38	135	20%	Azraff	21	175	12%
Fadjur	35	351	10%	Ferzon	22	120	18%
Indraff	30	254	14%	Rifraff	19	104	18%
°Witez II	29	211	16%	Yatez	20	138	14%
Ga'Zi	29	154	19%	Garaff	18	183	9%
°Count Dorsaz	25	124	20%	Imaraff	17	172	9%
Sureyn	25	132	19%	°Nizzam	18	120	15%
°Bask	25	115	21%	Ferneyn	17	145	11%
°Silver Drift	22	97	22%	Abu Baha	15	94	15%
				Al-Marah Radames	17	177	9%

(°SERAFIX and °SILVER DRIFT are full brothers and are first and second
respectively in highest percentage of champions)

SIRES OF THREE OR MORE 1970 CHAMPIONS

NAME	TOTAL 1970 CHS.	NEW CHS. 1970	NAME	TOTAL 1970 CHS.	NEW CHS. 1970
°Bask	19	5	°Count Dorsaz	4	0
°Serafix	13	5	Gazon	4	2
°Naborr	11	3	°Nizzam	4	3
Cedardell Heritage	9	7	Pulque	4	1
°Silver Drift	9	4	Tsatyr	4	1
Azraff	8	2	Al-Marah Radames	3	3
°Morafic	8	6	Amerigo	3	2
The Real McCoy	8	5	Antar (Egypt)	3	1
Ferzon	6	3	°Bajram	3	2
°Ansata Ibn Halima	5	3	Fadi	3	2
Bay Abi	5	2	Llano Grande Conquistador	3	1
Ga'Zi	5	3	Niga	3	0
Handeyraff	5	2	Pomona Ahmen	3	1
Ibn Hanrah	5	3	Radamason	3	2
Aahdin	4	3	°Raziri	3	3
Fadjur	4	1	Seraj	3	2
Ferneyn	4	2	Sotep	3	1
Comet (Poland)	4	2	Surf	3	1

(In 1970, 27 sires of 2 champions each; 37 sires of 3 or more champions;
191 sires of 1 champion each)

In order to evaluate a sire's record, the number of his champions
should be compared to the number of foals sired. This was done with the
high-ranked sires in the second chart. However, the number of foals

sired does not always tally with the number shown, since this includes only those registered in Vol. VII (1949-53) to Vol. XIX (1968). Although this does not eliminate older horses from being among the champions, it does nevertheless include the majority of the champions; and the closing date of 1968 allows two-year-olds to be of competitive age.

The list of sires of 1970 champions is included to show the trend, if any, in winning lines. Both new champions of that year and repeaters from former years are shown, indicating whether or not these stallions continue to sire quality foals. Age, of course, would be a factor in number by the old sires, in contrast to their record in their prime.

EXTENSIONS TO TAPROOT SIRES

Although grouped by country, these lines usually involve several countries when traced down to modern times.

Some confusion — as to country of origin — results from the fact that Lady Anne and Wilfrid Blunt maintained the Sheykh Obeyd Stud in Egypt for many years concurrently with Crabbet Park in England. Therefore many a Crabbet line may have been originally Egyptian although bred for several generations in England. This is also true in the reverse, with some Egyptian (R.A.S.) horses.

The BAIRACTAR line of the Weil Stud (Germany) is usually blended with other European lines, especially that of Hungary's Babolna Stud and Polish stock. Russian bloodlines are a combination of English, French, Polish and Egyptian. The SKOWRONEK line through NASEEM is especially cosmopolitan. It starts in England, where NASEEM was bred, then goes to Russia, where NEGATIW and *NABORR were bred, and then to POLAND and for *NABORR, to America.

Many of these foundation sires were named for their strain (or the strain of their sire, when imported to countries where the Bedouin system was not followed) or a combination of strains of both sire and dam, as for instance "Hamdani-Seglawi." None of this name is among the following taproot sires, however.

In several instances the horse's color distinguishes him from others of the same name (in the same stud), as JAMIL EL AHMAR is the "bay Jamil" and DAHMAN EL AZRAK is "the grey Dahman," while another use is of "older" as JAMIL EL KEBIR (the old Jamil) or similar meaning.

TM = Tail Male number, for reference to this number in the subsequent chart of sires of champions.

. . . .

The foundation sire is named at the left, and each name to the right of the preceding name is a son of that horse. Names in column are all sons of the preceding horse.

. . . .

EGYPT:

JAMIL EL KEBIR-JAMIL EL AHMAR-DAHMAN EL AZRAK-RABDAN EL AZRAK┬ SAMHAN II
                                                             │ IBN RABDAN ─┬HAMDAN
                                                             │ *NASR   │IBN FAYDA
                                                                            │*FADL

(JAMIL is often spelled GAMIL.)

TM NO. 1

. . . .

NABRAS
Desertbred — ENZAHI—*MOFTAKHAR

TM NO. 2

. . . .

SAKLAWI I —— FARHAN—— JAMIL III — MANSOUR —— NAZEER
   (FARHAN is also known as SAKLAWI II, and JAMIL III is known as
      GAMIL MANIAL)

TM NO. 3

EGYPT, ENGLAND:

SUEYD DB — SOTTAM — ┃IBN NURA I —— FEYSUL——┨RASIM ————— RASEEM — GREY OWL
┃   ┃IBN YASHMAK
┃IBN SHERERA — KAUKAB — SAHAB

TM NO. 4

· ·

ZOBEYNI ─┨HARKAN — AZIZ — MESAOUD ─┨*ASTRALED ——┨SOTAMM——NAUFAL— RIFFAL—ORAN
┃   ┃   GULASTRA
┃   ┃   RUSTEM
┃
┃   HARB — *RODAN
┃   SEYAL— *BERK
┃   NADIR— JOSEPH — DARGEE
┃
┃WAZIR — MAHRUSS I ─┨MAHRUSS II – RIJM ─┨*NASIK
┃   ┃   *NUREDDIN II
┃*IBN MAHRUSS

TM NO. 5
*Berk imported 1918, his only American bred son is RIBAL. *RODAN imp. en utero 190⁄.
*ASTRALED imported 1909. His only Americanbred son represented here is GULASTRA.

GERMANY (Weil Stud):

BAIRACTAR — AMURATH 1829 – TAJAR 1852 – TAJAR 1862 – TAJAR 1873 — AMURATH 1881 — AMURATH II
Desertbred
Imp. Germany 1817

TM NO. 6
(As these horses so often had the same name, the date of their birth is always included)

HUNGARY (Babolna Stud), POLAND, RUSSIA:

KOHEILAN-ADJUZE — KOHEILAN II – KOHEILAN IV — KOEHILAN I— PIOLUN — PRIBOJ — PIETUSZOK
Desertbred

(KOHEILAN I had been sold to Poland where he was given the number "I." He was later resold to Babolna where he
was given the number VIII. This explains the seeming error in sequence. PIOLUN was bred in Poland, and PRIBOJ and
PIETUSZOK in Russia. PIETUSZOK was sold to Poland)

TM NO. 7

POLAND:

ABU URGUB II ── ATHOS ── ALMANZOR ── ROZMARYN

Desertbred. Imp. Poland c. 1898

TM NO. 8

. . . .

HERMIT── DZINGISHAN III ── *CZUBUTHAN

Desertbred

TM NO. 9
  Imp. Poland 1910

. . . .

ILDERIM──BAKSZYSZ── FETYSZ──┤MIECZNIK──┤DOKTRYNER──┤GERWAZY (England)
Desertbred   *SULEJMAN AQUINOR   *MUZULMANIN

TM NO. 10
  Imp. Poland 1900

. . . .

KRZYZYK── KRZYZYK I── MLECH I──┤ABU MLECH── ENWER BEY── TRYPOLIS──┤*ARDAHAN
Desertbred   FAHER
Imp. Poland 1876   *CYTRYS
                                                      *MOHACZ
                                                      *PILOT
TM NO. 11   ├FARYS II── KASZMIR── GEYRAN   SEDJIWOJ

. . . .

KUHAILAN AFAS──┤BAD AFAS── ABU AFAS── COMET
Desertbred
Imp. Poland 1931 │ARCUS ──BRANIBOR

TM NO. 12

. . . .

KUHAILAN–HAIFI── OFIR──┤*WITEZ II
Desertbred   WIELKI SZLEM
Imp. Poland 1931   WITRAZ

TM NO. 13

══

POLAND, ENGLAND, RUSSIA:

IBRAHIM── SKOWRONEK──┤NASEEM──┤RISSAM── *NIZZAM
Desertbred   IREX──┤CHAMPURRADO──*NIMROD
Imp. Poland 1907   ALEXUS
                                  NEGATIW── *NABORR
TM NO. 14   ├RAKTHA──┤GENERAL GRANT
                                           INDIAN MAGIC
                                           *RITHAN
                                           *SERAFIX
                                           *SILVER DRIFT
                   ├*RAFFLES
                   ├*RASEYN
                   ├*RASWAN──FERHAN──INDIAN GOLD──┤*ROSANTHUS
                                                          *SUN ROYAL

SKOWRONEK imported to England 1913, and all his get are Englishbred.

NASEEM was sold to Russia, where he sired NEGATIW, but all his other sons on this chart were bred in England. Both NEGATIW and *NABORR were sold to Poland, and the latter eventually was imported to the U.S.

*RASWAN died shortly after importation and his line exists only from foals sired in England.

══

ENGLAND:

DWARKA── *ALDEBARAN
Desertbred
Imp. England 1901 TM NO. 15

TAIL MALE LINEAGE OF SIRES OF CHAMPIONS (and Reserves) 1953-1970 INCLUSIVE

This is based on Yearbook records only, and Junior champions are not included, nor are champions of other than Class A shows. Accordingly there are probably other champions to be credited to some of these horses, and especially so in those Class A shows which did not send results in to the Yearbook, as happened in the early years.

This is tail male tracing only, i.e. through sons only, never through daughters.

Underscored numbers are main branch or line total, those in parentheses following a horse's name are the number of champions sired by that horse, and numbers in brackets are those of a sub-branch total.

Read from left to right – sire, son, grandson, greatgrandson, etc.

Names in column and connected by a vertical line are sons of the preceding horse when there are two or more by the same sire. In some instances the line founder is sire of a champion. Example: *RAFFLES is the founder of one branch from SKOWRONEK. He is himself sire of nine champions, his son AARAF is the sire of ten, so is written AARAF (10), and he in turn is the sire of several sons, listed in column, as also are the many sons of *RAFFLES, listed in column below the name of AARAF, since he leads in alphabetical order.

Refer to preceding chart for founders of the various lines. TM = Tail male chart number.

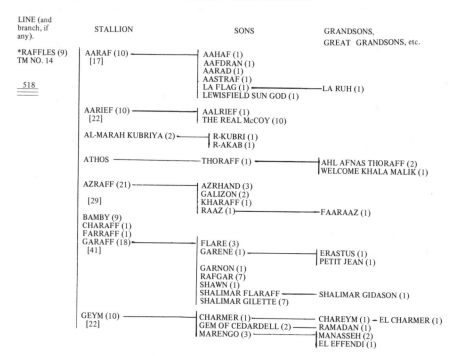

LINE (and branch, if any).	STALLION	SONS	GRANDSONS, GREAT GRANDSONS, etc.
*RAFFLES (9) TM NO. 14	AARAF (10) [17]	AAHAF (1) AAFDRAN (1) AARAD (1) AASTRAF (1) LA FLAG (1) LEWISFIELD SUN GOD (1)	LA RUH (1)
518	AARIEF (10) [22]	AALRIEF (1) THE REAL McCOY (10)	
	AL-MARAH KUBRIYA (2)	R-KUBRI (1) R-AKAB (1)	
	ATHOS	THORAFF (1)	AHL AFNAS THORAFF (2) WELCOME KHALA MALIK (1)
	AZRAFF (21) [29]	AZRHAND (3) GALIZON (2) KHARAFF (1) RAAZ (1)	FAARAAZ (1)
	BAMBY (9) CHARAFF (1) FARRAFF (1) GARAFF (18) [41]	FLARE (3) GARENE (1) GARNON (1) RAFGAR (7) SHAWN (1) SHALIMAR FLARAFF SHALIMAR GILETTE (7)	ERASTUS (1) PETIT JEAN (1) SHALIMAR GIDASON (1)
	GEYM (10) [22]	CHARMER (1) GEM OF CEDARDELL (2) MARENGO (3)	CHAREYM (1) – EL CHARMER (1) RAMADAN (1) MANASSEH (2) EL EFFENDI (1)

190

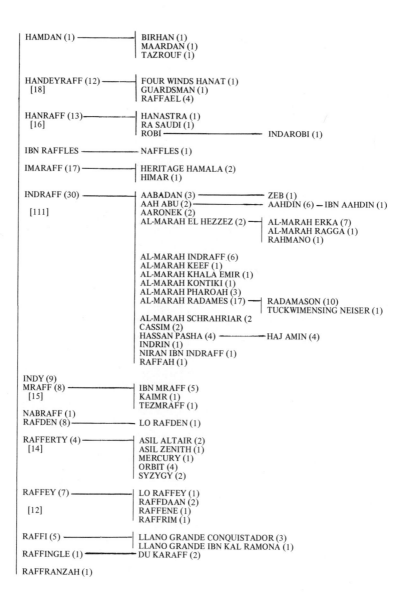

*RAFFLES
(cont'd.)

HAMDAN (1) ——————— BIRHAN (1)
MAARDAN (1)
TAZROUF (1)

HANDEYRAFF (12) ——————— FOUR WINDS HANAT (1)
[18] GUARDSMAN (1)
RAFFAEL (4)

HANRAFF (13) ——————— HANASTRA (1)
[16] RA SAUDI (1)
ROBI ——————————————— INDAROBI (1)

IBN RAFFLES ——————— NAFFLES (1)

IMARAFF (17) ——————— HERITAGE HAMALA (2)
HIMAR (1)

INDRAFF (30) ——————— AABADAN (3) ——————————— ZEB (1)
AAH ABU (2) ——————————— AAHDIN (6) — IBN AAHDIN (1)
[111] AARONEK (2)
AL-MARAH EL HEZZEZ (2) — AL-MARAH ERKA (7)
AL-MARAH RAGGA (1)
RAHMANO (1)

AL-MARAH INDRAFF (6)
AL-MARAH KEEF (1)
AL-MARAH KHALA EMIR (1)
AL-MARAH KONTIKI (1)
AL-MARAH PHAROAH (3)
AL-MARAH RADAMES (17) — RADAMASON (10)
TUCKWIMENSING NEISER (1)
AL-MARAH SCHRAHRIAR (2
CASSIM (2)
HASSAN PASHA (4) ——————— HAJ AMIN (4)
INDRIN (1)
NIRAN IBN INDRAFF (1)
RAFFAH (1)

INDY (9)
MRAFF (8) ——————— IBN MRAFF (5)
[15] KAIMR (1)
TEZMRAFF (1)
NABRAFF (1)
RAFDEN (8) ——————— LO RAFDEN (1)

RAFFERTY (4) ——————— ASIL ALTAIR (2)
[14] ASIL ZENITH (1)
MERCURY (1)
ORBIT (4)
SYZYGY (2)

RAFFEY (7) ——————— LO RAFFEY (1)
RAFFDAAN (2)
[12] RAFFENE (1)
RAFFRIM (1)

RAFFI (5) ——————— LLANO GRANDE CONQUISTADOR (3)
LLANO GRANDE IBN KAL RAMONA (1)
RAFFINGLE (1) ——————— DU KARAFF (2)

RAFFRANZAH (1)

191

RAFFLES
(cont'd.)

RAFISCO ——————— LO FISCO (1)
RAFMIRZ (11)——————— NEVER DIE ARION (1)

RAFOURID (1)

RAFGAR (7) ———————| IBN RAFGAR (1)
                   | KELLYAR (1)

RAPTURE (20) ———————| AL-MARAH CASSANOVA (2)
      [42] | DUMAH ——————————— IBN DU (1)
                    | IBN AL ——————————— SEAHORSE ALFAR (1)
                    | KOPTOS (1)
                    | LAUREN (1) ——————— LAUKIT (4)
                    | MISHMA (6)
                    | RAPSON (1)
                    | SYN RAPTURE (1)
                    | TAIB (2)
                    | TORRI (1)
                    | NAFSI (1)

RASRAFF——————— AZIZ (2)

TUT ANK AMEN (1)———————| EL DINARI (4) ——————— DARKITH (1)
                        | RAF-TUT (4)
                        | RAMOSE (1)

RIFFLES ——————— UDANDIE (1)

RIFRAFF (19) ———————| QADI (1)
     [23] | RAFFRAY (1)
                    | SEAHORSE THUNDER (2)

RUFFLES (4) ———————| RAUDI (1)
                   | RIPTIDE (1)

SHAYK (1)
SOTEP (6)———————| NA IBN SOTEP (2)
                | SO KET (1)

TIRAFF (3)

VICTOR HUGO (1)
WASL RAFFLES (3)

*RAFFLES was imported 1932
TOTAL *RAFFLES: 518

. . . .

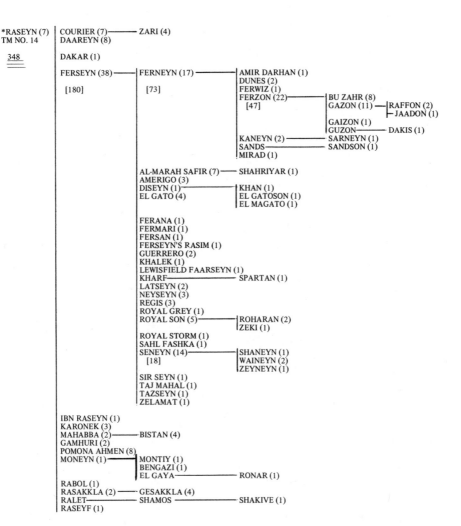

*RASEYN (7)
TM NO. 14

348

COURIER (7)——— ZARI (4)
DAAREYN (8)

DAKAR (1)

FERSEYN (38)——— FERNEYN (17)——— AMIR DARHAN (1)
[180]   [73]   DUNES (2)
                                         FERWIZ (1)
                                         FERZON (22)——— BU ZAHR (8)
                                         [47]   GAZON (11)——— RAFFON (2)
                                                                      └ JAADON (1)
                                                         GAIZON (1)
                                                         GUZON——— DAKIS (1)
                                         KANEYN (2)——— SARNEYN (1)
                                         SANDS——— SANDSON (1)
                                         MIRAD (1)

                     AL-MARAH SAFIR (7)——— SHAHRIYAR (1)
                     AMERIGO (3)
                     DISEYN (1)   KHAN (1)
                     EL GATO (4)   EL GATOSON (1)
                                          EL MAGATO (1)

                     FERANA (1)
                     FERMARI (1)
                     FERSAN (1)
                     FERSEYN'S RASIM (1)
                     GUERRERO (2)
                     KHALEK (1)
                     LEWISFIELD FAARSEYN (1)
                     KHARF——— SPARTAN (1)
                     LATSEYN (2)
                     NEYSEYN (3)
                     REGIS (3)
                     ROYAL GREY (1)
                     ROYAL SON (5)——— ROHARAN (2)
                                      ZEKI (1)
                     ROYAL STORM (1)
                     SAHL FASHKA (1)
                     SENEYN (14)——— SHANEYN (1)
                     [18]   WAINEYN (2)
                                    ZEYNEYN (1)
                     SIR SEYN (1)
                     TAJ MAHAL (1)
                     TAZSEYN (1)
                     ZELAMAT (1)

          IBN RASEYN (1)
          KARONEK (3)
          MAHABBA (2)——— BISTAN (4)
          GAMHURI (2)
          POMONA AHMEN (8)
          MONEYN (1)——— MONTIY (1)
                         BENGAZI (1)
                         EL GAYA——— RONAR (1)
          RABOL (1)
          RASAKKLA (2)——— GESAKKLA (4)
          RALET——— SHAMOS ——— SHAKIVE (1)
          RASEYF (1)

193

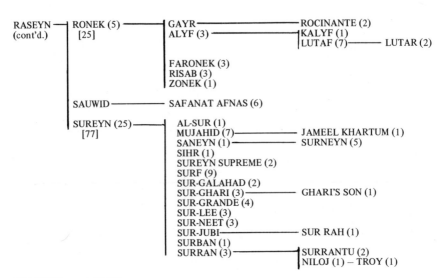

RASEYN — RONEK (5) ———— GAYR ———————————— ROCINANTE (2)
(cont'd.)   [25]   ALYF (3) ————————— KALYF (1)
                                                 LUTAF (7) ——— LUTAR (2)

                              FARONEK (3)
                              RISAB (3)
                              ZONEK (1)

             SAUWID ————————— SAFANAT AFNAS (6)

             SUREYN (25) ——— AL-SUR (1)
             [77]   MUJAHID (7) ————————— JAMEEL KHARTUM (1)
                              SANEYN (1) ——————— SURNEYN (5)
                              SIHR (1)
                              SUREYN SUPREME (2)
                              SURF (9)
                              SUR-GALAHAD (2)
                              SUR-GHARI (3) ——— GHARI'S SON (1)
                              SUR-GRANDE (4)
                              SUR-LEE (3)
                              SUR-NEET (3)
                              SUR-JUBI ——————— SUR RAH (1)
                              SURBAN (1)
                              SURRAN (3) ————————— SURRANTU (2)
                                                  NILOJ (1) – TROY (1)

*RASEYN imported 1926
TOTAL *RASEYN: 348

194

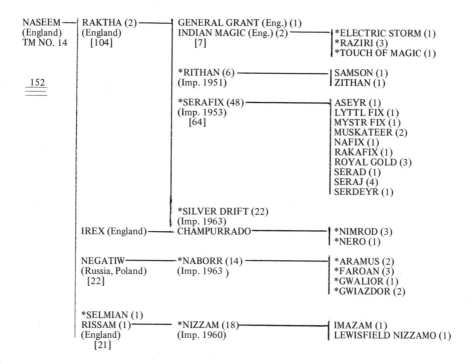

NASEEM —| RAKTHA (2) ——————| GENERAL GRANT (Eng.) (1)
(England) (England)   INDIAN MAGIC (Eng.) (2) ——————|*ELECTRIC STORM (1)
TM NO. 14 [104]   [7] |*RAZIRI (3)
                                                           |*TOUCH OF MAGIC (1)

                            *RITHAN (6) ——————————|SAMSON (1)
   152   (Imp. 1951) |ZITHAN (1)

                            *SERAFIX (48)——————————|ASEYR (1)
                            (Imp. 1953) |LYTTL FIX (1)
                               [64] |MYSTR FIX (1)
                                                  |MUSKATEER (2)
                                                  |NAFIX (1)
                                                  |RAKAFIX (1)
                                                  |ROYAL GOLD (3)
                                                  |SERAD (1)
                                                  |SERAJ (4)
                                                  |SERDEYR (1)

                            *SILVER DRIFT (22)
                            (Imp. 1963)
          IREX (England)——— CHAMPURRADO——————————|*NIMROD (3)
                                                  |*NERO (1)

          NEGATIW——————————*NABORR (14) ——————————|*ARAMUS (2)
          (Russia, Poland) (Imp. 1963) |*FAROAN (3)
              [22] |*GWALIOR (1)
                                                  |*GWIAZDOR (2)

          *SELMIAN (1)
          RISSAM (1)———————— *NIZZAM (18)———————|IMAZAM (1)
          (England)   (Imp. 1960) |LEWISFIELD NIZZAMO (1)
             [21]

TOTAL NASEEM: 152

```
*RASWAN———FERHAN——— INDIAN GOLD ─┐ ROSANTHUS (2) ──┤ KING FEISAL (1)
TM 14                              │ 14               │ HAZEM BEY (4)
                                   │                  │ IBN ROWHARA (1)
15                                 │                  │ MARGHEB (2)
══                                 │                  └ SILVER CRESCENT (3)—— Crescent's Ali (1)
                                   │
                                   │ SUN ROYAL (1)
```

TOTAL *RASWAN:

*RASWAN was imported in 1926 but sired no foals in America. The line survives through FERHAN only, in tail male, but he did sire two daughters, both of which were influential.

. . . .

TOTAL SKOWRONEK:1033

Through   *RAFFLES: 518
                  *RASEYN :   348
                  *RASWAN :   15

                  NASEEM   :   152

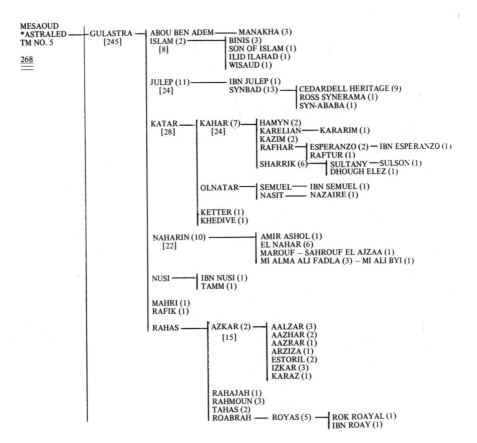

MESAOUD
*ASTRALED —— GULASTRA —— ABOU BEN ADEM —— MANAKHA (3)
TM NO. 5   [245]   ISLAM (2) ———— BINIS (3)
                                 [8]   SON OF ISLAM (1)
268   ILID ILAHAD (1)
≡   WISAUD (1)

                               JULEP (11) ———— IBN JULEP (1)
                                 [24]   SYNBAD (13) ———— CEDARDELL HERITAGE (9)
                                                                ROSS SYNERAMA (1)
                                                                SYN-ABABA (1)

                               KATAR ———— KAHAR (7) ———— HAMYN (2)
                                 [28]   [24]   KARELIAN ———— KARARIM (1)
                                                         KAZIM (2)
                                                         RAFHAR ———— ESPERANZO (2) — IBN ESPERANZO (1)
                                                                     RAFTUR (1)
                                                         SHARRIK (6) ———— SULTANY ——SULSON (1)
                                                                          DHOUGH ELEZ (1)

                                          OLNATAR ———— SEMUEL ——— IBN SEMUEL (1)
                                                       NASIT ——— NAZAIRE (1)

                                          KETTER (1)
                                          KHEDIVE (1)

                               NAHARIN (10) ———— AMIR ASHOL (1)
                                 [22]   EL NAHAR (6)
                                                 MAROUF – SAHROUF EL AJZAA (1)
                                                 MI ALMA ALI FADLA (3) – MI ALI BYI (1)

                               NUSI ——— IBN NUSI (1)
                                        TAMM (1)

                               MAHRI (1)
                               RAFIK (1)

                               RAHAS ———— AZKAR (2) ——— AALZAR (3)
                                            [15]   AAZHAR (2)
                                                          AAZRAR (1)
                                                          ARZIZA (1)
                                                          ESTORIL (2)
                                                          IZKAR (3)
                                                          KARAZ (1)

                                          RAHAJAH (1)
                                          RAHMOUN (3)
                                          TAHAS (2)
                                          ROABRAH ——— ROYAS (5) ——— ROK ROAYAL (1)
                                                                    IBN ROAY (1)

197

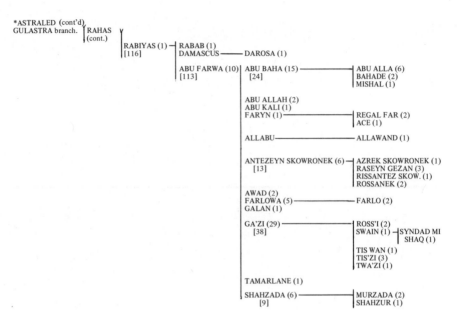

*ASTRALED (cont'd)
GULASTRA branch. RAHAS
(cont.)

RABIYAS (1) — RABAB (1)
[116]   DAMASCUS ——— DAROSA (1)

ABU FARWA (10) ABU BAHA (15) ——————— ABU ALLA (6)
[113]   [24]   BAHADE (2)
                                        MISHAL (1)

ABU ALLAH (2)
ABU KALI (1)
FARYN (1) ——————— REGAL FAR (2)
                   ACE (1)

ALLABU ————————————————— ALLAWAND (1)

ANTEZEYN SKOWRONEK (6) — AZREK SKOWRONEK (1)
[13]   RASEYN GEZAN (3)
                         RISSANTEZ SKOW. (1)
                         ROSSANEK (2)

AWAD (2)
FARLOWA (5) ——————— FARLO (2)
GALAN (1)

GA'ZI (29) ——————— ROSS'I (2)
[38]   SWAIN (1) — SYNDAD MI
                               SHAQ (1)
                   TIS WAN (1)
                   TIS'ZI (3)
                   TWA'ZI (1)

TAMARLANE (1)

SHAHZADA (6) ——————— MURZADA (2)
[9]   SHAHZUR (1)

TOTAL GULASTRA: 245

198

*ASTRALED — SOTAMM — NAUFAL — RIFFAL — VICTORY DAY II (1)
TM NO. 5   23   (England)   [23]   ORAN (2) ————————— SILVER VANITY (6)
                                          (England)   GRAND ROYAL —*ROYAL CONSTELLATION (4)
                                          [22]   (Eng.)
                                                           *ROYAL DIAMOND (1)

*ROYAL DIAMOND imported 1957, *SILVER VANITY 1962, *ROYAL CONSTELLATION 1957.

. . . .

TOTAL *ASTRALED: 268

Through GULASTRA: 245
        SOTAMM: 23

_____

NADIR branch TM NO. 5

    NADIR— JOSEPH — MANASSEH — *AANASSEH (1)
             (England)
           RISHAN — RADI—BRIGHT SHADOW— *BRIGHT DIAMOND (1) — BRIGHT JADIAMOND (1)
             (England)

. . . .

SEYAL branch TM NO. 5

SEYAL———— *BERK———— RIBAL— GHADAF (2)— MAHUBI (1)
                      15   JADIB (1)

   15   BORKAAN —— SARIF SERIK (1)
   =   GHAWI ———— HASSEN BEY (1) —— RASAN (2)— SHALIMAR TARDE (4)
                                                                   FAESON (1)
                            CARAVAN —— JUBILO (2)

. . . .

HARB branch, TM NO. 5

HARB — *RODAN — GHAZI— GHAZIBROA — GABILAN (1)
                  4   GHAZIDAH (1)
   4   GHAZITA (1)
   =   JEDRAN————————JEZAYAT ————JEZRA (1)

.. . .

TOTAL MESAOUD branch: 290

Through   *ASTRALED: 290
                   NADIR: 268
                   SEYAL: 3
                   HARB: 15
                                               4

199

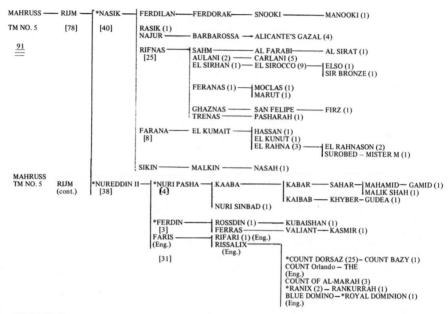

MAHRUSS ── RIJM ── ┌ *NASIK ── FERDILAN── ──FERDORAK── ── SNOOKI ───────────────MANOOKI (1)

TM NO. 5   [78]   [40]   RASIK (1)
                                 NAJUR ──── BARBAROSSA ──▶ ALICANTE'S GAZAL (4)

  91   RIFNAS──────── SAHM ──────── AL FARABI─────── AL SIRAT (1)
  ══   [25]   AULANI (2) ──── CARLANI (5)
                                                EL SIRHAN (1)── EL SIROCCO (9)──┤ELSO (1)
                                                                                │SIR BRONZE (1)

                                                FERANAS (1)──┤MOCLAS (1)
                                                             │MARUT (1)

                                                GHAZNAS ──────── SAN FELIPE ──────── FIRZ (1)
                                                TRENAS ──────── PASHARAH (1)

                                 FARANA──────── EL KUMAIT──────┤HASSAN (1)
                                 [8]   │EL KUNUT (1)
                                                              │EL RAHNA (3) ──┤EL RAHNASON (2)
                                                                              │SUROBED ── MISTER M (1)

                                 SIKIN ──────── MALKIN ─────────── NASAH (1)

MAHRUSS
TM NO. 5   RIJM   *NUREDDIN II──┤ *NURI PASHA ─── KAABA──────────┤ KABAR ─── SAHAR──┤MAHAMID── GAMID (1)
(cont.)   (cont.)   [38]   [4]   │   │MALIK SHAH (1)
                                                                 │KAIBAB ── KHYBER─ GUDEA (1)
                                                     └ NURI SINBAD (1)

                                  *FERDIN──────┤ ROSSDIN (1) ──────── KUBAISHAN (1)
                                  [3]   │ FERRAS──────── VALIANT── KASMIR (1)
                                  FARIS ──────┤ RIFARI (1) (Eng.)
                                  (Eng.)   RISSALIX──┐
                                                 (Eng.) │
                                  [31]   └ *COUNT DORSAZ (25)── COUNT BAZY (1)
                                                           COUNT Orlando ── THE
                                                           (Eng.)
                                                           COUNT OF AL-MARAH (3)
                                                           *RANIX (2) ── RANKURRAH (1)
                                                           BLUE DOMINO──*ROYAL DOMINION (1)
                                                           (Eng.)

TOTAL RIJM: 78

*NASIK imported 1926, *NUREDDIN II in 1933, *FERDIN imp. en utero 1926, *COUNT DORSAZ imp. in 1959.
Some sons of imported stallions, in this and other pedigrees, were foaled in other countries, and usually these
stay-at-homes are so indicated, as are foreign sires which sired horses which became American champions.

```
*IBN MAHRUSS ── EL SABOK── STAMBUL─┐ ALLA AMARWARD (1) ─┐ ALLA HANNA (1)
TM NO. 5                 [13]    │  [12]               │ WARDAMAR ALL (1)
Imp. en utero 1900,             │                     │ BACARAM (1)
    foaled 1901.                │                     │ ALLA JO (1)
                                │                     │ EL NATTALL (3) ─┐ EL NATTALL (3)
                                │                                      │ EL BIERNATT (1)
13                              │                                      │ EL NARAYIK (1)
                                │                                      │ RASOULMATALL (2)
                                │
                                └ BEDAWI ── CALIPH ── HAMIDA'S DAHMAN (1)
```

. . . .

TOTAL MAHRUSS: 91

Through RIJM: 78
*IBN MAHRUSS: 13

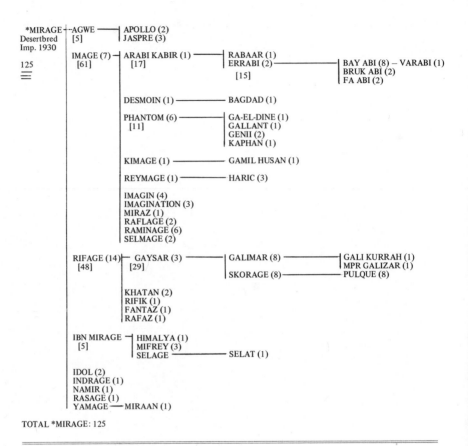

```
*MIRAGE ─┬─AGWE ──────┬ APOLLO (2)
Desertbred │  [5]       │ JASPRE (3)
Imp. 1930  │
           │ IMAGE (7) ─┬ ARABI KABIR (1) ──────┬ RABAAR (1)
125        │  [61]      │  [17]                  │ ERRABI (2)──────────┬ BAY ABI (8) – VARABI (1)
═══        │            │                        │    [15]             │ BRUK ABI (2)
           │            │                        │                     │ FA ABI (2)
           │            │
           │            │ DESMOIN (1) ─────────── BAGDAD (1)
           │            │
           │            │ PHANTOM (6) ─────────┬ GA-EL-DINE (1)
           │            │  [11]                │ GALLANT (1)
           │            │                      │ GENII (2)
           │            │                      │ KAPHAN (1)
           │            │
           │            │ KIMAGE (1) ─────────── GAMIL HUSAN (1)
           │            │
           │            │ REYMAGE (1) ────────── HARIC (3)
           │            │
           │            │ IMAGIN (4)
           │            │ IMAGINATION (3)
           │            │ MIRAZ (1)
           │            │ RAFLAGE (2)
           │            │ RAMINAGE (6)
           │            │ SELMAGE (2)
           │
           │ RIFAGE (14)─┬ GAYSAR (3) ──────┬ GALIMAR (8) ─────────┬ GALI KURRAH (1)
           │  [48]       │  [29]            │                      │ MPR GALIZAR (1)
           │             │                  │ SKORAGE (8)─────────── PULQUE (8)
           │             │
           │             │ KHATAN (2)
           │             │ RIFIK (1)
           │             │ FANTAZ (1)
           │             │ RAFAZ (1)
           │
           │ IBN MIRAGE ─┬ HIMALYA (1)
           │  [5]        │ MIFREY (3)
           │             │ SELAGE ─────────── SELAT (1)
           │
           │ IDOL (2)
           │ INDRAGE (1)
           │ NAMIR (1)
           │ RASAGE (1)
           └ YAMAGE ── MIRAAN (1)
```

TOTAL *MIRAGE: 125

```
*FADL (4) ──┤ ABOU (1)
TM NO. 1    │ FADDAN ──┤ FAD-ZARKA ── SA ZARKA (1)
            │ [4]      │ DAALDAN (1)
Imported 1932          │ MAHROUN (1)
                       │ SABDAAN (1)


113


            │ FABAH (2) ──── HADBAH (1)
            │ FADHEILAN (3) ─┤ FADEYN (1)
            │ [60]           │ FADJUR (35) ────┤ FADI (90)
            │                │ [55]            │ FADKI (1)
            │                                  │ FARJUR (1)
            │                                  │ IBN FADJUR (4)
            │                                  │ NADJUR (1)
            │                                  │ SHA RA ZADA (3)
            │                                  │ FLADJUR (1)

            │                │ ZURF ────────── ZURAMET (1)

            │ FA-EL-GEMAR (2)─┤ LDAF (1)
            │                 │ GULAM (2)

            │ RA RABDAN (1) ── ROJKIH (1)

            │ FA-TURF (1)

            │ FAY-EL-DINE (3)─┤ ATHI (1)
            │                 │ DISAAN (6) ────┤ CARASAAN (2)
            │ [25]            │ [12]           │ MAARDI (2)
            │                                  │ ROUSAAN (1)
            │                                  │ TISAAN (1)

            │                 │ GABBAR (2)
            │                 │ ZAB (6) ────────── DINERO (1)

            │ KHEBIR (1)

            │ FA-SERR (4) ──┤ FAARIS (1)
            │ [10]          │ FASEROUF (2)
            │               │ SERG (1)
            │               │ NEGEM (2)

            │ GAYF (1)
```

TOTAL *FADL: 113

. . . .

SAMHAN II ─ IBN SAMHAN ─ *ZARIFE (2) ─┤ HALLANY-MISTANNY (10) ─PRINCE HALLANY (1)
                                      │ ZARAK (2)

TM NO. 1

TOTAL *ZARIFE: 15 *ZARIFE imported 1932

```
*NASR ─────────┤ AMYR NASR (1)

TM NO. 1         SIRECHO (1) ───────┤ JORAMIR (2)
                                    │ ATIR (1)
Imported 1932      [5]              │ IBN SIRECHO (1)


                 PTOLOMY──────── HAMPTON (1)
 11              TIRS (1) ─────── ZINGARO (1)
 ══              UMAR AL KHAYYAM (2)
```

TOTAL *NASR: 11

. . . .

IBN FAYDA – EL MOEZ – SAMEH (3) – SULTAN (1)
TM NO. 1   (Egypt)
              (None of these horses were themselves imported, but are
              represented by imports which became champions)

TOTAL IBN FAYDA: 4

. . . .

HAMDAN – ANTAR (3)
TM NO. 1   (Egypt)

. . . .

TOTAL   RABDAN EL AZRAK: 146
           Through IBN RABDAN: 120 – (HAMDAN: 3, IBN FAYDA: 4, *FADL: 113)
           SAMHAN II: 15
           *NASR: 11

═══

```
NAZEER (5)──┤ *ANSATA IBN HALIMA (8)    (Imported 1959 as yearling)
(Egypt)       *GHALII (1)               (Imported 1960)
TM NO. 3      *MORAFIC (11)             (Imported 1965)
              GALAL (1)
 27           (Egypt)
 ══

              HADBAN ENZAHI – *DALIH (1) (Imported 1962)
                 (Germany)
```

TOTAL NAZEER: 27

═══

*MOFTAKHAR (4)   KAMIL IBN MOFTAKHAR (1)
TM NO. 2
Imported 1951
TOTAL *MOFTAKHAR: 5

204

```
OFIR ─────────┤ WITRAZ (Poland) (2) ─────────────── *BASK (25)
(Poland)      │ WIELKI SZLEM (Poland) (1)────────── CZORT (1) (Poland)—*CZORTAN (1)

TM NO. 13     │ *WITEZ II (29)─────────────┤ AHSAN (1)
134           │ [104]                       │ AWIZ (1)
═══                                         │ BLACK MAGIC (1)
                                            │ BOLERO (3)
                                            │ CAIRO (2)
                                            │ HIRZAN (1)─────────── SUGA (1)
                                            │ IWONKATEX (1)
                                            │ KUHAYLAN TEZ──── TEZ (1)
                                            │ CARTEZ (1)
                                            │ NATEZ (4)
                                            │ RIFTEZ (1)
                                            │ NITEZ (10) ────────┤ IMATEZ (1)
                                            │ [19]                │ NIGA (3)── GAMAAR (1)
                                            │                     │ GURTEZ (1)
                                            │                     │ GALAH (1)─┤GAILLAC (1)
                                            │                                 │GAYATH (1)
                                            │
                                            │
                                            │ WITEZAN (1)
                                            │ WITEZAR (4)─────── ZAZAR (1)
                                            │ WITEZRO (2)
                                            │ ZEST (1)
                                            │ YATEZ (20) ───────┤ AMZI (1)
                                            │ [23]               │ SHARR (2)
                                            │ ZITEZ (5)          │ ADIBIYEZ (1)
```

TOTAL OFIR: 134

      *WITEZ II imported 1945, *BASK 1963, *CZORTAN (en utero) 1962

ABU URGUB II
ROZMARYN (Poland) (1)
TM NO. 8

AMURATH SAHIB────┤ ARAX (Poland) (1)
              │ GWARNY─────────── *KIRKOR (1)

TM NO. 6
TOTAL: 2 *KIRKOR imported 1964

DZIGHISHAN III (Poland) — *CZUBUTHAN (1) — ROMBLON (2)

TM NO. 9

TOTAL: 3   *CZUBUTHAN imported 1938

```
FETYSZ ───|MIECZNIK─────── DOKTRYNER (1) ─|GERWAZY (3)
TM NO. 10 |                (Poland)        |(England)
          |                   [6]          |
          |                                |
          |                                | *MUZULMANIN (1) – MUZAMAR (1)
  24      | *SULEJMAN (6)──| JASUL (1)
  ══      |    [18]        | SHASUL (1)
          |               | SULMIR (1)
          |               | TOBRUK (5) ─────── IBN TOBRUK── ZABAD──TOBIZAB (1)
          |               |                                        ZABEZ (2)
          |               | KOMSUL (1)
```

TOTAL FETYSZ: 24
          *SULEJMAN imported 1938, *MUZULMANIN 1961

```
KOHEILAN I – PIOLUN – PRIBOJ – PIETUSZOK (5) – *BAJRAM (3)
TM NO. 7             (Russia)  (Russia, Poland)   (Imp. 1963)
```

TOTAL: 8

```
KUHAILAN AFAS ─| BAD AFAS──── ABU AFAS─────── COMET (10)
Desertbred     |                              (Poland)
               | ARCUS ─────── BRANIBOR (1)
TM NO. 7       |               (Poland)
TOTAL: 11
```

```
MLECH I ──| ABU MLECH ── ENWER BEY── TRYPOLIS (2) ─| *ARDAHAN (4)
TM NO. 11 |                          (Poland)       | *CYTRYS (2)
          |                            [15]         | FAHER (Poland) (2)
16        |                                         | *MOHACZ (1)
          |                                         | *PILOT (1) - TRYSEYN (1)
          |                                         | SEDZIWOJ (Poland) (1)
          |
          | FARYS II ────── KASZMIR ──────GEYRAN (1)
          |                              (Poland)
```

TOTAL MLECH I: 16
          *ARDAHAN, *MOHACZ and *CYTRYS imported 1961, *PILOT 1945

```
*DEYR ——— HANAD (1) —— NADDIE (1)
Desertbred        [51]       MAINAD ——— IBN MAINAD ——————— LADIGO (1)

Imported to U.S.           HANRAH (4)— IBN HANRAH (13) ——— FAYHAN (2)
1906                          [22]                            DON IBN HANRAH (1)
72                                                            DON FERSHEBA (1)
===                                                          BEAU IBN HANRAH (1)

                           ADOUNAD (1)—ADOUNAD'S LEGEND (1)
                           AMEER ALI——AARFAT (1)
                           HASAB ——— HASARIP (1)

                           IBN HANAD (6)—SUNNY ACRES TEQUILA (2) — SHAL TEKE (1)
                             [23]        TSALI (9)—TYSATYR (3)
                                         SUNNY ACRES CHEROKEE (1)
                                         SUNNY ACRES DARIUS (1)

          HARARA ——— ANTEZ ——————— ANKAR (3) ——— DAUFIN (2)
                                      [17]         BUNA (3)— HABU (6)
                                                   ANKAZAN (1)
                                                   JOANKAR — ALLA JO KAR — JOKKAR (2)

                                   *LATIF ——————— POTIF — NATIF ┤ BEHTIF (1)
                                     [4]           FERTIF (1)    └ YLIF (1)
                                                   ASSURBANIPAL — EL GRAND HALIFA — IBN HALIFA (1)
```

TOTAL *DEYR: 72

(ANTEZ was sold to Poland in 1934 or '35 and was re-sold back to the U.S. after siring only ten foals in three years.
However his Polishbred foals total 12, since one — *LATIF — was exported with his dam and the other was imported
en utero.)

```
*MUSON ——— LETAN ─┤ DHAREB (1)
Desertbred            │
Imported to the       │ ORIENTAL —— MUSTAKIM —— MUSTAFA (5) —— KIMFA (10) —— KIMKEM (1)
U.S. 1906             │ AKIL——————— RASSOUL (1)

TOTAL: 18
```

```
*ABBEIAN ——— ASHMAR ——— KOKHLESON ——— RALF (2) ——— EL IBITIDA (1)
Desertbred
Imported either 1893 or (less probably ) 1906.
```

```
*ALDEBAR—┤ KALAT ————— PADISHAH (2) ———JERAH (1)
TM NO. 15 │ DURRAL (5) ——— IBN DURRAL (1)
          │ BAAROUF (6)——┤MAIROUF (1)
          │              │ROUF (1)

Imported
1940
TOTAL: 15
```

```
*NEJDRAN——— NEJDRAN JR.—— ALCAZAR (1) —┤ ALHAAMED (1)
Desertbred                               │ KALUSTAN (1)
Imported 1904                            │ KATUN (1)-KULUN (1)
                                         │ KHALDI (4) — SHABURA (1)
```

```
*KISMET ───────── *NIMR─── KHALED┤ SIDI ── BABYAT──── YBABI (4) ────────┤ NA HAKIM (1)
Desertbred                        │                                     │ FE BABI (1)

Imported to
England 1882,                     │ RAAS ── RAASAUD ── RAASMARYN (1) ─ RAASWOOD (1)
and to U.S. 1891,
but died on arrival.
```

TOTAL: 8

GREY OWL (3)
(England)

TM NO. 4

---

*MOUNWER (1) — MOURNRI (1)
Desertbred
Imported 1947

---

*ZAMAL (1)
Desertbred
Imported 1947

TOTAL CHAMPIONS: 2051

Sire Line		Sire Line	
SKOWRONEK	1033	KUHAILAN-AFAS	11
MESAOUD	290	*NEJDRAN	10
RABDAN	146	KOHEILAN I	8
OFIR	134	*KISMET	8
*MIRAGE	125	NABRAS	5
MAHRUSS	91	*ABBEIAN	3
*DEYR	72	HERMIT	3
NAZEER	27	SUEYD	3
FETYSZ	24	AMURATH	2
*MUSON	18	*MOUNWER	2
*ALDEBAR	17	ABU URGUB II	1
MLECH I	16	*ZAMAL	1

The Legion of Merit winners are important to a degree, in that they reflect the performance ability as well as conformation and type of the horses involved. The award is based on points won at halter and in performance, and while most of the winners are champions, not all have attained that honor. Some are stakes winners in performance, others have made the grade with lesser wins but in greater quantity. While a good percentage of these are park horses, the majority have gained the award through pleasure classes. Others are jumpers, some are stock horses, and so on. I believe that show classes were the qualifying ones at first for the performance points, but that more rigorous types of performance are now, or soon to be, considered in this context. This would include racing, ranch horse trials, endurance rides and so on. Several of the best race horses are also show champions. An outstanding example is the great runner *ORZEL, now a show champion, after winning the "championship" in racing (1½ mile races, carrying up to 142 lbs.) in 1968. He also won as a three-year-old in Poland. Many ex-racers are now champions, including national championships, but most of these had been retired from racing when imported. In other words their performance points would not count here, for Legion of Merit. Usually these ex-race horses quickly qualify in a variety of classifications, usually park, so they are not so bad off after all.

While performance ability is often inherited more through the dam than the sire, the latter nevertheless is influential to a large enough degree to be noticable. Some are more noted for the performance of their get than for halter winners. Since the Legion of Merit is a sampling of the best looking of each sires' get, presumably the ratio is reasonably constant. Consequently the following chart may be pertinent, even though the owners of the horses and their interest in this award may have much to do with the percentages as does Lady Luck herself.

BINT SAHARA (Farawi-Bint Sedjur)

SAKI (Ferseyn-Ferdia)

SIRE LINES OF LEGION OF MERIT HORSES
(As of 1968)

(Branch includes all horses of that line which have sired champions)

Line	Leading Branches	Number of L. of M. Horses	Percentage Compared To Champions	Line Total L. of M.	Line Total Percentage
*RAFFLES	INDRAFF	11	12	39	8
	GEYM	2	19		
	GARAFF	2	6½		
	HANDEYRAFF	3	22		
	HANRAFF	3	20		
	RAPTURE	7	18		
	RIFRAFF	3	14		
*RASEYN	FERSEYN	8	6	31	10½
	RONEK	5	21		
	SUREYN	14	23		
NASEEM	*NABORR	3	30	9	9
	*SERAFIX	4	8		
GULASTRA	JULEP	3	27	24	12
	KATAR	1	3		
	ABU FARWA	14	15		
RIJM	*NASIK	3	7	3	4
*MIRAGE	IMAGE	6	11	8	9
	RIFAGE	1	7		
*FADL	FADJUR	2	6	4	5
*ZARIFE	HALLANY				
	MISTANNY	3	27	3	20
OFIR	*WITEZ II	10	11	11	10
DEYR	HANAD	3	7	4	6
*ALDEBAR	BAAROUF	1	12	1	6
*IBN MAHRUSS	ALLA				
	AMARWARD	1	9	1	10

Where only one branch is listed but the line total (percentage) differs from that of the branch it is due to lack of Legion of Merit horses in other branches of that line. Some lines have no Legion of Merit representatives at all, others have only one. The NAZEER line has eight champions and four Legion of Merit horses, so rates a high fifty per cent. ARAX has one champion, which is also Legion of Merit. Percentage-wise, that would give this Polishbred, Russian-owned horse a hundred per cent. The DOKTRYNER branch from ILDERIM, with one Legion of Merit out of three champions has thirty-three per cent, and PIETUSZOK has twenty-five per cent. The ORIENTAL branch from *MUSON has fourteen per cent Legion of Merit horses, simply by having one that qualified out of seven. Only in lines having many champions does the percentage show a reasonably true picture.

VII

THE FABRIC OF FAME

I had intended to relate short histories of stallions which had sired ten or more champions, but there are so many of them that to do so would take a book in itself. Moreover a good number of such sires are still comparatively young, so such histories would be only half accomplished. Therefore I shall concentrate mainly on the progenitors of these horses, other than those imported here who have already been dealt with. These will be taken in the same sequence observed in the sire line charts.

SKOWRONEK. This is actually the line of IBRAHIM D.B., but few people know of that horse, but everyone knows of SKOWRONEK (though none of us, probably, pronounce it properly). This horse is registered in the General Stud Book of England as follows:

> "Skowronek. A grey horse, bred by Count Joseph Potocki, at his Arab stud in Poland, in 1909, got by Ibrahim (A Kehilan-Ajuz), out of Yaskoulka, by Rymnik, out of Epopeja, by Dervish. Imported by Walter Winans in 1913."

A letter written by Count Roman Potocki to Mrs. Milton Thompson of Barrington, Illinois (owner of Tobruk, a son of the Polish *Sulejman) told of the almost accidental purchase of SKOWRONEK by the artist-sculptor Walter Winans. The Count's father, Count Joseph Potocki, Sr., owned a 10,000 acre deer park as part of his huge estate, where all sorts of deer, from Wapiti to Carpathian were kept. Also in the park were Aurochs, those wild cattle   straight out of the past, and which are so well represented in cave art. Since the old bull of the herd had started to kill the younger ones, it was necessary to save the youngsters that remained and kill the old warrior. Walter Winans wanted this rare trophy for his collection and arranged (for 1500 pounds) to go on the hunt. To get to the point, he shot his trophy all right, but also became entranced by the half Arabian geldings hitched to the carriage in which he followed a more conventional hunt (with hounds) after stags. He tried to buy the horses and equipment, and had almost reached a deal when he wanted the coachman too. So the whole sale fell through. However the Count asked him why not consider a purebred Arabian, saying "Buy a nice Arab stallion instead, you can have him for 150 pounds—that is his price. You will be glad to have him, he comes from excellent parents." And so, because of that Ice Age animal, the Aurochs, the most remarkably prepotent Arabian stallion of all time was sold for shipment to England. Actually this sale saved his life in all probability, for his sire and relatives were killed in the Bolshevik uprising several years after this 1913 incident. A year later SKOWRONEK was sold to Mr. Webb-Wares who used him as a hack during the war years. He was purchased in 1919 by H. V. M. Clark who gave him his first opportunity at stud with the mares FELUKA and NESSIMA, both of Crabbet breeding. SKOWRONEK was shown a few times during this period and that is where the eagle eye of Lady Wentworth noted the horse resulting in her determination to get him, which she did, in 1920.

SKOWRONEK (Ibrahim-Jaskolka)

NASEEM (Skowronek-Nasra)

*RAFFLES (Skowronek-Rifala)

*RASEYN (Skowronek-Rayya)

SKOWRONEK AND THREE OF HIS SONS

Of interest are the placings of **SKOWRONEK** and his rivals in those early years:

NEWMARKET 1919	RANELAGH 1919
1. Dolmatscher (Wiel Stud, Germany)	1. *Nureddin II
2. *Nureddin II	2. Yakoot
3. Skowronek	3. Skowronek
4. Yakoot	4. Crosbie
5. Fantass	5. Joseph
6. Crosbie	

LONDON 1920	LONDON 1921
1. Crosbie	1. Rasim
2. Skowronek	2. Skowronek
3. Nadir	3. Mutapha Kamil
4. Chandi	4. Crosbie
	5. Shahzada

LONDON 1922	LONDON 1923
1. Skowronek	1. Rasim
2. Rasim	2. Skowronek
3. Crosbie	3. Mustapha Kamil
4. Chandi	4. Shahzada
5. ?	5. Aldebaran (°Aldebar)

Skowronek means lark in Polish, and jaskoulka means swallow. SKOWRONEK had two brothers with equally avion names, and these were sold in 1914 to Cossacks in Kuban at 150 pounds each the same as his own price. This amount was only slightly more than SKOWRONEK eventually obtained as his stud fee at Crabbet Park. Although the pound sterling was then worth almost five dollars, this stallion's purchase must have been one of the greatest bargains in history.

SKOWRONEK was not faultless, but he had fewer and less serious defects than the average Arabian horse of his time. His main flaw was a rather straight and short shoulder with no withers at all. Along with his good points he also passed on this combination of forehand flaws. His lack of withers and equal lack of good layback of shoulder may be the major reason he was placed below RASIM (a very good horse, however) and °NUREDDIN II. He may not have moved out as well either. He was said to be not a very good hack, and a good, free way of going is part of a hack's qualifications. Certainly he did not show brilliant action, for every time any of her horses had this desirable attribute, Lady Wentworth mentioned it. Moreover those SKOWRONEK sons and daughters which lack such action horses in their pedigree as AZREK and QUEEN OF SHEBA rarely had more than average trotting ability.

Whatever faults he may have had, they were (except for the forehand) very minor; and after all, if American Arabian breeders wish to treat horses as if they were experimental guinea pigs rather than utility animals in the conduction of their inbreeding experiments, at least they chose one of the best Arabians of all time on which to base the inbreeding programs.

The pedigree of SKOWRONEK'S sire ends abruptly in the desert. While his detractors (any over-popular horse has them in direct ratio to his admirers) tried to claim SKOWRONEK was a part-bred because his sire came from Turkey and therefore was obviously a Turcoman or worse, it has now been proven he was indeed bred in the desert (and imported via Turkey), with the tribe that bred him identified, as well

RAKTHA (Naseem-Razina)

INDIAN MAGIC (Raktha-Indian Crown)

*SERAFIX (Raktha-*Serafina)

*SILVER DRIFT (Raktha-*Serafina)

RISSAM (Naseem-Rim)

*NIZZAM (Rissam-Nezma)

215

as the strain of his sire and dam. The long mysterious names (or so-called names) of IBRAHIM'S parents (Heijer and Lafitte) have at last been tracked down, and, as was rather obvious, they are a mangled version of the strain names. The dam of SKOWRONEK has a long and distinguished pedigree, and traces back in tail female to ILINIECKA, which old records give as a "Koheil a Dzius Um Argub." It does not take a linguist to deduce that this is Polish for Kehilan-Ajuz. IBRAHIM was a Seglawi-Faliti (hence the piratical sounding Lafitte) sired by a horse called HEJAR, whose strain is indefinite. IBRAHIM's strain as given in the G.S.B. is therefore in error. By some strain-theorists SKOWRONEK is called the "Seglawi-type," by others the "Kehilan type," so, since he is ' 'arf 'n 'arf" anyhow, both (or neither) can be satisfied. Actually his background includes many strains, Maneghi and Jilfan as well, but comparatively far back.

It should be noted here that the Polish and Weil Arabian pedigrees are the oldest Arabian pedigrees in the world, in that written records of these animals have been kept by the various stud farms at least since 1800. This was long before Abbas Pasha of Egypt had started his famed collection of desertbreds, and in fact he was not even born until 1813. These records varied as to method of recording, but they were available for the needed information when an official registry was founded and a stud book published in 1932. Some of the early records listed strains, others did not, just as our own Registry considers their inclusion without merit today. However, the very fact that the Polish Arabian pedigrees go back so far has allowed researchers to dig out horses with no strains; ones which came from Near Eastern countries other than Arabia; or ones with Persian names; and so on, and thereby claim that Polish horses are "impure." This seems a bit ridiculous when it is realized that the ancestral Arabian horse was of mixed ancestry to start with (when first acquired by the Bedouins, that is). The very type of Oriental horse that brings in such cries from impure minded people is of the same original blood as that of the Arabian, with breeding methods or environment making the distinction between the two. The Dickinson catalog of 1947 makes this comment:

> It is of interest that the taproot mares Iliniecka, the seventh dam of Skowronek, was accepted for the Polish Stud Book as a mare of unquestionable purity of Arab blood, and now believed to have been a Kehilet-Ajuz. As in the cases of the very few other Arab mares of the old historical studs of Poland which were in being before the modern system of stud books was established, and whose descendants now exists, as well as in the cases of the celebrated Arabs of the stud of Abbas Pasha, whose blood has been of inestimable value in the development of the peerless Crabbet horses to which Arab breeders are overwhelmingly indebted, something has to be taken on faith. These earlier breeders were fanatical in the desire to use only the purest blood. They went to extremes

216

hitherto unheard of to assemble studs of the finest available Arabs of the purest known bloodlines. The foundation stock was originally selected, later culled, and their descendants bred by men whose character, position, means and family pride give the highest conceivable assurance of excellence. While we grant the right of any person to like or dislike an individual horse or type, we have no patience with the gossip intended to reflect upon the forebears of Skowronek and other good horses simply because earlier breeders, in a different time and age, did not conform to present day methods of keeping stud books such as they never heard of. It may well be considered that such doubts pursued to their logical conclusion would raise serious question of the purity of all Arab horses bred by Bedouins who kept no written records.

Next to the lines of the imports *RAFFLES and *RASEYN, that of the elegant NASEEM is the most important of American lines today, and indeed the countrys leading sire. *SERAFIX is of this branch of the SKOWRONEK dynasty. NASEEM was noted for the extreme beauty of his head and neck and in most cases these attributes have been passed on down through the generations. He was rather shallow of body and his hind legs were not straight by a long shot, but nevertheless he gave the instant impression of great beauty, so decisive that his faults were often overlooked. Nevertheless the crooked hocks, sometimes to a sickle hocked degree, have been rather persistent, and they are transmitted quite often via horses which themselves have excellent hind legs. An example is NEGATIW and his son *NABORR, both of which need no apology in regard to underpinning or much else (other than withers) but occasionally a really over-angulated specimen shows up among the get of *NABORR. This is an inheritance from DAOUD, another crooked hocked stallion, who was sire of NASEEM's dam. NASEEM was an instant success from the day he was foaled—a stocking legged, grey beauty who dappled out in rocking horse perfection and eventually became silver white. He was foaled in 1922 and was out of NASRA. He was the most expensive of the group of Arabians sold in 1936 by Lady Wentworth to the Russian government. Estimates of the total price paid ranged around 50,000 pounds, which at the then current rate of exchange, would have been close to a quarter of a million dollars. These top Crabbet-breds, together with ones from previous Crabbet purchases, and a few from France with a large number from Poland (taken in war), form the basis of Russian Arabian stock, with lately a couple of additions from Egypt. From the combination of NASEEM and Polish stock the handsome NEGATIW was bred, with *NABORR (known as Nabor in Russia and Poland) being the next generation of the same blood. Both these horses were raced in Russia as two-year-olds. Each won two races—NEGATIW two out of four, *NABORR two out of eight. They were similar in that they each won two races and were unplaced in other starts. The show records of *NABORR's get have already been

NEGATIW (Naseem-Taraszcza)   °NABORR (Negatiw-Lagodna)

°ARAMUS (°Naborr-Amneris)   °GWALIOR (°Naborr-°Gwadiana)

SOME REPRESENTATIVES OF THE NEGATIW BRANCH OF THE
NASEEM LINE

touched upon. So has that of the RISSAM son, °NIZZAM, that eye-filling handsome bay from Holland. RISSAM himself was a well balanced, well built horse, with little fault about him, except from the hide hunters, who would object to the spot on his side, which however was low down, and near the girth.

RAKTHA, a grey, foaled 1934, was bred by Lady Yule at her Hanstead Stud and purchased when mature by Lady Wentworth. His dam was the foundation broodmare RAZINA, a really top mare, one that Lady Wentworth regretted selling. RAZINA was by RASIM, the nemesis of SKOWRONEK, and out of RIYALA. She had won several broodmare classes and a reserve championship. RAKTHA was a beautiful imposing stallion but would have been ideal if he had had a longer and better laid-back shoulder with higher withers. In fact he was about as remiss in regard to withers as was his grandsire. However that didn't stop him from being a winner, as witness his record in 1948 and 1949 when he won four championships and was said to have won more championships in less time than any other Arab on record, also winning get-of-sire classes. He was sold as an old horse to South Africa where he continued to sire prize winning stock. As the sire of °SERAFIX, he has earned his place in the hall of fame, though others of his get need not feel slighted because of the prominence of *SERAFIX. The latter's recently imported full brother *SILVER DRIFT, is making an impressive start as a sire as well.

RAKTHA's son, INDIAN MAGIC, has for years, been premier sire of C. G. Covey's Crabbet Stud which is based on stock of Crabbet Park. This 15-2 "pure white" grey is described in the Crabbet Park catalog (before Lady Wentworth's death) as "SUPREME CHAMPION INDIAN MAGIC Kehilan Dajania—dapple grey. A magnificent, very striking stallion with spectacular action and lovely Arab type, combining size with quality. 8 Firsts and Cups, First Grand Champion and Cup 1948, First and Champion, Royal Show 1953 and Reserve Grand Champion to *Grand Royal* 4 times . . . etc. . . . . Four leading horse judges and veterinary surgeons have pronounced him the best horse they have seen of any breed. Sire, *Grand Champion Raktha;* dam, *Indian Crown.*" He is truly a magnificent horse and might be called the crowning achievement of Lady Wentworth who was always trying for a good-sized Arabian with classic quality.

Now to return to the Americanbred stallions of the *RAFFLES and *RASEYN branches of the SKOWRONEK line.

As the chart so graphically shows, the oldest son of *RAFFLES is also the leading representative of that subdivision of this dynasty, which would be expected from the head sire of America's largest Arabian farm, Al-Marah, now located in Barnesville, Maryland. This is INDRAFF, the grey stallion foaled in 1938 at the Selby Stud. He was obtained as a colt by Donald Shultz who had been apprenticed by his father to the Selby Stud to learn the horse business. Apparently he learned it well indeed, for he traded a mare for the blaze-faced colt. James Dean, the manager of the Stud, reserved the rights to future services of INDRAFF which were subsequently taken. Actually the colt had been produced not so much by a scientific study of bloodlines, but simply because his dam was one of two mares which were easy to get in foal, and *RAFFLES, who had been considered sterile until experimental work and feeding was tried, was bred to these mares to see if they could catch. Both did, and *INDAIA was the first to produce her foal, thus INDRAFF gained his original first. Herbert Tormohlen, as his letter indicates, was the first to breed a mare to INDRAFF and thereafter returned several mares to him, by which time Dr. George C. Conn of Freeport, Illinois (author of two good books on Arabians) also was quick to realize this horse's potential. The first foal of INDRAFF to be registered was AADRAFFA, sold by the Ben Hur Farms as a three-year-old to the Joder Arabian Ranch in Wyoming. When INDRAFF was around six years of age Bazy Tankersley was told about him, so she went out to take a look. Instead, she took the stallion, at what turned out to be a bargain at ten thousand dollars, no sneezing figure today, but valued much higher in those "sound-as-a-dollar" days. INDRAFF was shown only two years, 1947 and 1948, and with one exception, he was undefeated at halter in his campaign of the East. His "National Champion" claim is through winning

RAPTURE (*Raffles-Rafla)

INDRAFF (*Raffles-Indaia)

GEYM (*Raffles-Rageyma)

IMARAFF (Raffles-Imagida)

RAFMIRZ (*Raffles-Mirzaia)

RIFRAFF (*Raffles-Rafissa)

LEADING SIRES OF THE *RAFFLES LINE

the Arabian championship at the National Stallion Show at Waterloo, Iowa. Like every horse, INDRAFF had his faults, the most noticeable being the typical SKOWRONEK shoulder, plus an apple rump and somewhat over angulated hind legs. He was also slightly back at the knees. His head was typical of the *RAFFLES line, and although it had the desired jibbah and dish, the nostrils were placed rather low. In January, 1961, INDRAFF suffered a stroke, but through dint of the efforts of the Al-Marah staff, INDRAFF, then twenty-three, was saved. He had fully recovered, or at least he was feeling fit by October, and the four foals by him, which arrived late in 1962, prove that the revival was real. But those four foals had nearly "missed the train." Many of the INDRAFF get were extremely cobby (thick-set, broad, short-legged, with heavy bone) although they have short and pretty heads, and arched if rather too cresty necks. But this was in the hey-day of the too fat show horse, and possibly some of this surplus breadth and bulk can be blamed on blubber. His tendency to sire horses with apple rumps was dominant. INDRAFF died almost within a year of the death of his arch rival FERSEYN. Among top winners by INDRAFF are TASLIYA, Reserve National Champion mare, and the Top Tens AL-MARAH, RUWALA, GEORGIA and IKHTIYARIN as well as a Canadian Top Ten winner, BINDAFFA. However his descendants in further generations are even more well-represented in the "top drawer." For instance AL-MARAH RADAMES sired the National Champion RADAMASON, and HASSAN PASHA is the sire of the Top Ten HAJ-AMIN, SAHRA BINT SABA and HASSA, with HAJ-AMIN in turn siring the National Champion HAJABABA+. AL-MARAH RADAMES also sired the Top Ten mare NEPTHYS+, and his son RADAMASON sired two others, GEYRADA and EASTERADA.

At the risk of having this become a dry repetition of statistics, other sires should receive their due, even though such lists are at best partial, leaving out all but the highest wins. GEYM is the sire of the Canadian Top Ten mare GEYNIMA and his son GEM OF CEDARDELL sired the East Coast Champion and Top Ten mare AABEEBE (originally Habeebe). AZRAFF is the sire of the Canadian National Champion COMAR BAY BEAU and the Top Ten stallion GALIZON. HANDEY-RAFF sired to Top Ten RAF-FARANA who also won innumerable park and harness classes. RAPTURE takes the credit for AMSHEH, a Pacific Coast Champion mare and zips clear across the country for the win of another daughter, HUNI, an East Coast Champion. His son AL-MARAH CASSANOVA is a Top Ten winner, as was another son, LAUREATE. Offspring of RIFRAFF to join the "Ten" club are SEAHORSE THUN-DER+ and SEAHORSE DAWN, while SEAHORSE AB-RIFA was a Canadian Champion mare. INDRAFF's full brother INDY is the sire of the Top Ten INDASAFA, and RAFFI's daughter KA-RAFKA is also such a winner.

The full brothers AARAF and AARIEF were more than just sires of halter champions—they were both top performance horses having action to spare, and moreover they transmitted it with fair consistency. Their sisters AARAFA and AARAFLA also won many park classes throughout of the East and Midwest. AARIEF went west, siring nine of his ten champions for the Lasma Stud in Arizona, but unfortunately he died when comparatively young. This group of horses were the sons and daughters of *RAFFLES and AARAH, thus doubling up on *BERK blood, as AARAH's sire was by RIBAL, a son of *BERK. Another action sire and park champion many times over is MRAFF a Top Ten stallion. He is a half brother to the brilliant park and harness mare ROSYRA who died young, sad to say. Their dam added two AZREK lines to that of their sires, so the intensification of latent trotting ability is not surprising. One of MRAFF's sons is the National Champion Gelding EL HADI+, which is worth a bit of pride in itself; but better yet EL HADI+ is a real worker and has the title of "World Champion Arab Cutting Horse" as well as "World Champion in Cutting Open to All Breeds." He also took time out to again stand still long enough to win the Great Plains Gelding Championship at halter. Another son of MRAFF is the Top Ten stallion KAIMR, and still another, ABU MRAFF, is a National Champion Trail Horse and Top Ten National Western Pleasure. In spite of his name he was not the "father of" (abu) MRAFF. When it comes to daughters MRAFF again can take a bow. One of them is the beautiful but durable MALIFA, a tough campaigner that makes every rival work not just a little but a whole lot harder. She has the high, fluid action characteristic of her lines (combining *Raffles with Alyf, and a Polish mare as her maternal granddam). Moreover she can turn on like a roadster and fly by the rest of the class as if they were in reverse, whenever the going gets hot enough that speed takes precedence over the proper park gait. Once she was allowed to flatten out and tear out at the trot, as she has always seemed inclined to do. This was in a roadster class, where speed is of the essence. BLUE VELVET took up her challenge and the two of them put on a battle royal that had the usually drowsy spectators on their feet and yelling, as if these were Standardbreds out for blood. The rest of the class was lapped several times by these two, with MALIFA winning out by holding her gait and speed. She was National Reserve Champion Park Horse and once Top Ten in that category.

FERSEYN had tenaciously clung to the top spot as Leading Sire for many years. This was in the face of new and formidable opposition from imports and ambitious young stallions, and his lead continued for a couple of years after his death. Not until 1968 did it succumb to the onslaught of the *SERAFIX forces.

Although registered as "dk. b." in Volume IV of the Stud Book, and as brown on his registration certificate, belatedly noted when he was sold at around twenty years of age, FERSEYN was a grey. He was foaled in

FERSEYN (Raseyn-Ferda)

1937 and was bred by the W. K. Kellogg Institute. His dam *FERDA had been sold, in foal to *RASEYN, to Fred Vanderhoof of Woodlake, California. She was then twenty-three years old. FERSEYN was foaled on the Vanderhoof ranch and was sent down to H. H. Reese's place in West Covina with a group of other young Arabians for eventual sale. However Reese was well acquainted with the breeding of this colt (after all he had been the manager of Kellogg's for years) and liked what he saw, so he bought FERSEYN himself. He operated what amounted to the first stallion station for Arabian horses, along with a sales stables, which accounts for the large numbers of foals sired by his horses, for he never turned down a mare if her owner had the cash (or a suitable trade). He did not believe in showing a horse once it made a good win, and he practiced what he preached. His advice to exhibitors was to retire a horse after winning a championship for it might never win again, and it might even lose in a small show, ruining the effect of the other win. Such advice would ruin horse shows, and fortunately no one (except himself) took heed. Nevertheless he did show FERSEYN once (holding to his rule) and the horse, as previously mentioned, was Reserve Champion at the Devonshire Downs show, judged by the Egyptian expert Dr. Ameen Zahir. When FERSEYN was twenty-one years old, he was sold to Frisco Mari of La Puente, California, and there he dominated the lives of the Mari family until his death in 1962. One of his last sons was

AMERIGO, out of the Polish import *SZARZA, already mentioned as a Reserve National Champion. A slightly older son is REGIS, who shares top billing at the Mari ranch with AMERIGO. FERSEYN was very similar to his sire in conformation but his head was more clean-cut and his eyes were larger.

FERSEYN nicked extraordinarily well with BINT SAHARA, owned by Mr. and Mrs. Frank McCoy of Chino, California, and eight of that great producer's ten champions were sired by FERSEYN. Although it is not obvious from the chart, this mare figures in the credits given FERNEYN (Ferseyn-Moneyna); for that stallion, bred to FERSARA (Bint Sahara's most famous daughter) sired Daniel Gainey's FERZON, and it is through most latter that the majority of the champions credited to the FERNEYN line trace. GAZON, by FERZON, is the sire of the National Champion RAFFON as well as the Top Ten winner GAZRAFF, while FERZON himself sired the Top Tenners BU-ZAHR, GAIZON and GA-RAGEYMA. FERNEYN sired one of these also, FERNEYNA. Not forgetting the source, FERSEYN sired a couple of Top Tens of his own, BREEZE and SAHARA QUEEN, and his sons ROYAL STORM and REGIS also contributed to this select group with one each. In addition, as with other sires (but not always), the FERSEYN line is responsible for countless regional winners and performance champions. An unusual one in the latter category is KONTIKI a son of WAIKIKI (by Waineyn), for this horse holds the American racing record (for Arabs) at a mile and a half, and except for one second place, was undefeated. North of the border, JOANA, by FERSEYN, was Canadian National Champion, and two other daughters, GAYE SEYN and WAHIDA won Reserves. The FERSEYN line nicks well with FADJUR, and SAKI, dam of seven of FADJUR's best champions, is a daughter of FERSEYN. Actually this is not too surprising, in the face of FERSEYN's equally fortuitous nick with BINT SAHARA, for that mare is the dam of FADJUR.

The *RASEYN sons include a number of horses with good action, just as was the case with *RAFFLES, but only when the dams brought in lines noted for this trait. For instance the Cal Poly (Kellogg) stallion COURIER is out of SHEHERZADE, herself a mare with good action; and she was a daughter of RAYIK whose dam was the great performance mare ROSHANA whose sire was *BERK. The grey stallion RONEK was out of *BAHREYN whose dam *BATTLA was out of BUKRA, the dam of *BERK, and through whom *BERK's action was inherited from AZREK (sire of Bukra's sire, Ahmar). RONEK has been prepotent in transmitting action to his get, of which the Kellogg show horse ALYF was one. *RAFFLES too usually did better as a sire of such trotting horses when he was aided by AZREK (and sometime *Rizvan) blood through the dam. He himself had *BERK in his pedigree, but when this was doubled, as it was in the case of AARAF and his siblings, the action potential was also doubled. AARAH, the dam of these "A" horses was

SUREYN (*Raseyn-*Crabbet-Sura)

COURIER (*Raseyn-Sheherzade)

FERNEYN (Ferseyn-Moneyna)

RONEK (*Raseyn-*Bahreyn)

FERZON (Ferneyn-Fersara)

GAZON (Ferzon-Scheraff)

SIRES OF THE *RASEYN LINE

by GHADAF, a son of RIBAL who was by *BERK. IMARAFF also traced to RIBAL.

The RONEK line, with its numerous branches, is worthy of note. This stallion was sold by the Kellogg Ranch to the Travelers Rest Arabian Stud when he was a four-year-old. There he was trained to the five gaits, emulating his sire. He was described in the Travelers Rest catalog as "Champion stallion and first prize Arab under saddle Illinois State Fair 1937. A show horse of brilliant action. Sold to California." Not only did RONEK himself have brilliant action but he and his offspring usually transmitted this trotting ability to some degree—also in some cases the inclination to gait. In fact the tendency to pace or slow-gait had to be trained out of ALYF. The later was one of RONEK's first foals, and the lovely mares BRIDE ROSE and GYM-FARAS were in the same distinguished crop. ALYF had been purchased at two weeks of age for the Kellogg Ranch, as a chestnut stallion of the *RASEYN line, as was desired, especially one which might develop action. But this "chestnut" turned grey before he was weaned and almost queered the deal, but he was accepted anyhow. It turned out well, in view of ALYF's show record and as a sire . . . not so much in the number of champions he sired as in broodmatrons. RONEK was unusually well conformed, about all that could be desired to make him perfect would have been a longer neck. He had been sold first to Donald Jones of Porterville where he sired RASUL, a chestnut parade horse without peer, with so much action he nearly "cut his knees on his teeth" as the saying goes. RASUL was so fiery he had to be gelded, but that fire made him a show horse deluxe and his high neck carriage probably helped elevate the knee action. He also was unbeatable in harness and in park classes, whenever they were judged by persons who realized that some Arabians *could* bend their knees despite the wording of the show rules. Another of the early California RONEKs was FARONEK, a liver chestnut streak of lightning who was as quick on his feet as a cat on that oft-mentioned hot tin roof. He displayed this ability in pole bending and stake racing as well as stock horse classes. RONEK was next sold to Robert Armstrong of Olympia, Washington, then a few years later, back to California where he was in different ownerships at times. When owned by E. E. Hurlbutt he sired the dainty champion and dynamic park and harness winner, ROSYRA; at the ranch of Leland Mekeel he sired another park winner and sire of others, RISAB; and in the ownership of Mrs. Kemp Dowdy he sired another king of the action classes, AL-HAKIM. Mrs. Dowdy gave an exhibition of RONEK at five gaits when he was twenty years of age at the San Francisco show in 1951, and he lacked none of the fire nor action of old. RONEK was also used for stock work, and all in all, he can be classed as one of the breed's most outstanding horses, not just a good sire.

SUREYN, an inbred SKOWRONEK, is the third of the main *RASEYN branch founders. His sire and dam (*Crabbet Sura) were both by that horse, as mentioned in the Kellogg chapter. He almost was lost to the breed, for along with nearly all the *RASEYN sons on hand when the Remount took over the Kellogg Ranch, he was issued as a Remount sire used only on grade mares. However he had caught the expert eye of Mrs. J. E. Draper of Richmond, California a few years after the Remount dispersal, when he was owned in Nevada and advertised at stud. Apparently he had sired no purebred foals until he was acquired by Mrs. Draper, with the first of his foals registered in 1952. This group of six contained the eventual National Champion mare SURITA and history was made by the SUREYNs on the occasion the first National competition was held. The first, that is, of the type now enjoying that title, although at this first show only one judge was employed, compared to the various (and occasionally disastrous) judging systems used thereafter. Not only was SURITA the National Champion mare, but MUJAHID+, also by SUREYN, was the stallion champion. SURITA is out of BONITA (Caravan-*Barakat), the dam of four other champions. CARAVAN is by RIBAL, while *BARAKAT is one of the Spanish mares imported by the Drapers. MUJAHID+ was bred by John Rogers and is out of the English mare *SILVER CRYSTAL, dam of six champions. MUJAHID+ is the senior sire of the Arabian Heights Ranch of Mr. and Mrs. R. E. Newman of Golden, Colorado, and he is the sire of several champions with the "Blue" prefix.

SUREYN is the sire of several Top Ten winners—SANEYN+, SUR-GHARI, SURI-LEE+, SUR-NEET+, SUR-KNIGHT and SUR-REYNA. A rather unique slant to the National scene is that he is the sire of the first and the latest (1968) champions, (or rather one of the latter), since the exquisite mare MI-FANCI+ was National Champion in that year. Some of the SUREYNS are too short in the neck, but this is also a complaint regarding others of the *RASEYN line; and at Kellogg's a nick that would overcome this was always sought—without too much success. Some of the SUREYNs have had action, with SUR-BUDDI+ (a Pacific Coast Champion at halter) going Reserve in the Pacific Coast formal driving championships. MI-FANCI+ too has won park and formal harness stakes. Another is SUR-BEN a Top Ten park horse as well as halter champion. All have RIBAL in their pedigree through their dams. As in the case of other sires, SUREYN has many regional champions, but in most cases these are too numerous to list along with the other references.

Leaving the SKOWRONEKs we now come to the MESAOUD line, which had its start in the United States seventeen years before the arrival of *RASEYN on these shores. However since it traces back to the importation date of *ASTRALED, who is represented by GULASTRA, who was foaled in the 1920s, the line actually did not have that much of a head start.

227

Before delving into the multi-floral branching of the GULASTRA family tree, a word on an Englishbred line with representatives here, that of DARGEE. This starts from MESAOUD through NADIR, JOSEPH and MANASSEH (not the horse of the same name in the U.S.) to the many times champion DARGEE. This compact chestnut was for several years a leading winner for Lady Wentworth, although he had been bred by G. H. Ruxton. He was foaled in 1945. DARGEE was owned by Covey after the death of Lady Wentworth, and after a semi-retirement from the show ring this flashy chestnut was exhibited again in 1960 at seventeen years of age, once more taking all honors. Unfortunately he died a couple of years later, not reaching the age customary in his line.

MESAOUD (Aziz-Yemameh)   AZREK D.B.

*ASTRALED brought the MESAOUD line to America in 1909. He was the last foal of the desertbred mare QUEEN OF SHEBA, so enthusiastically described by Lady Anne Blunt in *Bedouin Tribes of the Euphrates* in 1897, and termed "worth a king's ransom   if kings were longer worth ransoming." MESAOUD himself had been purchased from Ali Pasha Sherif in Egypt by Lady Anne and Wilfrid Blunt and was imported by them to England in 1891 as a four-year-old. There he sired ninety foals up to and including those of 1904, and he was then sold to Russia along with several other Arabians of the Crabbet Park Stud. His sire AZIZ was a blaze faced chestnut with four stockings, and he followed that pattern too. He also had some rather unusual dime sized white spots throughout his coat, which was liberally roaned at the flank and to a lesser degree on the barrel. An occasional spot was somewhat larger, including one about an inch long on his jowl, but these of course were not like the larger patches of white seen on so many of his descendants. He and AZREK were the best stallions of their time in England, and upon the latter's being sold to Cecil Rhodes in South Africa, MESAOUD had no other challenger, though there were several other good stallions at Crabbet. He was truly an outstanding individual but completely unlike the Egyptian horses of today in that he had heavy bone and was comparatively chunky. As to *ASTRALED's dam, QUEEN OF SHEBA, this mare is described in the General Stud Book thus: "A brown mare, foaled

1875, an Abeyah Sherrakieh, bred by Erheyen Ibn Alian of the Gomussa (Sebaa Anazeh) her sire a Managhy Hedruj, of Ibn Gufeyfi (Gomussa), purchased of Beteyen Ibn Mershid, Sheykh of the Gomussa, who owned her on shares with her breeder. A celebrated mare. Imported by Mr. Blunt in 1879."

*ASTRALED's history is given in the story of the Maynesboro Stud in a previous chapter.

*ASTRALED sired three foals at Maynesboro, and he died in 1924. Two of them have no descendants but the third more than made up for that. There is a coincidence here, in that *ASTRALED was the last foal of his dam, and his third foal of *ASTRALED's last crop was GUL-ASTRA, the last foal of his sire. GULASTRA, foaled in 1924, was a bright chestnut, marked with neat strip, a fore stocking and a hind pastern. His dam was GULNARE. In the 1934 dispersal list of the Maynesboro Stud he is tersely summed up as "Proven sire of big, able well-built foals. Ride and drive." His statistics were height: 14-2½, weight: 900 pounds, and his sire was termed the best in England. He was sold to the Hearst Ranch, San Simeon, California, but since that ranch had also bought his son RAHAS they sold GULASTRA some time later to the Travelers Rest Farm in Tennessee. There he remained a few years until again sold, apparently to a not too reputable person.

In a 1962 letter Herbert Tormohlen (Ben Hur Farms) told of GULASTRA:

> GULASTRA was rediscovered, brought back to life by us, brought here and fed up, reconditioned and used as a sire here one season. We found him sadly neglected, in a deplorable condition, in a filthy chicken coop in one corner of an old stable, down in Ohio where he had been sold by Dickinson. Skin and bones, rocking-chair feet. We made a deal to care for him with John Rapp whom we induced to buy him. We had him in fine condition, looking fine when we shipped him to Rapp, then owner of a ranch in New Mexico. We have never seen better mares sired by GUL-ASTRA that AALASTRA ex Nadirat 619 and AASTRA ex Aadura . . .
>
> It was from John Rapp that Howard Marks got GULASTRA after we had brought him back to life and condition. Bazy was here, saw AALASTRA and AASTRA then her desire to use him at stud. The last crop of foals were all colts, as we recall. She never realized her ambition to get fillies like our two.

The great park performers AARAF and AARIEF, and their full sisters AARAFA and AARAFLA, equally great action horses, were among the horses bred by the Ben Hur Farms.

While the arrangement mentioned in the foregoing letter is not too clear, it constituted an exchange on a transcontinental basis between Howard Marks and Bazy Tankersley for one season of the stallion INDRAFF and GULASTRA. This accounts for a number of California-

GULASTRA (*Astraled-Gulnare)

RAHAS (Gulastra-Raab)

RABIYAS (Rahas-Rabiyat)

ABU FARWA (Rabiyas-*Rissletta)

GA'ZI (Abu Farwa-Ghazna)

ABU BAHA (Abu Farwa-Surrab)

ONE BRANCH OF THE GULASTRA LINE

bred foals by the eastern based stallion. However when it came time to return GULASTRA, it was decided not to do so because of his age; and he died not long thereafter.

RAHAS, a chestnut, foaled 1928, was also bred by W. R. Brown. He was out of RAAD, and although this mare had no more white than a tiny star and one coronet, her son had a blaze and four stockings. Oddly enough her daughter RAAB, by the very flashily marked *ABU ZEYD, had only a narrow strip and a hind pastern white. RAHAS was described in the Maynesboro list in part like his sire's summary, but with an added note: "A proven sire of big, able, well-built foals. Ride and drive (I kept this horse as superior to Champion Bazleyd)." He stood 15 hands and weighed 1000 pounds. RAHAS was a good saddle horse, and a characteristic of his get is a fast flat footed walk with lots of impulse. He was purchased by the Hearst Ranch along with GULASTRA and was a leading sire, there, along with GHAZI.

The RAHAS son AZKAR is another of the GULASTRA line used at Ben Hur, and he is described by Tormohlen: "AZKAR was a distinctive Ali Pasha Sherif type and throw-back, more beautiful than any of the line from pictures which we have seen. He was loaned to Byron Good at Michigan State for the last 7 years of his life. Injured front foot from running with a band of a hundred Texas mares in his early life made it wise not to move him back home. I made 14 trips and back 190 miles up there with mares one season to breed, rather than take a chance hauling him back home. Then he died with melonic tumors." As might be guessed from the reference to melonic tumors, AZKAR was a grey, and such tumors occur mainly (or only?) with this color.

Of necessity confining these summaries to horses which founded many faceted branches, we have to by-pass several sires noted on the chart, which have only one line, if any, to carry on for them to date. So the next stallion is the five-gaited horse of Kellogg fame, RABIYAS. He has already been mentioned earlier but only casually. This horse, foaled in 1936, was out of the all time great performance mare, RABIYAT, but he did not display the bold brilliance at the trot that characterized his dam. He did however, have a quite good rack (for an Arab), and he could buzz on in fine fashion at this flashy gait, showing good elevation of knee action and plenty of speed. RABIYAS had a rather plain head, and a croup of the "apple" order, but he was an outstanding performance horse. For this reason an Arabian breeder in South Africa (where many Arabs are trained for five gaits) eventually purchased him. He had been sold to Donald McKenna after the Remount dispersal, and it was McKenna who sold him to that distant land. The gaited classes in South Africa still include horses by RABIYAS, and several have won championships in these events. He lived to be over thirty years of age, which his son ABU FARWA has also almost reached to date. A hot performer among the many sired by RABIYAS was RABAB, a truly spectacular horse with action

231

to spare. This stallion, at *sixteen years of age* won the Pacific Coast three-gaited (park) championship stake, ten years after his first in a series of stakes wins, and at twenty he again placed in the stakes event. There is something extraordinarily durable about this line.

The ABU FARWA dynasty is of course the most prolific in its number of champion-siring sons, many of which also have founded many branched lines. A champion at halter and in park, ABU FARWA was magnificent under saddle. He had the beautiful neck of the NASEEM line (through his dam) and this relationship also served to give his head more class than his sire's. He of course had plenty of action, and is noted for siring Arabians that "can do." He was foaled in 1940. I was then secretary of the Kellogg Ranch and had the duty of digging through Arabic dictionaries for suitable names, so used Abu (father) and Farwa (chestnut) for a combination name which supposedly means "Father of Chestnuts." Whether or not it would be so understood in Arabic, he did become the sire of many chestnuts. This stallion was sold as a weanling to a rancher in Northern California who decided he was too much of a handful at two years of age, and sent him down to the sales stables of H. H. Reese for resale. However Reese decided to buy him himself, and it was he who showed him a couple of times but no more, and kept him for many years at public stud. AB was eventually acquired by Charles Doner and he has remained ever since at the Elsinore Stud. He won a class for " Senior Sires" (over 15 years of age, and sire of champions) at Del Mar when he was twenty-four years old.

As obvious in the chart, ABU FARWA's most successful of many champion siring sons are ABU BAHA and GA'ZI, and moreover their own sons are running to form. The latter sire has an amazing record as a sire of winners in the Canadian Nationals. In 1963 GA'ZIMA+ and SIR LANCER+ were the champions of this event, and to take the two top spots is something in itself. But this was topped in 1967 when all four of the stallion and mare national championships and reserves were won by offspring of GA'ZI. They were FATEEN, MISS CENTURY 21, GANEYN and FAR'ZI. In 1968 the Canadian National Champion Mare and the same rank in geldings was won by LLANA and HAASSAN, both by that same stallion, GA'ZI. ABU BAHA is a chestnut, (a full brother of Shahzada) foaled 1948, bred by H. H. Reese, but owned ever since foalhood by James Ward of Mountlake Terrace, Washington. GA'ZI too is a chestnut, foaled 1949, and bred by Mr. and Mrs. Leland Mekeel of West Covina, California, who are also breeders of his full sister, the classic GHEZALA, whose head lives up to her name. Both of these great sires were themselves champions on several occasions, and GA'ZI was reserve Pacific Coast Champion in 1954. He was owned many years in partnership of Dr. E. E. LaCroix and Woody Madsen in Washington, dividing his time for a year or so between Washington and Arizona after

232

the Lasma Ranch was established in Scottsdale, although he eventually remained in Washington.

ANTEZEYN SKOWRONEK is the third ranking ABU FARWA son. This name and those of its ilk are very unwieldy to handle in a chart, usually having to be abbreviated to "Ant.Skow.," "Riss.Skow." and so on. It is a mystery why the Registry allowed such pedigree-in-a-word (or two words) names in the first place. In the second place the only bit of SKOWRONEK in the pedigree of "Ant.Skow." is way back, through FERSEYN and *RISSLETTA, themselves two   generations removed from SKOWRONEK. In other words the name is misleading, especially as in this case the horse is not of the SKOWRONEK sire line, but instead that of MESAOUD. In the case of AZREK SKOWRONEK, one would expect the horse to be a grey (Azrek meaning grey) but he is a chestnut, and didn't have enough of the desertbred AZREK in him to warrant the use of his name, except as was probably the case, in honor of that horse. Another name in this line is RASEYN GEZAN, which is nothing more than pirating of two names, and it's again hard to understand why the Registry allowed it. To top it off, the horse's dam is NADIR, another name taken from famous Arabians of old. To make it worse, this is of course a mare, while the original was a stallion. The confusion this could cause needs no amplification. These horses were bred by Carleton Cummings, originator of the Skyline Trust, which had done a great deal of good promoting Arabians, especially among youthful Arabian admirers. RASEYN GEZAN is Canadian Top Ten, while another by ANTEZEYN SKOWRONEK is the U.S. Top Ten mare KHATUM TAMARETTE. RISSANTEZ SKOWRONEK is the sire of the Pacific Northwest champion stallion WALLA NAR.

GALAN+, by ABU FARWA, is a Top Ten winner in both the United States and Canada as well as a winner of several park and harness events. FAROLITO+, another Canadian champion stallion (and U.S. Top Ten) is by FARLO+ (Top Ten park horse), a grandson of ABU FARWA. The line of FARYN does not contain as many halter champions as some others, but it can certainly turn out performers in park and related classes. One of these is TRACEYNAH, a daughter of ACE (who is by FARYN), Reserve National Champion Park horse to the Polish *BASK+. So it can be assumed that she had nearly as brilliant a way of going, other factors being equal. That she can move is not surprising for she has, besides ABU FARWA, the ubiquitous RIBAL and also the dam of RASUL in her pedigree, which has twelve lines to AZREK in all. SHARADA, by ANTEZEYN SKOWRONEK, was a Top Ten park horse in 1968. AFARI, an inbred ABU FARWA stallion (both sire and dam by that horse) is a reserve national champion stallion and a Top Ten park horse, while his sire AWAD was a stakes winner in park classes several years ago. AWAD is the sire of IBN AWAD, also a Top Ten stallion (halter). ZONGA+, another stakes winner in park events, was the winner of the Canadian National Gelding Championship as well. In addition to these, grandsons of ABU FARWA have been winners of the various types of Arabian races. One of these, like the others, but out of an ABU FARWA mare, is the indomitable and gallant grey KONTIKI, nearly unbeatable at 1½ miles; ARWALLANY, winner of one of these races; and MICHAEL who shared honors with OFIR as champion of the 2½ mile races of a few years ago. MICHAEL had previously won a couple of the Florida 100 mile trail rides as well. He is sired by RAFFEY but had none of the bulk of that horse, obviously. BARQ, a daughter of ABU FARWA and dam of several champions, is a former winner of stockhorse classes. These few serve as examples—but the list could go on and on.

The RAHAS line may be overwhelming in numbers of champions and in performance winners, but that doesn't mean that other GULASTRA sons were remiss in their duties. Some of them were outstanding in quality and performance, but simply contributed less through their sons, or had fewer sons, than did the aforementioned horses.

The next highest to RAHAS, in regard to the number of sires repre-senter by champions, is KATAR—that beautiful little bay stallion contri-buted by his breeder A. W. Harris, to the Remount as head sire for the Remount Arabian breeding program. KATAR was foaled in 1929 and was out of the English import *SIMAWA (Rustem-Sarama). RUSTEM is the sire of *FERDA and of RAYYA, the dam of *RASEYN. He is responsible for the doubling of MESAOUD lines in this pedigree, for RUSTEM is by *ASTRALED and was very similar in appearance to that horse.

KAHAR is the leading sire of the KATAR line, with RAFHAR and SHARRIK having the most representatives through sons and grandsons. Through the former branch, ESPERANZO can claim a real "doer" of a son in REY DE ESPERANZO, a stallion which in 1967 was in the Top Ten in four categories—formal driving, combination, English pleasure and costume. While that latter has little to add to a horse's fame, the others do. This horse was not like the usual jack-of-all-trades and master-of-none. He was definitely the master of each, for he had a beautiful way of going, free, effortless and high (where elevation was required, as in park and formal driving) and where he went, he went with class. Un-fortunately he died recently so cannot contribute to trotting action in the breed, other than what few foals he had sired before retirement.

The JULEP line is a distinguished one, noted for quantity and quality of its champions. He himself was foaled in 1939 and was bred by J. M. Dickinson. JULEP was out of the Egyptian mare *AZIZA, and although she had hind legs as crooked as her dam's, JULEP took after his sire and has straight hind legs. He seems to have inherited the best of the two lines, and transmits the same way. His son SYNBAD+ is a national champion as was a daughter, HIGH FASHION; and two others are Top Ten—JULIETTE and MINT JULEP. HIGH FASHION is also a Top Ten park horse. SPARKLES, by SYNBAD+ out of SILVER SPARKLE, was the National Park Champion in 1964, then came back the following year and was a Top Ten English pleasure horse. Her brother GRAN SALAAM, is a Top Ten gelding. These and HIGH FASHION are of the YATANA (Farana-Ghazayat) family, as is SYNBAD, while JULIETTE and MINT JULEP trace to ROSHANA in tail female.

The ISLAM (Gulastra-Nafud) line has done well through his son BINIS, and several good park horses have belonged to this line. Not the least of these is ROYAL BINIS (Binis-Hamnan) a National Champion in formal driving and in combination. This bold and handsome dark chestnut is inbred to GULASTRA, but of more importance in regard to action, he is also inbred to REHAL, since ISLAM and HABIBA (dam of BINNI) are both out of NAFUD, a granddaughter of REHAL. The latter is out of *RAMIM, a daughter of *BERK, and has been dominant in transmitting the ability to trot. That ROYAL BINIS can trot both high and fast has been demonstrated often, in his duels with other top performers. He would be ideal for roadster classes, if such were scheduled more often in Arabian shows. Among his competitors who made him step lively was HAAT SHAAT, a real hot shot in park classes, and he too is of the GULASTRA line, but of the RAHAS branch, since his sire is TAHAS.

Another high ranking park horse is of the GULASTRA line. This is ALHARIN, a son of NAHARIN (Gulastra-*Rimini). He was Reserve National Park Horse Champion. His dam ALLA KYAM, is double *ROSANTHUS since her sire and dam are both by that horse. The line of RISSLINA, a daughter of the famous mare RISSLA (she by *Berk), is also intensified in this pedigree. Despite all this English influence, ALLA KYAM is of a Polish family, that of *UGRA. The full sister of the latter is the celebrated SAGAR, leading money winner as a four-year-old and winner of both the Oaks and Derby (Arab) in Poland. So, as always, the winning park horses all seem to tie in with either AZREK (via *Berk or other lines) or Polish blood and sometimes Egyptian.

While the *BERK line may be represented mostly through other parts of the pedigree than tail male, his line is gradually increasing. His influence through RIBAL has already been shown in the few cases mentioned, but of course it is much greater than seen at first glance. Moreover the *BERK lines in England have helped improve action there as well as in the imported Englishbreds and their descendants here. RIBAL's grandson MAHUBI sired the versatile gelding SAN LUIS JOSHUA who cleaned up first as a jumper, then in various English classes all the way from pleasure to formal combination, in the latter going Top Ten at the Nationals. He has a very free and easy way of going, with plenty of action and style, but proved that he too could turn on speed, in roadster classes. The handsome old stallion CARAVAN, still alive and lively as of this writing at thirty-one years of age, proved to be a valuable sire in the Draper breeding program. Many of the mares which contributed to the phenomenal success of SUREYN as a sire in his relatively short time at stud, were by CARAVAN or his son JUBILO.

Many of the horses of the *NASIK and *NUREDDIN II lines have been mentioned under the Kellogg and Selby, as well as Harris, headings. However some top wins can be added: ALICANTE's GHAZAL sired the Top Ten GHAZIK, and in the RIFNAS group CARLANI was a Top Ten stallion, as was EL SIROCCO who sired the Reserve Great Plains Champion ELSO and the Canadian Top Ten MALAK ABYAUD. In the FARANA section, EL KUMAIT (full brother of the extraordinary foundation broodmare of the Cedardell Stud, Yatana) was sire of EL RAHNA whose daughter ROSE RAHNAFIN was a Top Ten mare. NUSIK sired several hard-running race horses, including NUSABRE, while another son, the champion NUSEYN, is the sire of the Top Ten park horse MASEYN, who is also a Legion of Merit winner. In the SIKIN branch, his grandson NASAH sired a Top Tenner in NADISA. From *NURED-DIN II, and via KAABA, GUDEA is the sire of a Canadian Top Ten, WILDWOOD FAROUK. Still in the KAABA groups, SAHAR is the sire of the Pacific Coast champion BINHARA, dam of BREEZE, who is a Top Ten mare at halter, also Reserve National Champion in western pleasure. In the *FERDIN branch ROSSDIN is the sire of the Top Ten stallion KUBAISHAN. The FARIS line came under the import section.

The *IBN MAHRUSS line was first referred to under the 1900 importation of the mare *BUSHRA, a daughter of AZREK. Her son *IBN MAHRUSS, imported en utero, is the founder of a sire line having two branches via STAMBUL, one of the early Remount stallions. Further details on STAMBUL's sire are given under the *BUSHRA heading. STAMBUL was a grey, foaled in 1926 and bred by A. W. Harris. He was a combination of early American lines, but of course had that one lone top cross to English breeding, because of his grandsire, which makes him belong to that sire line regardless of the preponderance of other bloodlines. He was stylish, but quite plain, and his neck was thick and underslung. His son ALLA AMARWARD was coarse, and his neck was extremely heavy, especially in his old age when it seemed thicker than his body. This animal was bred by Dr. W. W. Thomas of Merced, California and was foaled in 1935. As a four-year-old he was purchased by H. H. Reese because, as Reese said "he was a flaxen-maned chestnut and the price was right." It was low enough, all right, much less than generally secured even for a foal in those days. He was not a show horse; unlike the other Reese stallions (aside from Gezan) which were shown just enough to gain the title of champion, so he has no show record at all. Nor was he a riding horse—he just brought in income mainly as a sire of Palominos and other grades, but of course he was also used on purebreds at a low fee. This accounts for the large number of foals registered under his name, for up until 1963 he ranked fifth in registrations. ALLA had a habit of flattening his ears when anyone approached him, giving the impression he was mean, but he was instead quite gentle. This would be of no import at all except that his trait was inherited and many of his get and even later descendants are said to be sour in disposition because of it, yet many of them are not *really* sour, they too just faked meaness.

Since the show wins in this book are based on the Yearbooks, and don't start until 1953, this leaves out one of ALLA's best sons, EL NATTAL, as a champion to his credit. EL NATTAL did not resemble ALLA whatsoever, but instead was a dead ringer for his dam NATTA (Farana-Rahika) but of a less hot disposition. NATTA is also dam of VAN's NATTA, (full sister to El Nattall) who has nicked well with FADJUR and FERNEYN. Her daughter FER-NATTA is the dam of two Top Ten mares, BINT FERNATTA and FERNEYNA and the former (of these two) is also a Canadian Top Ten. EL NATTALL was champion at one of the Southern California all-Arabian shows, but more important he was the first Pacific Coast Champion Stallion. He died fairly young, but as the charts show, he sired three champions and several sons to carry on the line. One of these sons has a first to his credit too. This is EL BIER-NATT, winner of the first Great Plains championship. EL NATTALL was the light and life of his owner Mrs. Marietta Whitcomb of Riverside, California, and her place is named after him—Rancho El Nattall. Mrs. Whitcomb has already been mentioned as the importer of three English horses, these having brought over subsequent to EL NATTALL's death. EL NATTALL was a bay, foaled in 1944, and was bred by Ralph S. Vanderhoof.

BACARAM, a winner in the National class at Cheyenne, was also a pre-1953 champion sired by ALLA AMARWARD. He was out of the good mare *BABEL, a French import. BACARAM is sire of BAKAR, Great Plains Champion Gelding, and of THE ELECTRICIAN, former jumper who won one of the 2½ mile races.

The highlights of the *MIRAGE line are given under the Selby heading. The most important wins of this sire line at present are through the ARABI KABIR branch. This was a very classy chestnut horse who had won both at halter and in park classes, as he had very good action. If he had been as good in back of the saddle as he was in front he would have been hard to beat even now, but although his croup was good enough his hind legs were very, very over-angulated. This seems to have been counteracted in later generations however, and certainly his grandson, the National Champion BAY ABI+ not only has straight hind legs but he sires foals with the same sort. Indeed he is proving to be an outstanding sire. The other winner in the national category is IBN RAMINAGE, a Top Ten gelding.

IMAGE himself had sired IMAGIN, a Reserve National Champion stallion, and SANGE, a Top Ten mare. IMAGIN and his full brother IMAGINATION were many-time winners in park and harness classes.

237

IMAGE (*Mirage-*Rifala)

RIFAGE (*Mirage-*Rifala)

GAYSAR (Rifage-Ralouma)

SKORAGE (Gaysar-Rageyma)

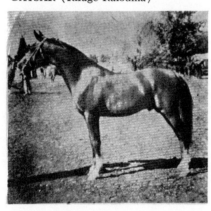

ARABI KABIR (Image-*Kareyma)

BAY ABI (Errabi-Angyl)

SOME SIRES OF THE *MIRAGE LINE

RIFAGE, full brother of IMAGE purchased from Selby by L. W. Van Vleet and featured in his Sunday exhibitions high in the Rockies, was more successful than IMAGE in high wins too. His daughter ROMINNA was National Champion, two others, RISHIMA and SHIHADA were Top Ten, as was a son, SULYMAN. His sons GAYSAR, a chestnut bred by Van Vleet and foaled in 1942 started quite a line through his two sons GALIMAR and SKORAGE. The latter could be called the foundation sire of Ed Tweed's Brusally Ranch in Scottsdale, for he not only sired most of their early stock, but he did about everything he was qualified for in the show ring as well. He proved it emphatically at the 1965 Scottsdale show, when he was eighteen years of age. He had been retired for several years, but when the Polish stallion *GWIAZDOR died on the eve of the show, SKORAGE was hurriedly entered as a substitute. Working by memory more or less, he cleaned up, winning three of the four classes in which he was entered and taking a second in the other. Included among them was the English pleasure stake, with thirty-nine entries. His son PULQUE+ and daughter SKORATA are Top Tens, and SKORENNE won the same honor in Canada.

In the *FADL line there is no doubt as to which is the star. Through the half Polish FADHEILAN and his son FADJUR and their descendants, thirty-nine of the *FADL line's eighty-four champions are accountable. Second highest is through the all Egyptian FAY-EL-DINE branch with twenty-two. *FADL is first referred to under the Babson importation heading, and most of the information about his line is given there. FADJUR was bred by Harry Linden of Spokane, Washington who then owned the soon-to-be famous BINT SAHARA who is now the dam of nine other champions. FADJUR is a bay, foaled in 1952. When he was sixteen years old (the oldest horse in the show) he won the Reserve National Stallion Championship, much to the near hysterical enthusiasm of his wildly-clapping admirers. While he has his faults, he also has great animation, and moreover rarely stands still long enough for the faults to become obvious, and it is the never failing animation, plus his style and beautiful head, that has earned him his gallery. He had been Top Ten on previous occasions, and his dark grey son IBN FADJUR has won a Reserve National Championship. The latter was also Canadian National Champion. He was killed in a fluke accident by electrocution in his own corral, so his spectacular record was cut short. Other wins by FADJUR get are the Canadian National Championship with SAKIFA, and Top Tens in that country by BINT FERNATTA (also U.S. TT), SAFAD, HI-FAD and JURNEEKA+, while ANTONETTE was Reserve Champion. FADJUR was purchased by the Jack Tone family of Stockton, California as a gawky yearling, but he showed his glamorous potential even then. FADJUR "made" the Tone Ranch, as far as the horse operation there is concerned.

In the FAY-EL-DINE branch, ZAB (whose grandsire is the English-bred *Aldebar) is the sire of the National Champion Gelding BAZREB and the Top Ten mare RUSA. A horse which may not be listed in the rarified atmosphere of national halter wins, but who deserves mention nevertheless is MAARDI. His sire and dam are both by FAY-EL-DINE (in fact *Fadl is three of his four greatgrandsires) and in conformation he is good except for short legs, a rather unexpected feature considering his breeding. The unusual thing about this horse is his versatility. He is one of the best and most willing jumpers, and has won, besides the common garden-variety pleasure classes, hunter, trail, reining and anything else that comes up. About all he lacked was action enough for park competition. The FA-SERR branch from FAY-EL-DINE on the other hand has produced some park winners. He sired BINT AAROUFA, Top Ten park, and his son FAARIS is the sire of FARR-RA, a national park champion. FA-SERR also sired a Top Ten in halter, SERR-RA.

*ZARIFE, an import of W. R. Brown, has been fleetingly mentioned. His son HALLANY MISTANY was bred by Travelers Rest Arabian Stud and sold to Northern California where he sired only one foal up until 1956, in which year he sired two. To backtrack a bit—the dam of this stallion was the beautiful *RODA, a level-crouped, arch-necked, beautiful-headed mare whose hind legs were not quite as crooked as were some of the NEGMA family to which she belongs. She has so far been mentioned only as an import by Brown in 1932. Dickinson had this to say about her:

> *RODA was the Reserve Champion Mare in a strong class of twelve entries in the National Arabian Show of 1933, second prize mare at Columbia, Tennessee, 1936, and first prize Arabian at Franklin, Tennessee, 1936. . . . At the age of two *RODA met with a serious accident which has left her permanently blemished. Notwithstanding, she is a mare of admirable conformation and development. Her head has been described by one of the most distinguished breeders of Arabs in the United States as perfectly representative of the classic type.

HALLANY MISTANY is registered as a black, foaled in 1937. He was discovered, salvaged actually, by Howard Marks of Tracy, California, in 1956, at which time the horse was already nineteen years old. Like SUREYN, he was nearly lost to the breed, and the same was true of *ASTRALED, but for the latter it was almost too late. HALLANY MISTANY is described succinctly in the Travelers Rest catalog:

> Sold 1940 to California and there a 1st prize winner. His owner described him as having 'the most exquisite rein, is as fast as he can be on his feet.' and described by a visitor as 'most beautiful black stallion I have ever seen.'

HALLANY MISTANNY became popular enough when Howard Marks first acquired him, but in his 1957 crop was the gorgeous bay filly HABINA, and as soon as she was old enough for the show circuit HAL-

LANY MISTANNY's stock soared. She became a Top Ten mare. The dark bay PRINCE HALLANY has been another big winner. Several HALLANY MISTANNY horses have been winners in hunter and jumper classes, others have done well in park as well as in the inevitable pleasure classes.

The *NASR line is represented in the upper echelons by the Top Ten gelding SELRUBA, but apparently no others in the Nationals. The NAZEER and *MOFTAKHAR lines are detailed under the import divisions.

With the appearance of the OFIR representatives in this country, competition definitely stepped up. *WITEZ II was of course the first here and the other two lines, represented by *BASK and WIELKI SZLEM have had previous coverage. However until a son of the latter sires some champions (*El Mudir is of this line), the line will stay where it is (on sire line charts), for the champion represented is a mare, *ARWILGA. As already mentioned, the get of *WITEZ II can and do win at any kind of performance. That they are not limited to the brawn division is proven by their wins at the national level. *WITEZ II is the sire of the Reserve National Champion stallion BOLERO, whose son ZARABO copied this achievement, then went on to take the whole affair the following year with his very popular National championship. BO-LERO was a Canadian Top Ten, his son was Reserve Champion there. Other sons winning the Top Ten spot were HIRZAN, NATEZ, WITE-ZAR and YATEZ, with TANGO, a full brother of BOLERO and NATEZ, taking the Canadian version. BLACK MAGIC, another full brother, was Reserve Canadian Champion. AMATEZ+ was Reserve National Champion Gelding and another, FARO IBN WITEZ was Canadian Top Ten, AMATEZ+ is a Reserve National Champion in English pleasure. *WITEZ II seemed to prefer colts, for his daughters were less well represented than his sons. However MITEZ did make the Top Ten plateau. NITEZ is a three-quarter brother of the foregoing group of brothers, in that his dam is the dam of NAFALLA. NAFALLA's dam is NAFA, who also produced the champions NAFATEZ and NAFASON in addition to NITEZ and NAFALLA. She is a daughter of NARASA who is the tail female family founder in IBN HANRAH's pedigree. And since NARASA is a full sister of FARANA who turned out to be such a good broodmare sire, there may be some connection here. This is of course the *FERDA family, that may be the clue. NITEZ has the most sons representing him of all the *WITEZ line at present. These NAFA and NAFALLA sons were bred by Robert McDonald of Sepulveda, California and represent quite an achieve-ment for a breeder with a broodmare band consisting only of a mare and daughter team at the time.

ZITEZ is the sire of ALSAGHEZ, a handsome chestnut stallion which is a Top Ten cutting horse, a National Champion stock horse and in his leisure moments, a Great Plains Champion at halter, and Top Ten.

OFIR (Kuhailan Haifi-Dziwa)

WIELKI SZLEM (Ofir-Elegantka)

WITRAZ (Ofir-Makata)

*WITEZ II (Ofir-Federacja)

BASK (Witraz-Balalajka)

STALLIONS OF THE OFIR LINE

YATEZ is the sire of the Top Ten mare TEENA, also the Top Ten park horse TERISSA; and NATEZ takes the credit for the National Champion mare INDIAN GENII. WITEZAR, who won the A.H.S.A. Horse of the Year Award, is the sire of the Reserve National Champion gelding BURRTEZ who also won the Great Plains gelding championship.

The *DEYR line is a very old one, antedating that of *WITEZ II for instance, by forty years. Not in pedigree, for *DEYR's pedigree stops in the Circassian village where he was purchased, while that of *WITEZ II goes back a hundred more years; but old in the time it was in this country. *DEYR has been discussed in the Davenport chapter. Suffice to say he is not the sort of horse anyone would inbreed to, and most breeders have avoided it. But now he is so far back that he really doesn't matter, except for those dominant faults that have been transmitted through his get. HANRAH was a very good-looking horse, which is not surprising, for even though his dam was by *RAHAL, that horse had some good points to contribute. The mare line is the notable one however, as it brings in GHAZI, *RIZVAN, *RODAN and *GHAZALA. HANRAH is the sire of the Canadian National Champion and Reserve U.S. National Champion IBN HANRAH. His dam in turn was RONARA, of the family line already mentioned regarding the phenomenal NAFA branch, but which here brings in ROAYAS as the sire of RONARA, and ROAYAS is by ROA-BRAH out of RASOULMA. A full sister of IBN HANRAH, LA BAHIA, is a Top Ten mare.

Unlike IBN HANRAH, IBN HANAD is all Davenport, but his champion get are all out of JOYE and STAR OF EGYPT (full sisters by *Raffles ex *Roda) and the Polish import *AENIZA, a fine group of mares. TSALI, out of another *RAFFLES mare, MY BONNIE NYLON, is the sire of the Top Ten winner TSATYR.

The adventures of ANTEZ were sketched in the Davenport section. The Top Ten gelding GHAMAR is by ANKAR and another Top Ten, the stallion HABU, is by BUNA. HABU in turn sired a Top Tenner in IBN HABU. *FERTIF, whose sire is out of the Polish mare *LASSA and his dam is by FERSEYN out of a FARANA mare, is the sire of the previously mentioned FER-NATTA, a Top Ten in Canada.

*ALDEBAR was one of the Babson imports and though this line does not seem to have halter champions of the national level, the fine park horse of pre-National days, ROUF, is of this line.

The remaining lines were covered under their importation dates, however *MOUNWER is the sire of a Top Ten stallion, MOUNRI.

The foregoing data makes monotonous reading, and although limited to the National wins for the most part, gives an inkling of the quality of the get of the various sires. It should be realized however that all the wins mentioned are but a part of the actual number of various championships acquired by these horses. Many of the Regional wins were made by the same horses that at least placed in the Top Ten competition. On the

243

other hand quite a number of Regional wins, unreported here, were made by horses whose owners could not afford to haul them halfway across the country to the Nationals, or did not want to. On top of the wins omitted because of lack of space (such as Regionals) there are sure to be many I just plain missed. Nevertheless the charts at least, since they reflect all regular show championships, are reasonably accurate and give the ratings at a glance.

I have emphasized park wins and skimmed over pleasure wins, because the former have to show a native talent for the work. They *must* have action. Of course judging in Arabian classes of this sort is often erratic, so some winners may have had no action at all, or else the wrong kind (goose-stepping), but hopefully the majority of the winners could trot. While park horses are of course three-gaited and therefore must perform adequately at the walk and canter, the truth is that most Arabians can walk and canter reasonably well, but not many can really trot with all the brilliance and action (remember its definition) demanded in a horse show. Consequently the first requirement is *action*. It is true that some of the best trotters may not like to either walk or canter, and accordingly they require more schooling in these gaits. The walk in such instances is usually almost a jog, even exceeding the springy walk that is permitted for a fired-up park performer. It should also be remembered that some of the most brilliant park (or harness) horses are rarely of the same temperament that characterizes a pleasure horse. The same nervous energy that gives them that about-to-explode attitude is exactly what separates the placid pleasure horse from the athlete of the show ring, the park horse. The latter seems to put every drop of energy into his work, as if in a hard fought finish of a race, and it may be this factor that makes ex-racehorses (Arabian) such good park horses. There are exceptions to this, of course. I believe it was President U. S. Grant who said "Never believe a generality, including this one," and that certainly applies to horses and their work. The ideal Arabian of this sort is one which can relax and go through all the motions of a pleasure class, then be collected to the required degree and made to step "high and handsome." And some do. Most do not.

There is a popular fallacy, generally held most strongly among those who own horses of strictly pleasure performance, to the effect that the Arabian's "natural action" is what is desired in a park class. Now just what is meant by "nautral?" As it was in the desert? Hardly. The Bedouins did not use this gait, so it was undeveloped to the point that Arabian horses were often described as two-gaited when first they were imported. Does it mean natural to the individual horse? That is altogether a different kettle of horseshoes. For there are about as many natural-to-each-horse ways of going as there are horses in this breed. Some have high, airy, well-flexed, and balanced action; others drag their toes and barely bend their knees; some have no flexion in front but too much hock action,

244

giving the riders a down-hill trip; and some go high in front but drag their hocks. Others have only moderate elevation and a free way of going. Of the bunch, the first and the last are good, depending on the purpose required, although a low-going horse is satisfactory for western use, providing it does not stumble over every match stick in the road and drag too much dust into the atmosphere.

Considering that the trot was an unused gait in the breed for countless generations, it seems to me that its progress is remarkable. There is still the strange conglomeration of ways of going, but nevertheless there are more *good* movers and the others are either improving somewhat or else going out of style. I rather think it is the latter, and that a better trot is a prominent part of breeding programs. It is true that there are still some "man-made" park horses, but breeders are generally aware of the degree of artificiality and use stallions which display the right sort of action, for after all the shoeing cannot be inherited, nor can an especially adroit trainer (except by other trainers). In other words, the action must be built in. Sad to say, however, there are still too many Arabian owners who cannot tell honest action when they see it, and they call any high action unnatural, even though the horse in question may be just off the track, and is either wearing racing plates or no shoes at all, and has never been trained for high action. This blindness to the fact that some Arabians *can* move is generally due to inexperience, the wrong information about Arabians, or prejudice.

It is this blind prejudice that so often holds back the breed, in that the Arabian is not allowed to exhibit its true potential in many lines of endeavor. Overall mediocrity seems to be preferred for the Arabian performance rather than allowing horses with latent ability in various lines show what they can really do.

It would take a book in itself to enumerate all the wins Arabian horses have made in endurance and trail rides. Unfortunately I have not kept records on these, so will have to just name, hit-or-miss style, a few examples. Competition in these is open to all breeds.

BINT GULIDA (Ghadaf-Gulida), a mare inbred to GULNARE and consequently also to °RODAN and °GHAZALA; with nine fairly close-up lines to MESAOUD, and also linebred to RIBAL, has a remarkable record in these affairs. She was 6th in the Western States 100-Mile Ride in July as a warm-up, then in September won the "Jim Shoulders 100-Miles-in-1-day-Ride" in the unprecedented time of 13 hours and 36 minutes. She finished the hundred miles more than five hours ahead of the second horse. She was owned and ridden by Linda Tellington.

Arabian horses have an enviable record in the famous Tevis Cup 100-miles in one day ride, over rugged mountainous terrain, from Lake Tahoe to Auburn, California. Wendell Robie's grey stallion BANDOS (°Nasr-°Baida) has the unique record of siring at least twenty-five finishers of the tough test. The parentage of this stallion makes him seem

245

fast just standing still, but of course a different type of speed and stamina is required in this affair. Included in this number are several winners of the Tevis Cup. However there were many other Arabians and half Arabians which won or completed this ride. A commemorative buckle is given to each person who completes the ride, and Wendell Robie, who made the first tour over the course to prove it could be done, has won ten of these buckles. Most other contestants are equally addicted to the sport.

An example of Arabian dominance of endurance rides, especially the 100-milers, is that of the 1969 Florida event, in which purebred or part-bred Arabians took eight of the twelve placings in the Heavyweight and Lightweight divisions. Lucille Kenyon, riding in her 58th 100-miler, won the Michael Trophy (named after that great endurance-ride winner who went on to become a champion of the 2½ mile races) for high point senior horse, and she also won the Heavyweight Challenge Trophy. Her mount was the purebred gelding PAZZAM. Losing the former by only a half point was another purebred gelding, KAMIN KU, ridden by Schuyler Hopper. However he won the Lightweight Challenge Trophy.

MAJUBA with Polly Johnson   SKOWREYM (Sauwid-Rafeyna)

AL-MARAH RAPTUROUS (Rapture-*Radeyra), owned and ridden by Mrs. William Hewitt, is unusual in that she won the Heavyweight Division of the Florida 100-Mile Ride while on the show circuit, during which time she had picked up a Canadian Top Ten, a reserve regional championship, and a U.S. Top Ten in English pleasure. Ordinarily show horses are too fat to even walk a hundred miles without foundering.

Another Hewitt winner is SKOWREYM (Sauwid-Rafeyma) who not only won several endurance rides, but also competed in a steeplechase and finished the course, which is more than some of the standard sized 'chasers did on this occasion. SKOWREYM has won combined training events as well. He is a small horse too, which is not surprising since he is inbred to SKOWRONEK, although through various lines—*RASEYN, *INCORONATA and *RAFFLES.

A true endurance ride was made by Polly Johnson on the stallion MAJUBA (Abu Zim-Zaza). His sire is by ABU FARWA and his dam by RAYHAK, a stallion bred by the Hearst Ranch and who showed magnificent trotting action, as might be expected since he was out of RAYIK. This is Maynesboro breeding. ZIYADI, the tough old ranch horse who showed so much speed in early day Arab races in California, is also in the pedigree as is *ZARIFE, of Egyptian breeding. The journey undertaken by Polly Johnson and MAJUBA was no overnight affair—it was one of 2250 miles, from Anchorage Alaska, down the rugged Alcan Highway, through Canada to the States. The stallion arrived in fine shape, but doubtless his rider was willing to stay off a horse for a while, after this three month trip.

Another recent long distance saunter was undertaken by Jefferson Spivey on a dappled grey gelding ROSE ARABY MR. SOL (Silver Crescent-Jawharah) loaned to him for the adventure by the Rose Araby farm. This trip in 1968, was from Santa Barbara, California to Rehoboth Beach, Delaware, a distance of 3,850 miles in slightly over six months. The danger of such journeys of course is that man-made monster that teems over the plains and everywhere else—the automobile. Aside from a loss of two hundred plump pounds, MR SOL was none the worse for wear. His sire is by the English horse *ROSANTHUS out of INDRIFF, while his dam combines JEDRAN, GUEMURA, *IBN NAFA and *EXOCHORDA. JAWHARA is a three-fourths sister of ANNE, the dam of the winner of one of the recent sprint races, RAFFHA.

A few years ago FERAL (Aldisa-Ferini) was the N.A.T.R.C. champion (over all breeds) in the Heavyweight Division. Two other trail ride champions were BILLY and SHAMUS, the unusual part oftheir accomplishment being that they were both by the same sire, MAINAD.

The winning of the $1000 Rein-Horse Championship Stake at the Grand National Livestock Show in San Francisco by RONTEZA (*Witez II-Ronna) has already been mentioned, but it was quite a feat, in that this mare was competing against the best rein horses of all breeds (at least all suitable for such work), and she won in both the Light and the Heavyweight classes. RONTEZA was owned, trained and ridden by Sheilah Varian.

Several Arabian jumpers have won in open competition, and as hunters too. Among these is the *WITEZ II gelding GALLAHER, the Arizona Champion Green Jumper and Reserve Champion Green Working Hunter. Another open winner was RAKIZ, by *ZARIFE, and the mare AANADRAH (by Aarief) also won in open competition. Another is PADISHAM, a bay gelding by PADISHAH, who won the Small Hunter High Point Award of the Virginia Horse Show Association, and fourth place in Junior Working Hunter. This was in the heart of hunting country,

247

as might be assumed. OVERBROOK'S JAFAR and ridden by a fourteen year old boy, is another Arabian with a number of hunter and jumper championships earned in open shows. There are many others of equal talent, proving that Arabs *can* jump.

The 2½ mile exhibition races held at major race tracks in the eastern states were first held in November of 1959. The premier was won by OFIR (Witez II-Tiara) in a battle down the stretch against MICHAEL (Raffey-Abuseyna), the latter losing by a half-length. Weight 115, for all entries. Time, 5:05 1/5. OFIR won the second race, in slightly faster time but did not have MICHAEL to urge him on. However in the third of these marathons, MICHAEL and OFIR battled it out again, OFIR forcing the pace to make MICHAEL set the (American) Arabian record for the distance, of 4:51 4/5. These two are the acknowledged champions of the 2½ miles races, OFIR winning three before an accident in a van stopped his race career, and MICHAEL winning four. KHALI (Kalun-Kaat) also won two of these events. The only comparable time (i.e. for distance) I happen to have is for the Russian Arabian SPORT, of 4:42.3 when he was five years of age, so he presumably carried at least 130 pounds—probably more, in view of his past performances. Russian dirt tracks seem to have less cushion than American, so may be fast.

An interesting sidelight is that AL-MARAH IBN INDRAFF, the "place" horse to OFIR in the second race and third in a couple of others in 1959-61, around *nine* years later was competing in the races (1½ miles) in Phoenix, where he won some newspaper acclaim when it was noted that he was a year older than his jockey. While he did not win, he managed to be close up in these as well as earlier races. Little SKOW-REYM was in training for the latter (in 59-61) too. No one can discount the durability of these horses, nor the pluck the Poles spoke of.

The races held under the auspices of the Arabian Horse Racing Association of America are the only one wherein pari-mutuel betting is allowed, and they are on regular tracks, on the same card as the Thoroughbred events. A number of races (1½ miles) were held in Louisiana, including the Arabian Classic, but most of the Arabian racing (aside from those held in connection with all-Arabian shows) has been in Arizona, with a couple of months in Colorado in 1969. The champion of 1967-68 was the Polish import *ORZEL (now a halter champion) already mentioned, with KONTIKI the runner-up. However in the last race of the 1968 season, at Phoenix, KONTIKI set the American record for the distance, 2:49 4/5ths. He carried the same weight as *ORZEL (who was not in this race) in the battle in which KONTIKI was second to that horse, 142 pounds. EL GOHARI, second in this race, also carried 142 pounds. He is the winner of the 1968 Arabian Classic (won by *Orzel in 1967) and also won the 6½-furlong spring championship (Arab) at Pike's Peak Meadows in 1969 in Colorado. KONTIKI (Camelot-Almiki) was unbeaten until he met *ORZEL. His sire is a son

First Arabian Race in the U.S., 2½ miles, Laurel, Md., Nov. 11, 1959

*ORZEL (Pietuszok-Ofirka)

Winning at Arizona Downs, Phoenix, March 30, 1968

249

of SENEYN and his dam (in the case of Michael) is by ABU FARWA. As already pointed out, EL GOHARI is by *MOFTAKHAR, who has sired several other American race winners. A winner of both 1½ mile races and sprints is BJD SKOWROEK, by ROMBLON, a son of *CZUBU- THAN. A tough veteran of show racing is NUSABRE by NUSIK (Sikin- Nusara) out of NEVADA STAR (*Lotnik-Tunis), who has won both of his sprint races. Another repeater is SARED (Satrap-Raqana). The grandsire of his dam is also *CZUBUTHAN. The Brazilian-Argentinian mare *NAHRAWANA is also in this pedigree. *FIREBRAND, a cham- pion son of *BASK out of a RAPTURE mare, was second in his first out- ing and won the second handily, so he is a chip off the old block.

Although there is no real way of comparing the times, the following are given for general interest. They are not, in all cases, records for the distance. There may be differences in the actual method of timing, i.e. when the barrier goes up (or gates open), or when horses are in stride, etc.; the difference between turf and dirt; the type of turf; the condition of the track; and the weight carried. So actual comparisons are impossible. Even the length of the track makes a difference, though most Arab racing (foreign) is on mile tracks or longer. Although actual weight is not given for the Russian horses, the minimum for 4-year-olds and up is 130 pounds. For 3-year olds, 128 pounds.

Distance	Time	Horse	Weight	Country
6½ furlongs	1:25 4/5	BJD SKOWROEK	120 lbs.	U.S.A.
1 Mile	1:46	BALANCE	132 lbs.	Egypt
1600 meters	1:47	SPUTNIK	?	Russia
1600 meters	1:48	KAHRAMAN	111	Egypt
1600 meters	1:48	KAYED	112	Egypt
1600 meters	1:53	ALLADYN	141	Poland
2000 meters	2:14	KOMPOZIDOR	?	Russia
2000 meters	2:14	PLASKA	?	Russia
2000 meters	2:15	AMIR EL LEWA	140	Egypt
2000 meters	2:29	FELLACH	139	Poland
2400 meters	2:43 3/5	EL MANSOUR	133	Egypt
2400 meters	2.41	PRIVET	?	Russia
2400 meters	2:49	PIEN	130	Poland
1½ miles	2.47 3/5	KONTIKI	142	U.S.A.
3000 meters	3:26	SPORT	?	Russia
3000 meters	3:26	LEOPARD	?	Russia
3000 meters	3:35	EQUIFOR	132½	Poland
4000 meters (nearly 2½ miles)	4:42.3	SPORT	?	Russia
2½ miles	4:51 4/5	MICHAEL	115	U.S.A.
7000 meters (4⅜ miles)	8:59.7	KNIPPEL	?	Russia

250

There is a popular misconception that Arabian horses can beat Thorough-breds at long distances (1½ miles on) but that is a complete fallacy. The endurance for which Arabians are famed was not at a dead run, and more often than not the horse was led beside a camel and only used in the short dashes and in-fighting of a raid. Whenever a long ride was demanded however, if the horse was run all the way it was either laid up for months, worthless thereafter, or it died on the way—which is the same thing intensified. This is according to actual reports, and even Arab bragging often ends up—on these tales of long rides—with the afterthought "but the mare died."

Wilfrid Blunt wrote:

> . . . even in war it is often a question of endurance rather than speed, which is the better animal; and where a real flight and a real pursuit takes place, the course is seldom a straight one, that it is often that the best-trained or the best-ridden mare gets the advantage, as the one which really has the speed. A mare celebrated for speed in the desert is as often as not merely a very well-broken charger. . . . The Bedouins must be very hard-pressed indeed if they keep on a steady gallop for more than a mile or two together. Their parties and expeditions even where is haste is necessary, are halts and dismountings, and a steady pace all day is not a thing to be thought of.

The fortitude for which the breed is noted is more the ability to endure great hardship and privation rather than the stamina demanded in a long race at a dead run. Nevertheless the Arabian is the fastest of the unimproved breeds (or rather, unspecialized breeds) and has been *the* racehorse of many countries. And even Mohammed said "The horse is created to run, otherwise he is as worthless as a wooden frame."

The times of Arabian races are much slower than in Thoroughbred races—in the time a good Arabian was completing a mile, a fast Thoroughbred would finish a mile and a furlong. But that's no reason for not racing Arabians. If competition for the specialists should stop Arabians from doing the same sort of work, then Arabs would not be shown in harness, in park classes, or cutting, reining, and so on, including jumping.

The Arabian has long been touted as the most versatile of breeds. It cannot be so in actuality unless it is allowed to perform various tasks to the best of its ability—whether this be action, speed, agility, or whatever. Not necessarily (in fact preferably not) by the same horse, but by those having a talent along certain lines. In other words the *breed* is versatile, not each member thereof.

To this point the lines have been traced through sires, giving a "view from the top" only. It is true that the sires can be more important than mares, not because of any dominance, but through percentages. While

251

a stallion can sire hundreds of foals in a lifetime, a mare averages around ten, though some produce double that number. They are rare, however. It is also presumed that a stallion will resemble his own sire, assuming that horse was worth his salt, or maybe will even be an improvement over him. A third point is that theoretically only good stallions are used at stud (in the Arabian breed this has been more theory than practice), while *all* Arabian mares are bred, if possible. This is true no matter how hideous the mares might be, their owners hopefully believing the stallion can improve the foal. Some of these nightmares however are "incubator" mares, and reproduce the sire's good qualities while adding none of their own unlovely points. While this is fine as far as the first generation is concerned, there is always the haunting fear that there might be throwbacks to the mare in future generations. One thing is sure, the breeder never intentionally lets the dam be seen when selling the foal, in such incubator cases. When a colt of such a mare is to be gelded, then there is no problem of this sort, but when the colt or filly is a breeding prospect, then the mare line is of much more importance. In most cases no horse is a stallion prospect unless his distaff side is as good as his sire line.

In view of the contribution of the distaffers, the following list and charts are of some value. They also provide a closer look at "the fabric of fame," providing the warp and woof, you might say, not just a single continuous thread, since the sires of their champion foals as well as their own sires are indicated. While these represent only the leading families, they at last give an inkling of the trend.

AARAF (*Raffles-Aarah)

AARIEF (*Raffles-Aarah)

252

LEADING BROODMATRONS
Dams of 3 or more champions, Class A Shows, 1953-1970 inclusive.

In order to give more depth to this survey, the sire of the dam (maternal grandsire) is given, which sheds some light on the better broodmare sires one generation back, not only the sires of the mares listed. In addition the stallions which sired the champion produce of the mares are given, in order to indicate the successful nick, or that the mare can produce champions by various sires and of varied bloodlines.

As in the Leading Sire list, this number of champions (or reserves) reflects the minimum number, as some are from unreported (to the Yearbook) shows, or of earlier periods than 1953. Also, some names were changed and could not be traced, so the parents of such do not get their credit.

The number on the "Family" column at right is that of the main tail-female family which is shown on a separate chart.

NO. OF CHAMPS.	MARE	COLOR AND DATE FOALED	PARENTS	SIRE OF DAM	SIRES OF MARE'S CHAMPIONS	TF FAMILY
10	BINT SAHARA	gr. 1942	(Farawi-Bint Sedjur)	Ribal	Ferseyn (8) Fadheilan (1) The Real McCoy (1)	No. 11 Sedjur
7	SAKI	gr. 1950	(Ferseyn-Ferdia)	Farana	All by Fadjur	Babe Azab No. 12
6	BONITA	ch. 1945	(Caravan-*Barakat)	Fondak (Spain)	Sureyn (4) Pomona Ahmen (2)	No. 14 *Meca
6	GAJALA	gr. 1943	(*Raffles-Rageyma)	*Mirage	Fay-el-Dine (1) Ferzon (3) Phantom (1) Niga (1)	No. 5 *Kareyma
6	*SILVER CRYSTAL	gr. 1937	(Rangoon-Somara)	*Nureddin II	Sureyn (1), *Serafix (3) Raktha (1) Grand Royal (1)	No. 7 Somara
5	FERSARA	gr. 1947	(Ferseyn-Bint Sahara)	Farawi	Ferneyn (4), Aarief (1)	No. 11 Sedjur
5	FEYN	gr. 1945	(Feyd-Kishta)	Akil	All by Ga'Zi	No. 3 *Felestin
5	JUBILEE	gr. 1946	(Jubilo-*Menfis)	Ursus	Sureyn (4) Sur-Grande (1)	No. 14 * Menfis
5	NARZAH	b. 1947	(Narzigh-Narlah)	Narkhaleb	All by Yatez	No. 9 Killah
5	POMONA AVESTA	b. 1944	(Farana-*Malouma)	Maloum (Egypt)	Ronek (1), Hasarip (1) Fadjur (1), Sha-ra-zada (2)	*Malouma
4	ABUSEYNA	gr. 1946	(Abu Farwa-Daanaseyn)	*Raseyn	Aah Abu (1), Imagin (1), Ruffourid (1), Hai-Amin (1)	No. 6 *Raida
4	BARQ	ch. 1947	(Abu Farwa-Antana)	Antez	Indy (1), Natez (2) Muskateer (1)	No. 1 Bazikh
4	CHLOEYN	gr. 1947	(*Raseyn-*Chloe)	Lirnik (Poland)	All by *Serafix	No. 16 *Chloe
4	GAY ROSE	ch. 1957	(Ferzon-Gali Rose)	Galimar	(Azraff (3), *Nizzam (1)	No. 6 *Rose of France
4	GHAZNA	ch. 1943	(Chepe Noyon-Ginnyya)	Bazleyd	Abu Farwa (3) Hallany-Mistanny (1)	No. 4 Gulnare
4	INDAYLA	gr. 1955	(Indraff-Shu Ayla)	Ptolomy	All by El Nahar	No. 3 * Ferdisia
4	MILANNE	gr. 1946	(Feyd-Kishta)	Akil	Rapture (3), Laukit (1)	No. 3 * Felestin
4	NAFALLA	b. 1946	(Alla Amarward-Nafa)	*Raseyn	All by *Witez II	No. 3 Farasin
4	RAZIMA	gr. 1950	(Rasan-Roseyna)	*Raseyn	Julep (2), Fa-Serr (1) Faaris (1)	No. 6 * Rokhsa
4	RONARA	b. 1946	(Roayas-Narlet)	Ralet	Hanrah (3), Al-M. Erka (1)	No. 3 *Farasin
4	ROSE MARIE	gr. 1947	(*Raffles-Rodetta)	Agwe	Indraff (2) Royal Diamond (1) *Count Dorsaz (1)	No. 13 * Roda
4	RULITHA	ch. 1954	(*Shamadan-Korlitha)	Kalat	*Serafix (3), Faserouf (1)	No. 10 Sultana

253

4	SCHERAFF	gr. 194	(Indraff-Scherazade)	*Al Mashoor	Ferzon (2) Galimar (1), Phantom (1)	No. 11 Domow
4	TAHIR	gr. 1942	(Antez-Setana)	Farana	Abu Farwa (1), Abu Baha (2) Ferseyn (1)	No. 1 Bazikh
4	TUWAISAN	gr. 1949	(Rossdin-Kotsi)	Caravan	Sureyn (2), Surran (2)	No. 14 *Meca
3	AL-MARAH RASHMA	gr. 1953	(Selmage-Rose of Luzon)	Gulastra	Zarak (2), *Aanasseh (1)	No. 6 *Rose of France
3	AL-MARAH AASABA	gr. 1949	(Indraff-Nafri)	*Nasr	*Royal Diamond (1) *Count Dorsaz (1) *Silver Vanity (1)	No. 10 Dawn
3	ARACHNE	gr. 1953	(Desmoin-*Azja)	Landsnecht (Poland)	Ibn Semuel (1) Niga (1), Ferzon (1)	*Azja
3	ARIFA	gr. 1940	(*Zarife-Arjemonde)	Aahmed	Alicante's Ghazal (3)	No. 10 Sheria
3	BALENA	b. 1945	(*Raseyn—Dirabba)	Rossdin	Gaysar (1), *Sulejman (1)	No. 6 *Rijma
3	BELGHRA	gr. 1949	(Afmaar-Fazala)	*Fadl	Ibn Hanrah (2), Mraff (1)	No. 13 *Bint Serra I
3	BINNI	ch. 1940	(Gulastra-Habiba)	Bazleyd	Sahar (1), Hallany-Mistanny (1) Aarief (1)	No. 4 Nafud
3	BINT ABOU	b. 1948	(Abou-Yatana)	Farana	(Imaraff (2), Synbad (1)	No. 4 Ghazayat
3	BINT HALOO	ch. 1945	(Kamil-Kutaia)	*Nuri Pasha	All by Ga'Zi	*Nufoud DB
3	BRIDE ROSE	gr. 1938	(Ronek-*Rose of France	*Raswan	Nitez (1), Galimar (1) Fay-el-Dine	No. 6 *Rose of France
3	CAPRICE	gr. 1955	(Gem of Cedardell-Barsha)	Tebruk	Hassan Pasha (1) Synbad (1) Cedardell Heritage (1)	No. 4 Ghazayat
3	DOMINICA	gr. 1942	(Hattal-Nasafa)	Rifnas	Rifage (2), *Zarife (1)	No. 6 *Rasafa
3	DORAZA	ch. 1956	(El Zarib-Doraz)	Miraz	Heritage Hamala (2) Fadi (1)	No. 13 *Maaroufa
3	EL LOUISA	ch. 1955	(Malik Shah-Zaaba)	Aabadan	Sir Seyn (1), Raffon (1) Bur-Loya (1)	No. 13 *Mahrouss
3	FAE	gr. 1950	(Indraff-Kae)	*Mirage	Julep (2), Rasan (1)	No. 10 Aatika
3	FADJURA	b/gr 1956	(Fadjur-Fer Natta)	Fertif	Rifraff (1), Seraj (1) Raamason (1)	No. 1 Bazikh
3	FARADINA	b. 1942	(Farana-Hazzadina)	*Ferdin	All by Ga'Zi	No. 6 *Rossana
3	FIALA	gr. 1952	(Indy-Barq)	Abu Farwa	All by *Royal Constellation	No. 1 Bazikh
3	FLAIA	gr. 1945	(*Raffles-*Indaia)	Raseem (Engl.)	Garaff (1), Ghadaf (1) Sunny Acres Tequila (1)	No. 2 *Indaia
3	FRANKOKHLA	gr. 1939	(Kokhleson-Franza)	*Mirzam	Rafourid (1), Rifraff (2)	No. 6 * Rose of France
3	GAY-NEGMA	gr. 1951	(Gaysar-Fay Negma)	Fay-el-Dine	*Fadl (1), Sahdaf (2)	No. 13 *Maaroufa

3	GEBINA	b. 1950	(Fa-el-Gamar – Bambina)	*Raffles	Image (1), Rasakkla (1) Fa-el-Gamar (1).	*Muha D.B.
3	GEYNIMA	ch. 1956	(Geym-Nima)	Image	Radamason (1), *Nizzam (1), Llano Grande Conquistador (1)	*Nedjme D.B.
3	GHARASITA	ch. 1950	(Gharis-La Placita)	Caravan	All by Sureyn	No. 8 Sura
3	GISELA	gr. 1940	(Akil-Shemseh)	*Nasik	All by Rapture	No. 6 *Rifla
3	GRIFFIN	b. 1953	(Garaff-L'Aida)	Abou	All by Tsali	No. 8 Il'id Ilkbir
3	*GWADIANA	gr. 1952	(Amurath Sahib-Gwara)	Wielki Szlem (Poland)	*NABORR (2) Comet (Poland) (1)	No. 16 Milordka
3	HAMANNE	ch. 1945	(Ptolomy-El Aroussa)	Ribal	All by Durral	No. 3 *Ferdisia
3	IDORA	b. 1952	(Amidore-Izmir)	*Ferdin	Zari (1), Shalimar Gilette (2)	No. 11 Moliah
3	IMAFARA	b. 1953	(Imaraff-Fa Rahna)	*Fadl	Tsali (1), El Gato (1), *Nizzam (1)	No. 4 Ghazayat
3	IMAJA	gr. 1956	(Image-Nimja)	Geym	Radamason (2), Nitez (1)	No. 7 *Selmnab
3	INDAIRE	b. 1946	(Indraff-Varioca)	*Czubuthan	Bamby (2), Himalaya (1)	No. 19 *Aire
3	INDRIFA	b/gr 1951	(Indraff-Rifa)	*Fadl	Handeyraff (2), Julep (1)	No. 4 Ghazayat
3	ISHMIA	gr. 1937	(*Selmian-*Rishafieh)	Jeruan (England)	All by Rifage	No. 6 Rish
3	JAWHARAH	gr. 1944	(Jidua-Suleika)	*Ibn Nafa	Silver Crescent (2) Aahdin (1)	*Exochorda
3	JOYE	gr. 1948	(*Raffles-*Roda)	Mansour (Egypt)	Ibn Hanad (2) Sunny Acres Darious (1)	No. 13 *Roda
3	JUBILEMA	gr. 1947	(Jubilo-*Menfis)	Egipto (Spain)	Sureyn (1), *Morafic (1) *Royal Diamond (1)	No. 14 *Menfis
3	KA-RAMONA	gr. 1945	(Ramon-Kalhana)	Katar	All by Raffi	No. 10 Sula
3	KAHLA	gr. 1955	(Moneyn-Fa Gazal)	*Fadl	All by Surf	No. 18 *Kostrzewa
3	KISRONA	b. 1950	(Faronek-Kiswah)	Abdullah	Ga'Zi (1), Mraff (1) Abu Baha (1)	No. 12 Kapiti
3	LASKA	gr. 1946	(Faronek-Mithra)	Akil	Khaldi (2), Shahzada (1)	No. 6 *Rifla
3	MAILATRAH	b. 1942	(Balastra-Mailat)	Farana	All by Baarouf	No. 8 Fadil
3	MARIFA	gr. 1946	(Abou-Safar)	*Sulejman	Imaraff (1), Hassan Pasha (1) Handeyraff (1)	No. 8 Il'id Ilkbir
3	MARZJA	b. 1957	(Azraff-Marhava)	Azarah	Geym (2), *Nizzam (10	No. 14 *Menfis

QUEEN OF SHEEBA DB

255

3	MERZEL	b. 1948	(*Raffles-Khymae)	Image	Image (1), Kimage (1) Lo Rafden (1)	No. 10 Aatika
3	MLECHA	gr. 1941	(Gulastra-*Aeniza)	Dzingishan III (Poland)	Mahabba (1) Rapture (1), Lauren (1)	No. 15 (Aeniza
3	NAFA	b. 1937	(*Raseyn-Narasa)	*Nasik	All by *Witez II	No. 3 Farasin
3	RAFALIA	b/gr 1953	(Rapture-Rosalia)	Abu Raseyn	Rafferty (1), Orbit (1) Szyzygy (1)	No. 12 Badia
3	RAFINA	gr. 1939	(*Raffles-*Rasmina)	Shareer (England)	All by Image	No. 6 *Rasmina
3	RHAPSODI	ch. 1946	(*Latif-Raihadeyna)	Ferdeyn	Padishah (2), Marengo (1)	No. 6 *Raida
3	RIHALLI	gr. 1951	(Rifage-Allifah)	*Zarife	Sharrik (2), Kahar (1)	No. 10 Sherah
3	RISHIMA	gr. 1952	(Rifage-Ishmia)	*Selmian	All by Sharrik	No. 6 *Rishafieh
3	RON RAFFIA	bl. 1955	(Raffnat-Ronekka)	Ronek	Gazon (1), Surneyn (1) *Aramus (1)	No. 7 *Simawa
3	ROSE OF LUZON	ch. 1942	(Gulastra-*Rose of France)	*Raswan	All by Indraff	No. 6 *Rose of France
3	*ROYAL SILVER	gr. 1952	(Grand Royal-*Silver Crystal)	Rangoon (England)	All by *Serafiz	No. 7 Somara
3	SAH-MIRADA	gr. 1958	(Mirad-Sahra Sauda)	Abou	Imagin (2), Rapture (1)	No. 8 *Haffia
3	SAHRA SU	gr. 1946	(Indraff-Fa Rahna)	*Fadl	All by Julep	No. 4 Ghazayat
3	SARA JEAN	gr. 1954	(Ferneyn-Fersara)	Ferseyn	The Real McCoy (2), Aarief (1)	No. 11 Sedjur
3	*SALINAS	gr. 1947	(Grey Owl-Shamnar)	Naziri (England)	All by Garaff	No. 6 Riyala
3	SCHERAFFA	gr. 1947	(*Raffles-Scheherazade)	(Al Mashoor D.B.	Raffi (2) Ibn Kal Ramona (1)	No. 11 Domow
3	SELMIANA	gr. 1940	(*Selmian-Nurselma)	*Nureddin II	Imaraff (1) Umar al Khayyam (2)	No. 3 *Selmnab
3	SHAMARA	ch. 1951	(Ankar-Panay)	*Nasr	All by Seneyn	No. 17 *Przepiorka
3	SILVER MIST	gr. 1951	(Hassan Pasha-Marifa)	Abou	Hanraff (1), Al-Marah Pharoah (2)	No. 8 Il'id Ilkbir
3	SILWARA	gr. 1955	(Dargee-*Silwa)	Raktha (England)	*Count Dorsaz (1), *Bask (2)	No. 7 Somara
3	SURIMA	b. 1955	(Sureyn-Bonita)	Caravan	*Serafix (1), Sur-Grande (1)	No. 14 *Meca
	SURRA	gr. 1947	(*Raseyn-*Zewa)	Kaszmir (Poland)	Surran (1), Saneyn (1) Fadjur (1)	No. 18 *Kostrzewa
3	*SZARZA	gr. 1956	(Ali Said-Salwa)	Kuhailan Abu Urkub (Poland)	Regis (2) Ferseyn (1)	No. 15 Mlecha
3	TANARA	gr/b 1956	(Bistan-Belara)	Ferseyn	Garaff (1), Petit Jean (1) Shalimar Gilette (1)	No. 10 Rhua
3	TELMRISS	ch. 1954	(Jedriss-Telmiz)	Rahas	All by Yatez	No. 1 *Bahreyn
3	TEZZA	b. 1955	(Yatez-Narzah)	Narzigh	All by Faro	No. 9 Killah
3	*THORAYYAH	b. 1946	Desertbred	———	All by *Serafix	*Thorayyah D.B.
3	UM EL SURAB	gr. 1944	(Adonis-Anah)	Kaaba	Ga'Zi (2), Aazhar (1)	No. 19 Sultana
3	VADRAFF	b. 1950	(Indraff-Invasia)	Valenskik	All by Gazon	No. 2 *Indaia
3	WAHIDA	gr. 1953	(Ferseyn-Tahir)	Antez	Ga'Zi (1), *Silver Drift (2)	No. 1 Bazikh
3	WITEZA	b. 1948	(*Witez II-Azefa)	Alla Amarward	All by *Serafix	No. 11 Moliah
3	ZAZI	ch. 1955	(Zitez-Narzawi)	Narzigh	Witezar (1), Imatez (1) Daareyn (1)	No. 4 Gulnare

256

FAMILIES OF LEADING BROODMATRONS

These are the foundation families to which the dams of three or more champions trace (other than desertbred, or those of foreign families which have no other branches here). Period is from 1953-70 inclusive. Name of sire of mare is in parentheses. Number at left is for referral to "Family" column on list of leading broodmatrons.

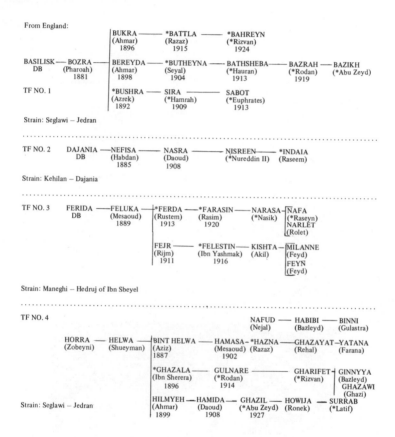

From England:

BASILISK—BOZRA
DB (Pharoah)
1881

TF NO. 1

BUKRA (Ahmar) 1896	— *BATTLA (Razaz) 1915	— *BAHREYN (*Rizvan) 1924			
BEREYDA (Ahmar) 1898	— *BUTHEYNA (Seyal) 1904	— BATHSHEBA (*Hauran) 1913	— BAZRAH (*Rodan) 1919	— BAZIKH (*Abu Zeyd)	
*BUSHRA (Azrek) 1892	— SIRA (*Hamrah) 1909	— SABOT (*Euphrates) 1913			

Strain: Seglawi — Jedran

. . . .

TF NO. 2 DAJANIA —NEFISA —— NASRA ———— NISREEN—— *INDAIA
DB (Habdan) (Daoud) (*Nureddin II) (Raseem)
1885 1908

Strain: Kehilan — Dajania

. . . .

TF NO. 3 FERIDA ——FELUKA —┬*FERDA ——*FARASIN —— NARASA—┬NAFA
DB (Mesaoud) (Rustem) (Rasim) (*Nasik) │(*Raseyn)
1889 1913 1920 │NARLET
│(Rolet)

FEJR ——— *FELESTIN —— KISHTA —┬MILANNE
(Rijm) (Ibn Yashmak) (Akil) │(Feyd)
1911 1916 │FEYN
│(Feyd)

Strain: Maneghi — Hedruj of Ibn Sbeyel

. . . .

TF NO. 4

NAFUD —— HABIBI —— BINNI
(Nejal) (Bazleyd) (Gulastra)

HORRA — HELWA —┬BINT HELWA —— HAMASA–*HAZNA——GHAZAYAT–YATANA
(Zobeyni) (Shueyman) (Aziz) (Mesaoud) (Razaz) (Rehal) (Farana)
1887 1902

*GHAZALA—— GULNARE ———— GHARIFET┬GINNYYA
(Ibn Sherera) (*Rodan) (*Rizvan) │(Bazleyd)
1896 1914 │GHAZAWI
│(Ghazi)

HILMYEH —HAMIDA—— GHAZIL — HOWIJA — SURRAB
Strain: Seglawi — Jedran (Ahmar) (Daoud) (*Abu Zeyd) (Ronek) (*Latif)
1899 1908 1927

257

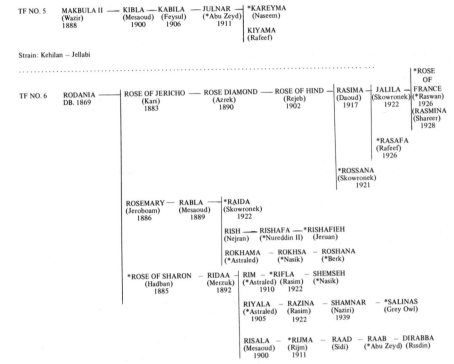

TF NO. 5 MAKBULA II —— KIBLA —— KABILA —— JULNAR ┬ *KAREYMA
(Wazir)   (Mesaoud) (Feysul) (*Abu Zeyd) (Naseem)
1888   1900   1906   1911
                                          └ KIYAMA
                                            (Rafeef)

Strain: Kehilan — Jellabi

. . . .

TF NO. 6 RODANIA ———— ROSE OF JERICHO —— ROSE DIAMOND —— ROSE OF HIND —— RASIMA ┬ JALILA ┬ *ROSE
         DB. 1869   (Kars)   (Azrek)   (Rejeb)   (Daoud) │ (Skowronek) │ OF
                      1883   1890   1902   1917   │ 1922   │ FRANCE
                                                                                 │   │ (*Raswan)
                                                                                 │   │ 1926
                                                                                 │   │ (RASMINA
                                                                                 │   │ (Shareer)
                                                                                 │   │ 1928
                                                                                 │
                                                                                 ├ *RASAFA
                                                                                 │ (Rafeef)
                                                                                 │ 1926
                                                                                 │
                                                                                 └ *ROSSANA
                                                                                   (Skowronek)
                                                                                   1921

                  ROSEMARY —— RABLA ——┬ *RAIDA
                  (Jeroboam) (Mesaoud) │ (Skowronek)
                  1886   1889   │ 1922
                                       │
                                       ├ RISH —— RISHAFA —— *RISHAFIEH
                                       │ (Nejran) (*Nureddin II) (Jeruan)
                                       │
                                       └ ROKHAMA — ROKHSA — ROSHANA
                                         (*Astraled) (*Nasik) (*Berk)

                  *ROSE OF SHARON — RIDAA ┬ RIM — *RIFLA — SHEMSEH
                  (Hadban)   (Merzuk) │ (*Astraled) (Rasim) (*Nasik)
                  1885   1892   │ 1910   1922
                                            │
                                            ├ RIYALA — RAZINA — SHAMNAR — *SALINAS
                                            │ (*Astraled) (Rasim) (Naziri) (Grey Owl)
                                            │ 1905   1922   1939
                                            │
                                            └ RISALA — *RIJMA — RAAD — RAAB — DIRABBA
                                              (Mesaoud) (Rijm) (Sidi) (*Abu Zeyd) (Rssdin)
                                              1900   1911

Strain: Kehilan — Ajuz of Ibn Rodan

RIDAA (Merzuk-*Rose of Sharon)

258

TF NO. 7   SELMA I

```
SOBHA ———— SELMA II  –   SIMRIEH  –   *SELMNAB
(Wazir)      (Ahmar)      (Seyal)      (Nawab)
1897         1894         1903         1920

             SIWA     –   SOMRA    –   SILVER FIRE  –   SOMARA        –  *SILVER CRYSTAL
             (Ahmar)      (Daoud)      (Naseem)         (*Nureddin II)    (Rangoon)
             1896         1908         1926             1930

                          SARAMA   –   *SIMAWA
                          (Daoud)      (Rustem)
                          1910         1915
```

Strain: Hamdani – Simri

. . . .

TF NO. 8   DAVENPORT mares:

```
*ABEYAH  –  *HAFFIA —— SABA   –   IL'ID ILKBIR  –   SAFAR
1896        1906       (*Deyr)    (Farana)          (*Sulejman)
DB          DB         1921

                       SAMIT ——— SURA    –   LA PLATA   –  LA PLACITA
                       (*Kusof)  (Oman)      (Akil)        (Caravan)
                       1914

                       FADIL   –  FAHM     –   MAILAT
                       (Letan)    (Stambul)    (Farana)
```

Strain: Abeyan – Sherrak

MAHOMET (Orjent-Pojata) Sire of *IWONKA III (Near side)

259

Dav. mares — cont:

TF NO. 9   *HADBA   —   KILLAH   —   NARLAH
            DB   (Gomussa)   (Narkhaleb)
            1900   1911   1932

Strain: Hadban — Enzahi

....

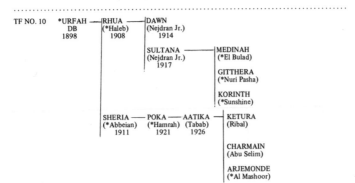

TF NO. 10   *URFAH —— RHUA —— DAWN
            DB   (*Haleb)   (Nejdran Jr.)
            1898   1908   1914

                          SULTANA —————— MEDINAH
                          (Nejdran Jr.)   (*El Bulad)
                          1917

                                            GITTHERA
                                            (*Nuri Pasha)

                                            KORINTH
                                            (*Sunshine)

                  SHERIA —— POKA —— AATIKA —— KETURA
                  (*Abbeian)   (*Hamrah)   (Tabab)   (Ribal)
                  1911   1921   1926

                                            CHARMAIN
                                            (Abu Selim)

                                            ARJEMONDE
                                            (*Al Mashoor)

Strain: Seglawi — Jedran

RULITHA (*Shamadan-Korlitha)

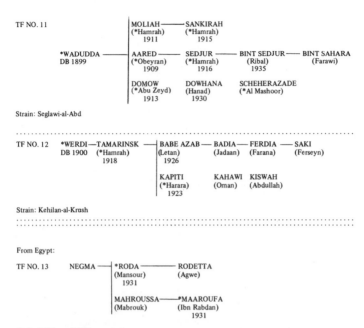

TF NO. 11

*WADUDDA
DB 1899

MOLIAH ——— SANKIRAH
(*Hamrah)   (*Hamrah)
1911   1915

AARED ——— SEDJUR ——— BINT SEDJUR ——— BINT SAHARA
(*Obeyran)   (*Hamrah)   (Ribal)   (Farawi)
1909   1916   1935

DOMOW   DOWHANA   SCHEHERAZADE
(*Abu Zeyd) (Hanad)   (*Al Mashoor)
1913   1930

Strain: Seglawi-al-Abd

TF NO. 12   *WERDI—TAMARINSK ——— BABE AZAB ——— BADIA ——— FERDIA ——— SAKI
             DB 1900 (*Hamrah)   (Letan)   (Jadaan)   (Farana)   (Ferseyn)
                      1918   1926

                                         KAPITI   KAHAWI   KISWAH
                                         (*Harara)   (Oman)   (Abdullah)
                                         1923

Strain: Kehilan-al-Krush

From Egypt:

TF NO. 13   NEGMA ——— *RODA ——— RODETTA
                      (Mansour)   (Agwe)
                      1931

                       MAHROUSSA ——— *MAAROUFA
                       (Mabrouk)   (Ibn Rabdan)
                                      1931

Strain: Kehilan — Jellabi

Paul Polk and FADJUR (Fadheilan-Bint Sahara)

261

From Spain:

TF NO. 14   SIRIA ─┬─ *MECA ─┬─ BONITA
                    │ (Ursus) │ (Caravan)
                    │ 1923   │
                    │   │ *BARAKAT ─ KOTSI ─ TUWAISAN
                    │   │ (Fondak)   (Caravan) (Rossdin)
                    │   │
                    ├─ *MENFIS ─ JUBILEE
                    │ (Egipto)   (Jubilo)

Strain: Seglawi-al-Abd

. . . .

From Poland:

TF NO. 15   MLECHA DB ─ ROZMAITA I ─ MLECHA   ─ MLECHA ─ MLECHA   ─ NIMFA   ─ FANFARA ─ *AENIZA
             Imp. 1845   (Elazus DB) (El Delami) (Bosak)   (Hafiz I)   (El Kebir) (Koheilan) (Dzingishan III)
                                                              1889   1900   1914   1931

Strain: Kehilan ─ Dajania

*IWONKA III and *SZARZA are of this family, but via another branch, from a full sister of ROZMAITA I

. . . .

TF NO. 16   MILORDKA ─ ZAIRA   ─ OSTROUSZKA ─ PRUSZYNA ─ GALICJA   ─ EUREKA   ─ ODYSSEJA
             1816   (Seglawi)   (Babilon)   (Krakus)   (Marymak)   (Arabi-Pasza) (Kohejlan-Dzedran)
                          1826   1837   1846   1867   1885

             continued: AMURATH   ─ HEBDA   ─ MALAGA   ─ *CHLOE ─ CHLOEYN
                           (Amurath 1881) (Hermit)   (Mazepa I)   (Lirnik)   (*Raseyn)
                                           1913   1931   1936

             (Amurath 1881   *GWADIANA also of the MILORDKA family, but different branch from PRUSZYNA
             is the sire of the
             mare of the same name. Date she was foaled not given)

Strain: Seglawi ─ Jedran

BONITA (Caravan-Barakat)

262

TF NO. 17 GAZELLA – GAZELLA I – LANIA – PAMELA – LANIA – ABRA   GAZELLA II
DB Imp. 1845 (Abiat DB) (Hami DB) (El Kebir) (Al-Nabi) (Anvil) (Kohejlan DB)
          1859   –   1890   1896   1904   1914

GAZELLA II cont: JASKOULKA II   –   *PRZEPIORKA
                    (Koheilan I)   (Almanzor)
                    1928   1934

                  ELEGANTKA   –   KAMEA   –   *WIERNA
                    (Bakszysz)   (Farys II)   (Ofir)
                    1923   1929   1938

Strain: Kehilan – Ajuz

. . . .

TF NO. 18 SWEYKOWSKA – TOR-KARSKA – METKA – LATKA – PERLA –   COMTESSA
           1810   (Janczar-Aga) (Kanarys) (Bon-Vouloir) (Iskander-Baszra) (Mahomet-el-H
                          1824   1831   1853   1858   1864

continued: MELODJA   –   ZALOTNA   –   LEZGINKA   –   KALINA   –   DZIEWANNA   – *KOSTRZE
            (Derwiz)   (Cyprian)   (Euclid)   (Ibrahim DB) (Bakszysz)   (Koheilan I
            1874   1882   1895   1909   1922   1929

No strain given

. . . .

From Brazil:

TF NO. 19 KARIBAN – MOHAREB   – RAHAT   – MELIHA   – RAIRA – *AIRE – CARIOCA
           DB 1895   (Marum DB)   (Racid)   (Mebruk)   (Rustnar) (Ali)   (*Czubuthan)
                       1902   1909   1921   1921   1929

Strain: Seglawi – Jedran

*KOSTRZEWA (Koheilan I-Dziewanna)

263

Bint Sahara and daughters: Sahara Rose, Sahara Dawn, Sahara Queen, Sahara Star and Sahara Lady (1970)

VIII
FROM WHENCE THEY CAME

The various countries contributing to the bloodlines of Arabian horses imported into America are worthy of detailed study in this regard. However the majority are already well documented through publications of assorted types—from stud catalogs to government booklets, and from all-breed books to those on Arabians only, and in the later category, on Arabians of each particular country. Some stud books, such as Egyptian (of the former Royal Agricultural Society, 1948), are also highly informative. At any rate only a sketch of this multi-national background can be included here.

The Babolna Stud of Hungary and the Weil Stud of Germany are quite inter-related in modern pedigrees as there was a regular interchange of horses between them. Babolna dates back into the tenth century but its breeding of purebred Arabians was not isolated until 1814. This stud bred two types of Oriental horses—the purebreds, termed "full blood" and the partbred Arabian, called "Arab race." Such terminology was used by other countries in early times also, and it can quickly be seen that a horses of "Arab race" would be considered by the uninitiated to be a horse of the pure Arabian breed. This has led to considerable confusion by researchers of old European Arabian pedigrees, wherein some halfbreds were considered by these researchers to have been listed as pure but whose pedigrees showed that they were not. In any case at the time the breeders and their contemporaries knew which was which, and kept the two strains apart—except for use of the purebreds on the halfbreds. This two-type registration was maintained by the Babolna Stud, but the Arab race is now popularly known as the Shagya breed, named after a foundation sire. Arabians are branded on the near side of the saddle place with the letter B and the Hungarian crown above it, while on the off side is the initial letter of the sire's name, and the numerals of the animal's date of birth. On the partbreds the B is on the off side, while the initial of the sire's name, his number, and the individual's number, are on the near side. So there is no possibility of confusing the two, nor individuals, especially as they are branded as foals. Both types are registered in the same stud book, but the purebreds are written in green ink, the partbreds in black. The system in naming is often cause for complications in newer pedigrees containing these names, for the mares are usually named after their sires. They inherit their sire's name, complete with any Roman

265

numeral suffix it might have, but their foal number is prefixed, and their broodmare number is suffixed to the name.   For example, the mare 24 KOHEILAN IV, whose own dam was 38 KOHAILAN-RASCHID, sired by a desertbred of that name, while the "38" mare was the daughter of 43 JUSSUF, a mare sired by JUSSUF.

While the Babolna Stud has now been cut down drastically in the way of Arabians, it has had much influence throughout the world, and especially in Polish Arabians, in part due to the purchase of a group of Babolna mares by Poland after World War II. These were obtained from the U.S. Army authorities, apparently as war reparations. They were, however, returned to Babolna in 1951. A Polish booklet describes these as "...all very typical, and almost all were deep and big, wonderful mothers with excellent pedigrees originating from Arabian imports." Some of them were given Polish names. For example 205 AJEEB-2 was re-named BRUZDA, and BAZA was orginally 212 ZUHAILAN-ZAID-2. These two names are good examples of the foal number (of foal by the sire named), which in the latter is the 212th by KUHAILAN ZAID, and the broodmare number indicates she is the second by that horse to become a broodmare. A strange appearing name is BRDA, re-named from the Hungarian 215 MERSUCH II-1. She is the granddam of ARAX, sire of *BOLTONKA. ARAX is now in Russia.

BAIRACTAR, a beautiful grey stallion whose descendants prove that his portrait was not idealized especially in regard to level topline, was imported by the King of Wurtemberg for the Weil Stud in 1817. He was used at stud there for twenty-one years, which accounts for his being in the pedigree of practically every horse bred there, over and over. The tail male line is represented through AMURATH 1881 and more recently by AMURATH SAHIB, a singularly successful broodmare sire who is also the sire of EQUIFOR (out of Forta, also dam of Czort), holder of the fastest record for the Arabian Derby in Poland, covering the 3000 meters in 3:35. Among the mares by AMURATH SAHIB are the dams of the American champions *GWALIOR, *ARDAHAN, *ARWILGA, *ARAMIS, *BASK, and *DORNABA.

A sire line noted for its well conformed horses is that from KOHEILAN ADJUZE, a desertbred foaled in 1876, bred by the Anazeh and imported to Hungary in 1885. His son KOHEILAN II 1887 (out of 91 Jussof, a daughter of the stallion Jussof) sired the famous KOHEILAN IV 1905. The latter was a Seglawi Obeyran, since he was out of 124 O'BAJAN (foaled 1898) who was sired by O'BAJAN out of the Seglawi mare 145 GAZLAN (1881). The name O'BAJAN would give the impression he was an Abeyan Sherrak, but apparently his sire was of that strain and he was named after him, for his dam was a Maneghi. With the "j" pronounced as a "y", it is easy to see what the original pronunciation was. Poland bought a son of "IV," and since he was the first of that line in Poland, he was dubbed KOHEILAN I, throwing the whole sequence

BAIRACTAR D.B.

AMURATH 1829 (Bairactar D.B.-Sady III)

AMURATH 1881 (Tajar-Koheil III)

AMURATH SAHIB (Amurath II-Sahiba)

HORSES OF THE BAIRACTAR LINE

out of kilter. However when this stallion, after many successful years at stud in Poland, was returned to the Babolna Stud, he was given the number VIII, and the sequence, despite some holes, was restored. SIG-LAVY-BAGDADY was another desertbred of note in this establishment, as well as a whole sequence of mares with that name, and at least three sons and grandsons (i.e. the numbers up to III at least) and their daughters. He was imported to Austria in 1902 and subsequently acquired by the Babolna Stud. MERSUCH is another desertbred whose name appears often in these pedigrees.

The Marbach State Stud in West Germany, which is also known as the Wurttemberg State Stud, since its foundation stock was imported or bred by the King of Wurttemberg on this site. Now used as top crosses are Polish and Egyptian stallions. A previous Egyptian import into Germany, JASIR, a coarse and singularly ugly horse considering his background, was the sire of some of the Marbach mares. A new Egyptian horse (by Nazeer), utterly different from the bulky JASIR, is the grey HADBAN ENZIHI, a beautiful-headed stallion with tiny,very smart ears. He is the sire of *DALIH and *SANACHT. Unlike the Communist countries (though a private stud or two is now operated in Poland) there are a good number of private breeders of Arabians in West Germany.

267

The history of the Arabian horse in Egypt is well documented by many publications, including the Stud Book of the Royal Agricultural Society, now the Egyptian Agricultural Organization; Dr. Ameen Zahir's *Arabian Horse Breeding and The Arabians of America;* H. R. H. Prince Mohamed Ali's *Breeding of Pure Bred Arab Horses;* Lady Wentworth's authoritative *Thoroughbred Racing Stock* and *The Authentic Arabian;* and so on, so there is no need to include other than the highlights here.

It is of interest however to note that the bloody-handed Mohamed Ali, who killed the Mameluke rulers of Egypt by a ruse and put himself in power, was not an Egyptian by birth. He was born in or near Albania and spent his youth in Macedonia, the historic land of northern Greece so famous for its horses. Philip II, the father of Alexander the Great, was so proud of his race horse which had won in the Olympic Games in 356 B.C. that he had a series of coins struck, varying as to workmanship but all showing a high prancing horse with Arabian tail carriage and high held head. Other Macedonian coins also featured horses. Of course this was over two thousand years before, but the horsey heritage may have hung on. Mohamed Ali had brought around two hundred of the finest Arabians to Egypt, but they died off due to the lack of care, insufficient feed, and even of lack of water, along with filthy conditions. Even well indoctrinated Arab horses cannot go long without water and *some* food. Abbas Pasha I was a grandson of Mohamed Ali (also spelled Mehemet Ali, Muhammed Aly, and so on) and showed the same, even more intensified interest in Arabian horses. But he too was not all Egyptian (the nationality of the mothers never seem to be given, but Circassian slaves were favorite harem inhabitants of sultans and pashas, so who knows...?).

This is not all of the foreign influence by any means. Mohamed Ali had brought with him from Macedonia a twelve year old boy, who eventually became the Wali (governor) of all Arabia, including Lebanon and Syria, along with other high offices in the Mohamed Ali regime. This was the father of Ali Bey, who will at once be recognised when two titles are added and the minor one (Bey) deleted—as Ali Pasha Sherif.

When Abbas Pasha died in 1854 his estate with nearly 600 horses and three stables, including the most famous, built of pink marble at a cost of 1,000,000 pounds, was inherited by his son Elhami Pasha. Elhami did not, however, inherit the same love of horses. So he held two auctions, the most important one in 1860, at which time 210 mares, 90 stallions and 180 colts and fillies were sold. Many went to European governments. One which can still be traced is GADIR, said to be a desertbred imported by Abbas, but if so, he would have been very, very old, unless he was a later import. This Seglawi-Jedran stallion purchased by the Weil Stud, is represented several times over in the pedigree of AMURATH SAHIB, through both sire and dam. He is quite close up in TAJAR 1873, as sire of OBEJA, that horse's dam; and TAJAR 1873 is in turn the sire of the

268

extremely influential AMURATH 1881. SAHIBA, the dam of AMURATH SAHIB, is the winner of the first Arabian Derby in Poland.

To return to Egypt, it was Ali Pasha Sherif however, who bought the majority of the Abbas Pasha horses. It is said that one of the Bedouins who were in charge of the horses had recommended to Ali Pasha the horses to buy, and that he had written his opinions and histories (pedigrees as related by Bedouins) in a book. These were incorporated into of the Ali Pasha Sherif's stud books, long kept out of public view. It is now thought that the books—in Arabic—now being translated are the long lost records. It is only in regard to a few lines however that they would amount to anything today, for many—in fact the majority—of the horses died during the two visitations of a horse plague that killed off all the Ali Pasha Sherif horses except those sent to a stable out of reach of its effects. In the last days of the stud, when the senile owner could no longer inspect his horses and operations of the stud, it fell into sad days. In addition to the plague, the grooms managed to further reduce the number of horses by selling off many of the animals and reporting them dead. Under such chaotic conditions, it is no wonder that absolute guarantee of bloodlines—other than that they were purebred—can be doubted. Lady Anne Blunt wrote:

"We all saw Ali Pasha's stud in the last hours of its disruption. Decimated by plague and weakened by years of inbreeding and gross neglect, the horses were of an ethereal quality and truly like gazelles, and with no more bone. It was 'Type' ethererealized almost to extinction."

The Blunts bought the cream of the horses, indicating that many of the remainder were not worth buying at any price. The best of the Blunt horses were sent to Crabbet Park, the rest maintained at Lady Anne's Sheyk Obeyd Stud near Cairo.

While many of the Ali Pasha Sherif horses were Abbas stock, he had already quite an extensive stable of his own horses before he bought these others. He was the richest of all the pashas and had the largest stud of Arabian horses of his time. He had twenty Circassian slaves as grooms and Circassians were also the favorite horsemen of Prince Mohamed Ali. While the Davenport horse *DEYR is said to have been purchased at a Circassian village on the upper Euphrates, Circassia itself is located on the eastern shores of the Black Sea, not too far west of the famous Tersk (Tiersk, Tersky, etc.) Stud of Russia—where *NABORR and other Arabians were, and are, bred. These south Russian people were also very popular with the Turks as slaves.

When the Arabian division of the Royal Agricultural Society was formed in 1914, horses were obtained locally, since desertbreds were either almost unobtainable or completely unsuitable. Many came from Lady Anne Blunt's stud; others from Prince Mohamed Ali and his relatives, Prince Ahmed Kamel Pasha, Prince Kamal El-Din Hussein, and the

Khedive (viceroy) Abbas Hilme II. In 1919 twenty Arabs were obtained from Lady Wentworth.

Prince Mohamed Ali is of course well known through his sales to the United States and through his two books already mentioned. He is a grandson of Abbas Pasha, and while some of his horses were descendants of the latter's importations, not all of them were, by any means. Although his horses were never ridden and were bred strictly for beauty, when he sold some for racing purposes, they did very well on the track. It is said that he compared the horses, individually, with paintings and old prints of idealized Arabian horses, using these as a "standard of perfection." Any that fell short of the ideal were culled. The Prince told of his efforts to encourage mares to have a black foal. He put black silhouettes on the walls of the stalls, with the expectation the mares would stare at them and get the idea. But none did, though they may have stared. However after he had given up on this practice, old NEGMA, a grey, produced a black foal by the dark chestnut IBN RABDAN. This is of interest, for a number of animals of these lines have produced blacks and near-blacks in America.

The R.A.S. Stud Book tells of the aims, and results obtained, of the Society, and also of the decision to use race horses of proven merit and authentic pedigrees, as far as ascertainable on desertbreds) for top crossing on the Society's original stock:

> To test their power of endurance, some are leased for racing purposes when they are three years old, and others trained on the Stud Farm at Kafr Farouk to test the value of their breeding stock. By such methods that Society assures the perpetuation of sound and enduring strains.

About inbreeding:

> For some time the Royal Agricultural Society strongly opposed introducing outside blood into their purebred Arab stock. This matter was discussed at several Committee meetings, and it was at last unanimously agreed that if the pure pedigree-bred horse were continually inbred there would eventually be 'all pedigree and no horses'. Experience has shown that continual inbreeding leads to deterioration, and that the introduction of new blood is essential. Establishments interested in breeding the pure Arab horse all over the world are convinced of this fact. For instance Poland, Hungary, Russia, America—in fact every country interested in the purebred Arab horse—have been compelled to go to Arabia to seek good outside Arab blood to introduce into their stock. For this purpose the Society, displaying great caution and after exhaustive enquiry into pedigrees, chose some Arab horses that had had good racing careers in Egypt and were passed as Arabs by the Jockey Club, the only organization to which all horses imported from the East, e.g. Syria, Iraq and Nejd, were submitted for classification.

270

Dr. Ahmed Mabrouk, former head of the Breeding Section, was delgated to study the breeding methods in Hedjaz, Nejd, Iraq, and Syria and to buy a few horses from those countries if he found any suitable ones, in order to revivify and improve the Egyptian stock. However Dr. Mabrouk found only one suitable horse, and that was in Beirut (therefore presumably a race horse). In his report to the Society, he gave the following reasons:

1. Lack of good stallions, which led to the deterioration of the Arab horse in its native land; and the lack of a stud book.

2. H. H. Prince Feisal refused to give a certificate of authenticity in his own name establishing the purity of the origin of the horses chosen by the Doctor for their fine lines and good conformation. This was because H. H. had confidence only in the horses bred in the Nejd, which were known to him personally, like the horses which he breeds himself or those descended from his horses.

3. In Dr. Mabrouk's opinion most of the Nejd horses were not worth importing into Egypt, as being unsound, having hereditary defects in their conformation, or undesirable markings, blemishes, etc., etc.

4. The Bedouin ceased to be interested in the breeding of thoroughbreds from the time they abandoned their nomad life and took to living in houses instead of tents. With the establishment of security among them, inter-tribal raids, for which horses are essential, have become a thing of the past.

5. The Bedouin care less for a horse's looks than for pedigree and action, and pay little heed to faulty conformation, with the inevitable result that the race has much deteriorated. Again, owing to the dearth of stallions they do not scruple to allow services on mares of their nearest kin, thus disregarding the example of their ancestors, who rightly believed that inbreeding led to levity and recklessness and therefore rigorously avoided it.

Levity must mean instability here, certainly not gaiety.

The stallions which had made good records on the track, and used as sires by the R.A.S. are listed in the 1948 Stud Book thus:

EL DERE—A horse belonging to the Royal Khassa; it is a Saklawi Sheifi with powerful muscles, strong tendons and beautiful appearance. It has won fourteen races. Presented to the Society in October 1934.

MICHAAN—A Koheilan Ajouz, belonging to H. E. Sheikh Fawzan El-Sabek, former Minister of Saudi Arabia; it has won twelve races.

NABRAS—A powerfully-built Hadban Enzahi horse, the property of Mahmoud El-Itribi Pasha which, like most of its sons, has won several races.

REGISTAN — One of Lady Wentworth's thoroughbreds, owned by Mr. T.G.B. Trouncer, breeder of Arab horses in Egypt.

ZAREEF—A pedigree thoroughbred whose dam was one of the late Prince Kamal El-Din Hussein's horses and whose sire

271

was Rustem, one of Lady Wentworth's horses which was imported by the Prince in 1920. It also belongs to Mr. T. G. B. Trouncer.

GHANDOUR—Out of Koheilet El Kurush, from Blunt's stables, by Marzuk (Merzuk?) an imported Arab and a very good racer, owned by the later Mahmoud Pasha El-Itribi.

GAMAL EL-DIN—A good race-horse belonging to Ahmoud Abu El-Fotouh Bey.

REGISTAN and ZAREEF of course are not "Thoroughbred," but the Egyptians and Arabs call the Thoroughbred an "English horse" while the only purebred—i.e. thoroughbred (thoroughly of Arabian blood)—was of course the Arabian. REGISTRAN was by SKOWRONEK and according to Lady Wentworth set a record for six furlongs. As is usually the case, his picture before exportation and one of him in training in Egypt are hardly recognizable as the same horse.

Among the well known imports tracing to these race horses are *MORAFIC, with EL DERE in the third generation; *MOFTAKHAR, with NABRAS as grandsire; while another race horse, EID, is the grandsire of *BINT BINT DURRA. Of present or former sires SAMEH is a grandson of EL DERE, and SID ABOUHOM is a son of EL DERE.

KAZMEEN (Sotamm-Kasima)   KASIDA (Nasr-Makbula)

The horses of the Crabbet group made a surprisingly strong contribution. For instance KAZMEEN (*SOTAMM-KASIMA) spelled KASMEYN in England, is the sire of BINT SAMIHA, dam of NAZEER, which means he is one-fourth Crabbet breeding, although KAZMEEN himself has several Egyptian lines, including two to MESAOUD. However he also has two to QUEEN OF SHEBA, as she is the dam of *ASTRALED and of AHMAR (sire of Selma II), in back of SOTAMM (*Astraled-Selma II). There is a very big fly in the ointment of KAZMEEN's pedigree in the ugly shape of the miserable mare KASIDA, but luckily she was not at all dominant—at least not enough to afflict KAZMEEN. She was the dam of KASIMA and was by NASR (Al Pasha Sherif stallion, not the import)

272

out of MAKBULA. If she is representative of the remaining Ali Pasha Sherif horses it is no wonder some were not worth buying as Lady Anne reported. KASIDA was the result of intense inbreeding, having four lines to ZOBEYNI fairly close up. Such sights may have fomented the Egyptian dislike of too close breeding.

Apparently a good dose of Maneghi blood improves Egyptian stock, for the best representatives in recent years have it. NAZEER has five known crosses to this strain—two through the QUEEN OF SHEBA, whose sire was a Maneghi, and two through OM DALAL, whose sire SABBAH also was a Maneghi. The latter is the dam of the much-used stallion SAMHAN and of the mare DALAL (as her name "Mother of Dalal" indicates) in the pedigree of NAZEER. DALAL is the dam of GAMIL (Jamil) MANIAL, the sire of MANSOUR. The foregoing SABBAH is not the same as the identically-spelled name in the pedigree of *BINT BINT SABBAH. The maternal grandsire of MANSOUR is MEANAGI-SEBILI.

The beautiful and spectacular chestnut ANTAR is one of the most admired of the E.A.O. horses, and at one time was the chief sire of King Farouk's prized Inshass Stud. ANTAR, through the most conscientious processes of genealogy, can be traced to QUEEN OF SHEBA by way of RUSTEM in the distinguished pedigree of his dam.

*ANSATA IBN HALIMA has identical Maneghi lines through his dam as through his sire, totalling ten. In other words, through his dam he brings in another KAZMEEN line, also MEANGI-SEBILI, GAMIL MANIAL and SAMHAN. It should be added, however, that these latter two horses were not, themselves, Maneghi, nor was OM DALAL, since the heritage was through the latter's sire. She, herself, was a Seglawieh Jedranieh of Ibn Sudan. Similarly, QUEEN OF SHEBA was Abeyah-Sherrakieh. The dam of *BINT MAISA EL SAGHIRA is out of ZARE-EFA, who was sired by KAZMEEN.

BALANCE, one of the best racers and sires of racers, was widely used at stud. He is the sire of ZAAFARANA, dam of the racehorse-turned-halter-champion, *TALAL, and also of *BINT ZAAFARANA. ZAAFAR-ANA has two lines to SAMHAN via BALANCE. Another of the best E.A.O. broodmares, MABROUKA, has two KAZMEEN lines, plus two to OM DALAL, giving the usual ratio of Maneghi, and in addition she has an EL DERE outcross.

From the foregoing it can be seen that the Egyptian lines are not "all Abbas Pasha" by any means, and the recent great improvement of Egyptian horses, especially with more strict attention paid to legs, may have something to do with the continued use of outcrosses. Line breeding is standard, just as it is elsewhere, but close inbreeding is rare.

Both MESAOUD and MAHRUSS are of the ZOBEYNI sire line. The former was by AZIZ out of YEMAMEH and although Seglawi-Jedran by strain he had, in the third generation, ancestors with these strains: Seglawi-Jedran, Kehilan Ajuz, Dahman Shahwan (twice), Dahman Najib, Shueyman-Sbah, Seglawi-Jedran, from top to bottom of that generation. MAHRUSS was by WAZIR, said to have been an unbeaten race horse, and out of BINT FARAS SAOUDA, whose dam, FARAS SAOUDA, was the famous parti-colored mare of Ali Pasha Sherif, imported by Abbas Pasha. She was a Wadnah-Hursah sired by a Shueyman-Sbah. The sire of BINT FARAS SAOUDA is unknown, at least unrecorded. WAZIR was by ZOBEYNI out of the Seglawieh Jedranieh mare, GHAZIEH. ZOBEYNI was desertbred, and was one of the Abbas Pasha imports in 1842. All of these are described and praised in various books and are famous horses.

In Egypt today all racing is performed by Arabian horses and they do a fine job. Some of the fastest times are recorded by Egyptian tracks, but the weights carried are not as consistently high as in Poland, nor are the races as long—although there are occasional long races and heavy weights. All the sport horses too are Arabian, and jumping is second nature to Arabians in Egypt, judging by the well filled classes. And in most cases the impression of both the race horses and the ones in sporting events, is of great beauty. They may not all stack up as well in close inspection, but in general appearance they average high in type and quality.

Aside from royalty, there were and are several other Arabian breeders in Egypt, and the traffic in horses was sometimes a two-way affair between some of them and the Society. One of the most noted was the successful race stable of Mr. T. G. B. Trouncer, a Scot who chose to live in Egypt. He obtained some of the best "royal" horses of the various princes or pashas, along with some Crabbet-breds (including the aforementioned Registan),   and a mare from the King of Mecca, as well as SIT SERRA, bred by the Sheyk Obeyd Stud but obtained from Prince Kamil el Dine. Among Trouncer's fine race horses was SID ABOUHOM, raced under the name of NABEEH, who later became one of the Society stallions, and in fact he had been bred by that organization. SID ABOUHOM raced for six years and retired sound. He won thirteen races, was second nine times and was third six times. His time for the mile, carrying 112 pounds, in 1:46 4/5, a time yet to be approached here, was nevertheless a fraction slower than BALANCE's 1:46 flat.

Other private owners supplied horses to the Society. Among them was Mr. Kasdughli, who had purchased several of the Blunt's Sheyk Obeyd horses. DURRA (Saadoun-Dalal el Hamrah), granddam of *BINT BINT DURRA, was obtained from this source. The latter's dam, BINT DURRA was by the race horse EID, owned by Mr. Kasdughli. Mohamed Abu Nafie Pasha presented NAFAA EL KABIRA and NAFAA EL SAGHIRA, to the Society. The latter mare is the dam of the influential stallion MANSOUR (sire of Nazeer, Sheik el Arab, *Roda). She was bred by Prince Youssef Kamal.

Dr. A. E. Branch, a graduate of the R.C.V.M.S. in England was the first manager of the Society's Arabian horse stud. He was succeeded in 1949 by General Tibor von Pettko Szandter, after a hiatus of several years following Doctor Branch's retirement. Von Szandter, formerly of the world-famed Babolna Stud in Hungary, carried on the good work of Doctor Branch, but culled the stock according to his strict standards. He chose NAZEER and SHIEKH EL ARAB as key sires, and the results of his breeding program are now obvious, with the international successes of the "new Egyptians." In 1959 the management of the El Zahra stud became that of Dr. Mohamed Marsafi, the first Egyptian to hold this post, and who had been an assistant of von Szandter. Upon Marsafi's being promoted to the directorship of the Animal Breeding Section of the E.A.O. Dr. Khalil Soliman became manager of the stud farm.

Although there are the usual types within the type, the average Egyptian imports have been especially noteworthy for long, well laid-back shoulders and high withers. Although some have had slightly meaty heads, the majority seem to have all the dry, breedy quality that would be expected. Not all have short heads by any means, but a short, broad head would not be consistent with the fine riding type that most of these animals portray. Their legs still leave something to be desired in a few instances, but that is true everywhere, to a degree.

Some inbreeding has been practiced of late without the total degeneration that was prophesied should this happen. It is quite possible that it is the climate of Egypt that cause the over-refinement mentioned by the Blunts and others, rather than too much inbreeding. For instance Maspero, in *The Struggle of the Nations* (1897), wrote:

"The horse, when introduced into Egypt, soon became fairly adapted to its environment. It retained its height and size, keeping the convex forehead—which gave the head a slightly curved profile—the slender neck, the narrow quarters, the lean and sinewy legs, and the long flowing tail which had characterized it in its native country. The climate, however, was enervating, and constant care had to be taken, by introduction of new blood from Syria, to prevent the breed from deteriorating."

This was of course in reference to the second millenium B.C., but the climate has not changed much, nor has its effect on horses, judging by the opinions of other writers, including those of modern times. If close inbreeding caused increased frailty, and "all type and no horse" as the saying goes, then many Americanbreds should be ethereal wraiths. They are, by contrast, either quite normal, or at their worst, absolute clunks, thickset, heavy-boned and hairy-heeled, depending on their breeders' "eye for a horse," or possibly, luck.

Going north now to England, a quite different type is found. Here bone is usually much heavier, and so are the horses. However as a rule they maintain a high degree of quality, and have that much-desired attribute called class. Generations of lush pastures and good English oats have fortified the framework of these horses until they tend to remind us that England is also noted for originating the world's best breeds of beef cattle, by virtue of that same English pastureland. Nevertheless the English Arabians have that certain something that spells elegance, and their arched necks and beautiful style is a hallmark. There are of course a great number with low backs, and some have apple rumps with low set tails. A short croup can cause hind legs to appear crooked, and in many cases this is the reason for this faulty conformation, rather than over angulation of the hocks. Most English Arabians appear to have good action, possibly due to their concentration of Crabbet lines, which usually include at least one line to the great sire of performance horses, AZREK. Once in a while the action is rather odd, in which the foreleg is brought forward with very little flexion, then the foot is thrown violently up and forward, resulting in a most peculiar foot-flapping way of going. It is admired in some sections however as an interpretation of "a deer trotting through fern," as Lady Wentworth described an airy trot. Others vehemently disagree that the foot-flapping trot has any similarity in this description whatsoever. At any rate, when good action is mentioned in regard to English horses, unless one knows which type is admired by the person describing it, the action could be the opposite of what he expects. That Lady Wentworth's idea of exceptional action must at least have some relation to that expected of a park horse here, is indicated by the fact that the very ones she mentioned as having brilliant action have transmitted really good trotting performance to their descendants.

Most of the early importations to England were individual horses, and the first group lot was that imported by Mr. Sandeman in 1874 and which included YATAGHAN and HAIDEE as well as two others. The next group was of horses selected by Major Upton from the Shammar tribe for Mr. Chaplain, imported in 1875. The best known of these was KESIA. In 1878 Lady Anne and Wilfrid Blunt imported HAGAR, DAJANIA, TAMARISK, JERBOA, and DAMASK ROSE, all their own selections from Mesopotamia; and also those purchased for them by Mr. Skene, the British Consul in Aleppo. These were SHERIFA, ZENOBIA, PURPLE STOCK, WILD THYME, BABYLONIA, and BASILISK. In 1881 the Blunts imported CANORIA, DAHMA, JEDRANIA, MESHURA, RODANIA, and ZEFIFA from the same area QUEEN OF SHEBA was imported in 1879. Imported from Egypt were the desertbred FERIDA, and the Ali Pasha Sherif mares BINT NURA II, FULANA, JELLABIEH, JOHARA, KASIDA, KHATILA, MAKBULA, SAFRA, and SOBHA, from 1891 to 1898; and AZZ II was brought in in 1910. Stallions also were constantly imported by the Blunts—from India (but desertbred), the desert, and Egypt. These were KARS, in 1878; HADBAN, 1883; RATAPLAN, 1884, PROXIMO, 1887; ASGHAR 1887; AZREK, 1888; MERZUK and MESAOUD 1891; MAHRUSS II, and PHAROAH, 1897; *SHAHWAN 1892; ABU KHASEB 1898; and FEYSUL, IBN YASHMAK, and IBN YAMAMA were imported in 1904. The stud was operated in connection with the Egyptian branch from 1878 to 1906 at which time Lady Anne retired to Egypt and died there in 1917. The legal wrangles of that time cause many turmoils at Crabbet but Lady Wentworth inherited the stud instead of Blunt acquiring control. It was in this time that W. R. Brown was able to buy horses that otherwise would not have been available. The size of this operation can be judged by the fact that in 1903 there were 29 stallions and 67 mares at Crabbet Park, exclusive of young stock. Sales were held biennially and were more of a social occasion than for any great monetary return. During Blunt's period of ownership he sold off many good horses, but even before that he was continually in conflict with his wife over selling what she considered some of the best stock, just to finance some of his political (or other) adventures. However this at least resulted in others being able to obtain excellent Arabians, and many countries throughout the world bought horses from this stud, especially Russia, Australia, South Africa, Poland, and of course the United States. Lady Wentworth is renowned not only for the adept management of Crabbet Park, but also for her many authoritative books on horses.

After the death of Lady Wentworth in 1957, C. G. Covey inherited most of the stallions and the best broodmares. Lady Wentworth's daughter, Lady Anne Lytton, inherited historic old Newbuildings, part of the original Crabbet holdings, around fifteen miles from the main stud. Lady Anne has many fine Arabians of her own breeding (of Crabbet stock) as well as the Polish import GROJEC, an outstanding sire. She too has written many articles on Arabians, but is an all breed judge of horses, not of Arabians alone.

While of necessity this must be confined to the first breeders of Arabians in England, the Courthouse Stud of H. V. M. Clark should be included, since it dates back to 1900, and was founded on Blunt stock. Early mares included FELUKA (dam of *Ferda), NESSIMA (full sister of *Nasik and *Nureddin II), and BELKA (Rijm-Bereyda). BELKA was a real performance mare. She took part in the first and third of the three 300-mile endurance rides held in England in 1920-22. She completed the course in the first and won the third. Moreover in 1924 she defeated the winner of the second of these events, in a mile race held under Pony Turf Club rules. That horse was SHAHZADA, later exported to Australia where his bloodlines are still important today. Clark has the strange fixation that no Arabian should stand higher than fifteen hands, basing this on a statement said to have been made by Lady Anne Blunt to that effect. Yet in 1906, when the Crabbet Stud was being divided, she had written that "Rijm is the ideal horse for this stud and cannot be let go," after she heard that an American was trying to buy the horse from Blunt. RIJM stood slightly over 15-2, and his grandsire MAHRUSS, an Abbas Pasha Sherif stallion, measured 15-2. Clark claimed that when

277

BENJAMIN (Champurrado-Baranova)　　　　GRAND ROYAL (Oran-Sharima)

*SILVER VANITY (Oran-Silver Gilt)　　　　SHAMNAR (Naziri-Razina)

*SILVER CRYSTAL (Rangoon-Somara)　　　　KARRAMBA (Witraz-Karmen II)

he saw the horses of Crabbet, around 1900 and thereafter, these "exquisite horses" were all under fifteen hands. This may have been before RIJM was mature (depending on the period he referred to), but NEFISA, the dam of NARGHILEH (dam of Nessima, etc.) stood slightly over 15-1. RIJM is also the sire of *CRABBET, winner of one of the Official U.S. Endurance Rides, and this tough, stocking legged chestnut stood 15-2 also. In view of these measurement of horses closely related to (or sire of) of Clark's own stock, it is hard to see how his theory came about, other than by reference to reports of half-starved desertbreds, stunted since birth. The Courthouse Stud has bred and shown some fine horses, including several champions. Among them are BENJAMIN, SHAMMAR, and BAHRAM. He also owned SAINFOIN and the bay beauty CELINA, that ex-racer turned broodmare to be then transfigured into something very representative of the horses in the painting so admired by Prince Mohamed Ali, when she won the championship at the Annual show. And don't forget that Clark also once owned SKOWRONEK and was the first to use him at stud.

The Hon. Miss Dillon was another early breeder of Arabs in England, some of her original stock descending from Crabbet horses, such as old HAGAR, the desertbred so admired for her stamina and speed by the Blunts. Another was the desertbred JEDRANIA. Others of her mares were imported by a few individual breeders—one of these was KESIA II imported en utero by H. Chaplain. KESIA's dam had been selected in the camp of the Gomussa tribe by them—Captain Roger Upton (author of *Gleanings from the Desert of Arabia* and *Newmarket and Arabia*) along with several others. Most of the Dillon desertbreds were purchased from their importers, but she herself imported EL EMIR, a desertbred allegedly taken to Algiers. An odd thing about the Dillon horses (judging by contemporary comments and pictures) is that they were uniformly plain, often leggy, and rarely typy, no matter what the strain nor from whom obtained. She seemed to prefer that type. She worked all her horses hard and even rode mares as hunters or show ring jumpers when they were heavy in foal. Her stallions were ridden and driven hard—they would have qualified for Pony Express mounts, in their unceasing, long distance travels. This, combined with poor condition, may be one reason that the horses had such a leggy and fine-drawn appearance, compared to the fat and happy Arabians of other establishments . . . but it did not account for plain heads and general lack of type. A number of Dillon lines can be found way back in American pedigrees, very few in English. RASCHIDA is one through which a number of these trace. She had won nineteen jumping prizes, one of them while her foal followed along behind her, presumably not over the jumps.

Originally the English Arabs were registered in the General Stud Book. So were the Barbs and assorted other Oriental horses, since after all they were the founding fathers of the Thoroughbred. In 1918 the Arab

Horse Society was founded, and a stud book was formed. Thereafter foals and imports were listed therein, and if acceptable, also in the G.S.B. if the breeder so desired (and most did). Shows were initiated under the auspices of the A.H.S., the first being held in 1919. The main event of the year is the Annual Show, at times called the Royal Show when it was held at Windsor Castle. Other shows are held during the rest of the year in connection with open shows, or agricultural fairs and so on, but the "national championship" though not so termed is that awarded at the Annual Show. In 1918 there was estimated to be only 120 mares in the country, approximately half of them at Crabbet Park. By 1965 over two hundred foals per year were registered.

With so many Arabs based on a limited number of horses, mostly from Crabbet stock, needless to say English Arabians were becoming noticeably interrelated. Some breeders considered this to be an unhealthy state of affairs, in that outcrosses were needed—
breeding programs everywhere in all sorts of livestock. This outcross was provided in 1957 by the introduction of Polish Arabians. These were brought in by Patricia Lindsay whose own purchase was the lovely KARRAMBA (Witraz-Karmen II) who made such a favorable impression that this became only the first of several "Polish invasions" of England, and which in turn spread to America. Another of this first group was CELINA, the bay mare so quickly purchased right there at the dock by Clark. The approval of such a connoisseur of Arabians as this old time breeder was not lost on other English Arabian breeders and may have further advanced the cause. At any rate, the new round of purchases included many eventual champions and reserve champions of the Annual show as well as at other events and in the performance categories. Not long thereafter the Russian imports made an impact, the higher class of these being well accepted, and the nineteen-year-old mare NAPRASLINA won the championship at a recent Annual show. Though Russianbred, this mare is a granddaughter of NASEEM. Miss Margaret Evans is the owner of most of the winning Russianbreds, and her stallion NAPLYV is another example of the cosmopolitan pedigree of these horses. His sire POMERANETS, a very beautiful horse, is by that highly successful sire of racers, PRIBOJ. This brings us right back to England, for the latter's dam is the Crabbet mare RISSALMA. Moreover the dam of NAPLYV (Nitochka) is a full sister of *NABORR, thus a granddaughter of NASEEM. The sun may have set on the British Empire, but apparently it will never fail to shine on the descendants of English Arabians, for not only are they represented in Europe, but as far south as South Africa, and equally "down under" in Australia; in North and South America, and all points of the compass. Therefore it often happens that the foreign horses aren't so unfamiliar after all.

The leading sire lines in England are reflected fairly well through exports, as noted previously. The use of Polish blood has already made

280

a noticeable improvement in regard to straightness of backs and often also in levelling the croup. For some reason, in countries where Arabians are raced, they seem to have stronger appearing backs (Egypt is another example) than in countries where riding of Arabian horses is restricted mostly to slow hacking and the like, or not indulged in at all. The emphasis being placed in England of late on the various horse trials, as well as ordinary jumping, is certainly a step in the right direction to counter the effects of generations of soft living.

A factor that favored the introduction of new blood into the English Arabs was the closing of the General Stud Book to all but foals of horses already listed therein. In other words, no imports could be registered, no matter how immaculate their credentials. They could, however, be registered in the Arab Horse Society Stud Book. There had long been a certain snobbish sense of superiority in having an Arabian eligible for double registry, that is in both the G.S.B. and the A.H.S.B. I believe *all* Arab registrations have now been discontinued by the G.S.B. just as had been done by the American Jockey Club several years earlier. At any rate the lure of double registration has lost its lustre . . . all horses are single but they are registered Arabian horses none the less. While you may not have any thought one way or another about this development in England, it should be of interest, for now the way is cleared for more importations of Americanbred horses. The snob appeal of double registration is gone, and the actual quality of the horse and of his antecedants is transcendant over this once popular attitude. The fact that a few scrubby horses of doubtful authenticity were accepted for early registration in the A.H.S. should not count too much against it—the same is certainly true of the G.S.B., not to mention some of the first registrees in our own A.H.C.R. stud books.

Speaking of stud books, Egypt still has no association which maintains a stud book for *all* purebred Arabians of that country The only one available is that of the former Royal Agricultural Society (1948) and its successor, the Egyptian Agricultural Society, which has recently issued a new edition. Apparently all other breeders keep their own records, although the horses are registered (in a way, but not the same as in breed registries) with the Jockey Club, if they race. By the way, all horses raced in Egypt must pass inspection as Arabs (as to type) before they can race, *including those bred by the E.A.O.* This prevents the off-type individuals, or culls, being used for racing instead of the better conformed animals.

In Poland all Arabians are raced, whether they look the part or not. The object is not to develop a strain of very fast Arabians, with the breaking of records under light impost as the goal. Instead, racing is the only test afforded aside from Military (3-Day Event) training, since there are no horse shows other than for jumpers, in Poland. Nor are there endurance rides or ranch horse trials, and so on. But racing

Mares at the Micholow State Stud, Poland

On the way to the starting post, Warsaw race track

Saddling paddock, Warsaw

has provided a fine test. Not only is it a test of speed and stamina, but also of soundness, constitution, and temperament. Any horse that is too nervous, or which will not recuperate quickly after an exhaustive effort, is not regarded as breeding material above and beyond his survival of a season or two of intensive testing without a breakdown. In addition type is considered, so with all of these elements combined an animal that is all type and no horse can't get by, any more than one that is the opposite, or one which is exceptionally fast but too nervous, and so on. Sometimes a really outstanding animal is only lightly raced, just enough to prove his durability and adequate speed, in order to retire him (or her) fairly soon to the stud. A rather unusual state of affairs is that the head stallions (Arab) also serve at the stallion stations in the production of Anglo Arabs and part Arabs. The Poles feel that the few purebred mares available are not a sufficient test of a sire's abilities, and his foals from assorted types of mares show his dominance in regard to various attributes. Also this would bring out any inherent faults. These vacations from the Arab studs at Janow-Podlaski and Michalow often extend over a two-year period. Young stallions are sometimes tried out in these stallion stations before being used with purebred mares. This program, of grading up peasant-owned stock, is not too different from the Remount system formerly used here. However the peasants often breed sport horses, as do some of the state studs, their well bred mares raising foals by Thoroughbred, Arab or Anglo Arab stallions. At three the animals are sold at auction, the better ones going into training for jumping and all the Olympic types of events. Many peasant horses have been purebred Arab mares, discarded from the state farms for a variety of reasons. Aside from lack of type, small size, and so on, a sure way for a mare to be eliminated is to be an irregular breeder, to have had trouble foaling; to be a poor mother, or, of course to be a bad broodmare in that she produced low quality foals. Many of the horses you see pulling the long, low slung, slat sided wagons are beautiful animals, and the nearer they are to the state Arab studs, the more all Arabian they appear. Some may even be purebred, as noted. Miss Lindsay rescued a fine mare that had been eliminated from a stud as being too small and had been sold to a peasant. After months of negotiations the mare was finally saved and taken to England.

As indicated regarding SKOWRONEK, Polish Arabian pedigrees are the longest continuous pedigrees in the world for this breed, as far as written records are concerned. Prince Hieronim Sanguszko for instance, sent an expedition to Arabia in 1803 for the purpose of obtaining blood stock, and after two years of search, his agent (who was also his confidential secretary) returned with five stallions and one mare. This was one of the first expeditions ever sent to Arabia for the specific purpose of exporting horses from that country. It was also before Mohammed Ali and his successors took so many horses back to Egypt, only to have them die of neglect and degeneration a few years later, in such strangely repetitive cases, although some were salvaged from the last two importations.

The Sanguszko family seemed to send an expedition after horses with every generation, for the son of each prince became an importer, in succession. Hieronim's son sent the expedition of 1816, and in this group of horses was the Jilfan stallion DZIELF and the Kehilan HAJLAN, both of which became important sires. SKOWRONEK's dam has six lines to this import and an equal number to HAJLAN. Ten stallions and four mares were obtained from 1821 to 1826, through the use of a Syrian Arab as agent. In 1844, Prince Roman Sanguszko (son of Prince Eustachy, whose father was Hieronim) tackled the journey himself, and obtained the Seglawi Jedran stallion BATRAN AGA from Musselin Batran Aga in Aleppo. It was only after extraordinary difficulties that he got the horse home, and even then Abbas Pasha did his best to buy the horse, presenting his offers through the Russian Consulate in Aleppo. BATRAN AGA's name appears twice in SKOWRONEK's pedigree. These horses all belonged to the Sanguszko's Slawuta Stud. Many additional desertbreds were obtained by Slawuta, including some imported by other breeders. One of the comparatively recent imports was ILDERIM in 1900, but the Satanow branch of Slawuta had brought in thirteen stallions and two mares up to 1912. This branch was owned by Count Josef Potocki of Antoniny, and among the stallions were the Crabbet import PHAROAH and EUCLID, a desertbred that had been very successful in races in India. But most important was IBRAHIM, imported by Count Potocki in 1907, for this was the sire of SKOWRONEK.

The studs of the Counts Branicki were equally old, originating with the former Szamarajowka stud founded in 1778 by the purchase of two stallions and thirty broodmares from the Tulczyn stud of Count S. Potocki. As shown by the stud books of Bialocerkiew, founded in 1803, 122 stallions and 15 mares had been imported from Arabia up to the year 1913. The over abundance of stallions is not only due to their easier purchase, but because they were used on grade mares, on the Remount system to upgrade cavalry prospects. In fact all the studs bred half breds as well as purebreds, the latter being the nucleus from which the stallions used for upgrading local stock were secured aside from imports. Some stallions imported by the "Emir" Rzewuski, who had lived long enough in Arabia to acquire that title, and who had written the first treatise on the Arabian horse (the first of any country), were obtained by the Bialocerkiew Stud in 1823. He had imported eight stallions and twelve mares in Arabia in 1819, for the Weil Stud in Germany and had established his own stud of desertbreds in Poland, which on his death were obtained by other breeders. Bialocerkiew obtained two stallions from General Narischkine in 1836, one of which was the noted sire WERNET. This is just a mere once-over-lightly of the many horses imported by this stud, or purchased from other breeders.

Count Juliusz Dzieduskycki imported several horses and mares of great potential influence in 1840 and 1845. These included BAGDAD, ABU-HEJL, ABIAT, and KOHEJLAN among the stallions, and the three taproot mares GAZELLA, MLECHA, and SAHARA. The acquisition of ABU-HEJL was accomplished under difficult circumstances. Count Juliusz, after a two-year sojourn in Arabia, discovered this Seglawi Jedran stallion in the Syrian desert. He was purchased from the whole tribe, as he was common property, but although an agreement was finally reached, some of his erstwhile owners reneged, wanting to keep the stallion until the best mares could be bred to him. The Count, having paid for the horse, ostensibly agreed to this, but at nightfall he mounted ABU-HEJL, and with his dragoman on GAZELLA (purchased from the same tribe) they took off for Damascus in something of a hurry. After a while, they heard the galloping of horses behind them, along with the punctuation of gun shots. The whole tribe was after them with the object of recovering their stallion. However, thanks to the swiftness and stamina of ABU-HEJL, and not to forget GAZELLA, they arrived safely in Damascus. ABU HEJL is the sire of KRYTYKA II 1858, who is the dam of CERCLE 1863, whose son KORTEZ sired the typy, beautifully conformed RYMNIK, the sire of JASKOLKA. Actually, as far as pictures prove anything, RYMNIK was infinitely superior to IBRAHIM, an indication that SKOWRONEK's dam (Jaskolka) may have contributed more to the excellence, and dominance, of that horse than did his desertbred sire, IBRAHIM. Going back to ABU-HEJL, if he had not been able to outfoot his relatives, what a hole that would have left in Polish pedigrees, not to mention all of those throughout the world which would have been minus SKOWRONEK. Also GAZELLA founded one of the most influential families of all time, and her loss would have been equally disastrous. So speed has its rewards in more ways than one.

A stallion named SEGLAWI-ARDZEBI, named like practically all the imports after his strain or strains, was one of the horses imported by Prince Roman Sanguszko in 1857. It was worth anyone's neck to even tour the Near East at that time, due to the recent conclusion of wars, the Wahibi uprising, religious turmoil and so on, and moreover an Austrian expedition was in the area for the same purpose of buying horses. But this particular horse was worth the trouble. Among others he sired the aforementioned CERCLE, and so founded the sire line to which RYMNIK belongs. This makes a comparatively short sire line in JASKOLKA's pedigree, but her family line goes back to the first decade of the 1800s. SKOWRONEK is used as an example here, since through his innumerable descendants, nearly everyone has a relative.

Taking the family point of view, these are among the better known horses which trace to GAZELLA in direct tail female: The sires WITRAZ, WIELKI SZLEM, NEGATIW, and COMET. English or American champions include *ARDAHAN, *ARWILGA, MIKADO, *ORZEL, and GRO-

JEC; a few Derby winners include MIR SAID, *MIRZAZ, HARDY and ORLA.

Not to slight the other two of his famed triumvirate of family founders, the line from MLECHA includes *AMFIBIA, *ARWISTAWA, *BASK, *BAJRAM, *CZESTER, *MUZULMANIN, *EL MUDIR, *WIRAZ, *SALINAA, the English champion ARGOS, and the Americanbred Reserve National Champion AMERIGO. The great race mare *SABELLINA is of this family also. She is the winner of the Oaks and the Derby, and a son and daughter (Sabbat and Santa) are also automatically of the MLECHA family and are Derby winners.

From SAHARA the line comes down to *EMAUS, *MADRYGAL, KARRAMBA, and the Derby winners BADIARA and KREZUS (all Derby references is to Polish Arab Derbies). All of these references are but a small segment of the vast number of fine horses tracing directly from the foregoing three desertbreds of 1845.

The first World War marked the beginning of the end of the royal studs of Poland. The famous Slawuta Stud was destroyed by the Bolsheviks and only a small number of broodmares was saved. These were incorporates in to the Gumniska Stud. SKOWRONEK's former home, Antoniny, was also destroyed but some of the horses were saved, thanks to the devotion of the personnel. These formed the nucleus of the new stud at Behen. The great Bialocerkiew studs were completely obliterated, while others were damaged (including loss of stock) to a similar or a lesser degree. The horses which survived this chaotic interlude were taken to the remaining establishments, headed by the State Stud of Janow-Podlaski, north-east of Warsaw.

In the short between-the-wars period some fine horses had been imported from England. Included was the champion RASIM, along with four mares, also from Crabbet—NITLA (*Nureddin II-Nashisha), FASILA (Rasim-Feir), RAMAYANA (*Nureddin II-Riyala), and SARDHANA (*Nureddin II-Selima). FASILA is the dam of the Polishbred *SULEJMAN and SARDHANA is the dam of the Englishbred *CRABBET SURA (dam of Sureyn). These had been imported to the Ujazd stud of Baron W. Bicker. Another mare owned by this stud was the Polish KARIMA (Farys II-Rusulka), and she FASILA and RASIM comprise the whole immediate background of CELINA's dam, due to close inbreeding. However CELINA herself is a product of an outcross, as she is by WITRAZ. CELINA it will be remembered is the mare which in the ownership of H. V. M. Clark became Supreme Champion of England.

The Breniow Stud of Mrs. T. Raciborska is one that went out of existence as a stud but lives on through some of its horses. One of these is the beautiful grey SAHIBA, winner of many races, including the Oaks and Derby. Mrs. Raciborska used stock from the Babolna stud as well the mare RUSALKA, descended from the Bialcerkiew horses. As the dam of AMURATH SAHIB alone, SAHIBA has left her mark on

Polish Arabians. A write-up on the stud said it was conducted "with a view to bringing out type and pluck in racing," and apparently it was successful. Certainly SAHIBA was both typy and plucky, as she won five out of her seven races, plus one second, at distances from 1400 meters to 2400 (1½ miles). NEDJARI, a beautiful fronted stallion from France with an excellent race record, was one of the stallions used on Breniow mares. He had also won a gold medal "for his exterior." His dam won a similar gold medal.

NEDJARI was owned by the Gumniska Stud of Prince Sanguszko, who had imported a couple of French mares as well. Unaccountably these have been called Maneghi, as was NEDJARI, but he was a Hamdani by actual strain, as was ARBA (one of the mares). In the third generation of his dam of those ancestors having strains listed, five are Hamdani, one is Hadban, two are Seglawi and two—in the middle of the pedigree—are Maneghi. His sire was desertbred, the tribe but not strain was recorded. Apparently the fact that he managed to beat all rivals gave him the label Maneghi, but Hamdani was his strain. Quite a number of modern horses descend from this brilliant performer. French Arabian bloodlines are said to be for sprints only, but this horse won at distances over a mile in every case, from 1800 meters to 2200. NEDJARI is the sire of PORTA, the dam of FORTA, and apparently the blood of that indomitable old French warrior bred on, for FORTA has been remarkable for the number of superior racers among her produce. Among them are the fine sire CZORT and the Derby winner EQUIFOR, whose time (3:35) is still unequalled. CZORT is the sire of three Derby winners. *FAROAN is also a son of FORTA and among his championships is a Canadian Top Ten. GRAND, a sire of many superior racers, was out of the Derby winning mare SAGAR, whose dam was DJEBALLA, the third of the French mares. Another horse important in today's pedigrees and which was owned by this stud was MOHOMET, sire of IBN MOHOMET. Since the latter sired the internationally celebrated *IWONKA III, he now is well represented through her grandson *BASK and others of this family, many of which are Americanbred.

In 1930 Prince Sanguszko organized a new expedition to Arabia, to add new blood to the Gumniska Stud. As should be obvious by now, the Polish breeders constantly added desertbred blood into their stock, and even in Egypt this was practiced, with both countries claiming deterioration if this was not done. The horses brought back on this memorable occasion a year later included the great KUHAILAN-HAIFI a stallion inevitably termed "all-Kehilan," yet his pedigree shows in the third generation Hadban, Hamdani, Shueyman and Seglawi, in addition to Kehilan. A second stallion, KUHAILAN ZAID, is also considered pure-in-strain Kehilan, but in the second, generation alone (I don't have his full pedigree) can be found Seglawi and Hadban, in addition to the Kehilan. In other words, each are at least half of other strains. But

Kehilan, Seglawi, Hadban or whatever, they were good horses, especially KUHAILAN-HAIFI, most noted as the sire of OFIR. KUHAILAN ZAID was sold to the Babolna Stud, where he became one of its leading sires. He had crooked hind legs, but did not seem to be dominant in this. His name can be found in the pedigrees of many of the mares of that stud which were used by Poland a few years after World War II. A third stallion was KUHAILAN AFAS, of strains bred for centuries—more or less—in Bahrein. His son BAD AFAS sired ABU AFAS, sire of the redoubtable COMET. The fourth stallion, KUHAILAN-KRUSZAN, was kept by the Gumniska Stud—or at least he was the only one of these horses still listed as being there in 1937. What happened to KUHAILAN-HAIFI is not mentioned (in the 1937 booklet), but he sired only fourteen foals, the last arriving in 1935. This establishment was completely wiped out by World War II, except for young stock which were at the race tracks, one of which was the bay GRAND.

The Janow-Podlaski State Stud was founded on mares from the Jarczowce Stud, GAZELLA II, POMPONIA, and ZULEJMA, which traced to the famed three mares of the 1845 importation; SIGLAVY-BAGDADY from Slawuta breeding; KALINA and ELSTERA from the Antoniny Stud; BIALOGRADKA (full sister of Mohomet), dam of *KASZTELANKA; KEWA from the Inocenzdvor Stud of Prince Odescalchi in Yugoslavia, and a few others. Stallions used included BAKSZYSZ, from Slawuta; ABU-MLECH and FARYS II of Jarczowce blood; BURGAS, imported from Syria; GANGES II; HARDY and FETYSZ. The last two were famous racers. In 1933 the celebrated OFIR was foaled at Janow-Podlaski, sired by KUHAILAN-HAIFI; and with his sons of 1939—the famous "W" trio of *WITEZ II, WIELKI SZLEM, and WITRAZ, we approach modern times, and the history covered under the heading of the *WITEZ II. Regarding one of the mares of this stud, namely GAZELLA II, it is worthy of note that three of her daughters produced the great sires WIELKI SZLEM, WITRAZ, and *NEGATIW, and she herself was the dam of HARDY.

A write-up on the Janow Stud gives these aims: "The State Stud took a lively interest in the Racing tests and sent its horses to the races at Lwow and Lublin.... Notwithstanding the success obtained, Janow did not aim at any records of speed, but considered these trials as only a test of endurance of its horses over big distances and under heavy weights. The Management of the Janow Stud gives its whole attention to upholding the desert type of purebred Arabs. Next to health and correct build, it considers racing trials as one of the necessary tests of efficiency, but certainly not the only one."

The races as conducted now start with 1600 meter (about a mile) events for three-year-olds in mid-year. Four-year-olds compete at longer distances, climaxed by the Derby (3000 meters—a mile and 7 furlongs), but the average distance is 2400 meters (1½ miles). Weights (standard) are 58 kg (128 lbs.) for three-year-old colts, fillies about two pounds less; four-year-olds 60 kg (132½ lbs.); at five years a horse carries 64 kg (141 lbs.), and from six up, 66 kg (145 lbs.), with the usual sex allowance for fillies and mares. The weights vary according to handicapping however. Some carry more than scale, others less in certain races, especially from four years on up. Nevertheless these weights bear out the attitude of the Janow statment. They are universally considered heavy, and they are greater than the standards for Thoroughbreds. An occasional Arabian is used for hurdle racing and show jumping also. For instance MIRAZ, full brother of *MUZULMANIN, won in both classifications, against Trakehner and Anglo Arab competition. The Trakehner, the East Prussian breed famed for jumping ability, is the foundation of the Polish halfbreds, along with an overlay of Thoroughbred and Anglo Arab blood. These halfbreds, and Anglo Arabs, supply a large proportion of sport horses to Europe and even to the New World, and they have been successful in Olympic Games. Some famous purebred Arabs have contributed to their bloodlines.

In the fall at the end of the racing season, the Arabians are judged by a hard-bitten group of horsemen, and type alone doesn't get far with them, any more than a superior race record does for a horse with no Arabian type at all. Not only the exterior is judged, but also performance, including the constitution of the horse—the way he recovered after a race, his temperament, and so on, not to mention any pampering needed to avoid breakdown. After the inspection some colts and fillies are kept in training, others are returned to the stud farm for breeding purposes, and some are put on the sales list. Most of the latter remain in training and if they develop especially well a few are re-judged and returned to the breeding farms. Many of the young stallions are immediately assigned to stallion stations throughout the country. There is a three-way pull regarding sale stock in Poland. Animex wants as many as it can get and the best ones it can get for sale abroad, in order to obtain revenue and in addition to maintain a good reputation through sale of superior animals The track management wants to keep all the Arabs possible, in order to have full cards for Arabian races. The stud managers want to retain the best young stock, for obvious reasons, maintaining that unless the breeding stock is the best, soon no one would go all the way to Poland for Arabian horses. Even when frustrated from obtaining your "heart's desire" seen in the Polish paddocks, you can't blame them for this.

The first stud book of the Arab Horse Breeding Society of Poland was published in 1926, but since only around 45 of the 400 broodmares of the pre-war studs were saved (or were still in Poland) a new, revised edition, Volume I, was published in 1932. A careful, detailed investigation of the ones registered in the first book, found some that were not purebred (nearly all of the studs bred halfbreds as well as purebreds, often with identical names); and these lines were omitted from the first volume of the present series, although several pedigrees of half Arabians were contained in their own section. But since that time they have not been continued in the purebred records. Volume II was published in 1938, Volume III in 1948, Volume IV in 1953, and so on. The present volume is No. VII, published in 1967. There are yearly supplements, listing each foal separately, by name. A full description of the markings is given along with color, sire, dam, and breeder.   In the following section each broodmare is listed, including those just entering the broodmare ranks, and along with her statistics (color, age, breeder, owner, sire, and dam) her current foal is named; or if no living foal was produced (or if the foal died) this is indicated, and the date the mare was last bred in the current year, and to what stallion, is also recorded. This gives a very complete check-up on every animal. Moreover whenever any marking color, etc., is not recorded exactly, a correction is issued in the next supplement. In the sire's section, their foals of that year are given under their names, and of course their own color, age and breeding is given too. There are usually long lists of exports listed in detail, grouped under the countries to which the horses were sold. To make the whole thing even easier to double check, or see at a glance, each stud lists its mares, along with the name of her foal and its sire. There are around a hundred broodmares, en toto; in addition to the State studs, there are now two private breeders. This may not be many, but it is an increase of a hundred per cent over a couple of years previous, and double that of the post war period. This is exclusive of peasants who own purebred mares, as they do not receive certificates—purebreds are sold without papers, as it were, and peasant mares are generally bred to halfbreds for production of sport horses.

In addition to this, the racing records of Polish Arabians can be found in the Racing Calendar. The last issue of each year contains a summary of leading money winners by age; and index of the horses and the races entered; a list of leading sires, and so on. This is in with the same data on Thoroughbreds and halfbreds, but easy to find, since each is in its own section. However the races are not separated—they are entered numerically and chronologically, so only by checking the number of a race in question (under the horse's name) can the details of the race be found.

All of this gives a quite complete picture of Arabian activity in Poland, even if there are no horse shows other than jumping contests in which Arabians can compete.

Publications on Polish horses include the excellent recent book by Dr. Edward Skorkowski—*Arab Breeding in Poland* along with government bulletins and Animex booklets.

As should be quite apparent by now, in view of the "requisitions" of Polish Arabians and purchases from England, Russia had quite an eye for an Arab; and starting in Imperialist times had a habit of collecting the best, either by war or purchase. The immortal MESAOUD was sold by Crabbet Park to Russia in 1903, along with several others from that stud. In 1936 a still larger and equally important lot was purchased. Along with MESAOUD, in the first draft was included NAAMAN (Mesaoud-Nefisa), ANBAR (Mesaoud-Queen of Sheba) and RISHAN (Mesaoud-Rose Diamond.) These three were colts. Mares and fillies were DIJLEH (Ashgar-Dahna), DINAZARDE (Rataplan-Dahna), JENEYNA (Azrek-Jerboa), MAKBULA (Wazir-Makbula I), and SABHA (Wazir-Selma I). In the second group the stallions and colts were: JERUAN (*Nureddin II-Rose of Persia), NASEEM (Skowronek-Nasra), RASEEM (Rasim-Rim), RYTHAM (Shareer-Rythma), FERHAN (*Raswan-Fejr), and SHAREER (*Nureddin II-Selima). The mares and fillies were: BISARIEH (Naseem-*Battla), GREY CRABBET (Raseem-Silver Fire), NASIFA (Skowronek-Nasra), NISSAM (Raseem-Neraida), NASHISHA (Rasim-Nasra), NAJERA (*Rahal-Nasireh), RASHIFA (Shareer-Rishafa), RIAMA (*Nureddin-Dafina), RIXALINA (Raseem-Rissla), RIMULA (*Nureddin II-Rimini), RISSALMA (Shareer-Rissla), ROSE OF AFRICA (*Nureddin II-Jalila), RUELLIA (*Nureddin II-Riyala), RUANDA (Najib-Rythma), SILKA (*Nuereddin II-Somra), and STAR OF THE HILLS (*Raswan-Selima). These are listed to show what a large piece of Crabbet Park went to Russia, and what good horses some of these were! It makes one somewhat envious.

RIXALINA is the dam of KOREI, sire of KOMPOZIDOR, record holder (co-holder, rather) of the record for 2000 meters, and of KNIPPEL, holder of the record for 7000 meters (4⅜ miles). RISSALMA is the dam of PRIBOJ, sire of three record holders. RADUGA, by RYTHAM out of RUANDA is in the pedigree of PLASKA, the mare who, with KOMPOZIDOR, holds the record for 2000 meters.

In 1939 the Russian armies "liberated" over fifty Arabians, mainly from Janow, including OFIR, SKRZYP (sire of Sputnik, record holder for the mile), HARDY, ENWER BEY, and KUHAILAN SAID (son of Kuhailan Zaid), as well as many of the best mares—even old GAZELLA II, DZIWA, TARASZCZA (dam of Negatiw), FRYGA II, and ELEGANTKA. In mares alone the number exceeded forty. Some French Arabs were purchased in the 1930s, and recently a couple of Egyptian-breds were added. One of these died after only a year or so at stud, but the other ASWAN (by Nazeer) is doing well and hope was expressed that this new blood will be of benefit. It is not without its problems, for as Mr. O. Balakshin, of the Horse Breeding Agency of the Ministry of Agriculture, said in this regard, "To my way of thinking the offspring of Aswan will be useful in the Tersk Stud, as the first offspring on the whole create a good impression, although some of them have the defects of their father—long, light cannon bone with tied-in tendon, and lack of muscling on the croup. I think that in the future these defects will be eliminated." All of which reflects the usual conflicts between type and

PROFIL (Priboj-Fadbanka)

The Arabian mare NAGRADA (Arax-Naparnitsa) winning for the second time the great inter-breed handicap at the All-Union horse competition in Russia.

ARAX (Amurath Sahib-Angara)

PIETUSZOK (Priboj-Taktika)

conformation even though the latter should actually be incorporated into the former.

Arabians are not pampered in Russia. They are put in preliminary training as long yearlings, and are raced in sprints under light weights, as two-year-olds. At three they are entered in longer races, and at that time the weights correspond with those of Poland—58 kg. (128 lbs.); but some much tougher distances are included—from the beginners' 1600 meters to the veterans' 2800, 3000 and 3200 meters, the latter of course a two mile distance. The Oaks (for fillies of course) is the same as in Poland, 2400 meters. The race equivalent to the Derby is named "Grand Prize at Pjatigorsk," also at that distance rather than Poland's 3000. The difference is that in Russia, with training stepped ahead a year, the Derby is run by three-year-olds instead of at four, as in Poland. Four-year-olds carry 59 kg (130 lbs.), and from this age and up the races average from a mile and a half to four and three-eighths. In addition Arabs can compete against Anglo Arabs, halfbreds and Russian breeds in certain races. Moreover once in a while they win. They have also won some of the cross-country events and military trials.

As previously mentioned regarding *NABORR, all emphasis is not placed on performance; for *NABORR won beauty prizes in halter competition, as did his sire; so presumably others do too.

Volume I of the Russian Arabian Stud Book was issued in 1965 and includes horses of the second Crabbet importation as well as the Polish war captives. In addition the few French and Egyptian purchases are listed. Even for a complete non-linguist, it is not too difficult to read the Stud Book, aided with a Russian-English dictionary. Stallions and mares are listed in separate sections, by number, but alphabetically. The foals of each mare are given under her paragraph. In addition to the usual information, the summary of each horse's race record is presented, along with any noteworthy times. Despite the Russian alphabet, these listings are comparatively simple to negotiate, but what *is* aggravating is the inability to read the pages relating the history of the breed in Russia. The Russian Arabs are branded as foals, which is also the case of the Polish horses. The foregoing have been the major contributors to American Arabian backgrounds, although Russia's is mainly through its Polish-English bloodlines.

A sketch of the Spanish Arabians was given in regard to the Draper and subsequent imports, in which it was obvious that many of the famous names of the country were involved in breeding Arabian horses. However it is the Government stud, the Yeguada Militar del Estado, which has been maintained the longest among those still in existence today. Many purebreds were lost in the civil war in Spain, or at least lost their identity, or rather, that of their foals. Many who were absolutely and obviously purebred could not be registered because of this lapse.

293

A resume of the Yeguada Militar is given in a booklet written before the Spanish civil war, in 1929, and is delightful in its Spanish accent:

> Great interest has always been taken in Spain in this privileged breed, considering it the most suitable for the improvement of its equine race and the important production which this horse since olden times exists in the country has of late been greatly developed.
>
> Our excellent Arab breeders, some of them imported, but the greater part born in the military Stud of the State, which is to be considered the finest in existence, formerly chiefly served for crossing purposes, as the stockowners disposed of but few mares of pure blood. When later the production of the military Stud at Jerez developed excessively, the Directors of that Institution justly decided to sell some of them and consequently there are now quite many stockowners who use the mares for the obtention of pure blood. First class specimens of these are put on the market and are sold at high prices.
>
> However, the State continues to be the most prominent producer, maintaining actually in the Arab section 170 head, 80 of which are breeding mares in full production.
>
> The Arab section of the military Stud at Jerez was started with mares and germinal horses imported from the Orient, which still from time to time provides beautiful specimens. Russia also furnished germinal horses and some were equally obtained in France and England.
>
> With the flourishing development of our Arab production and the casting abroad of our perfect breed, the demand for them becomes greater every day, and as a logical consequence to the perfect stock offered, we are—false modesty apart—in a position to compete advantageously with the most ancient and renowned markets of Europe.

The article wound up with a comment regarding racing: "The Spanish Arabs are not tested to the limit of their velocity power."

Argentina has just recently organized an Arabian Horse Breeding Association and the production of Arabians in that country has grown amazingly. However it is the home of the oldest and largest Arabian breeding establishment in the Americas, in that Hernan Ayerza imported several Arabians from the Near East at least as early as 1898 and has imported from other countries since, including several from England. The present Haras Santa Helena is owned by Mario Ayerza who inherited it from Alfonso Ayerza, the brother of Hernan. Ignacio Ayerza is president of the newly formed Arabian breeder's club. I know of no North American Arabian farm which has such a long continuous heritage. Further details on the Ayerza horses are given regarding the Dickinson imports *AIRE and *NAHRAWANA, obtained from Brazil but of Ayerza breeding.

While there are other major Arab breeding centers throughout the world, the foregoing countries are the ones which have contributed most generously to the background of American Arabians. Some have contributed more than just the background, as the show winnings of these imports attest. That the breed is more international than ever is obvious from the Arabians of America alone.

There have been some nit-pickers who point with glee to alleged "impure" horses in the background of certain foreign Arabians, ignoring the fact that no guarantee is available that these horses, identified only by name or strain, were not mistaken for purebreds of identical names. Or, when labelled as being from Persia, Turkey, or even Algiers, they can't say for sure these were not supposedly purebred horses obtained in those countries . . . where they were bred by royalty and high officials, and ridden by generals, and so on, as has been the case ever since. But even if these animals were impure, this introduction of mixed blood into a breed itself or mixed origin, and also *a hundred or more years before there was an official stud book for the breed* (there or anywhere else), can be of no consequence. It is not easy to prove impurity or its opposite in cases where no records of any kind exist, such as in the desert. Memory is not enough, especially considering the tendency of human nature to gloss over unpleasantries and exaggerate the good. Nor should one of Mohammed's many admonitions be forgotten, "Remember of geneaologies, only that which keeps the line pure." Although he was speaking of human family trees, what applies to one can apply with equal glibness to the other—the equine family tree.

If the Arabian had been a distinct sub-species, such as its unmixed ancestor undoubtedly was before the Hittites and others tangled with foreign invaders who brought along their own horsepower, then there would have been reason for concern about a new (hundred year ago) admixture of Persian, Turcoman, or whatever blood. But this is nothing more than a new dose of its own basic ingredients, though hopefully the Arabian has much less of the North than the South in its makeup, at this stage of evolution. As it happens the first homogenization started over three thousands years ago, and its too late to wrangle over it now.

In consideration of the fact that in countries where type, quality, conformation and performance were all appreciated along with bloodlines, there have been produced consistently more typy and beautiful Arabians than in Arabia itself; there should be a moral there somewhere. For it is said that (in the 1800s and early 1900s at least) the Bedouins thought only of blood, and nothing at all about the conformation or soundness of the animal. They admired a good head and also high tail carriage, but they did not deliberately breed for either, except where such attributes accompanied the blood. Whatver the method, the results can be seen by even the most biased. A first class, typy, and sound Arabian is almost impossible to find in Arabia or the surrounding deserts—the former cradle of the Arab. But they can be found by the hundreds in parts of the world where modern horse husbandry is applied. To quote the Spanish writer, in America too we can say—"false modesty apart"—that some of the best Arabians in the world can be found here. Some may have come from other countries, but they now are *here* in America.

The 19-year-old stallion °NABORR was sold at auction, to settle the estate of the late Anne McCormick in October 1969, for a world record price for an Arabian, of $150,000.00. Buyers were Tom Chauncey and Wayne Newton. At the same sale the Polish import °PALLADA was sold for $25,000.00 to Marianne Hannah. This was a record price for an Arabian mare sold at auction up to that date.

IX

THE STRAINS ... COMPOUNDED AND CONFOUNDED

Before bringing the various activities of the Arabian horse world up to date, a couple of items need clarification. One is in regard to family strains, mentioned as to origins on pages 19 through 21, but due to the proliferating of ideas that a certain type accompanies a strain name — regardless of the true strain of the horse — some additional comments are in order.

At first there was no problem whatsoever. There were around two hundred family strains in the desert, but less than twenty have any bearing today, and even in olden times there were always a handful (literally, for they would be counted on the fingers); the five, al-Khamsa, which were regarded as most numerous or most important, the exact make-up of the five depending on which strains were bred by the tribe whose spokesman was enumerating them. Kehilan (though this also meant "the Arabian breed" in its generic sense) was always included. Nearly always too was the Seglawi, and very often the Maneghi, along with two or three now rarely mentioned, other than "related to" the others. They, and others, have many spellings, but these are the American versions.

It was partly due to our Registry's discontinuance of strain listings that the eventual complete flop-over of the already misleading concept of the "Three-strain" theory occurred. For when people did not know (without a lot of research) the actual strain of their horse, they were perfectly willing to accept the idea that it was of the strain assigned to horses of a certain type. But this is in itself getting the strain before the horse, so to speak.

First it should be pointed out that although there are several types within the breed, Carl Raswan telescoped these into three, and did the same thing to the most important strains ... that is, the ones most numerous in America, not necessarily elsewhere. He was a prolific writer and also traveled widely, preaching his "three-strain" gospel wherever he went and, since it was obvious to anyone that there were different types within the breed, many people went along with the "type-goes-with-the-strain" idea. This was despite the fact that all too often the wrong type accompanied horses of the various strains (i.e. a Kehilan would be "Seglawi type," a Maneghi was of "Kehilan" build, and so on). As it happens, several of the European strain enthusiasts wound up with their own picture of strain types, with the result that in Poland, for instance, the "Kehilan" fits Raswan's "Seglawi" type, and vice versa — a complete 180-degree turnabout. This, of course, negates the whole force of the argument.

The Raswan thesis held out for a heavily-muscled, broad-headed, wide-chested "masculine" type for Kehilan, which he claimed "looked like a Morgan," later supplemented to include the Quarter Horse. His ideal for the Seglawi was a much slimmer (100 lbs. lighter) and elegant, though narrower-headed horse of good riding type, which he said compared to the "Kentucky saddle horse" (American

Saddlebred) in type except for a better head, and naturally high-carried tail; while his third type, Maneghi, was for a tall animal, "coarse, very fast up to 4 miles" and Thoroughbred in type.

Going on a tangent of my own for a moment, it is interesting to note that the Maneghi strain's image was based almost *in toto* on Wilfred Blunt's first description (which did not tally at all with Lady Anne's references to Maneghis in the same book)plus Davenport's nearly exact copying of the same comments, plus ditto by Randolph Huntington. They all agreed, simply because they were all copied nearly verbatim from the Blunt wording, and then Raswan copied the lot. The color, chestnut, was added as a characteristic of the family by Huntington, and so was the "tall" comment. The reason was obvious, for the Huntington "Maneghi" horses were all of the *NAOMI group (see pages 31-33). She herself was chestnut, she stood 15-2½ and she was rangy in shape and amazingly proficient in performance (hunting, jumping, and at the trot). She and her daughters were bred mostly to chestnut horses, so the offspring should usually also be chestnut, and she was used for a target for inbreeding, emphasizing her characteristics. But she was half Kehilan, and stallions to which she and her daughters were bred varied as to strain: *LEOPARD was a Seglawi, and so was KARS, while *KISMET and MAIDAN had no recorded strain in the G.S.B. (though *Kismet became a "Maneghi" simply by crossing the Atlantic, being so registered here). So, with all these non-Maneghi and "unknown" strains mixed in with the Kehilan sire of *NAOMI in her very inbred descendants, it can be seen that only the lone line of her dam can actually be called Maneghi, and it is very much in the minority. So right off the bat, the projected image for this strain, based on this dynasty, is wrong. Dr. Skorkowski said he used American studbook data (first volumes) to supply color facts for the strain, and accordingly he classifies chestnut as the "Maneghi color," since the *NAOMI lot preponderated in these early registrations. He, too, used the Huntington "type" description in forming his first opinion of the strain, for there are no Maneghi horses (by strain) in Poland, although they have it in the pedigree via other (than tail-female) lines — usually distant.

Somewhere along the line speed was added to the list of Maneghi accomplishments although the strain was — in the desert — invariably mentioned as being in "high esteem" and further referred to as being noted for stamina, hardiness and courage. Possibly because of the note as to HAIDEE (*Naomi's dam) being described as chosen "not for her appearance, but for speed and bottom," speed got into the later picture, although Huntington did not mention it. But both Raswan and Skorkowski did.

This brings in a coincidence. Although Thomas Darley's letter to his brother in England in 1703 had mentioned the Darley Arabian's strain, this fact was not published until a couple of centuries later, though the fact that he was a pure Arab was known with the quotation that "both by sire and dam he is of the race most esteemed by the Arabs." As it happens the knowledge of his strain seems to coincide with the sudden interest the French took in importing Maneghi sires (c. 1890), when previously their Arabian horses were of all the best-known strains, including of course Seglawi-Jedran and various Kehilan sub-strains, with one influential Maneghi line, carried on through BELLE PETITE, whose name suggests both beauty and small size. It was in the 1890s that Huntington bragged: "From the MANEGHI came the DARLEY Arabian," but earlier this horse's strain had been guessed to be Seglawi (by Lt. Col. Hamilton-Smith in 1841) and Ras-el-Fedawi by the Blunts in 1879 and just Kehilan by others but never Maneghi.

Then an odd thing happened . . . instead of making any claim that the Thoroughbred resembled the Darley Arabian (which it does not, of course) the advocates of Arabian strain-type reversed the affair and made that handsome and breedy stallion resemble the modern Thoroughbred a hundred percent, simply because he is the most successful of the three "founding fathers" in direct tail-male of the Thoroughbred. There were also a few hundred other Oriental stallions and mares involved, plus, of course, the native English stock, so to make the Darley the exact image of his much-mixed but very admirable descendant-breed, is asking a bit too much for anyone to believe. Yet some do . . . but then some people believe anything. At any rate, this seems to be one way in which the "speed" category got into the Maneghi strain-type file. Wilfrid Blunt had given that virtue to the Kehilan, along with the words to the effect that the Kehilan more closely resembled the English Thoroughbred than did any of the other strains. This obviously excluded the Maneghi. Oddly enough, all subsequent "copiers" always neglected to mention this.

To further show how far from the original desertbred concept this "Maneghi-type" caper came to be, the early imports of this strain (or ones mentioned in books) were rarely chestnut, and hardly ever "tall." FERIDA, founder of the *FERDA and FEJR branches (via Feluka) was a bay "with 3 white hairs in her forehead," and standing only 14. 1½; the two Maneghis described by the Blunts were scorned as "a mere pony" in the case of the one "looked upon with awe because of his bloodlines," a black; and the other, TAMARISK (not the import) was also called a pony. She was a "good-looking" bay.

The Maneghis in the Upton group (see *Naomi pages) were, in order, 14.2 the grey; 14.1½, bay; and the chestnut (Haidee) was 14.2. The Davenport import *HALEB stood 14.2 but *GOMUSSA was around a half-hand taller. By contrast many horses of other strains ranged from 15 hands onward, and HAGAR, the bay with the "strange, wild head" and who was described as "Looking very much like a Thoroughbred" was a Kehilan, and she was 15 hands; while the Wadnan-Hursan stallion MAHRUSS was 15.2 (Ali Pasha Sherif stable) his grandson RIJM (Crabbet Stud) was said to stand 15.3-¾ unshod. He too was Kehilan, and was sire of *NUREDDIN II, 15.2. The famous Seglawi-Jedran desertbreds of the Weil Stud, BAIRACTAR and GOUMOUSH-BOURNU both stood 15.2 hands, all of which would indicate that the freakish height of *NAOMI was untypical of her strain at that time when the Maneghi Ibn Sbeyel was in its relatively undiluted form.

This one strain is an example of how the original idea in this sort of thing (strain-type) can be wrong. Presumably the other two were almost as befuddled. At least it was not long after the original idea of "the Three" having their own characterisitics that it was obvious that this was not the case. Accordingly, Raswan modified his dogma, stating that it was not the true strain (i.e. the strain by which the horse was registered) that counted, but instead the preponderance of strains in its pedigree. For instance, if mostly Kehilan, that is what the horse was to be called, even though actually a Maneghi, and so on. That too was soon proven to be tricky, for all too often a horse "saturated with the blood of" a certain strain, would resemble one of the other two types, and be actually of a minority strain not in the Big Three. All other strains, by the way, were casually lumped together as "related to" certain of "the Three," a strange situation, indeed, since the Kehilan were often crossed with Seglawi, not to mention Maneghi, and when a horse is "arf n' arf," how much more related could it be?

The ultimate in complex and unreasonable reasoning, was reached when it was finally decided to give a horse a strain name according to the type into which it fit, judged by its appearance. This has nothing to do with time-honored strain names as used in the desert for a specific purpose (and elsewhere for reference or even romantic history), and therefore should not be used at all. Instead, types within the breed should be treated, or termed, just as within all other breeds of horse — if nothing better can be devised, then as "racy," "compact," "rangy," "cobby" and so on, or even as among Thoroughbreds, as "distance type" or "sprinter type." For all horses even Przewalsky horses, as well as among the several kinds of zebras, there are different types. So it is not surprising that the Arabian includes some variety, especially in view of its own distant and mixed origin.

As a further example of "type-setting" and alotting the strain names to each is the situation in Russia. At least there they frankly admit that the names do not necessarily belong to the type, and prove it by calling NASEEM (a Kehilan) typical of Seglawi type, and identifying two other Kehilans, RYTHAM and *NUREDDIN II, plus the Hamdani-Simri SHAREER, as being typical Hadban (a strain designated as tall, coarse and heavy-boned by the Russians). At least the "typical Kehilan," actually is Kehilan, namely OFIR.

There apparently are no Maneghi horses in Russia at present, although FERHAN was of this strain (imp. 1936) and is the sire of several foundation mares. So something else had to be saddled with the "tall, coarse," etc. category. Raswan's description of the Hadban as coarse, muscular, heavy-headed with straight profile, heavy-boned, (but not tall, averaging 14.3) would be reason enough for such affiliation. The only actual close-up Hadban blood seems to be the sire of KANN, a French import (who has only one distant Maneghi line, by the way, which is far less than in Polish, English, American and Egyptian, Arabs, etc., as a rule). KANN is termed a "Maneghi" by other than the Russians. The Hadban source is far back, overladen with other strains, but it is carried right up to DENOUSTE (Kann's sire) in tail-female, so that's what he, DENOUSTE, is. Ironically, this is the same strain as that of the very refined Egyptian sire, NAZEER, and it would take some strong peyote (or other . . .) smoking to dream up a vision of NAZEER in the Russian "mold" for that strain.

And then take NAZEER's situation. He is the sire of nearly a hundred foals, of which 35 are Hadban, 33 Dahman, 17 Seglawi and 11 Kehilan. According to strain-faddists, going by family only, these would resemble the strain-type assigned to each family, yet NAZEER was very dominant. While the mares may have passed on some of their own characteristics, enough to show a slight family resemblance, the general inheritance was "all-NAZEER." He, too, is mixed of ancestry, as to strains, that one Hadban line being all there is of that strain as far as is known — until the sixth generation, where another turns up. However, there are many desertbred "unknowns" involved by that time. NAZEER's great-grandsire was a Maneghi, making him "one-eighth" Maneghi right there, but he has four other lines to this strain as well, plus three Seglawi and various other lines. Such an assortment is customary in nearly all pedigrees today, so belief in "strain-type" is little more than a sublime faith in hash.

It should be emphasized that actual strains are still listed in studbooks of England and Egypt and a few other countries, and in these you can rely on the strain designation as such. They are of no special use, other than being an immediate indication of tail-female bloodlines, similar to the Bruce Lowe numbering system in Thoroughbreds. By the way, the main strains in Egypt are Hadban and Dahman, with the Kehilan and Seglawi a poor third in a near-tie. The Seglawi was nearly lost in England until mares of the Bint Helwa family were re-introduced from America, also some from the French mare *KOLA from the same source. So the "Big Three" applies mostly to American strains.

Moreover, it should also be remembered that what Raswan calls "Kehilan," Dr. Skorkowski calls "Seglawi" and vice versa. This immediately leads to complete verbal and mental chaos when people addicted to such terminology start a learned discussion on the subject without first clearing the air and saying which "language" they intend to use. This in itself should tell them something (that the whole idea is wrong, if two authorities are at a diametrically opposed difference of opinion) but it doesn't. Probably the most damage done is in books which have picked up the Raswan line and started a whole new generation off into mental limbo on this subject.

One author, who is now sorry she ever used such material is Erika Schiele, whose beautiful book *The Arab Horse In Europe* is widely read (and used as additional "proof" of the "three strain" theory). Since its publication Mrs. Schiele has travelled widely in Arabia and environs, and made much more intensive study than before (and that was a lot) on her own — at the sources — of other Arab-breeding establishments and countries, including Europe. In a 1972 letter she wrote: "Raswan's 3-strain-theory is really nonsense. I wanted to get information in Arabia about the Maneghi and the so-called (by Raswan) related strains. Nobody understood in Arabia of what I was talking. "Maneghi? Oh yes, a very famous and fine strain!" Since she has to re-write parts of the book for the next edition she is understandably upset at having been taken in by the wrong information at the outset and now being forced to correct it. It would take wholesale corrections to bring other writers up to date on this matter, but too many are content to just copy the other fellow, and let it go (forevermore) at that.

This "Three strain" theory contended that the Maneghi should never be mixed with the other two, predicting a halloween mishmash of disasters to follow if the advice was not followed. Well, it wasn't, and they didn't. This can best be seen in the statistics supplied by study of the sires of American champions. Of the 739 sires of champions from 1953 through 1970, only 13 of these sires had no Maneghi (or "related") lines at all, as far as could be traced. And not one of these 13 was on the leading Sire List (sires of 5 or more champions). This should indicate something. Moreover, the champions sired by this lonely 13 were all out of mares with Maneghi lines, so in the straight no-Maneghi category they could not make it on their own. It would seem that horses of the strain so universally given the "highly esteemed" title in the desert strictly on performance, had what it takes in the matter of conformation too, even if they were often considered "plain" compared to some of the other lines.

The second subject has to do with the horses called "parti-color" in Prince Mohamed Ali's publication of the Abbas Pasha records. Some people now contend that the word should be translated as a type of grey, and that the original documents are in bad condition due to age (they are nearly 150 years old) and the fact the Egyptian scribes worked in desert camps under rough conditions, resulting in possible misplaced dots and badly-done squiggles of the Arabic words. However Lady Anne Blunt translated the same passages, and she came up with "parti-color," not grey, and was assisted as to Bedouin idioms by a Muteyr tribesman. Raswan, too, claims to have translated these from the originals. He also calls the horses "parti-color" and even further differentiates between the word for this and for speckling, as for "fleabitten" or other "dotted" grey. No matter how much one may disagree with his various theories on strains, he must have had a good command of Arabic (despite the many dialects). Moreover, he would have preferred to have this word come "grey" or almost anything but "pinto," since up to that time he had maintained that such coloration indicated a "crossing of the strains," especially with Maneghi. (In view of the usually solid color of Maneghi horses, this was a peculiar opinion). Also, the granddam of MAHRUSS was one of these parti-color (grey?) mares, and some descendants of MAHRUSS had a body spot or two, although they could hardly have been considered to be pintos. This can be countered by the fact that MESAOUD sired more "spotted" horses (with under-body spots, not pintos) and had more such descendants. But he traced to MAHYUBI, a famous stallion in the desert in the early 1800s who is listed as sire of two of those "parti-color" mares, and grandsire of one with Hereford-like facial markings. It would be interesting to see how the Abbas Pasha scribes wrote the word now in contention, to find if it is the same as used by much earlier writers who described parti-color Arabian horses as to exact placement and amount of the white. These most certainly could not have been mistaken as "greys." And finally, the large numbers of Arabian horses now registered in America has brought out an equal increase in number, if not percentage, of actual pintos in the breed. These are of just as pure breeding as their more discreetly marked or totally unmarked (called "deaf" by the Arabs) — siblings. It is just an ancient color — at the very least 3400 years old by fact, not fancy, again coming to light.

RAKTHA (Naseem-Razina)

X
THE NEW AGE OF THE ARABIAN

The past four years have brought out some new developments along with the general increase in shows and resultant larger number of champions. Unfortunately, although there are more shows, the types of performance in all-Arabian shows have gone backward as to variety, instead of making progress into new realms as one might have anticipated. The heavy emphasis, almost to the throttling of other classes, is on "pleasure" events. Formerly these were only English and Western, but now are added Pleasure Driving and Combination and "Versatility" classes in which this is generally limited to the foregoing, instead of work that requires a variety of talent, agility, ability or speed. These classes are often further divided according to age and/or sex of the rider as well as that of the horses, resulting in "all-pleasure" shows that are anything but a pleasure to watch. This even extends to the National level. Now, however, classes have become so large in these categories that plans are being made to change the National image, and either make it an exhibitor's show, or a spectator show (aside from breeding classes) but not try for both, and possibly delete Half-Arabian classes, which have increasingly filled the entry lists.

Probably the most spectacular progress was made in high-class auctions, whether dispersals, semi-dispersals, production sales, or other types. These have now become a way of life — the first ones were those of Al-Marah many years ago, and now auctions are even part of the Nationals, where sale horses of the best bloodlines and quality are as much a highlight of this show as the National entries themselves. The famous "*Naborr sale" in 1969 started the current high-price binge. The bidding was lively on this 19-year-old stallion and had the rest of the gallery agog, never having heard such bidding on an Arabian before although it's common at the best Thoroughbred auctions. While his $150,000 bid has not as yet been equalled at Arab auctions, the sale-topper for mares, $25,000, was later more than doubled for several different mares, not just one at this price, at the Lasma Sale. The Rogers dispersal saw VIRGINIA BELLE bring around the same amount (i.e. over $50,000) too, in topping that hotly-bid auction, and at one of the National auctions $35,000 was paid for the aged stallion MRAFF. Recently *ALGORAB brought $23,000, a record for an Arabian race horse in training, at the Northeast All-Arabian Sale. Other mixed as well as annual (or every 2 or 3 years) sales have done extremely well too, and horses sold at private sale have also brought fair prices, such as $100,000 for *GWALIOR and a reported higher amount for *IBN MONIET EL NEFOUS, but the latter is said to have included mares and young stock, so his exact price is not known (at least not publicly). Stud fees, too, have soared with $1,000 and $2,000 and upward (to $10,000) not too unusual for the most popular and successful sires (or costly new imports of exceptional quality, even though yet unproven). This is fine in some ways, but way out of line for owners of a few good mares who want to breed to the best, but not at any prohibitive cost . . . and even $1,000 can "prohibit" most people.

So much for economics. While comparatively quiet compared to the auction trail, racing has also made promising progress. Even more than promising, it has actually produced. This is in the matter of comparative times, and the fact that two records have been broken by a second-generation Americanbred race horse in this instance, KEMAH's POLKA, son of the famous 2½-mile racer OFIR (page 248), the latter a grandson of the great Polish sire of the same name. In 1970 this handsome chestnut broke the American record for the mile in 1:46.3, just three-tenths off the record set by BALANCE in Egypt forty years ago. The times noted here are of course Arabian. Previously the mile record here was held by NUSABRE at 1:47.3, subsequently broken twice by *ALGORAB (Mir Said-Algonkina) in 1:47.2 and 1:47.1.

KONTIKI was the "glamor-horse" of racing, and was pleasing to the chauvinistic element in that he was all-American so much so that he represented just about all Arabian bloodlines (which of course all started here as imports). He was of the SKOWRONEK sire line via FERSEYN and SENEYN (sire of Camelot, Kontiki's sire), but has English, Polish, French, Egyptian, Saudi Arabian, and Syrian (Hamidie and Davenport imports) in addition to this Polish-English top line. Some of his exploits are given on page 248, but after a semi-retirement due to lack of competition worthy of his steel, he came back in 1971, thanks to the efforts of Mrs. Stanley Kubela who subsequently bought him. He won his first outing, a sprint of 6½ furlongs, in the record time of 1:24. A few races later he set the American record for 1¼ miles in 2:19.4, knocking six-tenths of a second off that set by BARBADOS (*Bajram-*Cosmosa). He won all his starts in 1971, climaxed by the National Championship two-mile race, under the impost (a staggering one in American opinion, if not in Polish custom for mature stakes-quality horses) of 149 pounds. He won in a leisurely gallop, although there was a ding-dong battle for second many lengths behind. The time was not fast, 4:00.2, but the startling fact is that it set the track record for the distance at Sunland Park, simply no thoroughbreds had as yet run that distance there.

Three months later KONTIKI had retired from racing and at Scottsdale was given a fling at showing, just for the fun of it. He won a resounding ovation by winning the reserve championship. Here an odd coincidence showed up – his only defeat in racing was at the heels of *ORZEL, and here too he was a notch in back of that fine horse (now a Top Ten halter champion in U.S. and Canada), although only figuratively, for *ORZEL had won the championship at Scottsdale a few years before. KONTIKI's next show was at Baton Rouge, where he was a popular champion, but sad to say he succumbed to colic shortly after his return to Texas. It was lucky, however, that he had already sired a few foals, so hopefully his heritage will be carried on, to the good of the breed in general. As yet KONTIKI's record for the mile and a half has not been lowered, and in view of the impost (142 lbs) it may be some time before it will even be equalled in all respects.

HAMLET (Camelot-Farnina) a bright chestnut by the same sire as KONTIKI but out of a half-Polish mare holds the record for a mile and a sixteenth, of 1:55, but unfortunately he met with an accident shortly thereafter and had to

304

be retired. KEMAH's POLKA followed up his own mile record with a record-setting win two years later for a mile and an eighth, only to have it broken a month thereafter by *ALGORAB, a Polish horse who seemed to have a knack for breaking records at various distances. CORJON, a grey gelding by *CORSAIR out of ABU WITA has won at least six pari-mutuel, plus other races, and held the first of the mile-and-an-eighth records, of 2:06.2. His dam is by ABU FARWA, further adding to the lustre of that "show horse sire" as a sire of dams of superior race horses. BAR-KINHACZ (*Mohacz-Kinza), a flashy chestnut filly is one of the few of her sex to compete (to date) in American Arabian racing and she has been singularly successful, winning several, and coming in a hard-fighting second to such horses as *ALGORAB and CORJON (who once was second to her, though giving away 11 lbs). EL GOHARI (page 248) holds the record for a mile and three-quarters, of 2:51.2, and it was not long ago that this was considered fast for the mile and a half. He, too, is a veteran of many years' racing (like Kontiki) but was kept at it more steadily, and he always managed to win the important races after a few stodgy efforts, which did not help his record but did cheer up his backers — IF they picked "his day." He is the only horse to beat *ORZEL in American racing, but then the latter won a race in which EL GOHARI came in third, more than evening the score.

These are just some of the recent racing highlights, mostly as to records. But interest is picking up and new horses are being added at increased tempo. It will be noted that some are extraordinarily durable, being in training — and winning — for years. And not to be overlooked are the converts from racing to the "beauty parades," namely *ORZEL and KONTIKI already mentioned, plus the newer import *SAMBOR, winner of both parimutuel and show racing (including the National Show stakes) and now a regional champion at halter and in Park; and FIREBRAND, first a halter champion, then a race winner, and again a champion, plus "most classic" Arabian. These are but a few of the "beautiful racers." When it is remembered that all (with only an occasional exception) the Polish imports three years or older have been raced, and that some of the Egyptian imports have also (or their sires were, and/or other relatives), then it should be obvious that correct basic conformation is equally applicable to the show ring as to the race course or other rugged lines of endeavor, and that Arabian *type* is no detriment to performance. There is one minor exception to this last — the very short-headed or extremely dish-faced horses do not seem to do as well in tough work where hard breathing is required, as do the ones with more normal proportions, in other words a matter of efficiency in breathing.

Racing is not confined to professional status, except in parimutuel events, and even there owners can get right into the thick of things (when licensed) as trainers. An example is found in the Fastnacht family, where its three members are owner, trainer and jockey, respectively — and this is in "professional" racing. Moreover, they train (and ride) for other owners. Hazel Lucas is even more renowned, for she is breeder of such excellent horses as NUSABRE already mentioned, and BEAU RESHAN (both by Nusik) the latter is a veteran of many "show race" wins. She also trains her horses and rides in show races on top of which she has been most active in all Arabian racing activities. And speaking of the ladies — Cheri Bayens was the first trainer of KONTIKI and was responsible for the excellent condition in which he arrived at the track for his first blitz on the awe-struck Arabian racing scene. And as a long-time supporter of Arabian racing (and all other types of real work) Mrs. Stanley Kubela is right at the top, breeding her own many entries, and buying a couple of others — the champion show-horse-turned-racer, METEOR, and "Mr. Big" himself, the immortal KONTIKI.

A second way to give Arabian horses a good workout, as well as country-wide publicity, is through the various types of long-distance rides (pg. 246-7). Here all the family can get into the picture (or saddle) and it is indeed often a family affair. Arabians and Half-Arabians continue to dominate this field. WITEZARIF (Witezar-Razifa) won the Tevis Cup Cup three years in succession — and this rugged 100-mile one-day ride is considered an accomplishment even to finish.

Competition has always been tough. In 1970 it was the hard-bitten gelding QUIST (Champion Endurance Horse of 1970 and 1971) who was runner-up for the Tevis Cup and in 1972 it was a three-quarter brother of the winner, EL KARBAJ. There is a double continuity here, in that QUIST was foaled on the Rushcreek cattle ranch in Nebraska and WITEZARIF was foaled on the Hyannis cattle ranch in the same state, and both — like the other Hyannis horses of long-ride fame, were never pampered in their youth, which was spent on the open range.

Secondly, there is a noticeable influence of the mare line in the case of certain Hyannis-bred endurance winners. These are out of daughters of ZARYF (Rifnas-*Ferdisia) a Kellogg-bred mare of the Maneghi *FERDA family (a reference of interest only to the "strain" people, though it ties in with the ancient reputation of this family for endurance and stamina). One of these daughters was RAZIFA, by the Egyptian stallion *ZARIFE, and the other was by AZYM, a son of *ZARIFE. RAZIFA is the dam of WITEZARIF, EL KARBAJ and RAZLIND, the latter almost a duplicate of his grandsire *RAFFLES, which is of interest, in that while all were of the same female family and of course the same strain, little RAZLIND bears the others no family resemblance at all — outwardly — but he is exactly the same as to rugged fortitude as his larger tougher looking half and three-quarter brothers. Such heritage of performance ability is often known to come through the mare line, not surprising, perhaps, but just less publicised, for stallions are expected to be all things to all people, and often have more chance to prove it (except in Arabian) than do mares.

ZARIMA is the dam of PRINCE KOSCA (KoKo), who tied with QUIST for the 1971 championship. His full brother PRINCE KOSIMA (Brumby) has also won several Rides. All of these Hyannis-bred horses are closely related, for both WITEZAR and KOSCIUSKO are by *WITEZ II, whose get are renowned for top-class versatility (as a group, if not individually). KOSCIUSKO is a working cowhorse on the Hyannis ranch and is the sire of other endurance horses in addition to the foregoing.

Another sire of such horses is GABILAN, of the large Lanigan ranch in California where the horses run almost wild from foalhood on. He is a grandson, in tail male, of *RODAN, of earlier endurance-ride fame (page 52). One of GABILAN's offspring is AGUILAR, another is LANESSA and the third of these three geldings is PEPILLO, winner of the Regional Championship and Light-weight over-all championship in points won against all breeds in the North American Trail Ride Conference (N.A.T.R.C.). A GABILAN daughter, ALVARA, finished in the Drakes Bay Ride, and had never been ridden (or broken) until March of the same year, but was not soft, having run at large on the Lanigan hills all her life.

As with the case of BANDOS (who was himself an Endurance horse, however) other sires show this continuity if given the chance (and if they pass on good

306

conformation, plus intestinal fortitude to their get), but those mentioned are a matter of record, to date.

A summary of 1971 Rides (Western States), compiled by Marion Robie (daughter of Wendell Robie) and a many-time winner on various horses including her own KOKO, showed, that out of 15 Rides, 5 winners were also Best Condition; 12 were won by Arabian geldings (80%) and 3 by part-Arab mares; QUIST won 3 Rides; WITEZARIF, PATHFINDER (Jurwadi-Sarma) and CRICKETT (part-Arab) won 2 rides each; 7 were won by chestnuts, 5 by bays and 3 by greys; KOKO, at 5 years was the youngest winner, RAZLIND (12) was the oldest. All but one had been raised on the range, with no pampering whatsoever in their youth.

The "family-inheritance" sort of thing goes with the riders too, as witness the Robies, but also the Pat Fitzgerald family, where Pat has an infinite variety of wins to his credit, most of the recent ones on QUIST, while his wife Donna beat him out in some events notably the Tevis Cup triple, with WITEZARIF, and even young Mike has placed with WITEZARIF in other rides.

KAMIN-KU (Izkar-Samia) has quite a record too, in that not only did he twice win the Florida hundred-miler in 1966 and 1968, but was runner-up in '69, '70 and '71. His dam is a foundation mare of the Kubela ranch in Texas, where also the horses are used for ranch work, but of record is the fact that SAMIA founded a family noted for accomplishments on the race track. The 1971 winner of this Florida Ride was IBN AAHDIN, champion gelding at halter in the Dixie Classic and also winner of some reserve championships, who proved that "beauty is as beauty does" by doing. The trophy for this event is the Michael Cup, and further ties in with racing (page 248).

This is just a sketchy resume of the long-ride winners, but it further proves that "show" bloodlines are in the background of these as well as of the race horses, although more emphasis may be placed on sound conformation than to garnishment of type. Most of all, however, it depends on the opportunity given the horse, boiling down to the inclination of the owner — just as in the case of owners of hunters and jumpers. The beauty of such rides is that the whole family can join in — whether in all of them riding, or just pitching in and helping care for horse and rider en route . . and before as well as after. Many of the Rides are through awe-inspiring mountain country, and are a pleasure in their own right, but of course where they are competitive, and with time a factor, this is secondary. Nevertheless it is one of the best forms of outdoor exercise possible.

Now to the show winners, but again just a partial summary, via top wins. An over-all indication of championship sire lines can be ascertained more accurately from the sire-line charts since these reflect all championship (or at least the minimum) rather than National calibre. Through 1971 *BASK remained the only National Champion to sire National (or Reserve) Champions, of which he had three, and also five in performance. Several of these repeated, and some were both halter and performance winners. The same with a few of the following horses, *SERAFIX had five at halter and three in performance; SUREYN, 4 halter; *NABORR three halter, three in performance. A National Champion who sired two National Champion performance horses (of divergent types of work) and a Reserve, is BAY-ABI. His son MIKADO won the Park class; another (ex the famous Ronteza) was winner of the Stockhorse class, and a daughter was Reserve in Western Pleasure. Another National Champion MUJAHID, sired two performance winners — BLUE VELVET, an excellent roadster but here Reserve in Pleasure Driving; and SACREBLUE, Reserve in Western Pleasure. Two "non-resident" sires (Polish, and now deceased) were unusual in that both have two and three offspring among National winners, one in halter wins, the other in performance. COMET sired *GDYNIA, Champion in English Pleasure and Reserve in Western; and *ZBRUCZ, Reserve in Park. AQUINOR is sire of the Canadian National Champion *ELKIN the Reserve *ELEUZIS and the Reserve mare *ELKANA. The unusual feature is their sires' alien status plus number of winners. Several stallions have sired two champions (National) in either halter or performance, but are at stud in America. A list of National winners since the first edition of this book was published is included here.

A list of recent imports is incorporated also, but of the earlier groups, some of the 1970 lot were not registered in time to be listed in the 1970 Stud Book, so are not shown here. Nevertheless, some of them require attention, since they are among the current winners, or are otherwise worthy of note. Unfortunately there is no way of knowing all data on these, nor even all of the horses, until the Stud Books are published, so several may be missed. The breeding of National winners is given on the list of these, so need not be repeated. Topping this group is the 1972 Canadian National Champion (and 1971 U.S. Top Ten) stallion *ELKIN, whose full brother *ELEUZIS was Reserve Canadian National Champion the previous year. From the same stable as *ELKIN is *ELKANA, Reserve Canadian National Champion mare for 1972, and *FANTAZJA, Top Ten in both countries (U.S. 1971, Canada 1971). A bold-moving newcomer is *BAJDAK a former chief stallion at the Polish state studs, winner of several championships and now a Canadian Top Ten. *CEBION (Negatiw-Cela) is an East Coast Top 5 champion, and *ALLAHABAD (Czort-Algonkina) is a similar winner in Region 7. A very important horse was inadvertently omitted from the 1967 list. This is *ARAMUS, imported by Lloyd Burton and Bill and Janet Lowe, Rice Lake, Wisconsin. He is the 1970 National Champion and is by *NABORR out of AMNERIS. There are many in this new group which are not yet shown, are just starting their career, or which are imported for breeding purposes only, being too old for showing or racing. Among them are *CEDR (Equifor-*Cosmosa), bred in Poland but purchased from Sweden. His sire still holds the Polish Derby (Arab) record. Another old timer is FORTEL(*Como-Forta). He is a half brother of CZORT, EQUIFOR, *FINISZ, *FAROAN and *FORTUNKA, in that all are out of the remarkable broodmatron FORTA. *FORTUNKA is dam several American champions and of FORNARINA, dam of *FRANTAZJA. More on CZORT and FORTA is given on Page 287. *CHUTOR (Chazar-Czatanoga) is a newcomer just starting his show career, and represents the *LOTNIK male line. Another freshman is *GRENOBLE (Celebes-Gryzelda); while *GAZDA (*Naborr-Gazella) is unusual in that he is an imported gelding, and now has won many championships. *PENTAGON (Czort-Penza) is a brand-new arrival, as is the excellent racehorse *REZONANS, winner of six races despite two years of constant battles with *FINISZ, who won the Derby. In fact all, or nearly all, the Polish imports had been raced, including even the rather delicate looking *ELKIN and equally refined *FANTAZJA. The derby time of *FINISZ was one of the fastest of recent years, clipping a second off that of *MIRZAZ (Mirza), but the best current time is the 3:37 of ELFUR (Czort-Ellora), only two seconds slower than EQUIFOR's record. ELFUR's Derby was in 1970. MIR SAID (half brother of *Mirzaz) also showed speed, his time being 3:39 in 1957. He is the sire of *ALGORAB, who set several records here. As in the case of FORTA, MIRA passed on racing ability, just as the aforementioned

308

dams of endurance winners contributed to the success of their offspring, and as so many mares have passed down the ability to trot(*really* trot,not just pitty-pat) to their produce.

*BUSZMEN is Dr. LaCroix's replacement of *GWALIOR, and seems destined for a spectacular career. He won his first outing, at Scottsdale, and won several championships thereafter. He is by NEGATIW out of BUSZNICA.

Several Egyptian horses were among the late-registered imports. Among them is *RAMSES FAYEK (just Fayek originally) already winner of championships. His sire is NAZEER and he is out of FAYZA II. Another is *FOL YASMEEN (Hamdan-Muneera), winner of eight races in Egypt before his retirement. *ZAGHLOUL (Gassir-Gharbawi) is another multi-race winner. *SHIAA (Ala el Din — *Berlanty) was imported en-utero and should have been included on the 1966 list, since that was when her dam was brought in from Egypt. *SHIAA has won many championships, including Regional and a Top Ten. A new country was heard from with the arrival of *SLOVENKA-24 KOEHILAN 19, only recently registered but imported in 1966 also. She was bred in Czechoslovakia.

There are several large new breeding establishments, so many in fact that none can be mentioned without taking up a half-chapter. However there are four owners who are in a special category, new to the Arabian field, at least new in this degree. This the "show business" angle, headed by the highly-successful motion picture, stage and TV personality Mike Nichols. He has proven to have as much acumen in the horse field as he has in his profession. Several of his horses were personally selected by him in several trips to Poland,England and other countries, as well as a number of Americanbreds. Among the latter is the youthful champion TALAGATO (*Talal-*Agata III). His Polish champions *ELKIN, *ELKANA, *FANTAZJA and *ALLAHABAD are already mentioned or on the "National" list. Another Polish champion is an en-utero import, *ALONDRAA (Grojec-*Almaviva). Nichols first National venture was in 1971, when both his entries, *ELKIN, and *FANTAZJA, were Top Ten, a unique accomplishment for a newcomer.

Wayne Newton, the well-known singer based in Las Vegas, started his stable with all-black Arabians but soon found that it was hard enough to acquire a good horse without limiting himself to color. He was half-owner with Tom Chauncey of *NABORR after that spectacular sale, and this marked his advent into big time showing, for thereafter he purchased the best horses he could get, regardless of color. He soon acquired a half interest in *ARAMUS with Lloyd Burton and that horse went on to win the National Championship soon thereafter. Later he bought other imports and Americanbreds, including the champion *TINIAN (Negatiw-*Tryncza) and *DERWISZ (Comet-Daszawa), winner of performance classes. Newton's narration and assistance with the International's promotional movie "The Proud Breed" is one of his major contributions to Arabian interests.

John Davidson, a singer and TV star who is now displaying his talents as an actor, is also a very popular member of the show-biz clan of Arabian owners. Not only does he exhibit at many shows, he often rides or drives his entries himself. His wife, Jackie, is an equally enthusiastic competitor. His first purchase was the former Cal Poly College trick horse, POLY ROYAL, a son of FARLOWA. This stallion is quite versatile and, along with stockhorse and similar work, has been a Top Ten champion in pleasure classes. Davidson occasionally puts him through his trick role, a rather nerve wracking affair just to watch (let alone be the trainer in the ring) for part of the exhibition includes such movie

309

horse tricks as charging the trainer, rearing and striking and pretending to bite. The pride of the Davidson stable is the new import *FINISZ, an elegant and eye-catching stallion, already mentioned in regard to racing.

Fourth of this group, and often teaming up with John Davidson in entertaining at shows or conventions, is Sue Ane Langdon, well know actress and singer and a star of the long-running TV series "Arnie." There is no more enthusiastic promoter of the Arabian breed than Sue Ane, and in her many TV interviews she never loses an opportunity to get in more than "just a word" about Arabians, and has even had her champion mare SUJA (also a Cal-Poly purchase, and by Farlowa) on camera to amply prove the truth of her statements.

Two new organizations were "spin-offs" of the International in recent years. One is a promotional organization, the Arabian Horse Society (not to be confused with England's Arab Horse Society) and the other is the World Arabian Horse Organization, devoted to welding together the various Arabian horse breeding countries of the world, with more or less standardized methods of registration and other matters, to enable the import-export activities among all these countries to continue with a minimum of problems. Moreover, it encourages importations from new countries, but more important, it does the same for exports from America. A trickle of horses have been exported, but only a few of top quality, and some have even been of bloodlines which have proven continually unsuccessful here. In view of the intense interest given a well-publicized import to any country, it is for the general good that top individuals are exported at first (and thereafter, cost permitting) in order to give a satisfactory impression in their new country.

One thing should be remembered by foreign buyers, and that is the fact that American Arabian horses are the most artificially presented of any country. They are taught to stretch and arch their neck, and to pose in an animated fashion that recalls classic artists' representations; their poll is trimmed far down the neck to give an impression of a slim throatlatch; the neck (especially the throat) is sweated to make this appearance a fact, and in the beautiful photographs taken of these brilliantly animated horses, sometimes (in head studies which include forehand) the photograph is slanted, to further improve the image and even to give more slope to the shoulder.

So *caveat emptor!*

Many of these horses are as dazzling as their photos indicate, but some are not. An example of the advantages of artful posing and training is seen by "before and after" photos of imports. First they are seen in their native land, posed hunter-style; with at least an inch of mane along the top of the neck in back of the ears, adding to thickness of throatlatch; and with only ordinary animation, if any at all. Then presto! In America they become super-Arabs, with long gorgeous neck, eyes popping (from whip-trained attention) and a terrier-like tautness that adds verve to the whole picture. It takes a good horse, generally seen in racing condition (in Poland) or rather thin (in Egypt) to show up well in the original case, which may explain their instant transition to show-horse glamor. Nevertheless this above-average image, as so consistently seen in innumerable horses pictured in our Arabian magazines, has to be lived up to — at least to a degree — in American exports, assuming a correspondingly good price is paid. So now the problem is to breed Americanbreds which live up to their advertised image. And surprisingly, quite a number do.

310

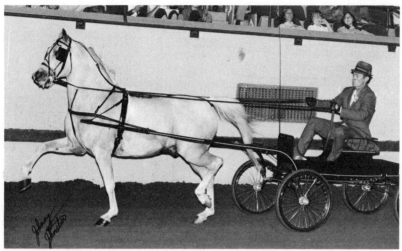
*MECZET (Comet-Mimika) 1972 Nat'l Park and Formal Comb. Ch.

The foregoing was written before the 1972 U.S. Nationals took place, and although the results are given in the charts, certain interesting aspects of this show were too late to be inserted into the text. The most unusual factor was the double championship in stallions (Canada and U.S.) and the near-double in mares (Res. Canada, Ch. U.S.) for Mike Nichols' *ELKIN and *ELKANA. Apparently this is the first time for an owner to score this sort of double (or rather, triple) and I can't remember an owner even getting both stallion and mare championships. To make this even more remarkable, these champions are both by the same sire, AQUINOR (Miezcnik-Amneris) and a full brother of *ELKIN, namely *ELEUZIS, was Reserve Canadian National Champion the previous year. Another tie-in is that AQUINOR is a half-brother of *ARAMUS, also a double winner of U.S. and Canadian National Championships. *BASK holds the record for siring most National Champions and Reserves of both halter and performance categories; *SERAFIX was first to sire National and Reserve Champions along with several Top Tens the same show; and MUJAHID sired both National Champions for the first National show, but the Nichols Arabians' accomplishment is nevertheless unique.

The nearly clean sweep of the "high action" classes in the 1972 show by the Polish import *MECZET is also unusual. Veteran of 32 races over a four-year period, carrying as much as 145 pounds in his later starts (and winner of 5), he won a pleasure class at Scottsdale less than six months after his last race, and now further emphasizes the versatility of so many of these ex-racers, by his conversion to the glamorous "formal" events. By coincidence, several of his erstwhile rivals on the track in Poland were also in the National classes which he won, namely *GWALIOR, *BAJDAK and *KLUSZYN. There were six imports among the Top Ten Park winners, five of them Polish, and one Egyptian.

Another example of real versatility is the winning of the Stockhorse class by ROUFER (Gassour-Roufer) who was also second in a large class of hunters in this show.

311

Stallions	Mares	Geldings
1968 CH:ZARABO (Bolero-Rizara)	MI-FANCI (Sureyn-Tuwaisan)	STAR-SIRZA (Sihr-NaZaba)
U.S. R: FADJUR (Fadheilan-Bint Sahara)	EL MALIKA (*Serafix-Witeza)	ASIL ZODIAC (Syzygy-Zareyna)
CanadaCh: COMAR BAY BEAU (Azraff-Rose of Mirage)	LLANA (Ga'zi-Zaryn)	HASSAAN (Ga'zi-Zaryn)
R: ZARABO (Bolero-Rizara)	SOLSKIN (Al-Marah Radames-Fashia)	LANIF (Lutaf-Talima)
1969 Ch: GALIZON (Azraff-Gay Rose)	FAME (*Bask-Wirdih Jameel)	BRUMARBA RAHZAM (Imazam-Romona)
U.S. R: *GWALIOR (*Naborr-*Gwadiana)	DANCING FLAME (*Bask-Habina)	BAARHAN (Baarouf-Wadi Sirhan)
CanadaCh: TORNADO (*Bask-*Silwara)	DANCING FLAME (*Bask-Habina)	SINIB (Binis-Tiffany Du)
R: NA IBN SOTEP (Sotep-Na Ilham)	*ESKADRA (*Naborr-Ela)	BRUMARBA RAHZAM (Imazam-Romona)
1970 Ch: *ARAMUS (*Naborr-Amneris)	DANCING FLAME (*Baks-Habina)	MOR-RAA (BuZahr-Balareynah)
U.S. R: *GWALIOR (*Naborr-*Gwadiana)	FIRE FLAME (*Bask-Aethena)	GRAND SALAAM (Julep-Silver Sparkle)
CanadaCh: *ARAMUS (*Naborr-Amneris)	GA-RAGEYMA (Ferzon-Gajala)	MEADOWLARK DRIFF (*Silver Drift-Kiswa)
R: BASKE-TU (*Bask-Naftu)	CENTURY 21 (Ga'zi-Wahida)	KAYLEK (Farjur-Darbana)
1971 Ch: ANSATA IBN SUDAN (*Ansata Ibn Halima-*An. Bint Mabouka)	*SERENITY SONBOLAH (Sameh-Bint Om Saad)	TAJ AMIR (Naharin-Zabira)
U.S. R: *GWALIOR (*Naborr-*Gwadiana)	GIOIA (*Serafix-Surima)	MR. CEDARDELL (Cedardell Heritage-Sahra Bint Sabba)
Canada Ch: *GWALIOR (*Naborr *Gwadiana)	BASQUINA (*Bask-Habina)	SILFAUN (*Silver Drift-Farnina)
R: *ELEUZIS (Aquinor-Ellenai)	SILHOULETTE (*Bask-*Silwara)	TAJ AMIR (Naharin-Zabira)
1972 Ch:*ELKIN (Aquinor-Ellenai)	*ELKANA (Aquinor-Estebna)	SILFAUN (*Silver Drift-Farnina)
U.S. R: KHEMOSABI (Ameriga-Jurneeka)	BASQUELLE (*Bask-Country Belle)	BLITZ (*Bajram-Aanadra)
Canada Ch:*ELKIN (Aquinor-Ellenai)	SILVER CHARM (*Bajram—*Silwara)	ROYAL AKAA (Silver King-Aakadina)
R: SILVER CENTURY (*Silver Drift-Century 21)	*ELKANA (Aqunior-Estebna)	ARC TENAYA (Negem-Schiba)

*ELKIN (Aquinor-Ellenai) National Champion Stallion, 1972

NATIONAL WINNERS, PERFORMANCE CLASSES 1968-72
(Sire's name in parentheses)

	1968	1969	1970	1971	1972
Western Pleasure					
Ch:	BAY ROD (*Nimrod)	MISS FARANA (Ga'zi) (Indian Magic)	*LEWISFIELD MAGIC (Indian Magic)	*NIHAL (Antar)	SKOVRAFF (Kharaff)
R:	STAR SIRZA (Sihr)	BAY KINRA (Bay Abi)	BAHADUR (Abu Baha)	SACREBLEU (Mujahid)	GAI-AMIR-AMAGE (Gani)
English Pleasure					
Ch:	*WIRGINIA (*Nabori)	ELNA (Yatez)	LE BASK (*Bask)	EL MALIKA (*Serafix)	BASQUINA+ (*Bask)
R:	BINT SURF (Surf)	DANCING FLAME (*Bask)	FIRE FLAME (*Bask)	CONTESSA-B (*Bask)	SKOVRAFF (Kharaff)
Park					
Ch:	*PROWIZJA (Ego)	SEAHORSE DUKE DORSAZ (*Count Dorsaz)	*EL MUDIR (Wielki Szlem)	MIKADO (Bay-Abi)	*MECZET (Comet)
R:	HILLCREST'S IMAZETTE (Imaraff)	ED-MAR BALEK (Safinat Afnas)	*ZBRUCZ (Comet)	*GWALIOR (*Nabori)	MURZADAE+ (Murzada)
Costume					
Ch:	KISHTEE TIMP (Mounri)	RAJAG (Rafur)	XANADU's HAJ-ABU (Haj-Amin)	*FALEH (Ala el Din)	ROSS'ZI (Ga'zi)
R:	AMIR DHARAN (Ferneyn)	*WIRGINIA (Nabori)	ROSS'ZI (Ga'zi)	KIMICIAA (Kimfa)	DOLCE-VITA (*Nizzam)
Stock Horse					
Ch:	ABIYEZ (Zitez)	RAFSI (Nafsi)	RAMIRAFF (Ghari)	BAY EVENT (Bay-Abi)	ROUFER (Gassour)
R:	TSATELLITE (Tsatyr)	SKORDONAS (Skorage)	DARODAN (*Cytrys)	GAJALA ETOILE (Ferzon)	BALI HAI TIKI (*Nizzeym)
Trail Horse					
Ch:	AADRIEF (Aarief)	TUGALOO (Apollo)	RINGMASTER (Daaryn)	IBN WITRAFF (Witraff)	TAZOMAR (Azlaf Omar)
R:	LITTLE ME (Ross'zi)	TAHLOW (Phaalow)	LAURGAY (Laureate)	ROUFER (Gassour)	RAMIR (Mraff)
Formal Driving					
Ch:	—	*ORAN VAN CRABBET (Oran) (Park Nat. Ch. in 1966)	SEAHORSE DUKE DORSAZ (*Count Dorsaz)	MURZADAE (Murzada)	*ARAMUS (*Nabori)
R:	—	RAMPAGE (*Bask)	ANCHOR HILL HADUD (Hadbah)	ABA BAHABAS (Ibn Semuel)	*MECZET (Comet)
Formal Combination					
Ch:	—	*ORAN VAN CRABBET (Oran)	SEAHORSE DUKE DORSAZ (*Count Dorsaz)	HMR PHAROD (Pharoh)	*MECZET (Comet)
R:	—	RAMPAGE (*Bask)	RAMPAGE (*Bask)	ABA BAHABAS (Ibn Semuel)	IBN RAFFI (Raffi)
Pleasure Driving					
Ch:	—	ELNA (Yatez)	MARJAN AZEM (Fadjur)	HILLCREST TISHAMBA (Tisaan)	SHIMMERING STAR (Syzygy)
R:	—	BLUE VELVET (Mujahid)	LE BASK (*Bask)	SILFIX (*Serafix)	MAGIC GENII (*Serafix)

XI
IMPORTATIONS AT THE CHANGE OF THE DECADE

IMPORTATIONS
1968

A.H.R.A.
Number

Imported by Bradford and Hanna Luise Heck, Queensville, Ont., Canada:

50737 *SERENITY SONBOLAH (Sameh-Bint Om el Saad) Ch. m. 1967. Breeder, E. A. O., Egypt.
50738 *SERENITY SHAHRA (Anter-Shahrzada) Gr. m. 1966. E.A.O., Egypt.
50739 *SERENITY SABRA (Sameh-Shahrzada) Gr. m. 1965. E.A.O., Egypt.
50740 *SERENITY SAGDA (Anter-Samia) Gr. m. 1966. E.A.O., Egypt.
50741 *SERENITY MONTAHA (Galal-Mona) B. m. 1966. E.A.O., Egypt.
56064 *(en utero import) *BINT ALAA ELDIN (Alaa El Din-*Serenity Sabra) Ch. m. 1969. E.A.O., Egypt.

Imported by H.J. Huebner, Silsbee, Texas:

50731 *GAMILAA (*Morafic-*Bint Hanaa) Gr. m. 1964. E.A.O., Egypt.
50732 *SAKR (Sultan-Enayat) Gr. st. 1968. E.A.O., Egypt.
50733 *DEENAA (Sameh-El Dahma II) B. m. 1967. E.A.O., Egypt.
50734 *BINT HANAA (El sareeri-Hanaa) B. m. 1959. E.A.O., Egypt.
56065 (en utero import) *HABEEBAA (El Araby-*Bint Hanaa) B. m. 1969. Bred by Ahmed Sherif, Egypt.

Imported by Leon Rubin, Hillsdale, New York:

Imported en utero, 1967:

48984 *DIMRAK (El Azrak-*Dimatra) B. st. 1968. Breeder, Janow-Podlaski State Stud, Poland.
48985 *KANGUR (Ego-*Kaniaa) B. st. 1968. Janow-Podlaski State Stud, Poland.
48986 *TRYNEG (Negatiw-*Tryncza) Gr. st. 1968. Janow-Podlaski State Stud, Poland.

Imported 1968:

50935 *BRAWURA (Wielki Szlem-Bryssaga) B. m. 1958. Breeder, Janow-Podlaski State Stud.
50936 *CECORA (Pietuszok-Celia) B. m. 1963. Janow-Podlaski State Stud, Poland.
50937 *PANONIA (Comet-Pandora) Gr. m. 1961. Janow-Podlaski State Stud, Poland.

Imported en utero, 1967 by E.J. Tweed, Scottsdale, Arizona:

50087 *BRUSALLY EL AZRAK (El Azrak-*Salinaa) Br. st. 1968. Breeder, Janow-Podlaski
                                                          State Stud, Poland.
50088 *BRUSALLY GWARNY (Gwarny-*Lawenda) Gr. st. 1968 Michalow State Stud, Poland.
50089 *BRUSALLY BULAWA (Almifar-*Bulawa) B. m. 1968 Janow-Podlaski State Stud, Poland.

Imported en utero, 1967 by William McCrea, Alliance, Ohio:

48982 *DOKTRYNA (Doktryner-*Kanossa) Ch. m. 1968. Breeder, Janow-Podlaski State Stud, Poland.
48983 *IBN GWARNY (Gwarny-*Leszczynol) Gr. st. 1968. Michalow State Stud, Poland.

Individual importations:

50735 *ANSATA ADEEBA (Anter-Ibtsam) Ch. m. 1966. Breeder, E.A.O., Egypt. Imported
                     by Mr. and Mrs. Donald Forbis, Chickasha, Oklahoma.
50736 *REFKY (*Morafic-Rafica) Ch. st. 1963. Breeder, E.A.O., Egypt. Imported by
                     David L. Hilsheimer, Siloam Springs, Arkansas.

Imported March 1970:

61769   *IBN HAFIZA (Sameh-Hafiza) B. st. 1959. E.A.O., Egypt.
         (Note: ANTAR is generally so spelled, but is registered as ANTER, and
         in some previous importations it is spelled as in the latter case.)

Imported by Simms Arabian Ranch, Albuquerque, N.M. and Scottsdale, Arizona (Sept. 1969)

61145   *SABELLINA (Abu Afas-Sabda) Gr. m. 1954. Bred by Janow-Podlaski State Stud, Poland.
61146   *SABALGO (Ego-*Sabellina) Gr. st. 1969. Janow-Podlaski State Stud, Poland.
61147   *GARUFA (Faher-Gastronomia) B. m. 1958. Janow-Podlaski State Stud, Poland.
61148   *GARYY (Caracyn-*Garufa) B. st. 1969. Janow-Podlaski State Stud, Poland.
61149   *FEREZJA (Doktryner-Forta) Ch. m. 1956. Michalow State Stud, Poland.
61150   *FESTYN (Celebes-*Ferezja) B. st. 1969. Michalow State Stud, Poland.
61151   *PURPURA (Anarchista-Porfira) Ch. m. 1961. Michalow State Stud, Poland.
61152   *POLANKA (Gwarny-*Purpura) Gr. m. 1969. Michalow State Stud, Poland.

Imported en utero:

61772   *SABSON (Czort-*Sabellina) Ch. st. 1970. Bred by Janow-Podlaski State Stud, Poland.
61773   *PAN-BAJDAK (*Bajdak-*Purpura) B. st. 1970 Michalow State Stud, Poland.
61774   *FENIKS (Elf-*Ferezja) Gr. st. 1970 Michalow State Stud, Poland.

Imported by Leon Rubin, Hillsdale, N.Y.   (April 1969 and Sept. 1969)

53653   *SAMBOR   (Czort-*Sabellina) Ch. st. 1965. Bred by Janow-Podlaski State Stud, Poland
53654   *ALGORAB (Mir Said-Algonkina) B. st. 1965. Janow-Podlaski State Stud, Poland.
60570   *BAJKAL (Comet-Bajdara) Gr. g. 1961. Janow-Podlaski State Stud, Poland.

Imported by Leon Rubin en utero 1968:

53651   *NEGOR (Negatiw-*Cecora) Gr. st. 1969. Bred by Janow-Podlaski State Stud, Poland.
53650   *PRAWEGA (Negatiw-*Brawura) Gr. m. 1969. Janow-Podlaski State Stud, Poland.

Imported by Halberg Arabians, Iron, Minnesota: (May, Sept. 1969)

60571   *HARBIT (Negatiw-*Harfa) Gr. st. 1964. Bred by Janow-Podlaski State Stud, Poland.
69572   *DERWISZ (Comet-Daszawa) Gr. st. 1965 Bred by Michalow State Stud, Poland.
60573   * BUFA (Negatiw-Busznica) Gr. m. 1964 Janow-Podlaski State Stud, Poland
60574   *MAGNAT (Aswan-Monopolia) Gr. st. 1966. Bred by Tiersk Stud, Soviet Union,
                                                                Imported from Poland.

Imported by Thomas M. Lazor, Woodside, California: (Sept. 1969, Feb. 1970)

61009   *DRUZBA (*Naborr-Druchna) Gr. st. 1964. Bred by Michalow State Stud, Poland.
61143   *CELA (Pietuszok-Celia) Gr. m. 1961. Bred by Albigowa State Stud, Poland.
61144   *MORWA (Wielki Szlem-Mordzana) Gr. m. 1956. Bred by Nowy Dwor State Stud, Poland.

IMPORTATIONS
1969-70

(In Vols. XX and XXI, imports of the previous year are occasionally included, as
are a few registrations of the previous year's Americanbred foals. Therefore date
of importation, if other than the above, is given. En-utero imports are usually,
but not always from dams imported the previous year. This lap-over of yearly
registration is seen in a few previous volumes also).

Imported by Gleannloch Farms, Spring, Texas: (Nov. 1968)

56066   *OMNIA   (Alaa El Din — Ameena) Gr. m. 1966. Breeder, E.A.O., Egypt.
56067   *NIHAL   (Antar — Neamat) Ch. m. 1966. E.A.O., Egypt.
56068   *OMAYMA   (Sameh — Nazeera) Gr. m. 1964 E.A.O., Egypt
56069   *KAHRAMANA (Antar — Kamar) Gr. m. 1966. E.A.O., Egypt.
56070   *FALEH   (Alaa El Din — Frashah) Ch. st. (Reg. as grey). E.A.O., Egypt.
56071   *NASHWAN   (Alaa El Din — Noosa) Gr. st. 1966. E.A.O., Egypt.
56072   *SOOMA   (Fattan — Thouraya) Gr. m. 1968. E.A.O., Egypt.
56073   *SOUFIAN   (Alaa El Din — Moniet El Nefous) Ch. st. 1968. E.A.O., Egypt.
56075   *MAGIDAA   (Alaa El Din — Maysa) Ch. m. 1964. E.A.O., Egypt.

Imported March 1970:

61769   *IBN HAFIZA (Sameh — Hafiza) B. st. 1959. E.A.O., Egypt.
         (Note: ANTAR is generally so spelled, but is registered as ANTER, and
              in some previous importations it is spelled as in the latter case.)

61770   *IZEES (El Sareei-Ghariba) B. m. 1964. Bred by E.A.O., Egypt.
61771   *BARAKAA (Sid Abouhom-Rafica) Gr. m. 1960. E.A.O., Egypt.

En-utero imports, foaled 1970:

64639   *IZIZA (*Ibn Hafiza-*Izees) B. m. 1970. Bred by Jack W. Walters.
64638   *DAHK AL RAKESSA (*Ibn Hafiza-*Barakaa) B. m. 1970. Bred by Jack W. Walters.

Imported by Clay and Struck Arabian Ranches, Madison, Wis. and Scottsdale, Arizona:

Imported en utero 1967

53647   *BINT BAJDAK (*Bajdak-*Bint Badiara) Ch. m. 1968. Bred by Janow-Podlaski State Stud, Poland.
53648   *CELFIR (Celebes-*Mafia) B. g. 1968. Bred by Michalow State Stud, Poland.
53649   *CELEGAL (Celebes-*Galicja) B. m. 1968. Michalow State Stud, Poland.

Imported by Dr. John C. Coles, Arva, Ontario, Canada: (Feb. 1970)

61766   *HEND (Alaa El Din-Mansoura) Ch. m. 1963. Bred by E.A.O., Egypt.
61767   *WATFA (Shahriar-Set El Wadi) Gr. m. 1967. E.A.O., Egypt.

Individual importations:

61010   *EXELSJOR (Aquinor-Eleanora) Gr. st. 1963. Bred by Janow-Podlaski State Stud, Poland.
           Imported from Sweden 1970, by Larry Black, Oakdale, Calif.
54962   *TELLSTAAR (Rissani-Sparkling Fire) Ch. st. 1965. Bred by Derry Arabian Stud,
           England. Imported by Max H. Campbell, Collingwood, Ont., Canada 1968.
55969   *NASRA (*Morafic-Zobeya) B. m. 1966. Bred by Sayed, Arei, Egypt. Imported
           by James G. Dowd, Decatur, Ill., 1969.
55968   *BINT SHAHBAA (Gassir-Shahbaa) Gr. m. 1960. Bred by E.A.O., Egypt. Imported by
           Trucilla L. Enz, Lakeport, Calif. 1969.
60297   *INDIAN VANITY (Indian Magic-Silver Ripple) Gr. st. 1966. Bred by Mr. and Mrs.
           R.G. Archer, England. Imported by Margaret D. Fifield, New Market, Ont.
60569   *ANSATA BINT ELWYA (Anter-Elwya) Gr. m. 1961. Bred by E.A.O., Egypt.
           Imported by Mr. and Mrs. Donald Forbis, Chickasha, Oklahoma 1969.

62564   *CANDAWA (GANDAWA, in Poland) (Grand-Gazella) B. m. 1961. Bred by Michalow
           State Stud, Poland, Imported by Vytenis and Irena Jonynas, Chesterton, Indiana, 1970.
61768   *SER EL SAHARA (Ibn Fakhri-Bint Kheir) Gr. m. 1966. Bred by Ahmed Hamsa, Egypt.
           Imported by Martin Loeber, Chicago, Ill. 1969.
56074   *SUBHAYA (Tuhotmos-Ilham) B. m. 1968. Bred by E.A.O., Egypt. Imported by Thomas
           P. McNair, Jr., Spring, Texas, 1968.
61142   *RAVLON SUNDOWNER (Count Manilla-Trix Silver) Ch. st. 1968. Bred by Ravlon
           Arab Stud, Australia. Imported by Newton Bros. Enterprises, Beverly Hills, Calif. 1969.

53652   *SILVER MOONLIGHT (Indian Magic-Silver Fire) Gr. st. 1949. Bred by Crabbet
           Arabian Stud, Englaind. Imported from Australia by Dr. Andrew G. Sharf, Glendale, Calif. 1969.

> (Vol. XXI of the A.H.R.A. Stud Book adds gratuitous asterisks (*) in front of
> names of parents of several imports, wherein these animals were not themselves
> imported, and to even things up, it left the asterisk off the names of several sires
> of dams which had been imported. Wherever possible, these have been corrected
> here. However, aside from dead ancestors, it is possible that some may be — or
> have been — imported after Vol. XXI was issued, and these of course would earn
> the star in later publications. This has already happened with some horses, such
> as *MORAFIC, imported after several of his get had come to this country.)

XII

PICTORIAL GALLERY

TABLE OF ILLUSTRATIONS

317

BOZRA

BUKRA

BAZRAH

BAZIKH

MARES OF THE BASILISK FAMILY

BOZRA is by PHAROAH D.B. out of BASILISK D.B. BUKRA is a daughter of
BOZRA, by AHMAR, and BAZRAH is a greatgranddaughter of a full sister of
BUKRA, BEREYDA. BAZRAH is by *RODAN while her daughter BAZIKH is
by *ABU ZEYD. BUKRA is the dam of *BERK, and it is through her that his
action was transmitted, as her sire was a son of AZREK D.B.

FELUKA

*FERDA

*FARASIN

NARASA

ONE LINE OF MARES OF THE FERIDA FAMILY

FELUKA is by Mesaoud out of FERIDA; *FERDA is by RUSTEM out of FELUKA; *FARASIN is by RASIM out of *FERDA, and NARASA is by *NASIK out of *FARASIN.

*WADUDDA DB

MOLIAH

MONICA

MONEYNA

SANKIRAH

MOLIAH is by *HAMRAH out of *WADUDDA; SANKIRAH is also by *HAMRAH, and out of his daughter MOLIAH; MONICA is by TABAB out of SANKIRAH; MONEYNA is by *RASEYN out of MONICA.

ONE BRANCH OF THE *WADUDDA FAMILY

*URFAH

SHERIA

POKA

*URFAH D.B. and ONE BRANCH OF HER FAMILY

SHERIA is by *ABBEIAN, and POKA is by *HAMRAH who was a son of *URFAH so POKA is closely inbred.

RABIYAT

ROSHANA

RAYIK (Rehal-Roshana)

"ACTION" MARES, bred by MAYNESBORO

*RAMIM

*RAMIM (*Berk-Rim) is the dam of REHAL (sire of Rabiyat, Rayik, Ghazayat, etc). RABIYAT and ROSHANA are half sisters, out of *ROKHSA.

DAOUD (Mesaoud -Bint Nura)

NASRA (Daoud-Nefisa)

DAOUD and his best-known daughter, NASRA.

Of the 28 foals sired by DAOUD only six were colts and none of them sired registered foals. DAOUD is represented therefore only through his daughters, of which NASRA has the most numerous descendants in American championship ranks.

323

KEMAH (*Nuri Pasha-Nanda)

*NURI PASHA (*Nureddin II-Ruth Kesia)

STAMBUL (El Sabok-Morfda)

KATAR (Gulastra-*Simawa)

KAABA (*Nuri Pasha-Ophir)

*SUNSHINE DB (DB St.-*Nufoud)

STALLIONS OWNED OR BRED BY A.W. Harris

NAUFAL (Sotamm-Narghileh)   RIFFAL (Naufal-Razina) at age 26

ORAN (Riffal-Astrella)

PROGENITORS OF THE SOTAMM BRANCH OF THE *ASTRALED LINE.

ORAN is the sire of GRAND ROYAL, *SILVER VANITY, *ROYAL DIAMOND and *ORAN VAN CRABBET.

325

*ZAMAL DB

*MOUNWER DB

*LEBNANIEH DB

*ARKANE DB

HEARST IMPORTATIONS

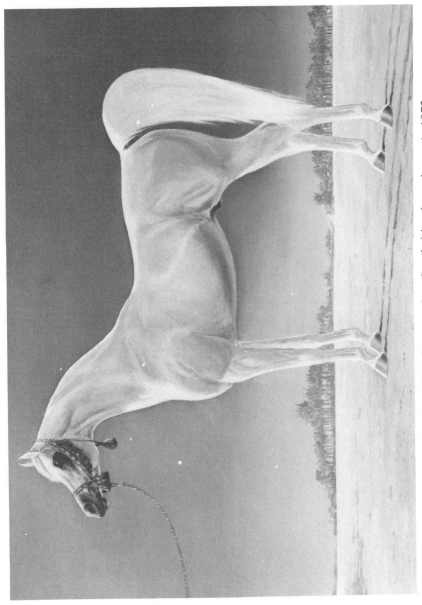

A painting of the Egyptian stallion NAZEER (Mansour-Bint Samiha) by the authoress in 1972

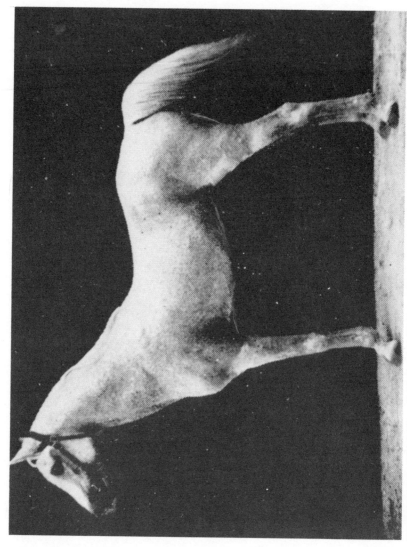

MABRUK MANIAL (Gamil Manial-Tarfa) Sire of MAHROUSSA, SAADA, AWAD & BINT RADIA

TALAGATO (*Talal-*Agata III)

AQUINOR (Miecznik-Amneris) Sire of *ELKIN and *ELKANA

KONTIKI (Camelot-Almiki)

*ELKIN (Aquinor-Ellenai)

*ELKANA (Aquinor-Estebna)

331

MIKADO+ (Bay-Abi+-*Naganka) National Champion Park horse for 1971
ridden here by Sheila Varian

*ARAMUS (*Naborr-Amneris)

*ANSATA IBN SUDAN (*Ansata Ibn Halima-Ansata)

*GWALIOR (*Naborr-Gwadiana)

THE REAL MC COY (Aarief-Fersara)

KHEMOSABI (Amerigo-Jurneeka)

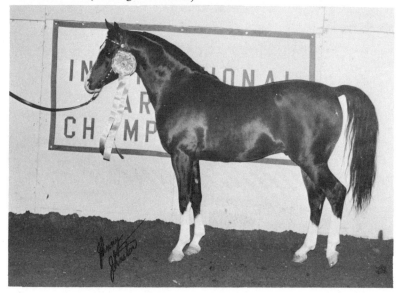

*SAMBOR+(Czort-Sabellina)coupled mile and ½-mile wins at 1969 O.C. Nationals

PONCHO (Faro-Tezza) 1972 I.A.C.H.A. World Ch. Cutting Horse

TAZOMAR (Azlaf Omar-Tabtaba) won $1000 Hunter Stake 1972 O.C. Nationals

ROUFER (Gassour-Roufa) Versatile stallion won 1972 National Champion
Arabian Stock Horse competition and was second in Hunter Stake class.

*BASK+(Witraz-Balaljka) A truly great stallion in the breed!

PARTIAL BIBLIOGRAPHY

Chapter I

Ancient Arts of Central Asia; Tamara Talbot Rice; Praeger Publ. Co., N.Y., 1965

Ancient Greek Horsemanship; J. K. Anderson; U.C. Press, Berkeley, Calif. 1961

Ancient Iraq; Georges Roux; World Publ. Co., N.Y., 1965

Ancient writers; Aelian, Herodotus, Xenophon, Strabo, etc.

Ancient History; Rollins, 1731

Ancient Mesopotamia; A. Leo Oppenheim; Crown Publ. Co., N.Y. 1964

Ancient Near East, The; James B. Pritchard; Princton Univ. Press, 1958

Ancient Records of Egypt; J. H. Breasted

Anthropology; A. L. Kroeber; Harcourt, Brace & World, Inc., N.Y. 1948

Arab of the Desert; H. R. P. Dickson; Allen & Unwin, London, 1949

Arabia Deserta; C. M. Doughty; Jonathan Cape Co., London, 1936 (1st ed. 1888)

Arabia Deserta; Alois Musil; American Geographical Society, N.Y., 1927

Arabs, The; Hitti

Arabs in History, The; Bernard Lewis, 1956

Archaeology of Weapons; Oakeshott

Art of the Steppes; Karl Jettmar; Crown Publ. Co., N.Y., 1966

Art of the Stone Age; Crown Publishers, 1961

Art of Warfare in Biblical Lands, The; Yigael Yadin, McGraw-Hill Book Co., N.Y., 1963

Asia, A Natural History, Pierre Pfeffer, Random House, N.Y. 1968

Authentic Arabian, The; Lady Wentworth; Allen & Unwin, London, 1962

Bedouin Tribes of the Euphrates; Lady Anne Blunt, 1879

Cambridge Ancient History

Cave Paintings; Roxane Cuvay; Crown Publ. Co., N.Y.,1962

Cuneiform Parallels to the Old Testament

Dawn of Civilization, The; ed. by Prof. Stuart Piggott; McGraw-Hill, N.Y., 1961

Earliest Civilizations of the Near East; James Mellaart; McGraw-Hill, N.Y., 1965

Earl Man in the New World; MacGowan & Hester; Doubleday-Anchor, 1962

Explorations in Turkestan (Prehistoric Civilizations of Aanau); Raphael Pumpelly, 1904

Fertile Sahara, The; Henri Lhote (in *Vanished Civilizations*)

Forgotten Kingdom, A; Sir Leonard Woolley; Pelican Books, 1953

Fossil Book, The; Fenton; Doubleday, N.Y. 1958

Historia Numorum; Barclay Head; Argonaut, Chicago, 1911

Historians History of the World

History Begins at Sumer; Samuel Noah Kramer; Anchor Books, Garden City, N.Y., 1959

History of Ancient Egypt; J. H. Breasted; Scribners, N.Y. 1912

History of Assyria, The; A. T. Olmstead

History of Domesticated Animals, A; F. E. Zeuner; Hutchinson, London, 1963

History of Herodotus; Rawlinson, 1862
History of the Persian Empire; A. T. Olmstead; Univ. Chicago Press, 1948
History of the Saracens; Simon Ocley; Geo. Bell & Sons, London, 1894
    from 3rd ed. 1757)
History of Syria; Hitti
Hittites, The; O. R. Gurney; Penguin Books, Baltimore, Md., 1952
Horses of the British Empire; ed. by H. F. de Traffard, Bart; London, 1907
Journal of the American Oriental Society; 84.3, 1964
Journal of Cuneiform Studies, V. XV 1961 "Early History of West Semitic
    Peoples"; I. J. Gelb
Journal of Cuneiform Studies, V. XII, Nos. 1 and 2 "Sumerian Proverbs and
    Fables"; E. I. Gordon
Journal of Heredity; June 1935, "The Oldest Pedigree Chart",
    Wolfgang Amschler
Journal of Mammalogy; May 1962, "Anatomical Variations of the Spine of the
    Horse", Robt. M. Stecher
Larousse Encyclopedia of the Earth; Prometheus Press, N.Y., 1961
Leo Africanus (in *Golden Trade of the Moors,* Bovrill)
Literature of the Ancient Egyptians; Erman
Manners and Customs of the Rwala Bedouins; Alois Musil; Am. Geo. Soc.,
    N.Y., 1927
Multiple Origin of Horses and Ponies; Prof. J. Cossar Ewart;
    Smithsonian Report, 1904
Muqaddimah, The; Ibn Khaldun
Newmarket and Arabia; Roger Upton; c. 1875
Nineveh and Babylon; Austen H. Layard; Putnam, N.Y., 1853
Notes on the Bedouin and Wahabys; J. L. Burckhardt; 1830
Oriental Assembly; T. E. Lawrence; Dutton, N.Y., 1940
Origin and Influence of the Thoroughbred Horse; Prof. Wm. Ridgeway;
    Cambridge Univ. Press, England, 1905
Origin of Domestic Horses; Animal Industry Report; Dept. of Agriculture, 1910
Origin of the Species; Charles Darwin; 1858
Pilgrimage to Nejd, A; Lady Anne Blunt; 1881
Prehistoric Art; T. G. E. Powell; Praeger Publ. Co., N.Y., 1966
Prehistoric Art; Robert Myron, Pitman Publ. Co., 1964
Prehistoric Investigations in Iraq Kurdistan; Braidwood & Howe;
    Univ. Chicago Press, 1960
Records of the Past; (texts of Assyrian and Egyptian inscriptions)
Royal Hordes, The; E. D. Phillips, McGraw-Hill, N.Y., 1965
Scythians, The; Tamara Talbot Rice; Praeger, N.Y., 1957
Secret of the Hittites, The; C. W. Ceram; Borzoi Books, N.Y., 1956
Seven Great Monarchies; Rawlinson; 1885
Struggle of the Nations, The; Maspero; 1897
Stud Book of the Przewalski Horse; Prague
Survey of Persian Art, A; Hersfeld & Keith; 1965
Thoroughbred Racing Stock; Lady Wentworth, Scribners, N.Y., 1938
War in the Desert; Lt. Gen. Sir John Glubb; 1960
World of Ancient Man, The; I. W. Cornwall; John Day Co., N.Y., 1964

Chapters II - VIII

The Arab and Anglo Arab; Poland, 1935

Arab Breeding in Poland; Dr. Edward Skorkowski; Poland, 1969

Arab Horse, The Spencer Borden; Borden Publ. Co., Pas., Calif., (1st. ed. 1906)

Arab Horse, The; (magazine) Coronation Issue, May 1937, England

Arab Horse in Poland, The; Dr. Edward Skorkowski, Poland, 1930

Arab Horse, The; Maj. Gen. Tweedie; Borden Publ. Co., Pas., Calif.,
    (1st ed. 1894)

Arabian Horse Breeding and the Arabians of America; Dr. Ameen Zaher;
    Cairo, Eg., 1961

Arabian Horse in America, The; ed. by Dr. Geo. H. Conn; Countryman Press,
    Woodstock, Vt., 1957

Arabian Horse in Fact, Fancy and Fiction, The; ed. by Dr. Geo. H. Conn;
    A. S. Barnes Co., N.Y., 1959

Arabian Horse in Egypt, The; Donald and Judith Forbis; *Your Pony Magazine,*
    1967-68

Asia Magazine; April 1929, "The Drinker of Air", Carl Raswan

Breeding of Pure Bred Arabian Horses; 2 Vol., H. R. H. Prince Mohamed Aly,
    Cairo, Egypt, 1935, 1936

Crabbet Park Stud catalogs; 1926, etc.

Davenport Farm catalog

En Buscar del Caballo Arabe Comision a Oriente; Spain, 1905

History of the Arabian Horse Club Registry of America; A.H.C.R.A., 1950

Horse, The; (magazine) July-August 1942, "From Needham Market to
    Oyster Bay", Thornton Chard

Horse, The; (magazine) Nov.-Dec., 1934, "Keene Richards' Importations",
    Thornton Chard
    (also by same author, "The Arabian and The Barb", *Western Horseman*)

Horse of the Desert; W. R. Brown; Shuler Publ. Co. (Reprint)

Horses of the Sahara; E. Daumas; London, 1863, (1968 reprint, Univ., Texas)

Maynesboro Stud catalogs; 1932, etc.

My Quest of the Arabian Horse; Homer Davenport; A.H.C.R., Chicago
    (reprint of 1907 ed.)

Raswan Index; Carl Raswan; 1960

Royal Agricultural Society Stud Book; Egypt, 1948. Includes "History of the
    R.A.S. Stud of Authentic Arabian Horses" by Dr. Abdel Alim Ashoub

Selby Stud catalog

Travelers Rest (Dickinson) catalogs

INDEX

343